"A Few
Acres
of Snow"

Books by Robert Leckie

HISTORY

Okinawa: Last Battle of World War II
From Sea to Shining Sea: 1812–Mexico, the Saga of America's Expansion
George Washington's War: The Saga of the American Revolution
None Died in Vain: The Saga of the American Civil War
Delivered from Evil: The Saga of World War II
The Wars of America: Updated and Revised, 1609–1991
Strong Men Armed: The U.S. Marines Against Japan
American and Catholic: The Catholic Church in the U.S.
With Fire and Sword (edited with Quentin Reynolds)
Challenge for the Pacific: The Struggle for Guadalcanal
Conflict: The History of the Korean War
The March to Glory: 1st Marine Division's Breakout from Chosin

AUTOBIOGRAPHY

Helmet for My Pillow • Lord, What a Family!

BELLES LETTRES

These Are My Heroes: A Study of the Saints
Warfare: A Study of War • A Soldier-Priest Talks to Youth

FICTION

Ordained • Marines! • The Bloodborn • Forged in Blood
Blood of the Seventeen Fires • The General

FOR YOUNGER READERS

The Battle for Iwo Jima • The Story of Football
The Story of World War Two • The Story of World War One
The War in Korea • Great American Battles
The World Turned Upside-Down • 1812: The War Nobody Won
The Big Game • Keeper Play • Stormy Voyage

"A Few Acres of Snow"

The Saga of the French and Indian Wars

ROBERT LECKIE

CASTLE BOOKS

This edition published in 2006 by

CASTLE BOOKS ®

A division of Book Sales, Inc.

114 Northfield Avenue
Edison, NJ 08837

This edition published by arrangement with and permission of

John Wiley & Sons, Inc.

111 River Street
Hoboken, New Jersey 07030

This publication is designed to provide accurate and authoritative information in regard to the subject matter provided. It is sold with the understanding that the publisher is not engaged in rendering professional services. If professional advice or other expert assistance is required, the services of a competent professional person should be sought.

Library of Congress Cataloging-in-Publication Data:

Leckie, Robert.
"A few acres of snow" : The saga of the French and Indian wars /
Robert Leckie.
p.   cm.
Includes bibliographical references and index.
United States—history, Military—To 1900. 2. United States—History—
King William's War, 1689-1697. 3. United States—History—Queen
Anne's War, 1702-1713. 4. United States—History—King George's War,
1744-1748. 5. United States—History—French and Indian War, 1755-
1763. 6. Great Britain—Military relations—France. 7. France—Military
relations—Great Britain I. Title.
E195.L43 1999
973.2'5—DC21   98-31023

ISBN-13: 978-0-7858-2100-7
ISBN-10: 0-7858-2100-7

Printed in the United States of America

Contents

Part VI   Seven Years' War, 1756–1763
(French and Indian War)

To our dear Kiawah Island friends—
Doctor Lynn and Jean Freeman—
With all affection.

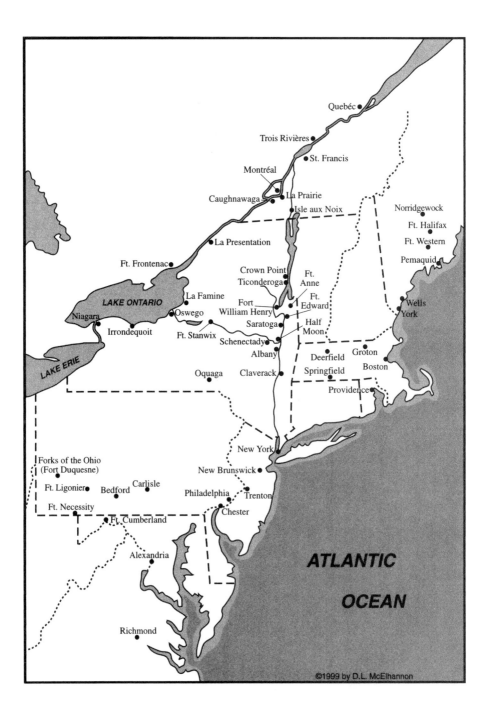

©1999 by D.L. McElhannon

King Louis XV of France was in conversation with Voltaire when he received the dreadful news that Canada was no longer French, but British. Aware of his sovereign's anguish, Voltaire spoke to him consolingly:
"After all, Sire, what have we lost—a few acres of snow?"

PART I

A Continent Is Discovered

CHAPTER 1

Christopher Columbus

SINCE THE FALL OF "invincible" Constantinople to the Muslim Turks in 1453, thoughtful men everywhere in Western Civilization shivered with fear and foreboding to behold a shrinking Christendom and an inexorably expanding Islam. It was the beginning of an astonishing and terrifying victory march of a century's duration. Each new kingdom or independent city of the East conquered by the Scimitar for the Crescent was another lost stronghold of the Cross. It was almost as though, to paraphrase St. Jerome upon his somewhat exaggerated estimate of the extent of the spread of Arianism: "The whole world groaned to find itself Muslim."

There were other, more subtle signs of the decline of Christianity than the trail of blood and ruin left in the wake of the dripping Scimitar, chief among them the absence of any new ideas in science or philosophy, and an alarming decline in enrollment at the universities. Eager young students flocking to the great centers of learning such as Bolonga, Salamanca, or the Sorbonne were bored by the insipid stale theories of masters seemingly interested only in "a good place" to enjoy a calm, comfortable life, and they turned away in disgust, embracing instead whatever was novel or thrilling; or they lost themselves in luxury or debauchery, preferring the sybaritic pleasures of a vanished paganism to the discipline and nobility of a Christianity still alive, though ailing.

Most of the great cities of the West were indeed splendid in their cathedrals, palaces, ports, and museums, many of them connected by roads and rivers, or able to conduct a thriving industry on the relatively safe waters of the Mediterranean. But these also could be regarded by Islam as routes over which the victory march could continue. Magnificent though these capital cities were, they were citadels of desperation and despair as well, teeming tenements into which the poor, the suffering, and the diseased were stuffed like rabbits in their warrens, while the faith that could comfort or console them with the barest promise of hope was slowly sinking into desuetude incurred by the unholy union of indifferent kings, a decadent aristocracy sated with privilege, and a worldly clergy.

All classes shared an unspoken dread of the appearance of the Muslim hordes, and if the roads, rivers, and ports of their kingdoms could link the trading centers, they could also become the corridors of conquest from the East; for if the unskilled peoples of Islam could never build a road—or even launch a galley, depending on construction of their fleets in the shipbuilding centers of Venice and Genoa—they could certainly follow these convenient, unguarded avenues of attack.

But in the final decades of the fifteenth century—the close of the Middle Ages—there were no great warrior kings to rally Christendom to the defense of these routes of approach from the East. Nor did spiritual leaders abound, for the Church was in the grasp of the corrupt Rodrigo Borgia, elected to the papacy as Alexander VI, celebrated for his steady accumulation of wealth, his harem of mistresses—and his bastard children. For half a century all the occupants of the chair of St. Peter proclaimed a crusade supposedly intended to repel the Muslim menace already in command of most of the medieval kingdoms of the East and preparing to hammer at the gates of Vienna. But the crowned heads of Western Europe regarded these appeals to duty as a pretext to raise money, and—except for Spain and Portugal—looked on them as an interference in their royal sport of small wars aimed at expanding at their neighbor's expense, or diplomacy (which all agreed to be the art of deception obtained by seeming to lie when telling the truth, or vice versa), or marrying off children trained to spy on their rivals.

Of all these kingdoms the most pathetic was the Holy Roman Empire, supposedly the secular arm of Christendom, which Voltaire described as "not holy, not Roman—not an empire." Emperor Frederick III was at best an amiable nonentity and so listless, so less than valorous, that at the first sign of danger he retired from his throne to dabble in astrology and alchemy. His son and successor was not even amiable, but actually only an egregious "gonter": "I'm 'gonter' do this, or 'gonter' do that."

Sadly, the corruption of these royals was so complete and contagious that it infected every walk of life. Licentiousness was rampant, indifference was a high art, and the singular or conspicuous masqueraded as distinction. As in our own modern age, every vice was cultivated everywhere, drink and sex leading the parade until, again as in our own time, it was augmented by drugs. As St. Augustine said of his lustful life in Rome: "Sensual love bubbled around me like boiling oil."

Yet Portugal and Spain, on the periphery of the Continent, remained loyal to the Faith. This is not to suggest that Iberians were paragons of purity, but their leaders during the fifteenth century were at least responsible. In Portugal, Prince Henrique, known to the Western world and posterity as Henry the Navigator, established his famous School of Navigation at Sagres on Cape St. Vincent. Although he made no great voyages of discovery himself, he directed, supplied and financed many along the coasts of Africa, while improving the compass and shipbuilding.

In Spain the "Two Sovereigns"—King Ferdinand of Castile and his consort, Queen Isabella of Aragon—were preparing to evict the alien Moors from their lands. Their counter-attack, begun in 1482, was completed with the conquest of Granada in 1492—a year that was to bring even greater glory to Spain, for it was then that Ferdinand and Isabella agreed to finance a lowborn illiterate named Christopher Columbus in his incredible if not actually lunatic proposal to open the fabled wealth of the Indies (Asia) by sailing west to them across the uncharted and storm-tossed Atlantic Ocean.

THERE WAS NO special aura about the birth of Cristoforo Columbo. No princes of the Church officiated at his baptismal Mass to enroll him in the Catholic Church of Jesus Christ. No soothsayers predicted mighty deeds or foretold fabulous fortune; nor did any astrologer search the night sky for those shooting stars or comet tails that might herald the appearance of a superman. No, Cristoforo was born to the woolen weaver Domenico Columbo and his wife, Susanna Fontanarossa, daughter of another weaver, in the ancient port city of Genoa, Italy, sometime between September and October 1451. If there was anything unusual about the child it was his size, for it suggested the tall and muscular stature that would be his at physical maturity, while his red hair, which would be snow white at thirty, and his bright pink complexion—so different from the smaller, dark-skinned Italians around him—indicated that the Columbos sprang from any one of the many races and tribes that had wandered and struggled across the face of Italy for so many millennia. This would explain—but never certify—why so many of his admiring biographers made Christopher "one of ours": a Castilian, a Catalan, a Majorcan, a Frenchman, a German, an Englishman, a Greek, a Corsican, a Portuguese, or an Armenian.

Though his demeanor was proud and his ambition would gradually become almost limitless, he saw nothing degrading in being the grandson and son of woolen weavers. Actually, his father, Domenico, was not an ordinary journeyman dependent on wages to support himself and his family, but was a master clothier who owned one or more looms, bought his own wool, and sold the finished cloth to merchants while teaching apprentice boys their trade. But Domenico was also a member of the local guild of clothiers and had thus gained a respectable position in the lower middle class. When he marched with his guild brothers on ceremonial occasions to attend a corporate Mass he always wore his chapter's arms. Much, much later, as Admiral of the Ocean Sea, his son Christopher quartered this device with the arms of Castile.

Yet Christopher and his younger brothers Bartholomew and Giacomo were loyal sons of their tradesman father, but sometimes as Christopher sat idle and dreaming at his loom—loathing a calling without glamor, respect, or wealth—he would fix his faraway gaze upon the blue Ligurian Sea outside the harbor mouth, and fancy himself aboard one of those great galleons or galleys arriving from or departing for the Aegean, the Levant or the coasts of Africa.

In 1455, WHEN Christopher was four, his parents moved to a finer home with a courtyard and garden near the Porta Sant'Andrea. On June 25—the feast of St. Christopher—the youngster attended Mass with his parents and received a glass of wine and a little pocket money from his father. This ordinary event made the boy acutely aware of his own first name, and how proud he was of it.

For the fifteen years following this little ceremony (was it a First Communion?), nothing is known of the activity of the Colombos. But in 1470, Domenico was placed on a guild committee to examine the rules of the master clothiers in nearby Savona, a thriving little seaport suburb of Genoa, with a view to adopting them in the city. Quickly convinced that his business would flourish more in the little town than in the big metropolis, in March of that year Domenico moved his growing family to Savona.

At nineteen Christopher was a fine figure of a man, a favorite with the young ladies, with his tall, strong body, red hair, and lighthearted personality. With Bartholomew now in his teens, the two would sit of a Sabbath in Savona's waterfront taverns sipping wine and listening enthralled to the sea stories of salty sailors, to whom, as neither youth suspected, all drakes would always be dragons.

Although Christopher never knew the exact date of his birth—most children in Catholic countries in those days celebrated the feast day of their patron saint rather than their own birthday—he had enormous pride in his Christian name, even more so than in his family name. In Greek it means "Christ-bearer." He believed implicitly in the legend of St. Christopher.

Supposed to have been a giant pagan, he had heard of Christ and went forth in search of him. A holy hermit told him: "Perhaps Our Lord will show Himself to you, if you fast and pray." Christopher replied: "To fast and pray I know not, ask me something easier." Immediately the hermit told him of a river without a bridge where so many travelers had drowned, telling him: "Do thou who art so tall and strong take up thine abode by the hither bank, and assist poor travelers to cross. That will be very agreeable to Our Lord, and mayhap He will show Himself to thee." So Christopher built himself a cabin by the riverbank, and there, aided by a tree limb he used as a staff, he carried many wayfarers upon his broad shoulders across the rushing stream.

One night while he slept in his cabin he heard a child cry, "Christopher! Come and carry me across." Out he came, holding his staff and sweeping the child upon his shoulders. But as he strode through the river his burden became so much heavier that he almost sank beneath it. Calling upon his great strength, he staggered up the riverbank, declaring: "Well, now, my little fellow, thou hast put me in great danger, for thy burden waxed so great that had I borne the whole world on my back, it could have weighed no more than you." Smiling, the child replied: "Marvel not, Christopher, for thou hast borne upon thy back the whole world and Him Who created it. I am the Christ whom thou servest by doing good; and as proof of my words, plant that staff near thy cabin, and tomorrow it shall be covered with flowers and fruit." Christopher obeyed, and awoke to behold a full-blown date palm.

The story of St. Christopher is, of course, one of those charming medieval legends churned out by overzealous hagiographers and has no more validity than similar confections composed by monks and priests eager to create a cult that would enrich the abbey or convent in which they resided and said their prayers. Of all these, the story of St. Christopher may be the most famous and familiar. Certainly in the heart of young and credulous Christopher Columbus the story was ever fresh. Devout Catholic that he was becoming, he might very well have believed that having received the name of that great pagan Christ-bearer he had also been given a command to carry the divine word of the Holy Child across the turbulent, terrifying ocean to lands populated by ignorant savages living in heathen darkness.

But Christopher gradually came to realize that to do great deeds he must be educated and that the exclusively non-written Genoese dialect that he spoke was no help to his mounting and now overpowering ambition. In effect, he was illiterate—and he knew it. He must learn to speak and write at least two languages: probably first Castilian Spanish, and then Latin. Actually Portuguese became his first language, because on his maiden voyage as an able-bodied seaman he was ship-wrecked in Portugal.

During the decade in which his sea voyages were mounted from Portugal, he learned that Castilian Spanish was the favored medium of the Portugese educated classes into which he hoped to marry. So he spoke that tongue before learning Castilian, which he always spoke and wrote but with Portuguese nouns and spellings. Whether he also knew Latin is not known, although surely a boy so devout would have served at Mass as an acolyte, and much of the language and rhythms of that ceremony would have entered his memory.

To his expanding familiarity with foreign languages was earlier added a growing grasp not only of charts and maps but also of map-making itself. Genoa had a celebrated school of mapmakers, and it is certain that young Christopher frequented these shops, and learned there the rudiments of cartography. Later, in Lisbon, he and his brother Bartholomew opened a shop of their own.

But above all, the boy Christopher loved the sea. How could such an ardent spirit not have, growing up in a great and ancient seaport?

In 1501 Columbus wrote to the Two Sovereigns: "At a very tender age, I entered upon the sea sailing, and so have I continued to this day. That art [of navigation] inclines him who follows it to want to know the secrets of this world. Already forty years have passed that I have been in this employment."

What the great Discoverer probably meant was not that "at a very tender age" he had commenced his seafaring career, or even sailed the coast as a part-timer on a short cruise, but that like healthy, high-hearted boys everywhere living on seacoasts or in ports, or on lakes and rivers, he loved to sail, but not as yet to earn his living before the mast. Probably Christopher's experiences on the open sea were overnight fishing trips, setting sail under the stars, then casting anchor to furl all canvas while fishing for sardines by torchlight; capering barefoot and half naked on the wooden decks while the little silver fish writhed and wriggled inside the nets. Finally, with the sun rising out of the sea due east of Genoa, they would unfurl the sails again and race each other with jeers and taunts to be the first in the market with the night's catch. For a fourteen-year-old, then, this was simply great fun and certainly not the dangers and drudgery, the poor pay, the wretched food, and the brutal discipline of life aboard a plunging, shivering ship.

From overnight fishing trips they would soon—especially if they were as tall and nimble and muscular as Christopher—be shipping aboard packets heading east and west from Genoa. It was sheer magic to watch with his heart in his mouth while a string of far-off islands might merge into a single great one, or when they entered strange ports and heard the weird jabbering of foreign sailors with the fierce, wild look of pirates. In shocked whispers they would ask each other if the girls ashore were pretty. Or obliging? But the enraged voice of the master soon put an end to such salacious sport, and the sound of it sent them scurrying barefoot to their stations.

Most of the trade along the Ligurian littoral was seaborne, and Domenico deliberately exploited his son's skill with small craft by buying a little, lateen-rigged packet for the young skipper to go coasting in it, taking aboard cargoes of wine, wool, and cheese while selling his father's cloth. The young master also had developed a sense of humor. It became apparent much later in life when he wrote in 1495 a now-lost letter to the Two Sovereigns. It described how in 1470 frightened passengers aboard a vessel bound from Marseilles to Tunis were fearful of being attacked by two stronger ships off Sardinia. Christopher agreed to hasten back to Marseilles for a stronger vessel and more people. At night, however, he doctored the compass to change course for Tunis, so that when the passengers awoke expecting to gaze in relief upon the towers of the Christian churches of Marseilles, they saw instead—and in consternation—the minarets of the Muslim mosques of the much smaller town of Tunis.

Whether or not this letter had actually been lost, it is more than likely that Christopher in 1470 was but a foremost hand and in his narrative had promoted himself to captain, a rank more suitable to his dignity as the renowned Admiral of the Ocean Sea. Nevertheless, it is a pleasure to relate that there might have been a twinkle in the eye of the greatest seaman of all time.

There can be little doubt that Christopher's brief coastal voyages at the helm of his father's packet had been to him like a release from bondage—or even better, from the oar of a galley. Actually, it had been a respite from the accursed clicking of the loom; and yet, instead of encouraging him to follow in the footsteps of his father in becoming a respected member of the clothier's guild of Savona, these marvelous moments in command of what was in effect his own ship encouraged him to make the final break with tradition and announce—in 1473— his determination to go to sea.

After all, he might have explained to his stunned father that he was already twenty-two and still knew almost nothing of how to "hand, reef, and steer," to estimate distances by sight, and to let go and weigh anchors properly. These, among the basic skills of seamanship, he would learn the old way, which is to say the hard way. So he left his family and his home and his beloved "noble and powerful city by the sea"—never to return.

ALMOST IMMEDIATELY, Christopher signed on at Savona aboard the ship *Roxana* for a voyage to Chios, an island in the Aegean off the coast of Turkey. Chios had been captured by a Genoese fleet in 1346, and the island prospered in the production of gum mastic until the nearby Turks appeared. *Roxana* was destined for trade and defense against the Turks. Columbus was surely aboard her, because her owner recorded the fact that besides sailors and soldiers she carried "workmen of Savona, including *tessitori*, or weavers." Columbus made one and possibly two voyages to the archipelago in *Roxana*.

Most of the seagoing Mediterranean nations were at war after Columbus returned from Chios, yet he shipped aboard *Bechalla*, a warship in a fleet being prepared by Genoa to protect a huge shipment of mastic bound for Portugal, Flanders, and England. On August 13, 1476, the Genoese formation was sailing off Cape St. Vincent when the sails of a Franco-Portuguese battle fleet led by the French naval hero Guillaume de Casenove appeared over the horizon. Although France and the Republic of Genoa were supposed to be at peace, when Casenove espied the flag of Burgundy, with which King Louis XI was then at war, among the Genoese vessels, he decided the entire convoy was fair game, and a bitter seafight ensued.

Surprisingly, the Genoese—respected as capable sailors but seldom feared as seafighters—not only held their own but actually gave more than they got. By nightfall three Genoese and four enemy ships had been sunk, and hundreds of men on both sides were either killed outright, or so badly wounded that they could not swim and drowned in the Atlantic; or among those unfortunates who so often go to sea unable to swim a stroke.

For the first time Christopher heard that wailing "music" of the cannonballs that can terrify some and exalt others. But because he was neither a gunner nor a musketman, he fired no weapon but simply did as he was told—until *Bechalla* was holed and began to sink. Though wounded, he leaped into the sea, struggling painfully to put as much distance between himself and his stricken vessel before it sucked him down with it; but then, seizing a sweep that floated by, he clambered aboard it and began paddling with his hands, managing to reach the shore six miles distant.

Meanwhile, the surviving ships had sheered off, some unharmed, others badly mauled—all seeking the safety of friendly ports for repairs and medical attention for their wounded shipmates. Columbus was among those so treated by the warmhearted people of Lagos, Portugal, after which he made his way to Lisbon, where he was graciously received and nursed back to health by a member of the local Genoese colony.

One more adventurous voyage awaited Christopher Columbus before he took up residence in Lisbon. In one of his many notes he wrote:

"I sailed in the year 1477, in the month of February, a hundred leagues beyond the island of Tile [what the Romans called Ultima Thule or "farthest North"] . . . And to this island, which is as big as England, come English with their merchandise, especially they of Bristol. And as the season when I was there the sea was not frozen, but the tides were so great that in some places they rose twenty-six *braccia* [about fifty feet], and fell as much in depth."

There is no doubt that Columbus's ship (no name is given) reached Iceland, for at the time there existed a brisk trade among Lisbon, the Azores, Bristol, and Iceland. He certainly visited Galway in Ireland, which was a natural port of call for Iceland voyages. But his tale of great fifty-foot tides at Reykjavik—the modern capital of Iceland—was one of those fantastic "sea stories" that mariners of those days loved to tell and hear. Spring tides at Reykjavik were only thirteen feet, in no way comparable to the swift-running rise and fall of seventy feet at the mouth of the Bay of Fundy in Canada or the thirty-six-foot depth at the port of Seoul in Korea, which was so troublesome to the U.S. Navy and the Marines of the First Division during their capture of that Communist-held city in 1950.

Actually, Columbus learned next to nothing from his Icelandic voyage except that "the northern ocean is neither frozen nor unnavigable." Apart from this, it seems that the Discoverer sounded somewhat disappointed, or simply didn't care, and that a possible reason for this was that his perceptive and speculative mind was already active with what he would always call *la empresa de las Indias*, or "the Enterprise of the Indies."

CHRISTOPHER COLUMBUS probably did not realize that the turning point of his life came in that sea fight off Cape St. Vincent and that his luckiest moment occurred as he struggled in agony and terror to stay afloat and that drifting sweep came to his hand like a life raft to deposit him on the beach in what was practically the front yard of the great Henry the Navigator. As his definitive biographer, Rear Admiral Samuel Eliot Morison, has written: "He was among people who could teach him everything he was eager to learn: Portuguese and Castilian, the languages of far-ranging seamen; Latin to read the geographical works of the past; mathematics and astronomy for the celestial navigation; shipbuilding and rigging; and above all, discovery."

Portugal, the ancient Lusitania of the Romans, was then the leading explorer nation of Europe, and had been steadily expanding the known world under the aegis of Prince Henry. Portugal not only discovered the uninhabited Azores but also had populated them. For almost half a century she had been sending vessels farther and farther out along the West African coast. They had eclipsed the Arab seamen, from whose language our word "admiral"—*amir-al-bahr*, commander of the sea—derives, and were learning to find their way by the stars, while the sons of Islam sank deeper and deeper into their "green sea of gloom." It was Henry, then, who was the living spirit of discovery—and, to quote Morison again, "not only guided it but organized it." At his headquarters at Sagres only a few miles away from where Columbus was washed ashore, he erected for himself a seafarer's town calculated to attract sailors and to supply them with every necessity, including all charts and sailing directions of the known world, while encouraging the more daring among the pilots to strike out from the shores of shallower waters into the deep, uncharted sea.

Columbus's exact activities during the eight or nine years he spent in Portugal can never be known, if only because the great Lisbon earthquake of 1755—having caused the death of some fifty thousand residents of that ancient city—also destroyed notarial and court documents that might have thrown some light on his movements. His first known decision was to join his brother Bartholomew in his chart-making shop. Though the younger brother by several years, Bartholomew had studied more frequently in the Genoa map-making centers and also had left that city before the Discoverer did. He left no description of Christopher, but a friend, Andres Bernaldez of Seville—who knew him well—describes him in his history as "a hawker of printed books, who carried on his trade in this land of Andalusia [modern Spanish province once held by Moors], a man of great intelligence though with little book learning, very skilled in the art of cosmography and the mapping of the world." Together the brothers profited handsomely, not only from making charts useful to the Portuguese maritime expansion but also from other articles similarly helpful.

Columbus's second decision was in taking a wife: Doña Felipa Perestrello e Moniz. He met her when attending Mass in the chapel of the Convento dos Santos in Lisbon. Little is known about her except that she was a member of one of the first families of Portugal. Nothing is known either of her appearance or personality. Yet, so many writers did not hesitate to call the marriage a mystery. How, they asked, could a lowborn foreign map-maker rise so high in Portuguese society that he could hope to marry into one of the kingdom's noblest families? A kinder biographer answered such scoffs and doubts with these words: "forasmuch as he behaved very honorably, and was a man of fine presence, and withal so honest." In other words, he was not such a bad catch, handsome and truthful, in his bearing and actions far more noble than most highborn courtiers. And he did seem to have a future. But Doña Felipa is as shadowy and mysterious a figure as the Discoverer's own mother. Felipa did have a child, however, Diego Colón, born in 1480, but rising no higher than as a member of the guards of both Isabella and Ferdinand. Even the date of her death is not known, except that it was before Columbus left Portugal in 1485, and might very well be the reason why he left.

During the Portugal sojourn, however, Christopher Columbus made many voyages—sometimes as a passenger accompanied by his wife, more often as a sailor or a sea captain eager to learn from his Portuguese shipmates, whom he truly admired as the world's finest mariners. They, in turn, were also unrestrained in their praise of this exceptional man. Here is a penetrating description of the Discoverer by Bartolmé de Las Casas in his *Historia de las Indias:*

> He was affable and cheerful in speaking and eloquent and boastful in his negotiations; he was serious in moderation, affable with strangers, and with members of his household gentle and pleasant, with modest gravity and discreet conversation; and so could easily incite those who saw him to love him. In fine, he was most impressive in his port and countenance, a person of great state and authority and worthy of all reverence. He was sober and moderate in eating, drinking, clothing and footwear; it was commonly said that he spoke cheerfully in familiar conversation, or with indignation when he gave reproof or was angry with somebody: "May God take you, don't you agree to this and that?" or "Why have you done this and that?" In matters of the Christian religion, without doubt he was a Catholic and of great devotion; for in everything he did and said or sought to begin, he always interposed "In the name of the Holy Trinity I will do this," or "Launch this" or "This will come to pass." In whatever letter or other thing he wrote, he put at the head "Jesus and Mary, be with us on the way," and of these writings of his in his own hand I have plenty now in my possession. His oath was sometimes, "I swear by San Fernando"; when he sought to affirm something of great importance in his letters on oath, especially in writing to the Sovereigns, he said, "I swear that this is true."
>
> He was a gentleman of great force of spirit, of lofty thoughts, naturally inclined (from what one may gather of his life, deeds, writing, and conversation) to undertake worthy deeds and signal enterprises; patient

and long-suffering, and a forgiver of injuries, and wished nothing more than that those who offended against him should recognize their errors, and that the delinquents be reconciled with him; most constant and endowed with forbearance in the hardships and adversities which were always occurring and which were incredible and infinite; ever holding great confidence in divine providence.

CHRISTOPHER COLUMBUS was deeply indebted to his Portuguese shipmates, and it was from their unconscious tutelage that he emerged as the greatest explorer of the Age of Discovery that had only just begun. They taught him the little things: how to claw off a lee shore, how to handle a caravel in high seas and headwinds, what kind of stores to take on a long voyage, and not only how to stow them properly but also how to consume them evenly to prevent capsizing, as well as what sort of trading trinkets to take along to gain the friendship of primitive peoples. He was pleased that his shipmates' confidence in God and their shipbuilders matched his own, and gratified to know that he had indeed learned the basic rule of sailing the sea, which was that to understand the prevailing winds was to conquer the oceans.

All this he needed, he knew, because on his return from far-off Guinea—his last voyage on a Portuguese ship—he was about to offer to King John II of Portugal nothing less than the passion of his very existence: "the Enterprise of the Indies."

AFTER THE legendary traveler Marco Polo returned to his native Venice in 1295, he was captured by Genoese three years later, and imprisoned in their city. There he dictated his famous travels, which almost immediately drew the wrath of those typical classroom minds that do all their traveling and adventuring in books, and who proclaimed Polo as the prince of prevaricators. Some critics, more derisive, pinned the sobriquet "Marco Millions" on him because he could speak of nothing—populations, wealth, spices, wonders, cities—in smaller denominations. But a famous Florentine physician-astrologer-cosmographer named Paolo dal Pozzo Toscanelli believed Marco Polo, and in a letter dated June 25, 1474, told King John II of Portugal that there was "a shorter way of going by sea to the lands of spices than that which you are making by Guinea." His proposal was based on Marco Polo's report of the vast eastward extent of Asia and the location of "the noble island of Cypango"—Japan (actually an archipelago)—"most fertile in gold, pearls, and precious stones," and they cover the temples and the royal residences with solid gold. Toscanelli confidently urged a trial of the westward passage, while enclosing with his letter to the king a copy of his nautical map of the Atlantic Ocean. There was no reply.

But in late 1481 or early 1482, Christopher Columbus heard of this letter and map, and it set fire to his already heated brain. He wrote to Toscanelli in a fury of excitement, requesting more information about the westward passage. In reply he received an encouraging letter, plus a copy of his Atlantic Ocean chart.

From mere rational conviction Columbus became a tireless, passionate advocate of the westward water route. In 1484 he made his first formal presentation of the Enterprise of the Indies to the king of Portugal. His striking physical presence and his polished flow of Spanish, as well as his personal charm, captivated John at first; but not after he related that he had "read a good deal in Marco Polo . . . [and] reached the conception that over this Western Ocean Sea one could sail to this Isle Cypango and other unknown lands." There it was again: wealth, wonders, precious stones, and precious metals, populations by the veritable millions just waiting to be exploited, rare spices of exquisite culinary delight; here indeed was history's greatest exposition of the hoary old adage: "The grass is always greener in the other fellow's yard." And with it, Columbus lost his listener. When he asked the king to equip and man three caravels for such a voyage, John "gave him small credit," finding Columbus to be "a big talker and boastful in setting forth his accomplishments, and full of fancy and imagination with his Isle Cypango."

Though inwardly crushed, the Discoverer still had enough brass to speak boldly and request that His Majesty should refer his project to a committee of experts. And John consented! He committed Columbus's proposal to Bishop Diogo Orriz of Ceuta and two Jewish physicians— Master Rodrigo and Master José—both celebrated for their knowledge of celestial navigation, and "they all considered the words of Christovao Colum as vain, simply founded on imagination, or things like that Isle Cypango of Marco Polo." Among the ignorant and illiterate who believed in the myth that the earth was flat, it was generally believed that Columbus was turned down because of his novel belief that it was round, when, in fact, the sphericity of the globe had been known by educated men and common sailors for centuries before Christ.

But Columbus did not surrender. Always optimistic in the face of opposition, he insisted that a directly westward voyage from the Canary Islands to Japan would be but 2,400 nautical miles. Actually, the king's committee concluded that the air distance from the Canaries to Japan was 10,600 nautical miles—and they were right. How could they recommend to their sovereign to invest in such a fantasy?

Nevertheless, in 1485, with the committee's concurrence, John had authorized two Portuguese—Fernao Dulmo and João Estreito—to try to discover the legendary island of Antillia, which the Portuguese called "the Island of the Seven Cities." They set sail in 1487 on a due westward course and were never heard of again. Unlike Columbus, who had not yet admitted to any mistake, they made the fatal error of setting out from the Azores in the high latitudes, where strong westerly winds made of their voyage a fatal fantasy.

The year 1485 had not been a happy one for Christopher Columbus. His wife, Doña Felipa, died then, and the Discoverer, accompanied by his five-year-old son Diego, departed from the country in which he had spent most of his adult life.

Moving to Spain, he was encouraged by the duke of Medina Celi, a wealthy shipbuilder of Cadiz, who might have financed three caravels for the expedition if the queen would give her assent. She would not; and because she wouldn't, and such an expedition must be a royal one, Columbus and his brother Bartholomew became convinced that success depended more on salesmanship than seamanship. They spent most of the next seven years in unsuccessful appeals to the crowned heads of Western Europe. Meanwhile, Isabella allowed a year to pass before permitting Columbus to appear before her.

Columbus was visibly impressed with Queen Isabella. She was a strikingly handsome woman, with regular features and a clear, fresh complexion, and her auburn hair was particularly becoming to her. Actually, this coloring was especially attractive to Spanish men because it was so rare, and whenever it was seen on the streets of the cities, among the elderly and the youthful the glad cry of "¡Rubiya! ¡Rubiya!" arose. Isabella's manners were friendly, but gracious and dignified. She was tactful, and received from her subjects an affection no previous Castilian monarch ever knew.* In her tastes she was simple, and in her diet temperate. In diplomacy she showed tenacity and skill. Once she had decided to support a policy, her loyalty was absolute. Above all, her piety and morality were impeccable.

Ferdinand did not quite excite the Discoverer. He was not very well liked, perhaps because of his frivolous love of diplomacy as a game in which he could outwit his friends. Louis XII of France was one of his particular dupes, and Ferdinand boasted openly and with twinkling delight in his shrewd eyes that he had gotten the better of him ten times. He was more intersted in his Mediterranean kingdom than

*She was joint sovereign with Ferdinand as Ferdinand V of Castile and Aragon.

those on the Atlantic. At once Columbus felt that he could not expect much from Ferdinand.

Many courtiers were shocked beyond belief when they heard the proposal of this handsome and poised appellant, and wondered if, in spite of all his charm, he were not a little mad. Basically the offer Columbus had made to King John requested (1) that the Sovereigns equip three caravels manned and provisioned for one year and loaded with trading trinkets; (2) that Columbus be created a *caballero* so that he and his descendants be styled Don; that he also be created "Admiral of the Ocean Sea" with all privileges of the admiralty; and be appointed perpetual viceroy and governor of all islands and mainlands he might discover; and (3) that Columbus receive a tenth part of all revenues and precious metals derived from these lands, and have the privilege of freighting an eighth part of ships trading with the countries he discovered.

Like King John, Queen Isabella appointed a commission headed by her confessor, Hernando de Talavera, archbishop of Granada. It was hardly less than a bald rejection. Columbus well knew that he was considered an unprincipled upstart with no academic standing, and although he was allowed to appear before Talavera's council and answer questions, he obviously suspected that the decision would be against him. And it was.

In the meantime, during an interval of waiting like a slow death, he became associated with a young lady of the royal city of Cordova. This was Beatriz Enriquez de Harana, the mother of little Ferdinand. Nothing is known of her appearance, personality or character. Columbus met her through his friendship with her cousin Diego de Harana. He did not marry her, even though his wife was dead, because, though she came from a respectable peasant family of wine pressers and gardeners, she was not a lady of rank, as Doña Felipa had been. Those were not prudish days, especially among those of the highborn or high-placed, when grandees and princes of the Church openly paraded their mistresses. Obviously, then, Beatriz could never appear at court. She survived Christopher by fourteen years, living comfortably on a pension provided by him. Nevertheless, for all his fondness for Beatriz, a peasant girl could hardly be an appropriate consort for a viceroy or the Admiral of the Ocean Sea.

IMPATIENT, HIS HAIR long since become a thick white crown, Columbus could not endure years of marking time while the queen's commissioners—now on one foot, now on the other—solemnly debated with the preconceptions of religion and imperfect science and the rigid error of precedent what was to be done about this mad map-making foreigner. Inevitably, Columbus remembered that King John of Portugal had bade him a friendly farewell. So he wrote to him, asking him for a safe conduct and freedom from the many debts he had incurred.

The king told him—"our particular friend"—to come ahead, his enthusiasm perhaps inspired by the dismal failure of the Dulmo-Estreito Expedition. There also had been no word from Bartholomew Días, who for seven months had been seeking an eastward sea passage to India. And this in Portugal's twentieth attempt in that direction!

Learning of this, the Colombos' spirits skyrocketed, until in 1488 they stood on a dock to watch with broken hearts as Días's three little caravels sailed triumphantly up the Tagus with the great news that they had indeed found a safe eastward sea passage to the Indies.

For a day or so—but no longer—the irrepressible Discoverer was sunk deep in despair, for Días's triumph had caused King John to lose all interest in the Columbos. If the eastward sea route was open, why bother with the other direction?

But then that indomitable faith in one's own convictions that issues from the soul of the great—and from that source only—filled the heart of Christopher Columbus as he reasoned with his crestfallen brother that the Portuguese success in the East would stimulate the interest of other investors in the opposite direction. Almost at once, while Christopher returned to Seville, Bartholomew set sail for England and France.

King Henry VII of England wasted no time on this brash appellant. As an island kingdom, of course, Britain was by nature a seafaring nation. But Henry Tudor was not accustomed to lending money for the fickle fortunes of voyages of discovery. He was a true miser who had accumulated enormous wealth, which he did not value so much for what it could buy, but rather because he had so much more of it than anyone else. So he barely glanced up from his beloved ledgers before saying, "No." King Charles VIII of France—the most valiant warrior-king in all that faineant Valois dynasty—was too much concerned with his Continental wars, and probably too much a land animal, to be interested in the risks and defeats of those sea animals of discovery. Moreover, he had been soured in the knowledge that he would die without an heir and thus would become the last Valois monarch. Nevertheless, encouraged by the support of Charles's elderly sister, Bartholomew remained in France, supporting himself as a map-maker until he heard the great news of his brother's discovery.

Christopher by then was beside himself with bitter outrage. Six and a half wasted years! All soured by the venom of jealousy, and by the taunts and jeers of brainless boobies who had emerged from gold-plated wombs and who found it most amusing to heap abuse on the head of a "nobody" motivated by a grand design. Columbus always resented his treatment at the hands of these useless courtiers, fawning sycophants in satins and silks, skilled in the art of flattery, whom he could not dare to duel in a contest of repartee. God take these scum! By San Fernando he had had them! I go to France!

But after Granada—the last stronghold of the Muslim Moors in Spain—surrendered on January 2, 1492, and Columbus experienced the great joy of marching in the victory procession, his spirits rose again. Surely the Two Sovereigns in their own exaltation would grant his appeal.

But they didn't. Many days later, in an audience with the Two Sovereigns, he was informed that his enterprise had been decisively and finally rejected. Gracious as always, they wished him bon voyage—and the queen presented him with a gift of money. Clutching it desperately, the Discoverer stumbled from the royal presence. He saddled his mule, packed his saddlebag with books and maps, summoned his great friend Friar Juan Perez, and set forth on the road to Cordova and a voyage to France.

AS THE DEJECTED pair slowly and silently clip-clopped away from Santa Fe, where the court was then residing, unknown to them a miracle had occurred behind them! Beyond question these two devoted devout Christians would have insisted that the spirit of the Holy Ghost had entered the soul of Luis de Santangel (keeper of the privy purse to the king), "who went in search of the queen, and with words which his keen desire to persuade her suggested, told her that he was astonished to see that Her Highness, who had always shown a resolute spirit in matters of great pith and consequence, should lack it for an enterprise of so little risk, yet which could prove of so great service to God and the exaltation of His Church, not to speak of very great increase and glory for her realms and crown; an enterprise of such nature that if any other prince should undertake what the admiral offered to her, it would be a very great damage to her crown, and a grave reproach to her."

Santangel went on to say that if money were a consideration he would be happy to finance the expedition himself. Impressed by the warmth and sincerity of his plea, Isabella said that she would reconsider Columbus's proposal, and then sent a messenger to recall him. Overtaken at the village of Pinos-Puente, four miles from Santa Fe, both travelers fell upon their knees and joyously offered thanks to the Almighty, while both repeated the saying with which Columbus began every written message from him: *Jesu cum Maria, sit nobis in via.* Jesus and Mary, be with us on the way.

So the great enterprise could begin, and it was fitting that Bartolomé de Las Casas, whose *Historia de las Indias* is considered by Columbian experts to be the finest work on the Discoverer and his enterprise, should write the reason why:

"When he had made up his mind, he was as sure he would discover what he did discover, and find what he did find, as if he held it in a chamber under lock and key."

CHAPTER 2

"*¡Tierra! ¡Tierra!*" "Land! Land!"

TO THE SURPRISE of everyone concerned, the terms of Christopher Columbus's enterprise, which King John of Portugal had rejected out of hand, were almost routinely accepted by Ferdinand and Isabella. Nevertheless, it required three months of negotiation before all was arranged, and Columbus, accompanied by the faithful Friar Juan—who had been his attorney during the talks—departed from Granada on May 12, 1492, for Palos de la Frontera on the Saltes River in the seaport city where the Discoverer had first entered Spain.

He arrived there ten days later. On the following day, Wednesday, May 23, in the Church of St. George, Columbus was somewhat mystified to hear the city notary read a letter from the Sovereigns to the people of Palos that "for certain things done and committed to our disservice you are condemned and obligated by our Council to provide us for a twelvemonth with two equipped caravels at your own proper charge and expense. . . ." There was a pause while an angry, excited buzzing arose in the church, puzzling Columbus still more until he learned later that a local "poet" had offended Isabella by dedicating to her an anonymous doggerel that did not celebrate her charms. As a result, the people of Palos would make full payment for the use of the caravels *Nina* and *Pinta*, while Columbus himself, through the investments of friends, would do the same for *Santa Maria*. All wages for the period would be paid by the royal couple. Finally, all this was to be accomplished within ten days.

Ten days! Momentarily, Columbus might have wistfully wished that it was Prince Henry of Portugal who was outfitting the expedition, for it was not until almost three months later that all was in readiness. Timber merchants, carpenters, ship chandlers, bakers, and provisioners—all had gone ashore—and all had performed for Columbus at the reasonable prices ordered by the Sovereigns, with no customs or excises to be imposed. All criminal and civil prosecutions would be suspended against anyone so charged who entered his service, this last giving rise to the malicious myth that Columbus's fleet was manned by cutthroats and pickpockets.

What Columbus himself did not realize was that, rather than to be on guard against common criminals who had come aboard as able seamen, he had better watch none other than Martin Alonzo Pinzon, the head of a middle-class seafaring family of Palos. Middle-aged but still ambitious and valiant, he was nonetheless a born schemer.

Fifty years later his lies would arise to haunt the Discoverer's family in a lawsuit that was celebrated worldwide but was still baseless. Pinzon claimed that a cosmographer in the Vatican Library had given him information that in the time of Solomon, the queen of Sheba had sailed the Mediterranean the length of Spain and had discovered an easy westward passage to the fabulous island of Cypango and that he, Martin Pinzon, had passed this information along to Christopher Columbus, along with other similar pertinent facts that were the true basis of the Great Discovery. Some suggestive notes in Columbus's splendid journal of his journey discuss Pinzon's interests in finding Japan, but the queen of Sheba tale is not even mentioned by the incomparable Las Casas.

None of this claptrap from cloud-cuckooland began to appear after Martin Pinzon took command of *Pinta* at the Palos with his younger brother Francisco Martin as the master, but only on the homeward voyage from the New World and after the death of Martin Alonzo. But his obstructionist activities and sometimes undisguised disobedience on the outward journey were far more abrasive of Columbus's peace of mind than the possibility of mutinous murderers among his crew. That, incidentally, came to ninety men: twenty-four aboard *Nina*, twenty-six aboard *Pinta*, forty aboard *Santa Maria*.

BEFORE DAWN OF Friday, August 3, the Captain-General, as Columbus was now called, received the sacraments of penance and the Holy Eucharist, along with all his officers and men and specialists such as surgeons, stewards, painters, boatswains, painters, caulkers, carpenters, coopers, and one *converso* or converted Jew named Luis de Torres, who had joined the company because he knew Hebrew and a little Arabic and might serve as an interpreter. Then they all went aboard their ships, everyone in high spirits. "In the name of Jesus," Columbus gave the command to get under way, after which cheerful chanteys were sung while creaking windlasses wound the anchors aboard. Without much wind the little fleet was sailing on the ebb, her sails though unfurled hanging limp while the sweeps were manned so the tide and the softly splashing long oars gained enough momentum to carry all three ships safely down the Saltes and over the bar into the open sea.

At last, Christopher Columbus might have thought. At last—at forty-one—I am finally on my way!

ONCE SAFELY AT sea, "a strong sea breeze" sprang up, preventing the trio of caravels from steering closer to the wind, or to make better speed than four knots. Within sight of land until nightfall, Columbus then ordered the course changed to south by west—straight for the Canary Islands. It was here that the captain-general's greatest sailing skill became apparent: his knowledge of sea winds. Unlike the ill-fated Dulmo-Estreito Expedition, which shipped out from the Azores and became a casualty of the prevailing westerlies in those high latitudes, he sought the protection of the Canaries because they were in the zone of the friendly northeast trade winds. Once out of them and on a westward course, he would enjoy a fair wind that would carry him—not to fabulous Cypango, land of his dreams—but to the unsuspected shores of unknown America.

Three days later the first of many minor emergencies arose: *Pinta's* big outboard rudder jumped its gudgeons, and Columbus came aboard, to be informed by an angry Martin Pinzon that this was the dirty work of the caravel's owner, Cristobal Quintero, furious at having his ship commandeered for the voyage. Columbus thought Pinzon handled the crisis with rare ability and calm, the only time he mentioned him in his outgoing journal. On August 12 the two other ships entered the roadstead of the island of Gomera, ruled by the strikingly beautiful widow Doña Beatriz de Peraza y Bobadilla. Columbus, who never could resist a beautiful well-born lady, was disappointed to hear that she was absent, but brightened when told she could soon return.

She was not back in Gomera until September 1. During the interval *Pinta* had been almost fully repaired and all three vessels replenished in every way. When the captain-general met Doña Beatriz, it was said, he fell instantly in love with her. Why not? She was still well under thirty and had been maid of honor to Isabella, until Ferdinand's roving eye fell upon her. But Christopher Columbus had a greater passion—his cherished great enterprise—and on September 6 the fleet departed under a full moon, after what had perhaps been a tender farewell between Christopher and Beatriz.

IN THE MIDDLE AGES the sailors of Europe who were on watch spent most of their time singing canticles, chanteys, and ditties to pass their time on deck or to speed their work. Daybreak aboard the vessels of

Columbus's little fleet was almost always saluted by a young gromet—or ship's boy—with the following ditty:

Blessed be the light of day
and the holy cross, we say;
and the Lord of Veritie
and the Holy Trinity.
Blessed be th' immortal soul
and the Lord who keeps it whole
blessed by the light of day
and he who sends the night away.

At sunset all hands joined in singing the great canticle to the Blessed Virgin, *Salve Regina*:

Salve regina, Mater Misericordiae
Vita dolcedo, et spas nostra salve
Nobis post hoc exsilium ostende. O—clemens,
O—Pia O—dulcis Virgo Maria!

There were other more solemn hymns usually sung on the Sabbath or on great feast days, among them *O Salutaris Hostia; Tantum Ergo Sacramentum;* and *Veni, Domine, Jesus.* These were not especially peculiar to sailing ships, but were, after all, also sung on land in the churches and cathedrals. Shipboard piety among the seafaring nations of Christian Europe, however, was always encouraged as an aid to nautical efficiency, and the rhythms of the canticles and hymns—and ditties as well—introduced a spirit of teamwork in group chores such as raising or lowering sails and anchors or stowing stores belowdecks. In those days of sail every language had an exact word for every shipboard activity, clear, strong words that could be shouted during a storm and heard and understood.

On a ship in Columbus's fleet there was only one meal, usually at about 11:00 A.M. It was never served, as it was in the officers' quarters. A man simply grabbed a few sea biscuits and a handful of garlic cloves, a chunk of cheese, a pickled sardine or two—and that was it for the day. Upon relief from watch, there was no silly or sissified notion of "undressing." Nobody undressed. The men merely raced each other below and flopped fully clad on some favored soft plank or any place where he might brace himself against the roll and pitch of the ship. Hammocks would not appear until much later. Relieving oneself was even less private or dainty, usually from open buckets slung fore and aft, and woe to the unwary who takes his ease against the winds, or to any infuriated shipmate within range. Imperishable in Spanish nautical lore is the story of the modification of one very reverend lord bishop compelled to ride aboard one of these swinging *jardines* and do his duty in full view of a convulsed ship's company. It is not known if His Excellency availed himself of the tarred rope end, a function that American seamen assigned to a corncob. Eventually compassionate shipowners provided space for such necessities inside the head or prow of the ship, from which in English it became delicately known as "the head."

To THE CAPTAIN or master of a sailing ship there was nothing more dreadful than the specter of a mutiny. No officer aboard any of the Discoverer's three caravels had ever been through such a trial—or if anyone had, he never adverted to it—and it might have been the captain-general himself who had noticed with growing horror that as his ships sailed slowly west—with so little wind on the stern that in six days they made only 382 miles—his sailors were growing restive.

At the outset of the voyage Columbus promised all hands that they would not have to sail more than 750 leagues—or about 2,250 statute miles—west of the Canaries before they sighted land. Their anxious glances toward the helmsman or the Captain-General himself suggested that they might be haunted by the ghosts of the Dulmo-Estreito Expedition. They might have begun to fear that they also were headed for some point of no return and needed to be reassured.

Now, this was still the Columbus of the Marseilles-Tunis deception, and he did not hesitate to begin to cook his books—that is, to falsify his daily journal.

For a while his trickery was successful, and it had to be, for only a few days prior to this report—September 21–22—the little fleet sailed smack into the Sargasso Sea, that vast oval in the mid–South Atlantic coiling and uncoiling like a living snake pit with bright green and yellow sargassum gulfweed. No one aboard—not even the captain-general—had ever seen anything like it before. Filled with alarm and fearing that their ships would be "frozen" in this evil morass, they demanded that the Captain-General change course to emerge from its clutches; but he, aware of the harmless nature of the seaweed, plowed straight through.

Three days later the entire fleet was thrilled after Martin Alonzo on *Pinta*'s poop shouted, "*¡Tierra! ¡Tierra! ¡Señor, alabricias!*" Land! Land! Sir, I claim the reward! A general scurrying across decks and scrambling up the rigging ensued on all three ships. Everyone declared that they saw land, and Columbus fell on his knees to thank God, while the *Gloria in Excelsis Deo* was sung by all hands. At daybreak, however, there was no sight of land—and deep disappointment, to be followed by the first stirrings of discontent, seized the hearts of the seamen. Columbus, however, was an experienced sailor who was accustomed to false landfalls. Usually it was a cloud on the horizon at sunset—which it actually had been.

Even the beautifully calm weather, the warm caress of the sun in what seemed to be the Sea of Eternal Summer, distressed them because it meant a lack of rain—and how was the Admiral of the Ocean Sea going to replenish fresh water on a salt sea?

As yet no leader of mutineers had emerged, no malcontent ready because of some petty punishment or mild rebuke to avenge himself on the entire fleet. He had not yet appeared, but his time might come. Columbus sensed this, for it had become more and more difficult to maintain morale. The fleet had now been three weeks without sight of land. Something must be done. . . .

Columbus knew that shipboard life is unique, in no way comparable to any existence on solid land. Wage slaves may and do hate their boss, but they are only at his call from nine to five and not at all on weekends. Officers in the armed forces are indubitably cruel and selfish, but a private can go on liberty or even a prolonged furlough, just as a cat may look at a king. Even in prisons men form friendships. But aboard ship—especially such tiny vessels as these caravels—there was nowhere that a man might find privacy. Instead they found only proximity. The same faces . . . the same voices . . . day after day . . . friends became enemies . . . *that son of a bitch who tried to spill me from the forward bucket into that sea of snakes . . . I'll get him! Just you wait and see. . . .*

Unhappy memories of those six-day doldrums when the fleet made only about sixty miles daily, at a speed of two knots, had not yet faded. At even twice that speed they could never return home. Ordinary grumbling—or even griping—the surest signs among soldiers and sailors that they are displeased but far from ready to take matters into their own hands, was being replaced by openly bitter complaint: in a word, incipient mutiny. This foreigner, many of the seamen were saying, would make himself a great lord at our expense. What lies ahead of us on this westerly course? Another one of the Devil's devices, like that sea of snakes? Food may not give out, but water will—for it never rains in this desert of salt water. Why should we all die for this upstart foreigner?

Columbus was well aware that they were turning against him. Usually his policy had been to speak to them with *palabras dulces*—soft words. But this time, when some of the officers insisted that he should turn back, he told them all that they might kill him and his officers if they wished, but it would do them no good. What would the Sovereigns say if they returned without them? *Could* they return without them? To their open scowls he replied with serene smiles and spoke to them encouragingly of the fortunes that would be theirs when they reached the Indies.

Suddenly in October the winds freshened and all three vessels seemed to bound forward. They averaged 142 miles daily for five days! On a single day they covered 182 miles, their speed rising to an unheard-of eight knots! Still, among a growing contingent of sullen Basques and Galicians—the soreheads of Spain—complaints were growing in number, and Columbus told these malcontents frankly that it was useless to protest, since he was resolved to reach the Indies and would continue until he found them, "with the help of Our Lord."

At sunrise on October 7 the second false landfall occurred, aboard *Nina*, actually ranging ahead of her sisters contrary to Columbus's orders, breaking out a flag at her masthead and firing a gun—again in violation of the Discoverer's instructions—the very signal for land dead ahead. Now the captain-general was so infuriated with all these bald-faced challenges to his authority that he gave orders that anyone who raised an untrue cry to *tierra* would be disqualified for reward, even if he eventually gave the true and accurate one.

Columbus was also irritated by Martin Alonzo's attempt to induce him to alter his course to southwest by west, but was so annoyed that instead he changed it to west-southwest, one point more westerly than the old sea dog from Palos had recommended. Suddenly the Discoverer heard above him the crying of great flocks of birds flying overhead to the southwest. He remembered that the Portuguese had been led to the Azores by birds. What he witnessed now was the fall migration of North American birds to the West Indies via Bermuda. He decided to follow these unconscious feathered guides rather than his inaccurate man-made chart—a decision that was vital to his own project and the whole future of Spanish colonization, as well as the entire quest for gold that was to begin at Hispaniola. Critics of the captain-general have tried to prove that the change in course came from Martin Alonzo, but Columbus's journal proves that the honor belonged to the birds of North America.

But at this most critical juncture, when all depended upon that decision, those stubborn Basques and Galicians aboard the flagship *Santa Maria* chose on October 10 to mutiny. But before it could spread to *Nina* and *Pinta*—where the men were almost as anxious to reverse course—the captain-general again spoke confidently of imminent success, and promised these flagship dissidents that if they did not sight land within two or three days, he would agree to turn back.

With this, the mutiny was quelled.

DURING THE ELEVEN and a half hours elapsing since sunrise on October 11, with a brisk trade wind and the heaviest following sea of the entire voyage, the fleet had made seventy-eight miles at an average of almost seven knots. At sundown the wind rose to gale force until all three vessels were rushing along with "a bone in their teeth," their speed rising to nine knots. At this point Columbus ordered the course changed from west-southwest back to the original west. He did not explain why, nor has anyone else. Perhaps it was just a hunch or a proud man's deep desire to prove that he had been right. At this speed *Maria*'s ever-cautious pilot Peralonso Niño—the seaman whose distance estimates had always been right, while those of the Discoverer had been almost unfailingly wrong—suggested that Columbus heave to for the night, since the brightness of a rising moon might make any shoals or rocks lying ahead invisible. Columbus said nothing, but kept on his course. Two or three days! he had promised the men. If there was no true landfall by then, he would have to turn back. No, this was no time for caution. Now was the time to continue the westing with such a God-sent gale at his back!

On the night of October 11–12 no one slept—perhaps excepting a few ship's boys—for all aboard realized that this might be a night like no other since the night Christ was born. Christopher Columbus aboard *Maria*; Juan de la Costa, owner of the indestructible *Nina*; and the Pinzons—all true believers in Christ, Jesus, and sons of Holy Mother Church—knew in their medieval minds so full of marvels and miracles that this was a night charged with unrivaled consequence for all humanity, and that their brave little fleet would enter history for a feat of seamanship never challenged by any ship on any sea.

Thus the tension mounted on all three ships: de la Costa and the Pinzons calling down nervously to their helmsmen, warning of the same fear that troubled Niño—that they would be among those treacherous rocks and shoals before they saw them. Alone on his poop, the Discoverer hoped there would be no more false landfalls. Yet there was—and by the captain-general himself! There was a light, "like a little wax candle rising and falling." In the next instant a few others said they saw it, and Columbus felt embarrassed that he of all men should have let his imagination deceive him! Perhaps it was merely a trick of the moonrise, becoming suddenly visible at 9:00 P.M.

Bathed in this light that was silvering both sea and sails and foaming water, the three ships swept on, buffeted by that gale, rolling and plunging, throwing up fountains of spray. *Pinta* was in the lead, and aboard her forecastle a lookout named Rodrigo de Triana, peering ahead toward the western horizon in high excitement, saw something like a white sand cliff gleaming in the moonlight—and then another! —with the dark line of land clearly linking the two, and a great shout of joy came bursting from his lungs.

"*¡Tierra! ¡Tierra!*" he bellowed above the wail of the gale, and this time land it was.

THE FIRST LAND of the Western Hemisphere sighted by Columbus was the eastern coast of an island in the Bahamas called Guanahani by the naked, docile, friendly, light-skinned aborigines who lived there; and who would eventually rue the day when "the men from heaven," as they soon called these fierce-looking armed invaders, came ashore on their island paradise.

Columbus, with his official party, promptly renamed the thirteen-by-six-mile coral island San Salvador in honor of Our Lord and Savior, although cartographers for some unknown reason would later add to it Watling's Island, and so it has stood for centuries.

With the Pinzon brothers in his boat, followed by other dignitaries, Columbus raised the banners of the expedition: a green cross with an F on one arm and a Y on the other. All knelt and gave praise to God, rising while the Discoverer took possession of the island in the name of the Catholic Sovereigns. To them he wrote the following letter, promptly printed in Latin at Barcelona upon their return and circulated with rejoicing throughout Europe:

> They are so ingenuous and free with all they have, that no one would believe it who has not seen it; of anything that they possess, if it be asked of them, they never say no; on the contrary, they invite you to share it and show as much love as if their hearts went with it, and they are content with whatever trifle be given them, whether it be a thing of value or of petty worth. I forbade that they be given things so worthless as bits of broken crockery and of green glass and lace-points, although when they could get them, they thought they had the best jewel in the world.

Unfortunately, the very generosity and lack of guile among these people would prove to be their undoing; and even Columbus, who was not a cruel or a greedy man, could not refrain form thinking on this very first day that they could be easily enslaved. After he left the island on October 13 he added: "These people are very unskilled in arms . . . with fifty men they could all be subjected and made to do all that one wished."

That would soon be reality—especially after gold was found on Hispaniola, a much larger island that would become the headquarters for Spanish colonization in what was soon to be called "the New World." But these gentle creatures could never endure hard labor, and would soon be ruthlessly exterminated, to be replaced by stronger and hardier black slaves from Africa.

Two days later Columbus and his party returned to their ships and unfurled their sails to set their course westward again for Cypango—which, of course, they never found, if only because the two huge continents of North and Central–South America stood in their path. The Admiral of the Ocean Sea was to make three more voyages to the New World, but he never set foot on North America. He did, however, drop anchor in a lonely harbor in what is now Venezuela, and he did eventually receive his promised rewards of wealth and glory, although his conduct as governor of gold-producing Hispaniola was a failure. He had not the tact required in an administrator, even though he was brave and resourceful in battle, ruthlessly putting down rebellions against his authority; as the historian Bartolomé de Las Casas wrote of Columbus, his brother Bartholomew, and son Diego, they "did not show modesty and discretion in governing Spaniards which they should have done."

This last proved his undoing, and the Two Sovereigns—themselves irked as much by his foreignness as by his high-handed rule—sent Francisco de Bobadilla to Hispaniola as royal commissioner, empowered to take complete charge of the colony in the Sovereign' names.

Having revoked in the name of the Sovereigns all the titles, honors, and emoluments they had granted the Admiral under the Articles of Agreement signed by them and Columbus, Bobadilla demanded that the three Columbos submit to his summons. Brother Bartholomew, now the *adelantado* and still at large with a formidable armed force, called upon Christopher to raise the standard of rebellion, but he refused and counseled his more fiery younger brother and his son Don Diego to do the same.

They did, and it may have been a mistake. The Columbos were not dissemblers, but more like Nathanael, "in whom there is no guile," while Bobadilla, a born civil servant, was, like Judas, full of deceit, and on the basis of all the perjured testimony he had gathered, he brought this innocent trio to trial, convicted them, and sent them back to Spain in chains.

Columbus could not be persuaded to accept the offer of his ship's captain to remove the fetters. He insisted that since they had been placed upon them by the Sovereigns' orders, only they could remove them. Upon his arrival in Cadiz and Seville a groundswell of sympathy greeted the Admiral of the Ocean Sea in both cities. Still, the Sovereigns waited six weeks before ordering the irons removed, and on December 17, 1500, the Columbos presented themselves at court in the Alhambra at Grenada.

Columbus spoke to the royal couple with tears in his eyes, apologizing for what had happened. They replied consolingly and commanded that all his rights be restored to him. They could not have meant it because it did not happen. When Columbus demanded that Bobadilla be recalled, and the restoration of all his rights, nothing happened there either.

Columbus then was penniless, and in his pride he asked for nothing, especially not from the courtiers who regarded him as a foolish knave who had not brought home with him as much as an ounce of Hispaniola gold. But Isabella softened this reproach by conferring two thousand ducats upon him, thus removing the sting of his having to beg for his food and lodging.

Even so, the Two Sovereigns, for all their kindness and sympathy, had still another mission for the captain-general. Chiefly to forestall the appearance of Portuguese explorer ships in what Spain now looked upon as *mare nostrum*—our sea—Ferdinand and Isabella ordered the Discoverer in 1502 to make his fourth and last voyage. It was largely a search for what Columbus might have called the Strait of Marco Polo.

On July 31, 1498, Columbus had sighted an island that he named Trinidad, for the Holy Trinity. Five days later he entered that Venezuelan harbor where he had first set foot on South America. Finding only naked savages and no refined and bejeweled gentlemen from Cathay or Cypango, he entered the Gulf of Paria, where he was astonished to find a vast flow of fresh water. This, he realized, was not the Indies, but an unknown land, meandering out from the Malay Peninsula. If so, there must be a strait through it, for Marco Polo had sailed home from eastern China.

But though he began to search for it, he never found it. Lady Luck, who had seemed so kind to him formerly, was now waving her wand elsewhere. Losing two of his four caravels off the coast of Panama, he barely made it to Jamaica with the other two—where he was marooned for a year before being rescued.

Upon his return to Spain as a forgotten explorer ("Christopher *who?*"), he was despised and derided. The Two Sovereigns considered the West Indies—his greatest discovery—of no value. He had given them a complete blueprint of how to colonize what he called *un otro mundo*—an Other World—but this, too, was ignored. Yet, out of his indomitable soul he could still declare:

"By the Divine Will I have placed under the sovereignty of the King and Queen, an Other World, whereby Spain, which was reckoned poor, is to become the richest of all countries."

Of this there was no doubt, but the great Discoverer was now but a shadow of his former robust self, a great sea soul who had spent his life voyaging and come home a wraith—dropping his last anchor in his final port. On May 19, 1506—at the age of fifty-five—he ratified his last will and testament. The next day he lay on his deathbed—his watery eyes turned heavenward, the walnut color fading from his shrunken cheeks—and murmuring the *nunc dimittus* of his last day—and then:

"*In manus tuas, Domine, commendo spiritum meum.*" (Into Thy hands, O Lord, I commend my spirit.)

It was then—and only then—that his great spirit left his lifeless body.

CHAPTER 3

The Colonizing Contest Begins

ALTHOUGH FERDINAND AND ISABELLA liked to pretend that the exploratory exploits of Christopher Columbus were really quite useless—some pearls, some gold in Hispaniola valued at about a million dollars in the peak year of 1512, and no bejeweled and gold-plated gentlemen from Cypango and Cathay—the fact is that the great Discoverer did in fact give to Spain an enormous head-start in the colonizing of the New World.

By 1600 these hardy and indomitable *exploradoes*—along with the fierce and ruthless *conquistadores* who had preceded them—had conquered almost all of coastal Central and South America, and much of the interior as well, down to the Rio de la Plata. In so doing they had laid the foundations of each of the twenty republics of Central and South America. The record is not only incredible, it is also unrivaled. No other nation in the history of humankind has conducted such a conquest in time as well as space. In a single generation the Spaniards seized more new territory than Rome could acquire in five hundred years. Genghis Khan in the twelfth and thirteenth centuries overran more territory, but he left only destruction and towers of skulls in his wake.

Spain not only conquered but also governed and organized all that it subdued, introducing the arts, literature, and architecture of Europe while converting millions to its Catholic Christian faith. The achievements of those brown-robed Spanish friars—without weapons save the crucifixes dangling from the rosaries wound around their waists—rivaled the triumphs of the armed and armored *conquistadores*, because they suffered and strove on the side of charity, seeking only the greater glory of God; and because they did do this, saving literally millions of Indians heretofore killed annually to appease the wrath of what they thought to be native, nonexistent deities. Cannibalism also was not absent from many of these detestable rites, especially among the Incas of

Peru and the Aztecs of Mexico. Inca children from four to six were murdered to keep the emperor in good health or to heal him if he were ill. For the same reasons widows were buried alive with their husbands. In the Aztec tradition a great victory in war would be celebrated in an enormous slaughter of enemy prisoners, usually begun by the emperor with an ever-plunging knife until he tired of the carnage and the bodies could be cooked and eaten.

So the greater triumph among the tribes and peoples of the New World was won by the friars, marching like any *soldado* alongside the fierce warriors of Cortes and Pizarro, hacking their way with them through the green hells of dense and dripping jungles, slogging across snow-capped mountains, trudging through the tall grass of seemingly endless plains, paddling rude canoes up and down foaming, roaring rivers—afflicted, meanwhile, and attacked by every unknown enemy of the New World's flora and fauna: yet never faltering, the one high-hearted, the other indomitable; the one seeking souls and salvation, the other gold and military glory. It was this pair, the friar and the soldier—originally led by the Spanish admiral from Italy—who gave to Spain the head start of a century over the rival English and French.

Better than this: Spain saved Western civilization. Spain saved Christendom from the Muslim Turks. The savior was Don John of Austria, the natural son of Barbara Blomburg and Holy Roman Emperor Charles V—who had earlier been king of Spain as Charles I. Born and educated in secrecy, Don John was the half brother of Philip II—most powerful of all European sovereigns—and chosen by one of the great pontiffs—St. Pius V—who had formed the Holy League of Spain, Venice and Genoa to repel the Islamic assault.

Until he died, the Turkish sultan Suleiman the Magnificent—with Saladin, the greatest of Muslim war chiefs—had dreamed of the conquest of Rome, where Christian popes resided. He called Rome "the Red Apple," but he perished five years before he could bite it. He had been waiting patiently for delivery of his war galleys from—but of course!—the shipyards in Genoa and Venice.

The mother of Suleiman's oldest son, Prince Mustafa—admired and beloved everywhere—was a Circassian beauty named Gul-bahar, or Rose of Spring. In Mustafa all Turks seemed to agree that here indeed was a warrior king: brave, handsome, intelligent, a lover of poetry—even though his own was commonplace—a darling of both the harem and the elite corps of Janissaries, the sultan's bodyguard, all born of Christian parents but trained from childhood to be Muslim warriors. In 1533 Suleiman approved Mustafa as his successor.

But the sultan had two other sons—Selim and Bayezid—both the children of Khurrem, a favorite harem slave nicknamed the Cheerful One; in actual fact her smile was an inscrutable mask from which—together with her harem skills—she could satisfy the sultan of his every wish. Eventually, grown religious in later years, Suleiman secretly married Khurrem—and slept with her alone. But now Khurrem was terrified. Prince Mustafa's growing popularity was a deadly menace to her own sons, for the Koran solemnly declares that upon the crowning of a new sultan all his brothers must be killed to prevent civil war.

Obviously, the Cheerful One's power had become at least the equal of the sultan's, and she began her infinitely sly intrigue against Mustafa by so defaming his mother that she left the palace to join her son in Magnesia. That left no one near Suleiman to protect Mustafa's interests. Subtle as the serpent, the Cheerful One never lied to her husband, thus establishing a reputation for truthfulness that enabled her to blacken the name of Mustafa.

In the end—in 1553—the unsuspecting Mustafa was now almost forty years old. Sultan Suleiman was out on campaign against the Persians. He summoned Mustafa to his tent. The prince entered alone and found seven huge deaf-mutes inside, each armed with a bowstring. But his father *was* there—watching from behind a screen—while these professional murderers, who could never testify to anything, seized and strangled him. In the morning his one small son was also strangled—for the Koran also states that royal blood cannot be spilled.

Now the sultan-designate became—by some small quirk of accident—none other than Khurrem's oldest son, Selim. Upon the death of his father in 1566 he was crowned as Selim II. Known almost everywhere outside the palace as Selim the Sot, he was on the Turkish throne armed with his ever-present bottle when the galley fleets of the Holy League decisively defeated the Turks on October 28, 1571, in the Battle of Lepanto, ending forever the Muslim threat to Christendom.

Eventually, the crushed and bewildered sons of Muhammad, unaware that they had been beaten in spite of their superiority in wind- and oar-propelled galleys, as well as about twenty thousand Muslim bowmen, could not defeat those six Venetian galleases armored with forty or more cannons apiece (thirty-pounders concealed abovedecks, fourty-pounders ranged below), because musclepower and spiritual power, even in combination, can never defeat firepower. Thus the weapon of naval gunpowder unveiled by the West at Lepanto became the dominant weapon upon the high seas, and Islam began to sink

deeper—ever deeper—into that long, long slumber from which it was
not aroused until more than three centuries later by that fortuitous
shower of liquid gold that is spelled:

O—I—L.

SO IT HAD BEEN Spain again, and in nine more years—even as the
rocket of Spanish prestige rose higher and higher in the view of the
world's civilized nations—the very globe itself seeming to be surrounded by its encircling wings, the left arm to the west coast of Mexico, the right arm to Manila in the Philippines—another stupendous
event staggered an envious family of nations: Philip II in 1580 succeeded to the crown of Portugal as well as the throne of his native
Spain. Could there be any realm more glorious? More powerful? More
successful? Any empire more extensive anywhere?

Ah, but there could. . . .

There could be because the discoverers and explorers were everywhere, now, for there was no longer any large body of salt water such
as an ocean or a sea that was unknown; or a homeland of sophisticated
races or ignorant savages unvisited by those "men from heaven"
whose reward for these friendly savages who received Columbus on
San Salvador had been so treacherous. No, the world had shrunk, and
the Mediterranean—the ancient and historic inland sea on the shores
of which so many bands of human beings were first to assemble as
tribes or races, and then as nations and empires—was now naught but
a calm blue lake.

But no.

Because eight years from the year of the dual ascension of Philip II
as king of Spain and Portugal, he had assembled a mighty armada intended to punish the Tudor dynasty for its forcible imposition of
Protestantism on the heretofore Catholic Kingdom of England and Ireland—and of which his dead wife, Mary Tudor, had been queen.

But no again—it was not to be. For beginning on August 7, 1588,
Philip's vast concourse of ships and soldiers was as decisively defeated as his own galleys had humbled the Muslim Turks only seventeen years earlier—and it was Spain now that was shocked and shattered and slowly sinking into a desuetude from which it is only now
beginning to emerge.

Spain's decline was not a free fall, a plummeting drop from the
zenith to the nadir, like the reversal of fortune that buried the nations
of Islam. The Spanish Empire expired slowly, under the winds of
change that had transformed those thirteen little seagoing republics of

England into the world's first truly independent democracy. It was the very birth of a genuinely free people: "We hold these Truths to be self-evident, that all Men are created equal, that they are endowed by their Creator with certain inalienable Rights, that among these are Life, Liberty, and the Pursuit of Happiness. . . ."

These were the words that inflamed all men of goodwill in Latin America. The great liberators of the South showed, by their contempt for place of power, their unflinching loyalty to the ideal of independence; that though the greatness and glory of Spain had declined, they were in their individuality the equal of Cortes, Pizarro, Balboa, Quesada and Alvarado, these fighters for freedom who unwittingly made Winston Churchill's credo their own: "in victory, magnanimity; in defeat, defiance." Their names were almost like a roll call of Spanish constancy: Bernardo O'Higgins, José de San Martín, Simon Bolívar, José Martí, Miguel Hidalgo y Costillo, José María Morelos—so many of these hundreds of Liberators who expressed their own truth with their lives: especially the last two, Hidalgo the highborn priest, Morelos the low-born, both the champions of the downtrodden Indians and mestizos. Because of them, by the time of that dreadful bloodbath in Europe of 1914–18, it is safe to say that most of the men and women of the Spanish New World were no longer slaves. Like the heroes of the American Revolution, thousands of noble Latinos suffered and died for their ideals; but in the end their constancy put an end to the tyranny and regimentation of Madrid.

ALTHOUGH THE GAZE of the princes of the Old World for some time had shifted from the Mediterranean—the birthplace of civilization—to the broad Atlantic, there was really no attempt at colonization in North America. Indeed, Juan Ponce de León had been granted Puerto Rico in 1501—providing he could conquer it, which he did. There were, however, few attractions to keep him there, especially at age fifty-three, which not too many hardy explorers of that century seldom reached and only a few ever passed. It was time, Ponce thought, to discover some sort of elixir to restore his high spirits, so he went looking for the fabled Fountain of Youth. Although he never found it—if he ever expected to—he did reach the eastern coast of what is now called Florida. Because the discovery occurred at Eastertide 1513, he promptly named it *Pascua Florida*—Flower of Easter.

By then, France had entered the competition. French fishermen sailing in the wake of John Cabot and the Azorean explorer Gaspar Corte Real had begun to fish the Grand Bank as early as 1504. While other

discoverers were still enchanted with the old lure of the hoary seagoing triumvirate—gold, jewels, and spices—these practical Gauls were
delighted with the unexpected substitute of fabulous catches of plump
and delicious cod falling from their nets into their hold in a golden
stream of squirming, stinking, silvery wealth to be taken home just in
time for the penitential season of Lent.

Twenty years later, the adventurous Jacques Cartier—the mariner
from St.-Malo in Brittany—made his first voyage to the New World
and focused the eyes of France on what was called Canada—an Indian
word for "place" or "town"—repeating the voyage two years later,
probably because he was unable to forget the mighty river he named
the St. Lawrence, and the majestic virgin forests of the Laurentians, or
the riotous glory of their autumn dress. Unknown to him, the St.
Lawrence—though only 750 miles long—was nevertheless one of the
world's major short streams, with a massive flow almost equaling that
of the Rhine, Volga and Nile combined.

Cartier spent his winters under the rock of Québec made welcome
by good-humored Hurons whose tall tales equaled those of travelers
anywhere. Chief Donnaconna delighted in regaling his visitor from
over "the Great Water" with lurid tales of a Kingdom of Saguenay in-
habited by similar white-skinned gentlemen whose mines disgorged
precious metals and rubies and whose fields were redolent with spices
sparkling in the sun. There it was again—the old trinity of gold, jewels, and spices—and who could blame these "ignorant" but humorous
Hurons if they nodded at their enchanted guest in gently smiling
approbation.

King Francis I of France, hearing about the same old lures, decided
to build a New World empire of his own by sending Cartier on a third
voyage, this time with a fleet of ten ships filled with veteran sailors
and explorers and so much equipment that the king of Spain thought
seriously of sinking it. Cartier's last voyage, of course, shattered the
Saguenay myth—which was only the name of a minor river—and the
civil wars that had begun to wrack La Belle France put an end to any
further expeditions.

In the meantime, the British entered the competition.

THE FIRST BRITISH attempt to colonize the New World was begun in
1584, when Walter Raleigh sent a reconnaissance fleet across the Atlantic to assess the chances of a successful commercial venture to the
future Croatan Sound in North Carolina, so named after a local tribe of
Indians there. Its leaders—Captains Amadas and Barlow—returned
with a glowing account of the climate, soil, and "friendly" Indians:

"most gentle, loving and faithful, void of all guile and treason, and such as live after the manner of a Golden Age."

Such arrant nonsense might have suggested to a hard-bitten pirate such as Raleigh—for all his literary and historical skills—that the good captains, so far from making the practical report that their master anticipated, were indulging in a fantasy intended to cover what may well have been a hostile welcome off the shores of Roanoke Island in what is now North Carolina. Enthused, the charming "favorite" —not to say lover—of the lasciviously impotent "Virgin Queen" Elizabeth, immediately set about organizing a colonizing expedition of starry-eyed pioneers similarly enchanted by the captains' tale, even though it had only hinted at the presence of precious minerals and fragrant woodlands filled with the willing naked daughters of these noble savages. After Raleigh had finished describing this report to the Pirate Queen, his enthusiasm was so infectious that she knighted him on the spot; and after she graciously permitted him to call his colony "Virginia"—by which she modestly meant all of North America—he formed his first group of about a hundred men. Departing in 1585, they did drop anchor off Roanoke Island, but found neither wood nymphs nor gold, nor jewels, nor spices, but rather snarling red men wielding sharpened stone tomahawks to protect their game, grain, and girls from these hungry, lewd intruders.

Fortunately for Raleigh's Englishmen, Sir Francis Drake—another of the Pirate Queen's freebooters—had been returning from his customary plunder of the West Indies and the Spanish king's bullion fleets, and dropped anchor off Roanoke for fresh water and a disappointing meeting with his friend Raleigh's unhappy colonists. They appeared to be walking skeletons, although an artist and a surveyor among them had been busy preparing the first illustrated account in English of the appearance and customs of North American natives, some of whom at that unpleasant moment were busily evacuating Roanoke Island, unaware that their unwelcome guests had asked Drake to take them home—and that he had consented.

Their tale of misery did not daunt Raleigh, who at once began organizing a second colony of 117 men, women, and children to found "the city of Raleigh, Virginia." This tiny colony might have prospered except that the times in 1588 were not propitious—the homeland frantically preparing to repel the Spanish Armada, and the Indian population being both hostile and numerous—so that the colony simply vanished. A third expedition sent out by Raleigh found only rotten chests filled with rusty armor and moldy maps and not a sign to be found of an English survivor, except for the tribal name CROATAN found carved on a tree, and suggesting that those "gentle, loving and faithful" aborigines had killed all their unwelcome visitors and adopted their children.

And so the sixteenth century came to an empty close, with neither England nor France having established a colony in the New World; with Spain still busily exploiting its claims in the West Indies and Latin America; and with Europe itself still tormented by the shipwreck of Christendom caused by the Protestant Reformation and the reaction of the Catholic Counter-Reformation.

EVEN THE CHAIN of trading posts established by the French in Canada at Port Royal, Québec, Montréal, and Trois Rivières to continue the lucrative exchange of metal tools and woolen cloth for the Indians' furs eventually fell into neglect and desuetude. All those hardy Frenchmen who had participated in this commerce had either died, been killed or returned to the mother country.

With one great exception: Samuel de Champlain.

PART II

Prelude to Wars

CHAPTER 4

Samuel de Champlain

IN THE YEAR 1603 a pair of lonely frail ships—one fifteen tons, the other twenty—entered the vast ninety-mile-wide mouth of the mighty St. Lawrence River, bound upstream for the Bay of Tadoussac, the center of the French fur trade among the Indian tribes of Lower Canada. Aboard one as commander was a merchant of St. Malo known as Pontgrave the Elder, and commanding the other was Samuel de Champlain, only lately invested with a patent into the untitled nobility of France; but even more important to him personally—a small pension from the slender revenues of King Henry IV of France, the first monarch of the Bourbon dynasty.

Samuel Champlain had been extremely proud to insert that particle *de* between his Christian and his family names, and though it was almost meaningless, to continue to serve his adored sovereign with every fiber of his adventurous, brave, devout, and devoted being. Champlain had been born in 1567 at the small seaport of Brouage on the Bay of Biscay. His father had been a captain in the Royal French Navy, and Samuel seems to have served briefly aboard a warship before fighting for the king on land.

Henry had been known as Young Henry of Navarre, a small northern kingdom that had once been Spanish. As a young man he had been attracted by the grim Calvinism of the French Huguenots. Becoming heir presumptive on the death of Henry III in 1589, he renounced Protestantism, entering Paris in triumph and with the typically lighthearted remark "Paris is worth a Mass." Young Champlain, also an earlier Huguenot, followed Henry IV back into the Catholic Church.

After the civil wars ended with the popular Bourbon sovereign Henri Quatre still on the throne, Champlain decided to visit the West Indies—to which the Spanish would permit no Frenchman to enter under pain of death—and this very peril, together with the young adventurer's yearning to bring back to the king a full report of Spanish exploitation, was an irresistible allure. In some way—his flair for the incredible but successful bluff was one of his chief assets—he managed to slip aboard a Spanish fleet bound for the West Indies under Don Francesco Columbo, probably a descendant of the Great Discoverer. Champlain spent two years on his West Indian adventure, visiting the island ports, making sketches of their defenses, journeying inland to Mexico City, and reaching Panama, where four centuries before the actual birth of the Panama Canal, his bold and penetrating mind conceived the plan for a ship-canal across the isthmus, "by which," he suggested, "the voyage to the South Sea would be shortened by more than fifteen hundred leagues."

Having made no effort to inform the Spanish crown of this veritable jewel of both sea-route control plus a steady, incredible revenue from passage charges, Champlain returned to court at Paris, bringing with him his fantastic journal of his travels. Here, in a clumsy, childish hand, were sketches combining the fantastic, the horrible, and the prosaic. Here were drawings of islands, ports, harbors, rivers, and forts done in the precise style of a master cartographer, and which someday might be of great value to some monarch seeking to expand at Spain's expense; but adorned by sketches done in that unstudied hand of fish, birds, and beasts native to the locale. Here also were joyous Indian feasts and dances, but also brutal scenes of priests flogging Indians for missing Mass, or of soldiers burning them alive for heresy, or of Indians working in the silver mines. Finally, this amazing record of his two-year journey contained descriptions of animals—some composed on the spot, others drawn from memory—such as a two-legged chameleon, or a man-eating griffin believed to haunt the heights of Mexico, a monster with the wings of a bat, the head of an eagle, and the tail of an alligator.

Except in the nautical and military charts there was no hint—nay, no attempt at—artistic skill; but Samuel Champlain's deepest ambition was to explore the lakes, rivers and rapids, cliffs and mountains, booming cataracts, and fog-bound seacoasts of the enormous wilderness of New France, his own land of heart's desire; there he could reach the consummation of a life both marvelous and noble by planting both cross and Fleur de Lis among the continent's naked savages and enlist them in the adoration of the risen Christ and the service of his anointed king.

Still on fire with this prospect, the old campaigner, whose experiences at thirty-six were worthy of another scarred and seamed soldier at sixty, arrived at court searching for a leader who could open to him the wide door of adventure. He found him in Aymar de Chastes, commander of the Order of St. John and governor of Dieppe. De Chastes had come to court to beg a patent from Henry Quatre, "and," said his friend Champlain, "though his head was crowned with gray hairs as with years, he resolved to proceed to New France in person, and dedicate the rest of his days to the service of God and king."

Costing nothing, de Chastes's patent for a monopoly of the Canadian fur trade was readily granted, and he immediately offered Champlain a post with the new company. Champlain consented, but only on the condition that permission be granted by the king, "to whom," he said, "I was bound no less by birth than by the pension with which His Majesty honored me."

Overjoyed, Samuel de Champlain hastened to the Port of Honfleur, where the St.-Malo merchant called Pontgrave the Elder had been busy outfitting two small ships for the Canadian adventure. He was pleased to see Champlain, for he had heard of him as a bold and brave adventurer. Soon these two small fragile vessels set sail from Normandy for the Gulf of St. Lawrence. Like cockle shells tossing on the surface of the great gray sea they plied their course steadily west, passing the tempestuous headlands of New Foundland, entering the great river and gliding deep into the heart of the Canadian wilderness.

To Champlain the soldier-adventurer and devout Catholic it was as though he were entering the Holy of Holies, where great deeds might be done in the name of the Lord; to the merchant it was to be the source of incredible wealth "beyond the dreams of avarice." Neither found either on this voyage, for as their fragile little craft held course up the mighty river they passed the abandoned trading center of Tadoussac, ghostly and quiet; navigated the channel of Orleans and gazed upward awestruck to the foaming, thundering cataracts of the Montmorenci; and high above them the silent, empty rock of Québec and beneath it its great blue basin gleaming in the sun; thence through the breathtaking Lake of St. Peter, a small but dangerous archipelago containing 142 square miles of water for the tiny visitors to thread—and, finally, the topline of a mountain beyond the forest-plain of Montréal.

All was silent. All was still. All was solitude. The kingdom of Hochelaga—like the mythical Kingdom of Prester John—had vanished. Of the Huron-Algonquin population Jacques Cartier had found here sixty-eight years ago, only a few wandering Algonquin remained, all speaking a different tongue and with a different tribal allegiance. Assisted by a few of them in a skiff, the bold Champlain sought to pass the rapids of St. Louis. Plying poles, paddles, and oars alike, they still could not penetrate their foaming surge, and the roar of their defiance was perhaps equally as daunting as their power.

Although the Indians boarded Champlain's little ship to draw rude sketches of the river above, with its chains of rapids, lakes, and cataracts, Champlain shook his head and turned his prow homeward. Following him came a dejected Pontgrave, thwarted in his quest for riches and perhaps even annoyed that his companion seemed not to regret this signal setback, but rather to be merely unsatisfied, his curiosity intact and his determination to return undeterred.

Arriving home in Havre de Grace, both men were shocked to learn that their patron—Commander de Chastes—was dead.

DE CHASTES'S PATENT of a monopoly of the Canadian fur trade was secured by Pierre du Guast, Sieur de Monts, gentleman in ordinary of the king's chamber and governor of Pons. He had petitioned His Majesty to colonize the enormous region of Acadia, an area stretching from modern Philadelphia to beyond Montréal. Sully, the king's minister, had opposed the venture on the eminently practical grounds that it would cost more than it was worth. But de Monts gained the grant.

Wisely enough, de Monts not only preserved de Chastes's old company but also expanded it, thus making partners of the chief losers in His Majesty's decision: the cities of St.-Malo, Rouen, Dieppe, and Rochelle. As almost a guarantee of trouble, a clause in his commission enabled him to impress idlers, vagabonds, and other scamps who might have been concealed criminals. Thus these ruffians, the worst of the dregs of the French ports, were crammed together with the nation's best in de Monts's two ships: well-born men such as Champlain and Baron Poutrincourt, as well as both Catholic priests and Huguenot ministers.

De Monts, with the first of his vessels and the merchant Pontgrave, sailed from Havre de Grace on April 7, 1604, the vessel laden to the gunwales with its cargo of useful metal tools, kitchen utensils, and useless trinkets such as bright buttons and caps, gay ribbons, and worthless rings for finger, nose, or ear—all of enormous profit when "traded"—if that is the correct verb—with the guileless Indians in exchange for their peltry of far greater value.

De Monts's vessel was hardly at sea before the priests and ministers fell into friendly discussion of points of doctrine, which, growing quickly heated, turned to quarreling and then to blows. Champlain was appalled, and wrote: "I have seen our curé and the minister fall to their fists on questions of faith. I cannot say which had the more pluck, or which hit the harder. But I know that the minister sometimes complained to the Sieur de Monts that he had been beaten. This was their way of settling points of controversy. I leave you to judge if it was a pleasant thing to see."

A Franciscan friar named Sagard, also aboard, was horrified to discover that after they had reached their destination, a priest and a minister died simultaneously, and the crew found it tickled their gallows humor to bury them side by side to see if they could possibly lie peaceably together.

Actually, de Monts, with his associates, found themselves more on an exploratory expedition than a colonizing venture, which delighted the ever-industrious Champlain. He was never so happy as when he was exploring and discovering—absolutely unbelieving when he sailed into the Bay of Fundy to find that the tides at its mouth sometimes rose and fell an incredible seventy feet! No one in the company was busier than Samuel de Champlain, taking soundings, surveying, making charts, entering an unknown river, questioning the occasional Indian who had ventured into the French camp.

When de Monts with Champlain and the others began to explore the Bay of Fundy, their first discovery was Annapolis Harbor, at first seemingly nothing more than a narrow inlet until, gradually, the little strait broadened into a wide and tranquil basin, encompassed by sun-bathed hills covered with the tender green of the verdant forests of spring—and laced with sparkling, foaming, musical waterfalls.

Baron Poutrincourt was enchanted, so taken with what he saw that he informed de Monts and Champlain that he would love to move here from France with his family and almost all that he possessed. De Monts, whose patent included almost half a continent, at once granted the place to his friend, who immediately named it Port Royal.

At last the restless de Monts decided on a site for his colony, choosing, at the mouth of an unknown river, a small island encircled by rocks and shoals that would certainly discourage an invader, but also if besieged and cut off, be just as completely starved into submission. De Monts seems to have given no thought to the second possibility as he and his friend Poutrincourt went about fortifying the island, while Champlain—too excited by the site's proximity to what would eventually become the beautiful northeastern coast of the United States of America—could do no more than name the stream St. Croix—or Holy Cross. For almost all the other pioneers at St. Croix life had become both tedious and unpleasant, while Champlain hurled himself with delight into a campaign of discovery and exploration along the American coast by which, as the historian Francis Parkman declared, "[He] threw light into the dark places of American geography, and brought order out of the chaos of American cartography."

There was little time for pleasure or leisure activities at St. Croix, while de Monts and Poutrincourt urged their assembled soldiers, sailors, artisans, and laborers onto their task of building a settlement; and before the brutal northern winter closed in, the island site was covered with structures surrounding a square in which a solitary tree was left standing, perhaps as some sort of grim reminder should misfortune overtake this lonely wilderness outpost. Next, the homes of de Monts, Poutrincourt, and Champlain were built, together with a workshop, lodgings for gentlemen and artisans, plus a barracks for the Swiss soldiers who had unwisely volunteered for the duty, much to their present regret. For Champlain—who loved gardens—there was a feeble attempt at planting one, and the beginnings of a cemetery as well, but both had to be abandoned as the riotous autumn colors daubed by the Almighty on his Canadian palate began to fade, a sure sign that the bitter winter that de Monts—who had been to the St. Lawrence once before—knew was on its way.

Poutrincourt, wiser and freer than all others, departed by sail for France almost the moment all labor had ended, announcing happily that he would return in springtime to take possession of his cherished Port Royal. His sails had hardly vanished beneath the horizon when the seventy-nine souls left behind at St. Croix felt the harsh cold breath of winter wind stabbing the backs of their necks.

It had come, and it came with a shriek and a howl.

Within a few frightening hours, the whirling, whistling, moaning snow had powdered the country around them with an obliterating blanket of white. In the gray light of morning it could be seen that the river was frozen. But soon, by the ebb and flow of its tides, a terrible crackling arose and the river was soon a mass of shifting ice slabs, sharpened like knives at its edges—impassable, and not only uncontrollable, but also isolating the settlement, cutting off all hope of gathering supplies of wood and water, without which they could not survive. It is not known what in that moment de Monts might have thought of his disastrous decision to choose such a frozen cul-de-sac for his settlement.

Soon cider and wine froze in the casks and had to be served by the pound. Then the dreadful scourge of scurvy appeared, riding among the company like one of the Four Horsemen of the Apocalypse, with its eyeless sockets and toothless gums and its head swathed in black. Such might have been a fair description of this horrible affliction. In those days the existence of such substances as citric juices that make vitamin C—which could contain and eliminate scurvy—were not known. In ignorance of their affliction, men began to slide slowly into debility, despair, and death. . . . They could not comprehend how or why they were falling apart, bit by bloated bit . . . the steady hemorrhaging . . . teeth falling from gums turned to sponge . . . apathy . . . anemia . . . oblivion. . . .

Of the seventy-nine men left behind, thirty-five died before spring, their frozen bodies awaiting incarceration in graves opened with axes rather than shovels. Yet, among all this gathering of shivering, chattering men crowding around their half-cold fires, their foul breath breaking from their mouths in vapor puffs, one man stood alone like a beacon of hope—indomitable, cheerful, a very apostle of deliverance: Samuel de Champlain.

SPRING CAME AT LAST, and with the drip-drip melting of the snow, the crackling breakup of the ice, the high crying of the returning waterfowl, the spirits of the surviving men slowly rose. Despair gave way to hope, hope was succeeded by suspense, and this sank back into a soul-annihilating torpor—until they saw:

A SAIL!

It was on the sixteenth of June 1605 that Pontgrave arrived with forty healthy men, all manner of food and drink and every conceivable replacement for all that they had lost to sustain life.

EVENTUALLY THE Sieur de Monts had come to his senses. He realized that St. Croix had been a snake pit, and he decided to look for some more amenable site upon which to rear the capital of the trackless wilderness that was his domain. Nevertheless, led by the tireless Champlain, neither his searching, scouting treks amid the forests, lakes, and rivers nor his months of cruising along the shores of what one day would be the northeastern coast of the United States uncovered a satisfactory site.

Until he thought of Port Royal.

True, it was to be the home of his friend Baron Poutrincourt, who had not yet returned to claim it; but he was certain the baron would be equally satisfied with another such paradise within his monopoly of millions upon millions of square miles. At once he resolved to move there, immediately beginning to transfer all that was portable from the miserable nightmare of St. Croix across the Bay of Fundy and into Port Royal.

But even as he began to settle in, another ship arrived—not bringing the baron back to Canada, but bearing the ominous news that de Monts's enemies in Paris were busily seeking revocation of his patent. Therefore he set sail, leaving Pontgrave in command at Port Royal, and Champlain and his friends to volunteer for a second winter ordeal in the wilderness.

CHAPTER 5

War in the Wilderness

IT WILL BE easier to understand these four wilderness wars of Colonial America with a knowledge of the weapons used, the means of transportation, the food, the clothing, the medicines or surgical practices in vogue, and the strategies and tactics of the protagonists during this period stretching from 1609, when Samuel de Champlain fired those first deadly shots on the shores of the lake that bears his name—and the climactic battle on the Plains of Abraham in 1759 when the golden lilies of France at last sank forever into the St. Lawrence, Canada then ceasing to be French and becoming British. That was a period of exactly 150 years of armed conflict, and during it none of the articles and attitudes quoted above had changed very much, if at all.

To begin: firearms. It is difficult to say exactly when firearms first appeared. It has been claimed—mostly by those people who assign to backward tribes or races the authorship of great discoveries—that gunpowder existed in China as early as the first century. If it did, it was only to make firecrackers for use at festivals, not to invent new and fearful weapons based on explosives and thus subjugate all humankind. Five hundred years earlier, the Greeks were pouring their terrifying "Greek fire"—an oily, tarry combustible—on invaders from land and sea.

There is, however, a tradition that puts the invention of gunpowder—and therefore of firearms—in the year 1320, when a German monk named Berthold Schwartz—a dabbler in the forbidden mystico-chemical delights of alchemy—sought to make gold by boiling a mixture of sulfur, saltpeter, quicksilver, oil and lead, succeeding only in cooking up explosions so violent that they sometimes wrecked his laboratory. Here was not gold but gunpowder. However, this curious and disobedient monk, whose last name, "Schwartz," or "Black," actually was a nickname derived from his habit of practicing the "black art" of alchemy (and also, one suspects, from his frequently singed appearance), was *not* the man who first thought of propelling a lead ball through a metal tube by exploding a charge of gunpowder behind it. Whether we wish to bless or to curse the true author of firearms, we do not have the gentleman's name. Suffice it to say that within eight years of Black Berthold's opening blasts, the French had cannons; and in another twenty the seafaring English were firing them from ships.

It is not really possible to establish at what date the first muskets and handguns appeared, although it is known that in 1537 King Henry VIII of Britain granted a charter to the Guild of St. George authorizing its members to practice with every form of "artillery"—bows, crossbows, and handguns alike. In every competition between both forms of bows and firearms until the end of the sixteenth century, the bow and arrow emerged victorious, usually by a score of something like 20 to 16. But the bows gradually fell out of favor, probably because they just could not match the range of the muskets or shoulder-firearm.

An informed guess would put the triumph of gunpowder over musclepower at the first decade of the 1600s. That was when the smooth-bore musket, with its various "locks," or firing devices—matchlock, firelock, wheel-lock, or flintlock—became popular, in that order. In the end the flintlock emerged as the universal favorite, probably because flint—a natural stone—was superabundant almost everywhere, more reliable and cheaper to obtain. It also could sometimes be fired in clammy weather or in a light rain because from the shower of sparks created when a small piece of flint struck a steel frizzen or hammer, at least one or two of them would fly through a touchhole and into the firing pan on which a few grains of gunpowder had been sprinkled, thus igniting the main charge in the barrel. This would happen almost instantly—between a tenth and a fifth of a second—though it takes much, much longer to describe it.

A flintlock musket was about five and a half feet in length, composed of a metal tube three and a half feet long, and a wooden stock of two feet, which was pressed into a soldier's shoulder to steady his aim. A matchlock was somewhat shorter, about the length of a modern carbine and therefore ideal for forest warfare. The bore—as the inside of the barrel is called—was a bit less than three-quarters of an inch in diameter. Because the bore was smooth, the weapon's accuracy was lamentably poor, and its range was miserably short. All readers of this writer's favorite book will remember that Robin Hood could fire an arrow a mile; but in actuality there is no record of an arrow having been fired any farther than six hundred yards anywhere.

A flintlock rarely hit its standing target at more than fifty or sixty yards, while to shoot at anything still visible at a hundred yards was simply a waste of ammunition. The bullet, incidentally, was a round lead ball weighing about an ounce and fitted loosely into the barrel to prevent fouling of the powder. Sometimes buckshot—that is, a cluster of small lead pellets—was used instead of the customary single ball. The gunpowder that propelled it was of the original black-smoke-making variety, and the smoke it produced was thick enough for it to be called "the fog of war."

It would be about two centuries before a shoulder firearm firing only a single bullet at a time became obsolete, succeeded by the amazingly accurate, long-range rifle, so called because armament manufacture had become all but a German monopoly, and the German word *rifeln* meant to groove. Usually four spiral grooves were drilled into the bore of a rifle, and these seized the bullet, giving it a remarkably rapid spin that vastly increased both its accuracy and its range. Somewhat later, rifles were equipped with chambers holding clips of from five to eight bullets, thus conferring an incredible advantage on the offense.

But the soldier or savage engaged in battle during the Colonial Wars still had to fight with the bulky, unreliable flintlock, about ten to fourteen pounds in weight and requiring many motions to load and fire it. First he must remove from the box at his hip a paper cartridge containing powder and ball. Next he must tear open the cartridge with his teeth, sprinkling a few grains of gunpowder into the firing pan, ramming some of the paper down the barrel with a ramrod, followed by the rest of the powder, the wadded cartridge, and then the ball—after which he could fire it.

It has been claimed that the average colonial militiaman could fire his musket five times a minute, but this is patently ridiculous, because each time he reloaded he would have to stop and take cover. If advancing, he could not fire so rapidly; if prone, to offer the enemy the smallest target, he dared not betray himself, squirming around like a stricken squirrel to make so many motions, or raising his head repeatedly to make sure of his target. At best a good soldier could fire his flintlock only twice a minute, and even this frequency could not be obtained if there were a bayonet plugged into the muzzle of his musket. Sometimes troops would load powder and ball without ramming, but this untamped charge fell harmlessly to the ground after about thirty yards. Most officers frowned on attempted rapid fire. James Wolfe was enraged to witness it.

"There is no necessity for firing fast," he said. "A cool well-leveled fire with the pieces carefully loaded is more destructive and formidable than the quickest fire in confusion." Notice that Wolfe said properly "loaded" rather than "aimed." Indeed, the word "aim" did not appear in the British manual of arms, and the celebrated—or accursed— British Brown Bess, named for the Pirate Queen, did not even have a rear sight!

Even before colonization of the New World, the Spanish had revolutionized warfare by introducing an improved matchlock and fielding units of professional foot soldiers called infantry. (The name derived from the custom of adopting Spanish princes, or *infantes*, as the honorary colonels of regiments.) With their new but clumsy six-foot muskets the Spanish foot soldiers were invincible, and their advent opened the age of modern infantry tactics. Deployment and maneuver on the open plain supplanted siege warfare.

Probably the most compelling reason for the flint's survival was its aforementioned durability, availability, and cheapness. After twenty or thirty shots even a carefully shaped flint would wear out, at which point it could be replaced by a new one. Flints were the lifeblood of all armies relying on firearms.

But the paper cartridge continued in use until the eruption of the American Civil War, although by then the powder charge was ignited by a percussion cap instead of a flint. Until it was abandoned, one requisite for a soldier was that he have a good set of teeth so he could bite off the end of the cartridge. Shirkers of the day avoided that dreadful bloodbath by having their front teeth removed. Fainthearted draftees during the two world wars sometimes would shoot off a toe or a finger on the premise that losing a few digits wasn't a bad way to save one's life.

Up until these even bloodier convulsions of humankind, soldiers were rarely taught how to fire their weapons accurately, probably because the costs of constantly drilling them in accuracy were too prohibitive. At most they "pointed" them rather than squinting down the rear and front sights to "aim" them; and also when lying prone to avoid being hit, lowering their piece almost level with the ground. Training in individual marksmanship in colonial days was still not in vogue, and those soldiers and savages of both sides who aimlessly exchanged shots rarely hit a running foe or one mostly concealed behind a tree.

Toward the end of the seventeenth century the much-derided musket took on a new menace. Some inventive soul thought of fitting a sharp-edged, pointed knife with a handle that could be jammed into the muzzle of a musket. Thus he inadvertently converted a firearm into a pike, whose row upon row of gleaming blades could terrify a reluctant soldier. Even more frightening was the device of another inventive soul who wielded what was to be called a bayonet to a socket that could be fitted around the musket muzzle. Thus he transformed the private soldier into a terrifying noise- and smoke-making machine. He could reload it again and again until he was concealed behind clouds of black smoke, and from which he could emerge with fiendish yells, brandishing his musket like a long, glittering pike. American colonials for decades could not stand against the European bayonet charge. One glimpse of those regulars in white or scarlet coats and pipe-clayed criss-crossed belts—all bellowing like the bulls of Bashan—was like an immense and horrifying starter's pistol sending them sprinting for the rear.

Of the other two "arms" of battle—cavalry and artillery—the horse troopers were practically useless in the American wilderness, although there were many forms of cannon, but none nearly as big as the great naval guns of World War II—the 14- and 16-inch mammoths hurling 2,500-pound shells at a range of up to 20 miles. The greatest land gun ever devised was Germany's "Big Bertha" in World War I. A 16.5-inch monster howitzer, it could hurl an 1,800-pound shell 9 miles, and it proved its worth by pounding Belgium's formidable Liège forts into rubble.

During the Colonial Wars there were three types of artillery: cannon of relatively long barrels; short-barreled howitzers; and even shorter, almost vertical "stovepipes" called mortars.

They also could be used as antipersonnel weapons, discharging a load of musket balls or clusters of small iron balls called grapeshot to break up an enemy charge.

Cannons were used to fire solid iron balls against forts, ships, or other defensive works such as wooden stockades, or stouter small redoubts of either timber-faced cribs filled with dirt or sturdier ones faced with stone.

Howitzers were short-barreled cannons capable of firing a shell on a curving trajectory that would take it inside an enemy defensive position or behind a hill where he was massing his troops. Mortars were very short and stubby, yet these beloved "stovepipes" have probably been the great killers of military history. They could lob a shell on a looping parabola that a really skilled gunner could actually drop down a chimney! All explosive shells were fitted with fuses, the length of which would govern the time it took between firing and striking its target. In the late Middle Ages—even much earlier than the Colonial Wars—a gunner might determine the time of flight to the target by mentally reciting the Lord's Prayer or the Apostles' Creed. All these guns were loaded at the muzzle—that is to say, its open mouth, for the period of breech-loading artillery at the bottom end was still centuries away.

The size of a cannon's bore was determined by the weight of the solid iron ball that fit into it, with a slight clearance of a fifth of an inch. A three-pounder had a bore of two and seven-eighths inches, a twelve-pounder four and five-eighths, while a huge (for those days) twenty-four pounder weighing up to almost three tons had a bore five and three-quarter inches across.

Inside forts a cannon was usually mounted on a low carriage with either two or four wooden or iron wheels. When the gun was to be moved, its trail, the rearward extension of its body, was attached to another wheeled carriage called the limber. Normally gun and limber were drawn by horses, but more often by oxen over the bumpy and potholed trails that the colonials dignified with the name of "roads."

When the expedition moved by water, the heavier guns were transported by flatboats or big *bateaux*; arriving at shallows or rapids, they were manhandled overland by the biggest farm boys available.

Howitzers and mortars were classified by the diameter of their barrel, six or eight inches being typical howitzer sizes, with ten and thirteen inches for mortars. Howitzers were mounted on a regular gun carriage, mortars fired from a simple flatbed with a round space to receive and immobilize the weapon's rounded bottom end. They could be carried to their firing position in a wagon or a flatboat and skidded into place with crowbars in the hands of those big farm boys.

All these pieces of ordnance—so-called at the end of the Middle Ages, when all military supplies were arranged in an "orderly" manner, from which rose the word "ordnance"—had a maximum effective range of about half a mile. Its extreme range, however, was much greater, but with less accuracy. To break down a wall, the shortest possible range in use was about two hundred yards. At this distance a bombardment could be remarkably accurate and effective, two successive shots landing almost in the same place. Range, or course, was lengthened or shortened by raising or lowering the barrel, which was done by means of a sliding wooden wedge for cannon and howitzer carriages. Toward the end of the Colonial period screw elevating gear had become available for some lighter field pieces. Mortar range could also be adjusted in this way, but the customary method of varying the range was by increasing or decreasing the powder charge.

Most veteran artillerists were agreed that bronze made the best guns, chiefly because it would not rust and—though expensive—was a stronger, more durable weapon than the cheaper iron cannon, typically mounted inside forts where its protected metal would not rust. Inside or outside, the bronze cannons were the best.

COLONIAL FORTIFICATIONS were usually of three kinds: wooden stockades or forts with walls made of timber- or stone-faced cribbing filled with dirt. The simplest and quickest way to build a frontier fort was the stockade. Generally it was a square enclosed by vertical logs set in a narrow trench three feet or deeper. Usually the logs were twelve to fifteen feet long. Firing loopholes would be cut into them, with barracks and storehouses built inside. Such positions were frequently built in a hurry to guard a threatened village or divert an enemy attack. If there were enough time, the ends of the logs were carefully dovetailed so that when they were fitted together snugly, whatever chinks remained between them could be filled with some form of mortar to make the walls bulletproof. A fort of this construction usually was safe unless it came under artillery fire. Young George Washington's famous Fort Necessity, which fell to the French with such infamous speed, was one of these stockades.

Fort William Henry on Lake George was a bastion of far more solid construction. Built of timbered cribs filled with earth, it could withstand heavy bombardment, but after a number of years the dirt inside the timbers would rot the wood and the whole structure would collapse. Also, William Henry was not very formidable, for Montcalm had no trouble taking it. The same could not be said of the French Fort Carillon at Ticonderoga. Here the cribs forming the walls were stone-faced.

Besieging a fort followed formal rules, which for some unknown reason were seldom violated. It began by bringing up heavy ordnance to knock down the fort's walls, or to blast a hole in them through which the position could be stormed. If the besieger made such a breach, it was acceptable for the fort's commander—if he had done everything possible to hold the fort—to surrender without reproach or censure. However, if the breach had to be stormed with great loss to the attackers, the garrison could expect no quarter; but rather, slaughter. A surprise attack by men swarming up scaling ladders could be a success if the defenders were actually taken unawares, depending more upon the strength of their walls rather than their own prowess as fighters.

But forts almost always fall. Indeed, to rely upon the physical strength of any fortress in any era generally has been a mistake. Of all the means of conquering a fixed position, however, the most successful have been trickery and betrayal.

Troy was deceived and undone by the ruse of the wooden horse. Jericho was betrayed to Joshua by the harlot Rahab. Jerusalem crumbled under the catapults of Titus; Constantinople was stormed by Crusader and Saracen alike; Québec, if not actually surprised by Wolfe, was indeed betrayed from within by the profiteering traitors who thwarted every one of Montcalm's wise provisions of defense; and finally, Vicksburg succumbed to siege guns and starvation. Century after century bears doleful evidence of the crossing of impassable waters, the scaling of inaccessible cliffs, the march through impenetrable swamps or the bursting by force of arms or the opening by guile or deception of unbreakable walls.

And the fall of the absolutely impregnable Maginot Line in World War II? Here indeed was military history's greatest example of mankind's immemorial bad habit of mistaking the part for the whole. The Maginot Line was not intended to protect all of France against a second soul-shattering visit from her brutal German neighbor. The Maginot was not completed west to the sea and thus to hold the attacking Huns at bay. No, it was rather intended to be the shield that would deflect the marauding Teutons in that direction, where the Sword of France—the reserve—would destroy them. Instead, through that unguarded gap the invading enemy hordes came pouring once again.

COLONIAL YOUTH DID NOT exactly make good solders, chiefly because they were free men who hated the iron discipline of armies and did not believe they had sacrificed their freedom when they "listed" in the "milishy." For the most part they were willing farm boys, fishermen, mechanics, sailors, clerks, handy-men, carters, and jobless drifters. Their only military experience was at monthly meetings of the "milishy," which actually were more like social gatherings or picnics with refreshments, cider or beer for the adults and sweetmeats and hot chocolate for the children. After a half hour of leisurely drill with the drums rattling gaily and the fifes raving away, and every "sojer" having two left feet and guiding on himself, the true purpose of the gathering became apparent:

Yankee-doodle keep it up, Yankee-doodle dandy,
Mind the music and the step, and with the girls be handy!

Their leaders were hardly better, politicans with little or no knowledge of war or the equipping and raising of armies, although most of these tyros were public-relations types whose chief function was to persuade those big farm boys to enlist. Junior officers were struck from the same mold who *had* to be popular with the men to be chosen for commissioned rank, and also to hold it once it was theirs. George Washington, upon arriving in Boston to take command of what would be the Continental Army, nearly had apoplexy when he saw captains shaving privates. If the Father of His Country had any *bête noire* it was what he called "the New England leveling spirit," and he happily reported to Philadelphia that he had "made a slam" among those officers who were infected by it.

All the officers of the formations serving during these four Colonial Wars had to a greater or lesser extent to be responsive to the wishes of the men. Those who commanded regiments or battalions had been the leaders in social life: the squire, the tavernkeeper, or the merchant—indeed, if teachers and parsons were included, the only persons who could read and write—translated by the emergency of a war into military commanders.

Because they were hunters—especially the Pennsylvanians and Virginians, with their long rifles—they did fairly well in battle, although Washington did grow so tired of their pop-pop-popping in the Boston encampment that he sent most of them home. But the Colonial Wars were never periods of constant combat, but rather a few military episodes in which a few Americans were killed or wounded.

Battle was only occasional, separated by long intervening months of indolence and ennui, which might instead have been used to make soldiers of them by weeks of drill, target practice, and the building of reads, forts, and camps. Instead they were allowed to degenerate into dirty, lazy loafers. In the summer of 1756 an officer was sent to Fort William Henry to report on conditions there. Here it is:

> At Fort William Henry, about 2,500 men, 500 of them sick, the greatest part of them what they call poorly. They bury five to eight daily . . . [They are] extremely indolent and dirty to a degree. The fort stinks enough to cause an infection, they have all their sick in it. Their camp nastier than anything I could have conceived, their necessary houses [latrines], kitchens, graves and places for slaughtering cattle all mixed through their encampment, a great waste of provisions, the men having just what they please, no great command kept up . . . not in the least alert . . . no advance picket . . . no scouting party out during six days. . . . The people extremely indolent. . . .

The sick or wounded soldier could not expect much from the medical service of the armies of those days. Normally each battalion or regiment had its surgeon, and perhaps also an assistant surgeon. Both countries established hospitals, mostly in buildings but sometimes under canvas. British regulations allowed four women per company and six to a regiment to act as laundresses and hospital nurses. They drew a soldier's ration. In those days many women accompanied armies in the field. Many were the wives of soldiers. The British garrison at Québec in the winter of 1759–1760 included 569 women, which was about 1 for every 13 soldiers, so that it is possible that some of these ladies earned money from occupations other than nursing.

Dysentery—or what was then called "the bloody flux"—was the most common disease among armies of the day. Failure to provide sanitation in the latrines—where disease-bearing flies gathered—was the most likely cause. Another was that it was just not possible to make lazy troops realize the importance of cleaning their latrines.

Smallpox was another widespread disease, but just as common among civilians as among soldiers and sailors. Scurvy was the naval curse, which was not recognized until the middle of the 1700s, when it was realized that it could be prevented by a steady diet of vegetables. Scurvy sometimes broke out among military expeditions, and especially during the brutal winters of Canada. The first French garrison of a hundred soldiers established at Niagara by Governor Denonville in 1687 was reduced by scurvy and famine to only twelve survivors because their provisions became spoiled and it was too late to plant vegetables.

The basic food in the armies that marched in the American wilderness was salt pork packed in barrels of brine that would preserve it for months—that is, until unscrupulous and greedy wagoneers began to drill holes in the barrels so that the brine would leak out and the meat spoil. The French were almost never without their wine, and their heroes were the brave ship captains who ran the British blockade to bring it to them. The French also made their own brandy, which they traded to the Indians for furs. When beer and rum ran out among the British colonials, they resorted to making spruce beer (no one would think of touching water except for washing clothes and the body), which was quite tasty and may have been an effective remedy against scurvy.

Soldiers in the Colonial Wars were not overburdened with clothing, except for the French of the regular regiments. In 1755 a French regular arriving in Canada was given more clothing than five British regulars and three American colonials combined. He received a coat, a sleeved jacket often worn as an outer garment, breeches, hat, three shirts, a pair of gaiters, two pairs of shoes with two spare soles, two pairs of socks, and a black stock. Sometimes he only got the leather for the shoes and had to pay a cobbler to make them. He also was issued a blanket, a haversack, a knife, a fork, and a spoon, as well as an awl, some thread, and six needles. To shave he had the use of one of the five razors issued to every company of sixty men. Musket, bayonet, and ammunition were also supplied. In cold weather he received a bearskin, as well as cloth from which he was to make his own mittens.

British soldiers got no more than a coat, trousers, and a pair of boots once a year; the remainder of his clothing needs had to be purchased out of deductions from his meager pay: the stingy daily sixpence. A colonial was expected to bring his own gun, receiving a small bonus to defray its cost, and was issued a blanket, a coat, and a "soldier's hat." American militia never had uniforms—at least not the enlisted men—turning out for drill in everyday clothes, and certainly not their best. If he were issued a musket because he brought no firearm of his own, it was usually one discarded by the British Army after it had been worn out by war in Europe.

CHAPTER 6

Champlain Founds New France

THE WINTER OF 1605–6 had been unusually mild, in no way comparable to the Gethsemane that all but exterminated the settlement at St. Croix. It was not until January that the pioneers at Port Royal began to wear their doublets for warmth, and they actually spent as much time in the open as within their flimsy huts and buildings. Hunting and fishing parties were common. "I remember," said Marc Lescarbot, the poet laureate, historian, and merrymaker of Port Royal, "that on the fourteenth of January, of a Sunday afternoon, we amused ourselves with singing and music on the River Equille, and that in the same month we went to see the wheat fields two leagues from the fort and dined merrily in the sunshine."

Feasting and wine-drinking became almost common inside the quadrangle, and the fifteen principal members of the colony partook with great gusto of the shipment of sweetmeats sent to them by the ever-generous de Monts. It was actually only the icing on the cake; even before its arrival, Baron Poutrincourt on his return had seen to it that this winter would be no repetition of the agony of St. Croix. Pleased to have so many convivial friends as guests in his domain at Port Royal, he also made certain that his table would sag and groan beneath the weight of the viands and *vin* piled high upon it noon and night.

Champlain, as might be expected, formed the fifteen chief gormandizers and wine fanciers into an order christened *L'ordre de Bon-Temps*, or The Order of Good Times. Each member was Grand Master of the Feast in his turn. To exercise his charge he spent several days hunting and fishing and bartering for provisions with the Indians. All the meats that the forest could provide, the fish from the sea, and the shellfish of the rivers and brooks found their way onto Poutrincourt's table. On it lay the flesh of deer, moose, and caribou; beaver, otter, and hare, bears and wildcats; with ducks, geese, grouse, and plover; sturgeon as well and freshwater clams and mussels, trout and scallops—

sometimes even lobsters gleaming red among all the silvery denizens of the deep piled around them, netted, hooked, or speared through the ice of the Equille, or drawn from the depths of the bay.

As was customary then among the wellborn, the bounteous repast was begun at noon. Upon the striking of the hour the Grand Master entered the hall, a linen napkin over his shoulder, his staff of office in his hand, the collar of the Order about his neck. His brothers followed, each bearing a dish. Indian chiefs were the invited guests, and how they did savor that great culinary skill of the French! Mingling among their hosts, they took great pleasure in their friendship. Seated on the floor were the humbler folk: warriors, squaws, and children, all covetous of biscuit and bread, a novelty of food they found delicious.

"Thus," said Lescarbot, finishing his own duty as Grand Master, "whatever our gourmands at home may think, we found as good cheer at Port Royal, as they at their Rue aux Ours* in Paris, and that, too, at a cheaper rate."

Great cries of merriment greeted such bold pronouncements of independence, bringing the noonday banquet to a shouting climax.

With the gourmands barely recovered from the length and variety of the noonday feast, the evening meal was only a bit less bountiful, more inclined to soaking than gorging; and as the winter night closed in and the flames flickered and logs crackled and the sparks streamed upward through the wide-throated chimney, the founders of New France, with their copper-skinned friends—sometimes allies, occasionally enemies—gathered around the blazing fire to sing or chant, while the retiring Grand Master conveyed his collar and staff to his successor and both toasted each other in a cup of wine.

Thus did those ingenious Frenchmen and their Indian friends defeat the evil winter of their confinement.

BUT THE GOOD TIMES were not destined to continue, although it is probable that the good cheer and high spirits might have saved the company from scurvy, and though toward the end of winter the weather turned severely cold, only four men perished. After the snow thawed and the ice melted, the colony began to hum and buzz once more with activity, until one morning in late spring a small vessel was seen moving slowly through the outer passage, lowering its sails to anchor before the fort. She was commanded by a young seafarer from St.-Malo named Chevalier, and the news he brought was calamitous.

*Then one of the most famous restaurants in Paris.

The Sieur de Monts's monopoly had been revoked! The enterprise was dead. It could no longer be supported, for revenue from the fur trade would cease, and thus provide no funds to pay the workers employed by the company. Worse, the conniving Dutch had entered the St. Lawrence to carry off a rich harvest of furs. Other interlopers had stripped the coasts bare of pelts, while the merchants and fishermen of the Biscayan, Breton, and Norman ports, having been provoked by the unilateral settling of the mantle of de Chastes on the shoulder of de Monts—a decision in which they had had no voice—and exasperated at being excluded from the fur trade, as well as enraged by the high-handed confiscations that followed, had brought all their considerable influence and wealth to bear at court and so achieved this result.

So Port Royal became a ghost settlement—as Tadoussac still was—and as the last boatload of departing French was rowed out to the waiting ship that would take them home, the lamentations arising from the inconsolable savages these pioneers had befriended and treated with Christian charity and kindness were like the cries of the bereaved. There were tears in the eyes of the French as they clambered aboard their waiting ships, and as the sails of their homeward-bound fleet dropped slowly beneath the horizon, the unassuaged grief of those they had left behind rose like a mighty hymn of heartbreak to the heavens above them.

SAMUEL DE CHAMPLAIN, having been among those pioneers compelled to return to his homeland in 1607, was yet in Paris in 1608, still dreaming of that imperishable Land of Heart's Desire: its fog-bound coasts slowly steaming in spreading sunshine, the pungent odors of its pine trees innumerable in number and variety, the music and magic of its coasts and water courses. He longed to return to unveil its mysteries, to tame and civilize its savages, to plant in the wilderness his two imperishable faiths: the Cross and the Fleur de Lis.

Five years earlier he had explored the St. Lawrence and had found at Montréal what he believed could become the perfect settlement: a fortified post from which to follow from its base those mingling and mighty waters that would lead westward—by land, this time—to China and Japan. He spoke of this and his dream to the Sieur de Monts, who—though having lost heavily in the Port Royal fiasco—was still not exactly destitute, and who immediately proposed to outfit two ships: one to be commanded by the aging Pontgrave, who seems to have had more pleasure from prospecting than from profit, and the other by Champlain. Pontgrave departed first, laden with goods for the Indian fur trade, leaving Honfleur on April 5, 1608; followed eight days later by his bold, cheerful, and fearless companion, bringing men, arms, and supplies for the trading post at Tadoussac.

In fine sailing weather Champlain was on the Grand Bank by May 15, passing Gaspé on the thirtieth, and on June 3 was nearing Tadoussac, about a hundred miles ahead. He saw no sign of life, but then his heart began to sing.

Dead ahead lay Tadoussac, nestling on the right bank of the Saguenay as it emptied into the St. Lawrence. Then—at last!—he saw living creatures. White whales were cavorting in the bay, blowing and spouting their streams of water. Wild ducks and geese were diving, some of them disappearing under the approaching vessel's prow, reappearing on the other side like dolphins. Champlain was thrilled, for he could hear the squawking and high crying of the waterfowl flying in formation high above him.

Then he frowned. In the still anchorage beneath the cliffs lay Pontgrave's ship, ominously still and silent.

Arriving a few days before, the elderly entrepreneur had found a Basque vessel flying the flag of Spain and doing a brisk but illegal trade in furs among the Indians outside their cabins alongside a cove. It was an angry Pontgrave who read them the letters signed by His Majesty the king of France claiming by right of discovery all the waters, lands, and coasts of New France. He demanded an immediate cessation of this prohibited traffic, and probably a return of all peltry illegally obtained as well.

The Basques—sullen and belligerent as usual—told the irate Frenchman that they would trade with whom they pleased in spite of their king. Without hesitation they fired at Pontgrave and his men with cannon and musketry, wounding both him and two of his men and killing a third. Unrepentant, they boarded the French vessel and carried away all its armament and ammunition, loftily implying that all would be returned when they had finished trading and were prepared to sail homeward.

About then the sails of Champlain's ship had come into view. In all probability the Basques watched it warily, while Champlain ordered a boat lowered and was rowed ashore, where he found his partner in pain and dismay. By then the Basques had learned—probably from the Indians—who it was who had just arrived; and perhaps knowing him by reputation, were having second thoughts. They were still strong enough to fight a battle, but chose instead to come aboard and submit to terms. A peace was therefore signed and all differences referred to the judgment of the French courts. A kind of uneasy harmony was restored, and the Basques—still scowling—and barred from expanding their store of priceless pelts, were obliged to surrender those they had gathered, changing instead with the customary bad grace to the more dangerous, less profitable, and more arduous pursuit of catching whales.

IT IS NOT KNOWN when Samuel de Champlain changed his mind about founding his great military base at Montréal, with its forest plain and manifold watery openings to the West, but he had needed only to look upon the rock of Québec to see that here indeed was a natural citadel, one that could make even Gibraltar look puny in comparison.

The fortress city of New France, standing on its great rock and then being built in 1608 by Champlain's workmen, lies roughly 700 miles above the Gulf of St. Lawrence and the Atlantic Ocean. Between two streams—the mighty St. Lawrence and the much smaller St. Charles emptying into it—Québec's front is like the prow of a ship jutting out into the great basin below formed by the widening St. Lawrence. Below it also was a narrow shelf of waterfront land to be known eventually as the Lower Town. Above it along the circuit of both rivers towered the rocky cliffs of the Upper Town, almost all of them at least 200 feet higher than the great river, rising steadily as they marched their way westward to the great long rocky hump of the precipice of Cape Diamond, nearly 350 feet above water.

As Samuel de Champlain moved among his workmen in the Lower Town, pointing and shouting, his ever-present pencil poised above his sheets of foolscap, designating to these men the size and shape of the building he wanted and where to build it, it did not occur to him that he was improving upon the incredible strength of this natural citadel in order to repel the attack of some European monarch anxious to evict his own sovereign, but rather constructing nothing more than a small city on a great rock sufficiently organized to discourage any foolish assault by any or all of the badly armed and badly led Indians in the area. So he watched as a strong wooden wall was erected, surmounted by a gallery loopholed for musketry and enclosing three other buildings. Within it would be quarters for himself and his men, together with a tall dovecote like a belfry. A moat or dry ditch was dug around the whole, with two or three small, loaded cannons mounted on platforms and aimed at avenues of approach. A large storehouse was also raised nearby, and part of its grounds was laid out as a garden, probably the place dearest to the heart of this valiant, resourceful commander. Well might he quote:

The kiss of the sun for pardon,
The song of the birds for mirth;
You are nearer God's heart in a garden—
Than any place else on earth.

In this half-completed garden one morning the pilot Tetu came to him asking for a private word. Both men withdrew to the privacy of the woods, and Têtu, visibly upset, told him that a locksmith named Antoine Natel was plotting to murder him and deliver Québec into the hands of the Basques still at Tadoussac. Another locksmith, named Duval, was the ringleader with three others as accomplices, Tetu said. At once Champlain told him to bring Antoine Natel into his presence. He soon appeared, trembling and so frightened that he revealed the entire conspiracy without hesitation.

Champlain next called upon a reliable young man in charge of a small ship built by Pontgrave at Tadoussac and now anchored near the encampment. He gave him two bottles of wine given him by his Basque friends at Tadoussac, he said, and instructed him to invite the culprits aboard. When they arrived they were seized and secured, white with fear at the sight of Duval's body swinging from a gibbet, with his bleeding head stuck up on a pike. Duval's trio of accomplices were also seized and sent back to Paris with Pontgrave to serve their sentences as galley slaves.

Champlain now held Québec with twenty-eight men, and three weeks later it was no comfort to him to see the surrounding woods and hills cloaked in their autumn glory—the gay forerunner of the gloom of winter. Soon its iron claws would clutch the little company in its grasp. Even so, the misery at Québec was in no way comparable to the agony of the Algonquin tribes of Acadia and the lower St. Lawrence, who had never known the barest hint of husbandry, unlike their neighbors to the south, who could till the soil and plant and raise crops. They subsisted in those dreadful winters like wild animals, gnawing on a bone or piece of flesh torn from the kill of some predator, or on what these newcomers to their ancient precincts might mercifully grant them from their abundant tables. Champlain wrote of a party of Algonquins marooned among pack ice. Desperate, they drove their canoes into the drifting floes, screaming as their craft were ground to pieces, and hurled themselves into water so cold no one could live in it more than a few minutes.

Those who survived came to the fort, gobbling the crumbs of a meal given to them by the French; and then, perhaps as a kind of dessert, fell upon the carcass of a dead dog Champlain had left in the snow a few months back as bait for foxes. Thawing it, tearing it into pieces, they fought over it like wolves, gulping it down with menacing growls—and woe to the child who sought to snatch a morsel from the dripping mouth of a warrior.

Toward the end of winter, when a spark of hope began to nourish failing spirits, scurvy broke out again, with all the virulence of the St. Croix horror. Only eight of the twenty-eight survived, and of these, half were stricken by an unknown malady. Champlain was among the healthy few, a tower of inner strength and a picture of outward health—and his joy on the fifth of June 1609 was boundless when he saw a sailboat rounding the Point of Orleans. A son-in-law of Pont-grave named Marais was at the tiller, and he told Champlain that his father-in-law was then at Tadoussac.

Champlain quickly hastened downriver to confer with his old comrade of so many trials and triumphs. They agreed that the aging merchant should take charge of Québec, while Champlain pursued his long-cherished ambition to discover a western route by land to China, as La Salle would attempt seventy years later.

But there was a difficulty in Champlain's path: much more than a mere inconvenience, he was warned by friendly Hurons and others, but rather a veritable roadblock of inimical and murderous humanity that could never be encountered at sea. It was now spring and all those warlike, scalp-taking tribes that were the scourge of the forests—especially those fierce Iroquois—were everywhere: in the streams, along the trails, bursting among the unwarned villages.

Champlain pondered his chances of success and they did not seem great, even when accompanied by a dozen or more of those hardy Canadian bush-rangers who were at least the equal of the Iroquois in forest craft, and because they had had long experience with firearms and edged steel weapons, were just that much more superior in combat. But just as he began to conclude that he might have to wait until fall before beginning his westward trek—which direction would take him at least closer to the sun—a young Ottawa chief entered the fort of Québec with what seemed to be a solution to the problem.

DURING THE PREVIOUS autumn this handsome, high-hearted young sachem had been at Québec and had been amazed at what he saw among the "Norman" warriors, as the Indians sometimes called the French. These were their war armor and weapons, especially what he called "the thunder horns," his own picturesque term for the French arquebuses, or ancient firelock muskets, and their cannons.

Aware of this superiority in battle not duplicated anywhere among the five hundred Indian nations of North America, he was overjoyed to think that he might now persuade the Father of New France to join him and other enemies of the Iroquois in deliberate war against them. Sensing by the sudden glint in the white sachem's eye that he had struck a responsive chord, he hastened to explain that Iroquois was the name of "the Five Nations"—Mohawk, Oneida, Onondaga, Cayuga, and Seneca—living in palisaded villages in that order among the forests of what is now New York State. They were the daily dread of all the surrounding tribes: killing, torturing, eating, or enslaving them, while imposing on some the humiliating epithet of "women" or exacting from others a ruinous tribute.

Should Champlain join with this Ottawa chief and his kinsmen, as well as with the Hurons and Algonquins, who were also friends of the French, he might make himself the ally and leader of all the tribes of Canada. Surely his thunder horns would humble the haughty Iroquois.

With hardly a moment's reflection, the Father of New France consented, for this had been the opportunity he had been seeking for so many years in the wilderness. It was an invitation to seize power among the savages and thus execute French policy in the New World. Unlike those English who had settled in 1607 at Jamestown in what is now Virginia, or the other "God-damns," as the French had called them ever since the days of Joan of Arc, who might at this very moment be crossing the Atlantic to form another colony far to the south, the French had never held aloof from the Indians, or like the Spanish followed a policy of enslavement to work the gold mines that once were theirs, or to seize their land like the British, knowing full well that it was held in common and that its owners by necessity must be murdered.

Yet Champlain did not pretend that the French were in Canada for purely unselfish motives. No, of course not: They were there to profit from the fur trade, not merely to exploit the hunters who trapped or shot the animals, like the greedy Spaniards would have done, nor deceitful like the English, but to share with the Indians in a prosperous partnership. Neither was this relationship wholly altruistic, but rather simply just less immoral than either of these, even though the profits from the fur trade might help finance the underlying desire to push both the cross and the Crown deeper into the westward wilderness.

Although it is doubtful that the young Ottawa chief ever fully understood the niceties of the French position as presented by Champlain—if they were not actually extremely subtle casuistries—his eyes nevertheless lighted up with the purest joy when the Father of New France signified his intention not only of joining the war party but also of leading it.

CHAMPLAIN KEPT HIS WORD, though by the middle of June he had become slightly impatient for the arrival of the braves from the upper reaches of the St. Lawrence. When they did not appear, he reluctantly put himself at the head of a band of Montagnais—not exactly ferocious warriors—and began moving up the great river in a shallop, or light, open boat driven by oars or a sail or both. He soon found his Huron and Algonquin allies among the lodges of their camp on the northern bank of the river. Few of them had ever seen a white man before, and they crowded around him in speechless wonder, fingering the steel of his armor, hefting his matchlock, or testing the edge of his sword, recoiling at the sudden emergence of blood on their fingers. Then they escorted him to the lodge of their chiefs, for each tribe was led by a sachem. Then they all descended to Québec, for the marvels of its architecture had reached even the recesses of their distant forests.

The cluster of huts, hovels, and a few buildings comprising the capital of New France actually stunned them. Tepees, yes, they knew; or even the wonder of lodges of woven boughs; but not the splendor of these structures made of wood—yes, wood—some of them planed and cut of every thickness and length, fitted together in uncanny fashion, with openings for cannon and loopholes for matchlocks. Then they heard the explosions of the firearms, holding their ears and screaming as they ran to their camps in terror, where they were gradually calmed by their sachems, who patiently explained that gunpowder was not a device of the devil. Still trembling slightly, they arrayed themselves in feathers and paint for the war dance.

In the still black night the yellow flickering flames of their fires made patterns on their naked copper bodies, falling on tawny limbs convulsed with gestures and fierce foot-stamping; on twisted facial features contorted with feigned menace and hideous with war paint; and everywhere, everyone brandishing on high their Stone Age weapons—stone war clubs, stone tomahawks, stone-pointed spears— while the drums maintained their steady hollow boom and their blood-curdling cries rose, mingling together in the cool night air.

For Champlain it was an exhilarating spectacle, but as it continued for perhaps an hour, much to the exhaustion of the participants, there came an interval of rest before the war feast followed, and then on the following morning—June 28, 1609—he led the war party south to the Iroquois country.

With Champlain in his shallop were eleven men of Pontgrave's party he had chosen to accompany him on his campaign. They were armed with the arquebus, a firelock or matchlock, actually a short musket similar to the modern carbine and also a fine weapon in the close quarters of forest warfare. Champlain looked about him in deep satisfaction at this great concourse of war canoes following behind him on either flank. The river was dotted white upon the entrance and withdrawal of thousands of paddles and oars into and out of its depths, stroked by hundreds of muscular arms by turns tawny, coppery, or sun-burned red.

Reaching the Lake of St. Peter—a vast archipelago of islands small and large—they threaded their way through its snakelike channels and so on to the mouth of the river called variously the Richelieu, the Iroquois, the Chambly, the Sorel, or the St. John. Here, probably at the site of the future town of Sorel, they halted while for two days they took their ease hunting and fishing, and regaling each other with fresh fish, venison, and the flesh of waterfowl. Then—as usual—the tribes and totems fell to boasting, and then to taunting and finally to outright quarreling, so that, to Champlain's great dismay, at least four-fifths of their number refused to continue, reboarding their craft in high dudgeon and paddling homeward; the sullen, set faces of some of them perhaps concealing a reluctance to try occasions with the Iroquois. The remainder—shouting insults and taunts at the defectors—continued on their course toward the Richelieu.

At this point Champlain and his French warriors disembarked from their shallop to make a personal reconnaissance of the territory ahead. Unknown to them—but not to their tawny allies, who watched them disappear—they were on the edge of the watery warpath followed for centuries by these mutual foes, and what was to become, for a century and a half, the same invasion route for the warring French and English. It was a lake-and-river chain descending from the St. Lawrence River—the Richelieu River—Lake Champlain—Lac St. Sacremont (Lake George)—the Hudson River, in that order or the reverse. Leaving the shallop guarded by four armed men, Champlain, with seven others, pushed forward toward the sound of tumbling waters, stumbling and tripping over a tangle of creeper-rot-and-vine that nearly brought them to a halt. Bursting through thickets and kicking away at rotten logs, they glimpsed at last water rising in thick spume, plunging over ledges, boiling in chasms, leaping over huge boulders. Here were the rapids of the lower Richelieu: impassable by boat, almost impenetrable by men loaded down with weapons and food.

Champlain called a halt, and his men could see from the scowl on his face that their beloved commander—always the perfection of calm—was now so flushed with anger that they hesitated to look on his features. At once he spun around and strode back to the shallop, where the remnant of his allies had gathered. He spoke to them mildly, for he had recovered his forbearance, gently rebuking them for their bad faith in informing him that the lake-and-river chain was indeed navigible by boat. Turning to Marais, Pontgrave's faithful son-in-law, he told him to sail the sloop with seven others back to Québec, while he, with two trustworthy bushrangers who had offered to stay, would push farther south on foot.

With this, Champlain's Indian allies lifted their canoes from the water and carried them on their shoulders through the forest to a calmer stream about two miles away. There the chiefs counted twenty-four canoes and sixty warriors, not by any means a formidable force, Champlain reckoned, against such an enemy as the Iroquois, who seldom took the warpath with fewer than two hundred or three hundred braves. From here they put the rapids behind them, paddling silently upriver and gliding into the lovely long lake that still bears Champlain's name. From here they planned to enter Lac St. Sacrament—to be renamed Lake George a century later by a toadying Indian agent after the Hanoverian monarch of that name who could not speak anything but German to any of his Scots, Welsh, Irish, or English subjects. From there they would strike overland to the Hudson River to raid a Mohawk village.

But Champlain and his allies did not traverse the full length of the watery warpath. The young Ottawa chief's scouts were reporting bands of all the Five Nations moving north. An ambush might await them, Champlain counseled, and gave orders for movement at night only. By day they lay hidden in the forest, sleeping, awaking to gnaw on the dried pemmican that sustained them on the warpath, smoke the tobacco of their own patches, lounge and beguile the daylight hours with jests and banter of customary obscenity.

Now the scouts reported enemy braves as thick as the leaves upon the trees, and on the morning of July 29, 1609, Champlain and his allies hid as usual in the forest. Trail-weary, hungry, and thirsty, they slept where they fell, while Champlain—who normally did not dream—stretched himself upon the ground and fell instantly asleep. This time he did dream, beholding all the Iroquois drowning in a lake, crying out piteously for help. As he moved to rescue them, an Algonquin told him that they were evil and worthless, and Champlain desisted.

Awaking, he found himself surrounded by eager warriors, asking him, as they had on all previous mornings, if he had dreamed. When he replied that this time he had, and revealed to them his auspicious vision, they were overjoyed, and at nightfall they reembarked, now fully confident of victory, boasting of how many scalps they would take, how much Iroquois blood they would drink. At about ten o'clock that night, nearing a point of land that was probably Ticonderoga, they became aware of a flotilla of Iroquois canoes on the lake—heavier and slower than theirs because they were made of elm bark.

Each party saw the other, and the night resounded to the peal of war cries across the water. The Iroquois who were nearer the shore—never having the stomach for a sea fight—landed first. Making the night hideous with their howling, they began to barricade themselves. Champlain could see their shadowy forms in the woods, busy as beavers, hacking down trees with iron axes taken as trophies from fallen enemies.

Champlain and his allies remained on the lake, a bowshot from the barricaded enemy, their canoes lashed together with poles. Hearing the enemy begin their war dance, they did the same, but with much less vigor, lest they sink their frail craft and drown themselves. At least, Champlain must have thought, the enemy will be far more exhausted.

When daylight dawned on Lake Champlain, the commander of that name and his two bush rangers began to vest themselves for battle in the light armor of the age. Dressed in the doublet and long hose then in vogue, they buckled steel breastplates over the doublet, backpieces next, and then cuisses of steel to protect their thighs. Finally a steel casque was placed upon their heads. Across their shoulders hung their bandolier or ammunition box, at their sides swords, and in their hands matchlocks.

Each of the three Frenchmen lay forward of their allies on the bottom of a separate canoe, either thus concealed or covered by an Indian robe. They approached the shore and landed without opposition from the Iroquois some distance away. The enemy came filing slowly out of their barricade, tall, strong men, smoothly muscled and extremely lithe. As they came they excited the admiration of Champlain and his comrades, for their stride was cadenced and purposeful. Champlain's allies marched to no such discipline. Nor were they armored like most of their enemies, some carrying shields of wood and hide, others protected by vests of woven twigs. Among them were three chiefs crowned by tall plumes on their heads.

Still the young Ottawa chief ordered his war canoes ashore, where they were beached and emptied. Growing anxious, his warriors called loudly for the Frenchmen to advance, opening ranks to permit their passage.

Just three men against two hundred, and the silent, invincible warriors of North America stared at them in speechless amazement.

"I looked at them," Champlain wrote, "and they looked at me. When I saw them getting ready to shoot their arrows at us, I leveled my arquebus, which I had loaded with four balls, and aimed straight at one of the three chiefs. The shot brought down two and wounded another. On this our Indians set up such a yelling that one would not have heard a thunderclap, and all the while the arrows flew thick on both sides.

"The Iroquois were greatly astonished and frightened to see two of their men killed so quickly, in spite of their arrowproof armor. As I was reloading, one of my companions fired a shot from the woods, which so increased their astonishment that, seeing their chiefs dead, they abandoned the field and fled into the depth of the forest."

Champlain's allies dashed after them. Some of the Iroquois were killed and more were taken. Camp, canoes, provisions, all were left behind in the mass flight of the vaunted enemy, and many weapons flung down in the terror and panic of their departure.

Exultant, the allies closed on the deserted camp. They took the scalps of the fallen—both living and dead—and seized prisoners, on whom they commenced those foul tortures that turned the stomachs of their mighty allies. At night the victors led out one of the prisoners, told him that he was to die by fire, and ordered him to sing his death-song if he dared. Then they began the tortures that so sickened Champlain, and when he demanded the right to shoot him, they refused—and he turned his back on them in anger and disgust. It was then that they gave him leave to shoot the wretched man, and a single shot from his matchlock ended his agony.

But Champlain's horror at the spectacle of his allies drinking the blood and eating the hearts of their victims—which, if they had been the victors, they would certainly have done to them—would have been magnified up to the limits of even his considerable forbearance had he suspected that his victory in this first pitched battle between French and Indians on American soil would produce in the hearts of the vanquished Iroquois a horrible ache for revenge.

FOR TWELVE MORE YEARS Champlain continued to command at Québec, although the so-called colony was hardly no more than a trading post. In 1629 disaster struck when the piratical Kirke family of

England sailed up the St. Lawrence to attack Québec, then held by
Champlain and sixteen starving pioneers. It was no contest; Champlain
capitulated, and he and his comrades were carried off as prisoners. But
fortune intervened as King Charles I of England, still waiting for the
overdue final payment of $240,000 from France on the dowry of his
queen, agreed to return both Québec and Acadia if the payment
would be made. It was, and all prisoners were returned three years
later—among them, Champlain.

MISFORTUNES OF A NEW and detestable variety had begun to unravel
the legend of the indomitable Father of New France. By 1620 his forest
roving and sea sailing was over. Although he had found it more con-
genial to do battle with naked savages or to behold the sight of silver
waves breaking on some heretofore undiscovered shore than to struggle to nurse a puny and neglected colony into strength and growth, he
gave to this latter occupation the same unflagging devotion he had
lavished on these earlier and more amenable pursuits.

He was still the commander of Québec, but in actuality he commanded hardly more than his sleigh. Québec's permanent residents
did not number more than fifty or sixty persons, and it was itself half
trading factory, half religious mission. Champlain had seldom deceived himself, and at this juncture he realized that the true authority
in New France was wielded by those fur-trading merchants who had
never left the snuggeries of their homeland. Everyone was in their pay,
and while each was jealous of the other, all were envious of Champlain. Some of the merchants were from St.-Malo, some were of
Rouen; most were Catholics, but a good number were Huguenots—an
excellent prescription for endless religious bickering.

All exercise of the Calvinist faith in New France had been forbidden, but the Huguenots ignored the prohibition, tirelessly provoking
fistfights by bellowing out their psalmodies from their ships in the
river—not daring to venture ashore, where they had lost too many
brawls—while the heretical merchants of Rochelle who had refused to
join the company of the monopoly had slyly set up a highly profitable
if illicit traffic in furs along the borders of the St. Lawrence. They also
annoyed Champlain and his followers by selling firearms to the Indians, just like their coreligionist Dutch brethren would soon be doing in
New York.

The colony, though designed to increase, could not, if only because
the commercial interest, the fur traders, did not want it to increase and
did all they could to prevent it. They feared that the de Monts calamity
might overtake them as well, so they sought to suck out of their mo-

nopoly the last *sou* before it was lost. Because they had no permanent stake in the country, those in their employ who formed the scanty population of Canada also could not care less. Few if any indeed brought wives to New France, agriculture was simply not attempted, and all that sustained them came from the Mother Country.

Competition—the soul of any modern capitalist country—just could not exist under the monarchies of the day, and Champlain would have been an original thinker indeed had he proposed throwing all trade open to all. To have done so would have been akin to treason, and so on his frequent visits to Paris he asked only that the monopoly be bound to stricter regulation. In this attempt he was at least partially successful, and it was in this newfound buoyant hope of success that he brought back to Québec—much to the colony's amazement—a young wife so beautiful and so gentle that the Ursuline nuns in Québec informed Champlain that the male Indians, if they could have, would have worshiped her as a divinity. She was only twelve when she became the commander's wife, a young age indeed, but in those times—and in a kingdom as dissimilar as France in its racial types—marriage at twelve or fourteen would be as acceptable in, say, Marseilles as it would never be in Brittany.

Champlain, however, paid little attention to whatever exclamations of impropriety might have been heard in the town, but he was thoroughly horrified to discover that his lovely young wife had been instructed by her father—a concealed Huguenot—in the heretical tenets of John Calvin. At once with the typical restraint of his generous soul, he sought to convert her to Catholicism, as he had been, and was eminently successful. During the four years she spent in Canada she was almost adored by the Indian squaws, and beloved of the children she instructed in the catechism. But on her return to France she was determined to become a nun. At first Champlain withheld his consent, but because she had been childless, he agreed to a separation. After his death she joined the Ursulines, founded a convent of that society in Meaux, and died revered as a saint.

CHRISTMAS DAY 1635 was a sad one in New France. On that day the valiant, devout, and generous heart of Samuel de Champlain ceased to beat. In a chamber of the fort he had caused to be built lay his cold and lifeless body. It had withstood the trials of war, the torments of the wilderness, and the storms of the sea—surviving even the ignominy of defeat and imprisonment. After being stricken with paralysis at age sixty-eight, he was dead two and a half months later.

Samuel de Champlain was easily the most versatile of colonial founders in North America. Soldier and sailor, discoverer and explorer, artist and scholar, he has unwittingly left to posterity his own description of what an honest man should be. It exists in his *Treatise on Seamanship,* and it describes "the Good Captain" that he always was and what all others should be:

"An upright, God-fearing man, not dainty about his food or drink, robust and alert, with good sea legs, and in a strong voice to give commands to all hands; pleasant and affable in conversation, but imperious in his commands, liberal and courteous to defeated enemies, knowing everything that concerns the handling of the ship."

To Samuel de Champlain, honor was everything. Always and everywhere, at all times and in all places, he was exactly what he wanted to be: *le preux chevalier*—the gallant knight.

CHAPTER 7

King Louis XIV of France

THE YEAR 1638 MARKED a turning point in the heretofore miserable history of the pathetic little French colony along the great Canadian river: for in that year there was born the child who was to enter history—and long remain there—as King Louis XIV of France.

His was a strange birth indeed. His royal parents were among the mismatches of history: King Louis XIII, sickly and introverted, but still the bear hunter of the mountains, overjoyed to consign his kingdom into the capable hands of his sinister minister, Armand Duplessis, better known to the world as Cardinal Richelieu. It may seem strange that a man who found pleasure in tracking man-eating beasts should be repelled by any contact with women, especially one as beautiful as his wife, Anne of Austria. It was not that he was a homosexual, just introverted and unhealthy. For years he did not deign to consummate the marriage, and had been all but dragooned into her bed by the great cardinal himself. In that unromantic way there had been a pregnancy, but one that ended in a miscarriage.

Queen Anne's formidable animal passion remained unrequited until the eruption of that violent, blessed, fortunate, and heavenly rainstorm that left the king between beds: his own that had gone far ahead of him, as was the custom of crowned heads on a progress, leaving him to have recourse to Anne for supper—and thence even to her bed. From that unlikely evening—the king unwilling, the queen awaiting with all that penned-up desire that so discouraged him—was born this beautiful male child immediately celebrated throughout France as Louis Dieudonné, or Louis Gift of God.

His father realized that his life was nearing its end, and Richelieu had departed—unmourned by the reigning pope, who said: "If there is no God, Cardinal Richelieu has had a successful life; if there is a God, he has much to answer for." Now Louis decided to invite Richelieu's protégé—the young Cardinal Jules Mazarin, a consummate

Italian diplomat—to be the dauphin's coregent with Queen Anne upon his own demise, and thus cleverly thwart all her Hapsburg instincts so constantly embarrassing to his own Bourbon loyalties.

Louis XIII did die—on May 16, 1643, four months short of the memorable event of September 5 five years before when his first son and heir was born. The king had died yearning that his armies would triumph over those of Spain and a few days later Paris heard the stupendous news that the duke of Enghien had won a great victory over the Spanish at Rocroi. What an auspicious beginning for the reign of Louis XIV, one that was to last almost an eternity—in actuality, seventy-two years!

The moment the dying monarch had drawn his last breath at Château St. Germaine, the palace guards surrounded the little boy who was now king to protect him from possible danger. This was only a customary precaution, but Anne of Austria had carefully arranged for it weeks before, trusting no one—but suspicious of many. At once she rushed to the child's side, knelt before him, and did homage to "my king!" The whole court echoed her cry, and within an amazingly brief few hours Anne and the young king and almost the entire court packed their belongings and headed for Paris.

Behind them, the corpse of Louis XIII was entrusted to embalmers, physicians, monks, and faithful servants of the household. This was a custom of the Bourbon dynasty: After the king died, everyone who was anyone departed from the palace, bound for the capital. And what a great concourse it was, hurrying toward the Seine and the streets over which the new king and his little three-year-old brother Philippe and his mother rode, wildly cheered and pelted with flowers. Everywhere a great cry was raised: "The king is dead! Long live the king!"

Few tears were shed for the dead monarch. Remote and ineffectual, he had never been popular with his wars and the exactions necessary to finance them; his reliance upon courts and prisons and galleys to order his realm; fearing rather than loving his people. At every village the priests who showered blessings upon the royal family were smiling, and the people were singing, church bells were ringing, cannons were booming, muskets rattling, bonfires and fireworks glittering, drinking and dancing in the streets with free wine for everyone. By the time the procession reached Paris the streets were so crowded that even the royal carriage had difficulty forcing its way to the Louvre.

All the way the handsome, robust, solemn little boy nodded his gratitude at the cheers and the kisses blown his way by pretty girls; and throughout the city they were telling the charming story of how the hussar at St. Germain had asked him, "Monseigneur, if God takes your good father, would you wish to be king in his place?" and how the boy-king had burst into tears, crying, "*Non!* I do not wish to be king. If he dies, I shall throw myself into the moat of the château."

And now that Louis le Dieudonné was in fact the king of France, under the coregency of the gracious and beautiful Queen Anne and the affable and subtle Cardinal Mazarin, the education of the boy-king would begin.

IT WOULD SEEM LIKELY that this high-spirited five-year-old was worthy of the highest compliment that can be paid by an American to an attractive youngster, and that was that he was indubitably "all boy." Perhaps even better, he seldom sought the company of adults—especially the sycophants who gathered around his mother complimenting her on his robust health, his solemn dignity, his grace and noble bearing—none of which pleased him and all of which bored him. Rather, he loved to hammer his drums trying to imitate the beat of the Swiss guards, or else to call out the commands of close-order drill for the little troop his own age of which he was the leader.

For Louis to love the martial spirit of the age was only natural, for the Thirty Years' War had not yet ended, and since the adults of his acquaintance spoke of nothing else, Louis was delighted by the war-like atmosphere of the court and the tales of combat he would hear from the colorful guards, or the marching bands that gave his surroundings such a constant military flavor.

He also had a program of physical exercises that helped to strengthen the obviously sturdy physique that would be his upon maturity. At seven he learned to shoot at a target, and soon became a crack shot. At that age also he was taken from the supervision of women and placed under men. Anne appointed Mazarin as supervisor of his education, and a host of other teachers and specialists became his instructors in mathematics, writing, horseback riding, fencing, Italian, drawing, and dancing—all the skills of royalty so necessary for one who would enter a gilded world under the sobriquet of *le Roi Soleil:* the Sun king.

At twelve Louis could speak and write elegant French, unlike both his mother and Mazarin, both of whom spoke with a thick and sometimes untranslatable accent that the boy-king fortunately did not try to imitate. He also handled Italian with ease, probably with the assistance of Mazarin, and Anne's impeccable Castilian only natural to a Habsburg would also be useful. Meanwhile, he had also acquired more than just a little Latin, enough to translate Caesar's *Gallic Wars* and so astonish his teacher. Of classical antiquity—with its ideas and accomplishments—he knew next to nothing, and could not have cared less.

His skills were neither literary nor intellectual, but rather mostly athletic. He had become an excellent horseman, an agile fencer, and an accomplished dancer; all of these were the result of a grace and physical coordination that was often the envy of the young nobles of his entourage and the admiration of the young ladies.

While many priests undoubtedly contributed to the boy-king's religious education—until his dying day the Sun King never could forget the gentle goodness of St. Vincent de Paul, who had been with his father when he died—it was certainly the queen mother herself who formed most of his religious beliefs and ideas. Anne had grown up in the court of her father, Philip III, better suited to an altar than a throne, and under his supervision she had become a complete Catholic in private devotions as well as externals. This combination of religious values—which also had animated her husband—she conveyed to her son-king. She saw to it that he was always with her on her numerous visits to the chief churches of Paris, or her pilgrimages to the great cathedrals of France. She also spent much time on her knees on her *prie-dieu* impetrating the Virgin—to whom she dedicated everything— to make her son a great king and a good man. For all her gentle love, she was an unbending disciplinarian, sending Louis to his room for the slightest infractions, once even imprisoning him for two days when she heard on his lips language that would shame a stablehand.

IN THE SUMMER of 1658 an indefinable epidemic, probably typhoid fever, began to appear all over France: in the peasant's hovel, the doctor's office, the convent and the monastery, the army and the navy, and in the Royal Palace as well.

At the end of June—two months before Louis's twentieth birthday—the young king complained of a severe headache and took to his bed. The next day he had a high fever. Two days later his doctors sorrowfully informed Queen Anne that in spite of her son's robust health he was now in grave danger. On the sixth of July Louis received the Holy Eucharist, and preparations were made for the application of the holy oil of Extreme Unction, the sacrament of the dying. But such plans were canceled, for on the eleventh the fever began to break and on the thirteenth he was out of danger.

While the *Te Deums* of thanksgiving were being sung all over France, Queen Anne and Cardinal Mazarin—themselves weeping with joy—realized that Louis must now sire an heir. Louis must marry. Anne hoped his bride would be the Spanish Infanta Marie-Therese, the most eligible woman in Christendom. Mazarin agreed, but France, as he carefully observed, was at war with Spain. Yes, but Marie-Therese wanted Louis, the most eligible prince in Christendom. A way must be found. . . .

At this juncture Anne and the cardinal were stunned to discover that Louis, upon his recovery—having attributed it to the grace of God—fell deeply in love with a niece of Mazarin's named Marie Mancini. She had been in Paris for some time, living in happiness among the young people who made up the king's entourage. Louis had barely noticed her.. She, too, had passed through a soul-shattering experience. Having grown up like Cinderella in the shadow of her two older and prettier sisters, her superstitious parents—fearing she would bring the family bad luck—put her in a convent at the age of seven. Two years later—sick unto death—she was brought home, coming to France after Mazarin called her family to Paris.

Having forgotten Marie, now the cardinal must see her. He was astonished. She had become beautiful beyond belief; and while she had been an ugly duckling, she had consoled herself with poetry, music, and the visual arts, achieving a cultivation and wit quite the equal of her physical attraction. At once the cardinal realized that if Louis rejected Marie-Therese and chose Marie, it would torpedo all chances of peace with Spain. Instead, the fires of war would burn ever brighter in the misplaced motives of mutual hatred: Philip IV of Spain offered an insult no Habsburg monarch could possibly accept—the Infanta rejected in favor of an Italian commoner—and young King Louis embarked upon a bloody revenge.

Again and again Cardinal Mazarin wrote to Louis beseeching him to change his mind and reject this awful alternative, attractive as it must have been to himself, a young man infatuated by a beautiful, intelligent, and witty young woman. In his letters he held up to him all that he and his mother had done in the way of preparing him to become a great and glorious king of France. He spoke of resigning his position to retire "to some corner in Italy, to pass the rest of my days and to pray God that His action will . . . produce the cure that I hope for." He even threatened his young charge with the wrath of God.

But in the end, it was Marie—not Louis—who broke off the relationship. Clear-minded as ever, she realized that the negotiations between the emissaries of Spain and France had reached such an unfriendly impasse that there was no longer any hope for her to marry the King. The alternative—to become the King's mistress—never seems to have occurred to her, nor did Louis ever suggest it.

The turmoil caused by what the chief members of the royal household called "the Mancini Crisis" seems surprising, granted the subtlety and diplomatic skill of Cardinal Mazarin. Perhaps in his eagerness to train the young king to emerge as the perfect sovereign, the sudden shock of learning that Louis actually *was in love with his niece* may have caused him—and with him, Queen Anne—to lose his balance. Certainly the tenor of his letters to the youthful monarch who, after all, was his master, sounded more like the scolding of a wrathful parent. They could only produce a reaction of resentment and resistance.

Obviously, the fact that Marie was a commoner was the sticking point. In the simplest terms, for Louis to marry Marie would so alienate Philip of Spain that all hope of peace would vanish. But why could not this astute and silken prince of the church have written to Pope Alexander VII explaining the situation and requesting him to raise Marie Mancini to the rank of a papal countess? This, it would seem, would delight the young couple—thus earning for Mazarin their undying affection—and give no provocative rebuke to Philip.

But it did not happen, and instead, Louis did marry the infanta, Marie-Therese: a devout Catholic, a devoted mother—and a dull wife. How often would Louis XIV after he had taken possession of his throne wonder what life might have been like with Marie Mancini if Mazarin had died a little sooner.

THE EFFECT OF THIS unfortunate denouement tending to become the true romance of the centuries—ending perhaps in some great personal tragedy rivaling in reality Shakespeare's myth of *Romeo and Juliet*—had to have had an almost shattering impact on the soul of the young king. He became once again the pliant, obedient, solitary student in the Royal School of Kingship conducted by Jules Cardinal Mazarin and Queen Anne of France. But he would recover his growing independence, for he was not yet twenty-one and his soul would yet again be buoyant with the resilience of youth; but he also knew that the champagne that might have been his with Marie was not to be, and that henceforth he would have to be content with the stale beer of a steady procession of mistresses.

ON THE MORNING OF March 9, 1661, King Louis of France was awakened with the sad news that his great and faithful counselor, Jules Cardinal Mazarin, had died during the night, calmly accepting death, courteously apologizing to the physicians he had accused of killing him—and receiving the last sacraments of the Church and the consolations of a gentle priest who remained with him to the end.

LOUIS ROSE QUICKLY, and with that peculiar custom of the Bourbons—who seemed to be unwilling to admit death into their household—paused only to order full mourning for his minister, a gracious gesture never afterward repeated for anyone outside the Royal Family—before joining the vast concourse of nobles, churchmen, and other dignitaries hurrying along the roads to Paris. His first act was to order all the members of his government to meet with him on the morning of the following day. His speech on that March 10, 1661—when he was still five months away from his twenty-third year—quickly became famous. Addressing the chancellor, he said:

> Monsieur, I have called you, together with my secretaries and ministers of state, to tell you that up to this moment I have been pleased to entrust the government of my affairs to the late cardinal. It is now time that I govern them myself. You will assist me with your counsels when I ask for them. Outside of the regular business of justice, which I do not intend to change, monsieur the chancellor, I request and order you to seal no orders except by my command, or after having discussed them with me, or at least not unless a secretary brings them to you on my part. And you, messieurs, my secretaries of state, I order you not to sign anything, not even a passport . . . without my command; to render account to me personally each day and to favor no one . . . And you, monsieur the superintendent [of finances], I have explained to you my wishes; I request you to use M. Colbert whom the late cardinal has recommended to me. As for Lionne, he is assured of my affection. I am satisfied with his services. . . .

Even more famous was Louis's answer to the president of the clergy when he asked to whom he should henceforth address himself for the settlement of business.

Without hesitation Louis replied: "To me, monsieur the archbishop, to me!"

A momentarily shocked silence descended on this distinguished company of nobles and officers of the government, to be broken by loud gasps and exclamations of disbelief. *No minister to keep the wheels of government spinning?* Unprecedented! But the young king had not been striving for effect. He meant exactly what he said. *À moi!* That was exactly what he meant and what Mazarin had warned him against doing. He needn't have worried, for Louis was his own master who would lead, but never be led; who had "collaborators" rather than ministers and superintendents. Almost all his projects and policies were his own ideas, and perhaps dearest to his heart among all of them was the colony of New France.

CHAPTER 8

The Kingdoms and Their Colonies

IT IS POSSIBLE—even probable—that part of young King Louis's education under Cardinal Mazarin was the delightful requirement to read the reports of governors and viceroys from distant possessions all over the world. Again probably, those thrilling and interesting him most came from those hardy pioneers and Indian-fighters in far-off Canada: men of character and devotion to the Cross or Crown, men such as martyrs like Breboeuf or Isaac Jogues, or captains and explorers like Cartier and Champlain. Interspersed among them like a kind of seasoning were horrifying tales of battles with the savages, as well as descriptions of their disgusting primitive customs, especially the torture and eating of their captives. Also included—and these might have excited the young monarch's appetite for power and possessions—were tales of Canada's incredible natural resources: its lakes, rivers and mountains, as well as its enormous landmass, still not exactly known but undoubtedly vast, and beside which the great kingdoms and empires of Europe and Asia were merely large blotches on the map. It was thus that the welfare of this surpassing wilderness grew ever closer to his heart, so that very soon after his accession to the throne he began to take an active interest in it.

First of all, he was shocked to learn that Canada's entire population—explorers, priests, nuns, traders, and settlers—did not exceed twenty-five hundred human beings. Even though he had begun to send shipments of settlers to Canada as early as 1659, he did not begin his regular shipments of three hundred men every year for a decade until 1661, the year of his accession.

To govern the colony he created the posts of governor-general and intendant: the former usually a military noble of high rank, the latter of modest birth and usually drawn from the legal class. The intendant was also the king's agent and his spy, this silent, unsmiling, efficient, self-effacing man in black who would control finance, the royal courts, public works, and all the administrative business of the colony. In 1664 Louis appointed Daniel de Remy, Sieur de Corcelle, governor, and Jean Baptiste Talon intendant.

It was Talon who actually organized the peopling of Canada, taking charge of each summer shipment of immigrants, and binding them on their arrival to enter into the service of colonists already established. They were not indentured, like the English immigrants who signed a contract to work for a specific number of years unpaid but long enough to defray the costs of their voyage and upkeep. In the French system the king paid for their transportation and necessities until their arrival in the New World, and their employer paid their wages until the term of three years expired and they became settlers themselves.

Agents moving through the provinces picked up the immigrants, conducting them to the ports of Dieppe or Rochelle, from which they embarked. However, the influential Bishop Laval was disinclined to receive recruits from Rochelle, "that ancient stronghold of heresy," and so sturdy peasants of the northern and western provinces were chosen instead. Some of them—not many—could read and write, and a few even left France with money in their pockets. Intendant Talon on the whole was satisfied with the immigrants, but his appeals for more were so frequent that Jean Baptiste Colbert, former intendant of Mazarin's household and now the king's chief minister, complained that his master did not intend to people Canada by depopulating France. King Louis also sent to Canada many of the discharged soldiers of the regiment of Carinan-Salieres, famous for its actions against the Turks. Both enlisted men and officers who agreed to immigrate to Canada and settle there were well rewarded by King Louis.

For all his energy and devotion to duty, Intendant Talon seemed not to understand that a country barren of the fairer sex cannot be populated by single men alone. But when he realized that wives were desperately needed, King Louis quickly responded to his plea. In the first year—1665—a hundred took ship for Canada, and nearly all were quickly provided with suitable husbands. Two hundred more arrived the following year, almost all strong, healthy peasant girls accustomed to hard work, for among the earlier arrivals many were city *mademoiselles* indifferent to labor and made miserable by the Canadian winter. Officers also wanted wives, and in 1667 Talon was pleased to announce a consignment of 109 eligible young ladies.

As might be expected, all immigrants were not always ladies and gentleman of impeccable virtue. "Along with the honest people," Mother Mary of the Incarnation complained, "comes a great deal of *canaille* [rabble] of both sexes, who cause a great deal of scandal." It was also discovered that some of the young women married in Québec had left husbands behind them in France. To prevent such bigamous unions, Colbert ordered each girl to be provided with a certificate from the *curé* or magistrate of her parish certifying her single status. He also added: "The girls destined for this country ought to be entirely free from any natural blemish or anything personally repulsive."

Actually, beauty could hardly compete with utility in a climate as harsh as Canada's in winter. As Count Frontenac remarked upon his arrival as governor in 1672, "If a hundred and fifty girls and as many servants had been sent out this year, they would all have found husbands and masters within a month."

Inevitably, the indefatigable Colbert informed Talon that the king also extended his generosity to the children of already established colonists. "I pray you," he wrote, "to commend it to the consideration of the whole people, that their prosperity, their subsistence, and all that is dear to them depend on a general resolution, never to be departed from, to marry youths at eighteen or nineteen years and girls at fourteen or fifteen; since prosperity can never come to them except through the abundance of men."

Talon at once introduced a policy granting to every youth who married before age twenty the sum of twenty livres, and the same to every girl wedded before turning sixteen. This was called "the king's gift," and was apart from the customary dowry presented to newlyweds. It varied in form and value: a house filled with provisions for eight months, or often fifty livres in household supplies, besides a barrel or two of salted meat.

Obdurate bachelors could not hope to profit from such an exclusionary policy, and no mercy was shown them. Unmarried men presumably still potent were forbidden to hunt, fish, trade with the Indians, or go into the woods under any pretense whatsoever. They were thus made as miserable as possible—and in those less than liberated days, no plea of a different sexual preference was possible—so that Colbert added infamy to penalty, writing that such men should also be "excluded from all honors."

From all these encouragements for the fecund, a bounty on children was almost inevitable. The king himself in Council passed a decree "that in future all inhabitants of the said country of Canada who shall have living children to the number of ten, born in lawful wedlock, not being priests, monks, or nuns, shall each be paid out of the moneys sent by His Majesty to the said country a pension of three hundred livres a year, and those who shall have twelve children, a pension of four hundred livres; and that, to this effect, they shall be required to declare the number of their children every year in the months of June or July to the intendant of justice, police, and finance, established in the said country, who, having verified the same, shall order the payment of said pensions, one-half in cash, and the other half at the end of each year."

Earlier Colbert had offered a reward intended for the better classes of twelve hundred livres to those who had fifteen children, and eight hundred to those who had ten. All these rewards and encouragements seemed to be working, for Talon in 1670 reported that most of the young women sent out the previous summer were already pregnant, and that in 1671 from six hundred to seven hundred children had been born.

Yet, during the ten-year period of organized immigration to New France, and for all the zeal of the king and the energy of Talon, the census for that time span showed an increase of fewer than twenty-five thousand souls, certainly not an inspiring result. One explanation for the failure of King Louis' indubitably noble attempt is that all the candidates for the New World were single men and women. Whole families did not immigrate, at least not to Canada, and this was because of one of the faults of monarchy. Also this oversight cannot fairly be blamed on Louis, for all reigning monarchs of the day sought to populate their colonies with unwed men and women, and it was not until after the United States achieved its independence that whole families of Europeans did indeed immigrate to the Land of Opportunity and almost always at their own expense. A king's personal purse is not unlimited. Generous though Louis was, he could not afford very much more than single candidates for immigration.

Also, Canada is a cold country, and its winters are usually brutally bitter. Some of it is even north of the Arctic Circle, while the American states—except for Alaska—are mostly in the North Temperate Zone, and more than a few of these are actually semitropical, especially in summer.

This disparity of population and climate between these two neighbor nations—both enormous in landmass—living amiably side by side, speaking or at least understanding the same language and enjoying the same liberties as neither enjoyed during their infancy, is nothing short of incredible. It might also have continued for the five centuries since Columbus discovered the New World, had not the mutual antagonisms of the colonizing powers of Europe produced an interval of hostilities between 1689 and 1763: the four wars of the Anglo-French struggle for Canada, which began almost from the moment their rival colonies faced each other across the great St. Lawrence River.

Thus the two most probable reasons for King Louis' failure to colonize Canada to any practicable degree of permanence: first, the decision to send only single immigrants to New France, and second, the harsh climate.

WHENCE HAD THEY COME from, these "Englishmen" who within much fewer years than another century would be calling themselves "Americans"? And whence derived that spirit of independence so fierce that an absolutely new phenomenon had appeared in the history of humankind?

In the main they came from the Western Islands—England, Scotland, Wales, and Ireland—what came to be known as Great Britain or the United Kingdom, although not too many of those bellicose Celts—Scots, Welsh, and Irish—took too kindly to the designation "British." At first they came mostly as fugitives from religious persecution: the Puritans of New England fleeing the mild persecution of the Anglican Church, and Quakers of Pennsylvania fleeing harassment from the same quarter; Catholics of Maryland fleeing rigid Protestant discrimination; and French Protestants (Huguenots) of the South fleeing persecution in Catholic France. After them came Germans, avoiding military service and the harsh rule of their petty princes and electors; then Lutheran Swedes, settling in Delaware; and finally the hard-bargaining, opportunistic Dutch, supposedly buying Manhattan Island from the Indians for a few strings of beads.

Here was the first of those astonishing real estate deals in which these land-hungry Europeans fleeced the trusting red men out of their hunting grounds. Of the aboriginals to whom Columbus had mistakenly given the name Indians, there were only a few hundred thousand occupying this marvelous land, so vast that its length and breadth were immeasurable and its natural riches so incalculable that even to think of exploiting them staggered the imagination. So these few tens of thousands of Europeans settled along two thousand miles of seacoast that were eventually to be organized into thirteen little seagoing republics that would receive additional hundreds of thousands of fugitives—again chiefly from the Western Islands—risking the terrifying, long ocean voyage and seeking sanctuary for different reasons.

William Bradford led his Separatists to New England to found a New Jerusalem that was based solely on the Bible, thereby laying the foundation of that grim Congregational church that installed a theocracy more intolerant than the faith the Separatists had fled. When Cromwell and his Roundhead Puritans defeated and beheaded King Charles I, many of the king's Cavalier followers sought refuge in Virginia and New

York. Upon the restoration of the Stuart monarchy under Charles II,
those now-proscribed Puritan regicides fled to New England. After
them came the Scottish Covenanters, or Presbyterians, rebelling
against the autocratic Charles's attempt to impose Anglicanism on
them, only to be crushed in 1679 at the Battle of Bothwell Bridge. Military disaster also overtook a fiercer breed of Scot, the Highland followers of Bonnie Prince Charlie, who sought to restore the Stuart dynasty by wresting the British throne from its Hanoverian kings, only to
be utterly crushed at the Battle of Culloden in 1746. For these once-
proud warriors, now outlaws, dispersed and hunted down like rabbits
in their Highland warrens, America was the only hope; they found
their refuge on the western frontiers of the Carolinas. The western portions of Pennsylvania and Maryland attracted Catholic Irish seeking
sanctuary from Cromwell and Charles II, while fleeing the famine and
poverty imposed by their rent-wracking Protestant landlords. From
the Protestant North of Ireland came the Scotch-Irish, militant Presbyterians so-called either because they were the "Plantation Irish," transplanted to lands seized from their Catholic owners by the persecutions
of King James I of Britain or Cromwell, or because en route to the
colonies as fugitives from the bitter conflicts dividing their homeland,
they had stopped in Ireland under the protection of its British army of
occupation. Finally, there were the Welsh, many of them Quakers, who
found sanctuary in William Penn's colony of Friends.

These were the first arrivals, of whom the overwhelming majority
were English. They were bound together by a common Christianity
and a single English language, even though they had also brought
with them the divisiveness of sect and race. For the most part, then,
they were noble human beings—which could not exactly be said of the
second wave of immigrants arriving in the eighteenth century.

UPON THE DEATH OF the Pirate Queen in 1603, Britain, except for
Raleigh's two unhappy attempts at colonization—the first failed, the
second destroyed—had yet to establish any form of settlement in the
New World. But three years later, a joint stock company was created to
finance a colony in Virginia. This was an admirable vehicle by which
private enterprise—rather than some royal personage suffering from
Unilateral Disease—would raise the money for the venture, and many
small investors would share in its profits.

The stock would sell at about $62 in gold a share, the whole to be
administered by a governor, treasurer, and assistants elected at quar-
terly meetings—all in London, the single great metropolis of about

250,000 human beings then, and the capital of a kingdom of close to 5 million souls. Announcement of this venture spread rapidly throughout the realm, including "public-spirited"—not to say profit-seeking—Britons of all classes: churchmen and laymen, nobles and knights, merchants and trade guilds, farmers and freeholders, all eagerly subscribing to the undertaking. King James I (formerly James VI of Scotland), having already distinguished himself in a similar scheme, whereby he had torn the Catholic Irish from their lands and farms in the six northern counties, repopulating the same districts with his own Calvinist Scots, now graciously gave a charter to the new Virginia Company, and on December 20, 1606, in three small vessels—*Susan Constant, Godspeed,* and *Discovery*—about 120 eager colonists set sail for the New World.

Captain Christopher Newport led this fleet to Virginia, raising the Virginia Capes on April 26, 1607, after nearly eighteen frozen weeks at sea. Captain Newport and his council, which included Captain John Smith among others, explored the lower reaches of the Chesapeake, searching for a suitable colony site; but finding none, he settled—like most newcomers to the New World—for a low, swampy island. This they named Jamestown in honor of the aforesaid King James, and there they began going ashore on May 14. Spring came much earlier in the American South than in the Canadian North, and there was time to build a fortified trading post consisting of wattle-and-daub thatched houses and a storehouse of similar construction. It was finished just in time to repel an Indian attack twelve days later, probably by natives similar to those of Roanoke Island's "most gentle, loving and kind, void of all guile and treason" who dispatched Walter Raleigh's second colony but who were not quite as successful farther north.

Even so, Jamestown did not prosper. After Captain Newport departed for England in June, he left behind him 104 men and boys, and within six months 51 of them were dead. Most or all of the survivors might have perished, too, except for Captain John Smith's diplomacy in cultivating Chief Powhatan, and perhaps also his daughter, somewhat more comely and certainly more famous. The forbearance of Powhatan lasted long enough for Captain Newport to reappear with a supply ship and 70 to 100 fresh pioneers. But they were actually not of the hardy type needed to found a successful colony in the wilderness of the New World. As Captain Smith wrote, "In Virginia, a plaine Souldier that can use a Pick axe and spade, is better than five Knights."

Evidently there was a surfeit of knights and a shortage of horny-handed soldiers at Jamestown, and as a result the colony once again faced the fate of its predecessors. Upon word of its impending demise reaching Britain, a rescue fleet of nine ships under command of Sir Thomas Gates—the largest such expedition yet sent to America—was mounted from the Mother Country. Arriving in May 1610, Sir Thomas was horrified to find that he had saved a community of shadow men: diseased and discouraged, starving and self-pitying. Having eaten all their livestock not stolen and consumed by their Indian neighbors, barely surviving in the ruins of their hovels, subsisting on half-ripe nuts and berries, they appeared to Sir Thomas almost ready to expire before he could put them aboard his ships and take them home. In June they were all on deck when a gig bearing Lord de la Warr—the new governor—sailed into the harbor with the good news that his rescue ships with 300 men were becalmed down the bay.

Once again Jamestown was saved from death or extinction but might have been spared only to die of despair and inanition. Introduction of a military system meant only for the hard life of the soldier on campaign did more harm than good, but four new reforms did lead to salvation. They were (1) tobacco, the seeds of which were furnished by the lovely Pocahontas, who married—not Smith, but John Rolfe; (2) the institution of private property; (3) freedom, meaning that they would enjoy "all liberties . . . to all intent and purposes as if they had been abiding and born within this our realm of England"; and (4) SEX. There had been a few women in the colony, but they had not withstood the hardships as well as the men. Now the company began to recruit "young and uncorrupt maids" to marry the eligible bachelors of Jamestown, and every such couple had a right to build a house for themselves.

These were all wise changes, and under them the colony of Jamestown began to prosper. Without them Virginia Dare—the first child born of English stock in the New World—would not have appeared, nor would have the world heard of this first "American."

Unfortunately, as the colony stood plump and purring on the brink of a lasting prosperity, an almost fatal indifference to the needs of defense against marauding redskins almost destroyed it. It had been naively believed that the marriage of John Rolfe to the friendly Powhatan's lovely daughter would keep Jamestown free of Indian attacks. But no one, it appears, had given thought to the possible death of their protector, or even the separation of Rolfe from his wife, to the ultimate distress of the colony.

But it happened. Powhatan died in 1618, to be succeeded by his brother Opechancanough, who, like a precursor of the vengeful Tecumseh—greatest of Indian chiefs—had begun to resent the encroachment of land-greedy settlers on his cornfields. So he decided to put a bloody end to it.

In a sudden, secret onslaught he led his Algonquin braves in a screeching surprise attack that killed 347 colonists, at least one-third of the white population of Jamestown. Even so, the colony survived; but it still had to pass through a few more shattering revisions of its structure and safety before entering, in about 1625 under the watchful but generous eyes of Charles I, the son of James I, an era of continued growth and prosperity.

Yet, by the mere quirk of the same name not always meaning the same thing, the Northern Virginia Company was the mother of the Plymouth Company, the first permanent settlement in New England. And another similar ordeal caused by misplaced trust in a friendly Indian chief—in this instance the genial Massasoit, friend of the palefaces and chief grantor of Wampanoag lands to the insatiably land-hungry Pilgrims—culminated in a terrible bloodletting between the red and white races that has gone into history under the name of King Philip's War.

CAPTAIN JOHN SMITH, having made no headway with the desirable Pocahontas, if indeed he had actually courted her, and being an old sea dog reluctant to be saddled with a wife and family, and—worse— life as a landlubber, had accepted the Northern Virginia Company's offer to explore the northern coasts of what was already being called New England. He wrote a description of the area that was published in 1616 and came to the attention of a group of Puritans who had left the Church of England to settle in the Netherlands. Their leader was William Brewster, who had found the Dutch something less than genial hosts—though sharing the same joyless Calvinism—and through his powerful friend Sir Edwin Sandys had obtained a patent to establish a "particular plantation" in southern Virginia.

Poor in funds but not in spirit, they had no recourse but to raise the money needed for a ship and a settlement site by indenturing themselves for seven years to a group of London loansharks. Four years later—in 1620—they cleared England in their ship the *Mayflower*. After a rough voyage of sixty-four days they sighted Cape Cod on November 9, but found the wind and shoals so frightening that they came about and headed for Cape Cod harbor (now Provincetown).

But because this area was outside Virginia, their patent was useless.

Still, enough tough pioneers in their midst decided that "when they came ashore they would use their own liberty, for none had power to command them." Brewster, with William Bradford, Edward Winslow, Miles Standish, and others, drew up an agreement that almost all the males signed and that was called "a civil body politic" promising "all due submission and obedience [to] just and equal laws."

Finding Cape Cod a barren desert, the Pilgrim Fathers, as they are now called in American history, decided to settle at the place that Captain John Smith had already named Plymouth. Their delay in departing from Britain was almost fatal, for it brought them ashore in the approaching and bitter New England winter, so that all but 50 of the 102 immigrants perished. But hope returned with spring, "when the birds sang in the woods most pleasantly." By then more Pilgrims had arrived, eager to plant their New Jerusalem on the shores of Cape Cod, and in their grim and unbending bylaws set up a theocracy far more binding and intolerant than the comparatively mild persecutions of Archbishop Laud and his Church of England. By then also they had met the aboriginals, whom—following the misnomer of Columbus—they also called "Indians"—in this instance the Wampanoag tribe.

AT FIRST THESE RED MEN had treated the new arrivals in their lands with a friendship and a courtesy that—when exploited by the white men—would ultimately and severely weaken the Wampanoags. They taught the colonists how to plant corn and tobacco and the other crops native to America: peas, beans, squash, pumpkins, melons, and cucumbers. They showed the colonists how to harvest maple sugar, how to make canoes, how to use fish for fertilizer, how to hunt and trap. Because they had no experience of private property but held land in community—that is, as a tribe, not as an individual brave—and because they were guided by the spirit of an agreement or the sacredness of a promise, rather than by the letter of those contracts so dear to the colonists or the legalisms that often were intended to deceive, they were at first willing to make treaties ceding their land. In their simple, letterless society, trickery was not esteemed, which is why they were enraged to discover that they were constantly being swindled.

The shabbiest instance of so-called hard bargaining by the colonials was the infamous Walking Purchase of Indian lands in Pennsylvania. The Indians accepted an offer for an area of land that a man could walk around in a single day, which, at a normal pace, would come to about twenty square miles. But the colonists used relays of runners to cover an area many times larger. To the outraged Indians, this was plain deceit and trickery; to the colonists, a clever ploy to obtain more land for the money. No wonder Pocahontas could say that the British "lied much" or that they "spoke with a forked tongue." No wonder that more than a century later, the great Tecumseh could point to thousands of such treaties violated by the false and devious white man. Not only were the Indians gradually becoming uneasy at the steady encroachment upon their ancestral lands, they were also infuriated by the arrogance and intolerance of the Puritans' imposition of the white man's customs and religion upon them.

CHAPTER 9

Iroquois Revenge
and King Philip's War

IN 1641 THE IROQUOIS were ready. An entire new generation had brooded over the insult dealt to the brethren of the Long House. Only fear of the French thunder horns had restrained them. But now Dutch traders at Fort Orange—renamed Albany, after England acquired New York and New Jersey—had supplied them with firearms.

With these in their hands, they boasted that they would wipe the Hurons, the Algonquins, and the French off the face of the earth. They vowed that they would carry the "white girls"—the nuns of the colony—back to their villages. Regarding themselves as peerless warriors destined to conquer all mankind, they went on the warpath; to the west the Senecas and the others attacked the Hurons, while to the east the Mohawks struck at the French and their allies.

There were seven hundred to eight hundred Mohawk braves, three hundred of whom carried arquebuses, and they came very close to exterminating the three hundred French colonists at Québec, Three Rivers, and Montréal.

In parties of ten to a hundred men, they paddled down the river that gave them their name, entered the Hudson at Albany, and stole north along the traditional invasion route. Reaching the St. Lawrence, they lay in ambush for canoes coming downriver with cargoes of fur or outgoing boats bringing supplies to the missions and trading stations in the Great Lakes region.

No one was safe from them. To hunt or fish alone was to risk the war whoop, the sudden shot—and the scalping knife in the brain. Small parties of French soldiers or bush rangers who rushed to the scenes of ambuscades rarely found more than a mangled corpse or heads stuck up on poles, and sometimes, scrawled on trees stripped of their bark, the crude picture writing of the Iroquois vaunting their latest massacre and promising destruction to all who opposed them.

Against the Indian allies of the French they aimed a particular ferocity. They drove the Algonquins from their hunting grounds deep into the wilderness, pursuing them there to destroy their camps and boil and eat the enemy slain in the sight of the survivors. "In a word," wrote the missionary Father Vimont, "they ate men with as much appetite and more pleasure than hunters eat a boar or stag."

But those who were merely killed and eaten were comparatively fortunate, for the Iroquois had brought the practice of torture to an indescribable degree of perfection. In justice to them, it must be stated that none of the Indians regarded cruelty as being wicked. Indeed, its very opposite—pity—was a weakness in their eyes. Compassion in a warrior seemed nothing less than cowardice. To eat the heart of a fallen foe or to drink his blood was to partake of the dead man's courage. To torture a prisoner was not only pleasant, it also gave an enemy the opportunity to show by his stoicism that he was a brave man. At times a victim's fortitude so excited the admiration of the Iroquois that they conferred upon him the highest honor, adoption into one of the Five Nations.

Nevertheless, they were savages, and if some well-manicured moderns may be able to rationalize their cruelty as being nothing but the ungentle customs of primitive peoples, those who suffered under it had a different explanation.

"They are not men, they are wolves!" a Frenchwoman sobbed after describing how her baby was burned before her eyes.

Human wolves that they were, they would have devoured New France had they possessed the slightest understanding of the art of warfare or of that discipline that is the chief mark of a military organization. The Iroquois, however, could only make forays or raids. A battle was won or lost in an instant's rush. Stealth and surprise comprised their tactics. A siege was to them an incomprehensible bore, to maneuver in the open a madness. Even so, skulking in the forests by day, charging with a yell out of the dark by night, the Iroquois struck terror into the hearts of the French and came close to achieving the extermination of their enemies.

Gradually, however, the warpath wore them out. Their victories exhausted them, their villages fell silent, and by the year 1660 the Iroquois could count only twenty-two hundred warriors, of whom more than half were adopted prisoners from the Hurons, Eries, neutrals, and various Algonquin tribes.

❊   ❊   ❊

BECAUSE CANADA WAS the only colony of New France and was also martial in spirit and autocratic in government, the settlers built their homes in mutually supporting lines along the mighty St. Lawrence, which also had the military virtue of providing quick and easy transport for troops. In times of danger a single cannon shot would summon all to their appointed forts under command of the local *seigneurs*, or officers of the French Army leading detachments of trained soldiers.

The portion of the 750-mile-long St. Lawrence exposed to attack was only 90 miles, while the borders of New England were from 200 to 300 miles in length. The settlers of New England were never organized for military use with forts and blockhouses as in Canada, but were rather nothing more than lonely farms or small hamlets and villages loosely scattered in the wilderness of primeval forests. Mutual support such as the French of Canada enjoyed simply was not possible. Enemy war parties composed of Indians and French bush rangers could approach their objectives swiftly and secretly, dividing into small bands and falling at once—usually in the dead of night—upon the isolated houses of a wide region, where they could almost unfailingly inflict widespread havoc on their unsuspecting victims with little danger to themselves. Butchery of livestock as well as friends and family was not only a tragedy but sometimes also a catastrophe, for the cattle either driven off or carried away as meat not only denied the settlers the steady supply of milk and cheese to which they had been accustomed, but also curtailed or ended the reproduction of farm animals. During summer strikes, fruit trees were stripped and their yield carried off, after which they were deliberately cut down.

Even in villages the houses were far apart and therefore much more vulnerable to surprise attack than those along the great river, and this was because—except for those who lived on the seashore and therefore drew their income and sustenance from the sea—most of the people of New England in the later seventeenth century lived by farming. Though the New Englanders were not especially martial or organized for war like the Canadians, they would learn from the sad experience of King Philip's War not only how to fight but also how to fortify their dwellings.

As in any rustic society, most of the males were handy with ax and saw, hammer and nails, and were therefore able to fence their dwellings with palisades, or to build them of solid timber drawn from those incredible virgin forests, actually making them like blockhouses with loopholes and a projecting upper story, enabling the defenders to fire on any enemy crouching underneath and mistakenly thinking himself concealed. In the larger settlements these fortified houses were held in time of danger by armed men, serving as sanctuaries for families from unfortified homes. These were "garrison houses" properly so called, although the designation was also given to fortified dwellings occupied by only a single family.

Indians alone rarely attacked true garrison houses, and certainly never true forts, and this was because their tactics were those of the predatory beasts that gave them so much of their food, clothing, utensils, shelter, and weapons. Like these beasts, their only stratagem was pounce-and-withdraw. Even those bush rangers who paid their Indian brethren the great compliment of imitation had not the slightest knowledge of the tactics of siege warfare then in vogue among the kingdoms of Europe. There was very little maneuvering—that is, by turning movements, penetration, or feint, because the objective was usually stationary: a city or a castle. To conquer either or both the only tactic in use was circumvallation—that is, to surround it and to work gradually toward it by digging ditches called "approaches" for concealment and safety. Static lines faced both ways: inward toward the objective, outward to intercept any relieving force.

Besides the military value of a short front and a swift major river to move troops quickly, the French missionary priest—either Jesuit or Recollet—was another great asset through his almost absolute control of his mission Indians. Two very fine historians—Francis Parkman and Samuel Eliot Morison—have both insisted, however, that these priests did everything in their power to excite the warrior spirit of their charges, rather than to tame it and turn it instead toward peaceful pursuits. The priests taught temperance, conjugal fidelity, devotion to the rites of their religion, and submission to the priest, but they left the savage a savage still.

And how did the English Protestant colonists south of the St. Lawrence improve their Indians? They so abused them and ridiculed their devotion to the Great Spirit, among many other expressions of their own haughty and intolerant character, and actually printed such absurd untruths, that an Abenaki chief named Bomazeen "when a prisoner at Boston in 1696 declared that they told the Indians that Jesus Christ was a Frenchman, and his mother, the Virgin, a French lady; that the English had murdered him (Jesus) and that the best way to gain his favor was to avenge his death." Apparently it did not occur to Parkman, who wrote those lines, that this particular sachem was a prisoner in the power of his enemy, and that to ingratiate himself with his captors he could have invented these calumnies himself. Also, no

Catholic priest would remain long in Holy Orders if it were known that he sought to save the souls of his charges by lessons in blasphemy.

Only as an afterthought, Parkman deigns to mention that early in the War of the Grand Alliance, the French priests in Canada—as well as Catholic laymen—adopted the practice of ransoming English captives brought north of the border after a bloody raid. Instead of the adults being tied to a stake and tortured or burned alive and eaten, and the children either incinerated or enslaved, this practice saved many English lives. Only occasionally were some of these captives who had been spared obliged to work for their benefactors. The vast majority of prisoners, however, were freed upon payment of the ransom by the French, and were treated well and often with such kindness that many of them refused to be exchanged and became Canadians by adoption.

These, then, are the great exceptions to the bloody barbarity on both sides that characterized the backwash of the War of the Grand Alliance. It was a small war, indeed, on this side of the Atlantic, even though it sputtered on from 1688 to 1697 and was ended by the Peace of Ryswick, with France expanded somewhat upon land and British naval power increased at sea.

However, inasmuch as there is no such thing as a peaceful war or a bloodless battle, anyone who has survived the crucible of combat can tell you that if you lose your life or your limb, the size of the war you lose it in is completely irrelevant.

THAT THE TOLERANT French rather than the haughty English should have been the first to incur the wrath of the red men is one of the ironies of American history. True enough, French policy toward the Indians was not one of unmixed altruism: if souls were to be won for the cross, there were also furs to be gained for the crown. Yet on balance the French treatment of the Indian tribes seems to have been more humane.

French agents lived in Indian villages and learned their languages. The Indians were befriended and flattered. Whenever they visited a French fort they were saluted with cannons and rolling drums. They were given medals and French uniforms and flags. Their customs— even the most savage ones, especially when they could be turned against the English—were rarely mocked or ridiculed.

IT WAS OTHERWISE with the English. First and foremost, the English colonists sought land. They had come to stay. This, of course, joined to the corollary necessity of learning to govern themselves, was to prove their strength, just as the paternalistic character of the French colony was to be its undoing. But in the beginning this passion for land was the disturbing quality that the Indians marked in the English. Not only the Indians, for the famous fighter for religious tolerance Roger Williams once observed: "I fear that . . . God Land will be as great a God with us English as God Gold was with the Spaniard."

English officials were often overbearing in their dealings with proud Indian chiefs. More often than not, the English emissaries among the Indians were the fur traders who were universally hated and despised as "rum carriers." Some Indians who had beheld the swift, curt justice of French military law were filled with contempt for slower English civil courts, confusing the Englishman's elaborate machinery for safeguarding civil rights with a weak uncertainty. Finally, although there were Protestant ministers such as John Eliot who were as zealous for souls as their Papist rivals to the north, Puritanical colonial legislatures passed blue laws applying to all Indians, converted or not. Thus, in Massachusetts, Indians as well as whites were liable to the death penalty for blasphemy, interpreted to be the denial of God or deprecation of the Christian religion; while in Plymouth no Indian was allowed to fish, hunt, or carry burdens during the white man's Sabbath. Such intolerance only served to aggravate the Indian's growing anger at the greatest provocation of all: the shrinking boundaries of his ancestral home.

True enough, the colonists were scrupulously careful to obtain titles to Indian lands; nevertheless, it was different for the red man to realize that in bartering away hunting preserve for guns or horses or casks of rum he was actually giving up all rights to hunt or fish there or to grow corn on unused parts of it. It might be that the genial Massasoit, friend of the Pilgrims and chief ceder of Wampanoag land, did not complain; but his far fiercer son, King Philip, came to see that the inexorably expanding whites would not be satisfied until they had all the land.

KING PHILIP RECEIVED his unusual name after his father had asked the General Court in Plymouth to give English names to his two oldest sons, Wamsutta and Metacom. The English, recalling the kings of ancient Macedon, named the former Alexander and the latter Philip. On the death of Massasoit in 1661 it was Alexander who succeeded to the chieftainship.

The new sachem quickly showed that he did not share his father's easy trust of the English. Although Alexander did not attack them, he tried to rule his people independently of them. Summoned to appear in Plymouth to give evidence of his loyalty, Alexander refused to go. But colonial soldiers made him go, and he was subjected to a haughty and humiliating interrogation, during which time he contracted a fever that killed him.

King Philip succeeded him, fired by a burning resolve to avenge his brother's death and a determination to wean his people away from the corrupting influences of the white men. Although Philip was only twenty-four, the fame of his ability as an orator and ruler was already great. More warlike and decisive than his brother, he saw with a painful clarity that there was no possibility of compromise for his people: they would either be overwhelmed by the colonists, or they would turn and drive the whites into the sea. He realized early that his own outnumbered forces were fragmented, cut up by the sharp knife of tribal jealousies. By the time of the outbreak of King Philip's War in 1675 there were about forty thousand whites in New England, all of whom would certainly close ranks in the face of Indian menace, against twenty thousand red men who would rather worry some old bone of tribal contention than rally to a common danger.

Nevertheless, King Philip prepared his war. For thirteen years he patiently sought to bind the Indians into a unified whole. By the end of that period, however, it did not appear that he could produce any valid reason for taking up arms.

Then, in January 1675, John Sassamon, a Christianized Indian who had been educated at Harvard College and had served as Philip's trusted aide, came to Plymouth to reveal to Governor Josiah Winslow all the details of Philip's "conspiracy" against the colonists. A few days later Sassamon was found murdered in a pond. The enraged authorities immediately blamed King Philip. They arrested three Wampanoags and put them on trial. Philip protested that the whites had no right to try red men for crimes committed against other Indians. But the trial went forward, the three men were found guilty, and on June 8 they were hanged.

Twelve days later a group of young Wampanoags came into the settlement at Swansea and shot some cattle. A young colonist retaliated by wounding an Indian—and then, painted and feathered for war, Philip's braves came swarming out of Mount Hope. They surrounded Swansea and shot down settler after settler, until by the night of June 21, eleven English had received their death wounds.

New England was shocked. From Boston and Connecticut, parties of hastily formed militia came hurrying to Plymouth's rescue. Philip quickly evacuated Mount Hope. His position on the peninsula in

Narragansett Bay was untenable. He moved west, to the mainland of Rhode Island, while the colonists occupied Mount Hope. From there, Benjamin Church, a colonist knowledgeable in Indian affairs, led a party eastward in pursuit. But they blundered into country infested with rattlesnakes, to the disgust of Church, who thought his men were more afraid of the rattlers "than the black Serpents they were in quest of." Suddenly the "Serpents" appeared and drove the colonists back to Mount Hope.

King Philip now had his war. It had been forced upon him unawares, and there was nothing to do but to unleash the ferocity that might rally all the wavering tribes to him while paralyzing the English will to fight. Moving rapidly, he struck against settlements in Rehoboth, Taunton, and Dartmouth, forcing the residents of Middleborough to flee their village and spreading the dread of his name right into nearby Plymouth. Soon, as he expected, news of his triumphant sorties brought hordes of other tribesmen to his side. Gradually, the fire and ruin, the blood and agony of the tomahawk and the flaming arrow were spread up and down the Connecticut River Valley. It was warfare as barbarous and as pitiless as the horror the Iroquois spread along the St. Lawrence. Massacre followed massacre, and midnight raids succeeded daylight ambush. With such terror Philip hoped to paralyze the English. But Philip had underestimated his foes. He was the first of the enemies of this country to mistake the peaceful man for the pacifist, and to confuse unreadiness for war with unwillingness to fight. So also were these colonists the first Americans to expose the guardians of their frontiers to a hopeless and bloody fight against overwhelming odds. Even so, the dripping hatchet plunging into the brains of defenseless women and children was also to cut away the last restraints of the English. All their own disciplined ferocity was now let loose upon the Indians. Scalps were taken by whites, bounties were offered for Indian heads, and captive red men were sold into slavery in the Mediterranean and the West Indies.

Six months after Philip had begun his war, the crucial battle was fought, on the western side of Narragansett Bay, where the United Colonies of Massachusetts, Connecticut, and Plymouth had raised a force of a thousand men. A few miles to the southwest of them three thousand Indians commanded by the Narragansett sachem Canonchet were entrenched in a fortified village built on an island in a marsh known as the Great Swamp.

On December 19, a cold, snowy day, the colonists marched toward the fort. They crossed the frozen marsh and came upon a walled village protected by masses of felled trees and piles of brush heaped in front of a stockade. There was one gap in the walls, directly opposite the colonists, and they charged it.

Fighting for their lives, the Indians drove the English back with a volley of musket fire. But the colonists rallied and charged again. They fought their way inside the village, and a fierce hand-to-hand fight raged among the wigwams. Then the English set fire to the lodges, and the battle swirled on amid flames and smoke until, as the dusk of a bitterly cold night began to descend, the Indians broke and fled. Now the flames were beyond control, engulfing the Indian dead and wounded, so that, in the words of Cotton Mather, six hundred men, women, and children were "terribly barbikew'd."

Such a defeat might have discouraged a less ardent spirit than Philip. But he fought on, assisted by the able Canonchet, with whom he had made rendezvous in central Massachusetts. Throughout the winter Philip counseled his allies: burn every house, destroy every village, kill every white man. Before the thaws of spring set in, the war parties set out along the frozen streams, and terror was renewed. Town after town was put to the torch. Canonchet struck steadily south until he had reappeared near the scene of his Great Swamp defeat, and King Philip devastated Rhode Island and swept east into Plymouth itself, burning sixteen houses.

Of ninety white settlements in New England, fifty-two had been attacked and twelve had been destroyed. The flower of its manhood was perishing in the battle. However, at the very peak of success, with his goal of utter annihilation almost within his grasp, Philip's own weaknesses became rapidly and ruinously apparent. He had no solid base of operations, no impregnable position to which he might return to regroup and replan. He had no stores. His war parties lived off the land. Now it was spring, and the Indians, denied old hunting and fishing lands, needed to search out new ones if they were to prevent their women and children from starving. And so, one by one, the war parties slipped away, to be defeated piecemeal by the rallying colonists or to be brought over to the English cause.

In April Canonchet was trapped and captured. He was sentenced to be shot. "I shall die before my heart is soft, or I have said anything unworthy of myself," the proud chieftain said before his death. His loss depressed King Philip. It discouraged Philip's followers still more. One by one, the war bands deserted their chief. One of them went straight to the enemy. A chief dispatched by Awashonks, squaw sachem of the Sakonnets, came to Benjamin Church and said: "Sir, if you will please to accept of me and my men, and will head us, we will fight for you, and will help you to Philip's head before the corn be ripe."

Church accepted. Plymouth authorized him to lead a party of colonists and the treacherous Sakonnets against Philip. On July 20, 1676, Church surprised Philip in a swamp, killing or capturing 173 Wampanoags. Philip escaped, but his uncle and adviser was among the slain; his wife and son were among those captives sold into slavery. Now the manhunt began in earnest. Philip flitted from haunt to hideout, never tarrying for fear some new piece of treachery would betray him. His followers were now few. After one of them advised Philip to make peace with the English, he ordered the man killed—setting in motion the final betrayal. The executed man's brother, an Indian named Alderman, deserted to Church and promised to lead him to King Philip.

The Indian leader, like a wild beast coming home to die, had returned to his ancestral stronghold at Mount Hope. In the dead of the night of August 11, 1676, Church led eighteen English and twenty-two Indians across the bay to the peninsula. They surrounded Philip's camp. To the rear of the camp, Church stationed an ambush. Then, at dawn, he attacked.

Driven from their quarters by volleys of musket balls, the startled Wampanoags reacted as Church had envisioned: they turned and fled. Most of them ran straight into the ambush. One of them came sprinting toward a man named Caleb Cook and the traitor Alderman. Cook's gun misfired, but Alderman's double-barrelled weapon roared twice. The fleeing Indian toppled to the ground. Alderman ran forward and rolled the body over. It was King Philip, and there was a hole in his heart and another one two inches above it.

Thus ended King Philip's War. It had been the opening round of a racial conflict that was to rage intermittently for two centuries until it came to its climax on the western plains. And if the colonists of New France had learned about war by fighting Indians, so had the settlers of New England.

Sooner than the French could believe, the Iroquois had returned to the warpath. In August 1689 the Five Nations had concluded that the time had come to lift the tomahawk against the French once more. So many of their tiny settlements along the St. Lawrence were either lightly defended or so completely unguarded that there would be a great harvest of scalps as well as much blood to drink. If they were again defeated, it would mean that the Great Spirit no longer protected them.

Goaded by the British, armed by the Dutch, still savoring the sweetness of vengeance more than the fruits of victory, they stole silently north toward the little French trading settlement of La Chine on the shores of Lake St. Louis, a widening of the St. Lawrence just above Montréal.

The Iroquois were down to about fifteen hundred warriors, when they had once numbered their braves by the thousands, and half of these were the adopted prisoners from the Huron, Eries, neutrals and various Algonquin tribes. As darkness on the night between August 4 and 5 concealed their approach, they heard the rumbling of a thunderstorm forming in the north. A sudden thunderclap crashed above them. In its light flickering on their coppery bodies smeared with war paint, it briefly illuminated the settlers' houses. No sound came from the village. Everyone was asleep. In silence the Iroquois posted themselves among the homes.

Suddenly a horrible screeching and whooping commenced. Lanterns flashed alight inside the houses. Men sought their muskets, but they never reached them . . . women began to scream . . . children sobbed. . . . The most hideous massacre in Canadian history had begun. . . .

The butchery was complete. Those who died beneath the tomahawk or the scalp knife were fortunate indeed. Not so the women and children seized in the light of burning homes and spitted on the sharpened ends of saplings carried for that purpose and thrust into the flames that roasted them like so many Christmas geese. Soon the attacking Indians were roaring drunk on the brandy they had taken from the houses of the traders. Reeling, chanting war cries, gnawing on the singed bodies torn from the fires, they staggered into the woods—where they continued to screech and dance.

In the neighborhood were three stockade forts, all of them garrisoned with militia. About two hundred regulars were also encamped, about three miles away, under the command of an officer named Subercase, who was then returning from an evening in Montréal with Governor Denonville. At four o'clock in the morning Subercase arrived to hear a warning shot from La Chine, and at once ordered his men under arms.

Soon after, the troops saw a terrified man running toward them, pursued by a band of hideously painted Indians. They turned and fled upon seeing the soldiers. Subercase ordered his troops to march, and they were soon joined by about a hundred armed inhabitants. Daylight was now high, but as Subercase's command reached La Chine they found some of the houses reduced to piles of smoking ashes, others still burning slowly. Bodies were strewn all over the village, many still tied to the stakes on which they had been tortured. Other bodies— mostly of spitted children—lay half-eaten in the now-cold fires.

Strengthened by troops joining him from the other forts, Subercase prepared to attack the Indians carousing and chanting, capering drunkenly in the woods. When he saw some of his men weeping uncontrollably, he knew that he need not command them to show no mercy to such howling werewolves. Before he could give the order to enter the woods, however, there appeared the Chevalier de Vaudreuil, just come from Montréal with orders from the governor to run no risks and to stand solely on the defensive. Subercase could not conceal his contempt for Vaudreuil, though he admired Denonville, and tried to ignore an order he doubted had ever been issued. Vaudreuil was probably trying to protect only himself. But Subercase was overruled by this obvious *poltrone,* whom he despised, although he could not have known that his grandson of the same name would be even less valorous when he deliberately issued the same kind of timorous commands to betray Québec and all of Canada seventy years later.

Furious, Subercase was compelled to lead his troops back to Fort Roland, where about five hundred regulars and militia were now collected under command of Vaudreuil. On the following day a detachment of eighty men from Fort Remy tried to join them, but were intercepted and cut to pieces in full view of the fort. All were killed or captured—the lucky dead ones roasted over fires in the woods, the unlucky prisoners taken back to the long houses, where, during the few nights left in their lives, they would hear the sachem's dreadful cry, "Come, my children, let us caress our captives!"

Montréal went flabby with fear. Its terrified residents knew that there could be little hope of protection behind the flimsy palisades erected since the War of the Grand Alliance began that year in Europe. But they took comfort in Subercase and his soldiers, whom they admired. He knew that the redmen never tried to attack a fortified position except in the certain prospect of surprise. So the savages kept to the woods, holding undisputed possession of the countryside, scalping and pillaging over a twenty-mile area.

No attempt was made to send the town's soldiery against them, much to the deep shame of veterans yearning to retaliate. But Vaudreuil, in his pretense of superior military wisdom, still counseled Governor Denonville with his gospel of defense. Denonville himself was a fearless soldier devoted to the service of King Louis, and proud to have served under the great Count Frontenac during the War of the Grand Alliance. It is most doubtful that he ever gave the order relayed to Subercase by the cowardly Vaudreuil. Denonville was deeply distressed when he arrived in New France as the colony's latest *onontio*, as the Indians called the French governor. With so many tiny settlements strung out along two hundred or three hundred miles of the St. Lawrence, any attack by a true military force would end only in its destruction.

After he took over from Governor Lefebvre de La Barre, a timid, deceitful, boastful, and pretentious soldier, he quickly wrote Canada's epitaph, declaring, "If we have a war, nothing can save the colony but a miracle of God."

Even the departing Iroquois realized that Denonville was a true commander indeed. As they turned their canoes southward—fully loaded with loot and terrified, bound prisoners—they cried, perhaps in the delusion that they were mocking La Barre, "*Onontio*, you deceived us, and now we have deceived you."

But La Chine was their last massacre, and in fact these warriors, once so dreaded by their neighbors, were in reality only the scourge of women and children. Even when armed with the white man's weapons, they had never attacked a heavily fortified position.

And now, with the red men reeling on both sides of the St. Lawrence, the English to the south and the French to the north would soon be fighting each other.

PART III

War of the Grand Alliance,
1688–1697 (King William's War)

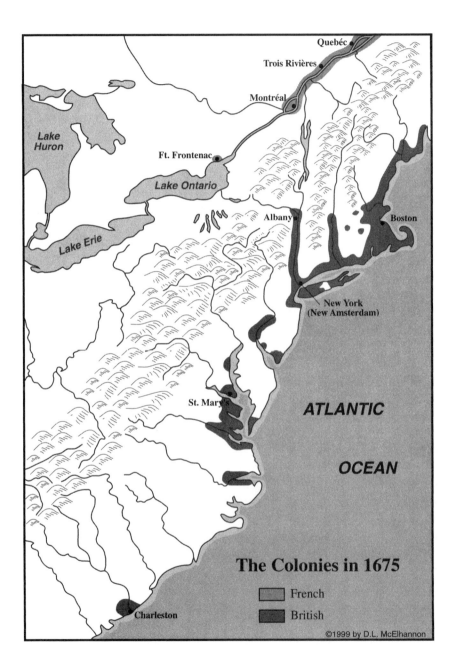

Quebéc

Trois Rivières

Montréal

Lake
Huron

Ft. Frontenac

Lake Ontario

Lake Erie

Albany

Boston

New York
(New Amsterdam)

St. Mary's

ATLANTIC

OCEAN

The Colonies in 1675

French
British

Charleston

©1999 by D.L. McElhannon

CHAPTER 10

Count Frontenac

LOUIS DE BUADE, the Count Frontenac, a fiery, contentious, self-centered, impossible, but absolutely fearless and successful old war dog of fifty-two years, came of an ancient and noble family said to be of Basque origin. His very physique suggested those broad-shouldered, thick-chested warriors, who in their pagan days worshiped their idols among sacred groves of oak trees as sturdy as their own bodies. Only five feet, five inches tall, with close-cropped, bristling hair; small, sunken, but shrewd eyes; a heavy face and blunt nose, all reddened by the burning sun or biting winds of a score of battlefields, he was not one of those dainty, simpering courtiers in silks and satins one would expect to find lounging in the marble halls of the gilded French court at Versailles.

His father had held a high post in the household of Louis XIII, who became the child's godfather and gave him his own name. As a boy little Louis was headstrong and given to outbursts of rage, a personality that his disturbed parents at once recognized as suitable for a soldier.

At the age of fifteen Louis was sent to the war in Holland to serve under Prince William of Orange, whom he despised as a pervert whose great wealth often blinded his fawning sycophants to his inability to command. At eighteen Louis was a volunteer at the siege of Hesdin; in the following year he was at Arras, where he distinguished himself during a sortie from the fort; and later at Callioure and Perpignan. At age twenty-three he commanded the regiment of Normandy in many battles and sieges of the Italian campaign. Often wounded, he broke an arm at the siege of Orbitello. In 1646, at age twenty-six, he was raised to the rank of *maréchal de camp*, the equivalent of a modern brigadier general. A few years later he was at his father's house in Paris, where he met a beautiful sixteen-year-old spitfire every bit as bad-mannered and ill-tempered as he was arrogant and overbearing.

Her name was Anne LaGrange-Trianon, the only child of the Sieur de Neiville, a widower at fifty who had placed his daughter in the care of a relative, Madame de Bouthillier. The lady did not care for the robust young firebrand and did everything she could to discourage her charge from seeing him. But Frontenac nonetheless fell in love with Anne, as was his custom with anyone or anything that appealed to him. The matron insisted to Anne's father that for all his noble airs, her suitor was hardly better than a pauper. His daughter, typically, took umbrage at the insult and accompanied her importunate lover to the little Church of St. Pierre in the vicinity, which boasted the odd privilege of uniting couples without the consent of their parents.

Unfortunately, marital bliss could neither smooth nor shine either of these abrasive personalities. Anne's was not a tender or loving nature; her temper was imperious and explosive, and she had a strange craving for excitement. Frontenac, whom the battlefields had taught the folly of vainglory, was nonetheless a French husband accustomed to what St. Paul has called "the *debitum.*" This, Anne was not accustomed to render, although she did give birth to a little boy named François Louis, whom she promptly placed in the care of a foster mother. She was now free to resume her close relationship with Mademoiselle de Montpensier, the granddaughter of the late King Henri IV, and daughter of Gaston, duke of Orleans, and a princess in her own right. Anne and "La Grande Mademoiselle," as she was called, became close friends, and Anne was often a visitor to her home at St. Fargeau. So was Frontenac. On one occasion he spoke to his beloved of her duty to remember St. Paul's dictum, whereupon she tore her hair and ran off crying and screaming in such a maniacal seizure that her hostess quickly sent for a *curé* to bring holy water to exorcise the devil that had possessed her.

Inevitably the marriage failed, although Frontenac was never averse to dropping in on Anne's close friend. Whether the attraction was the princess herself, or her great wealth—she was certainly the richest woman in France, if not also in Europe—Count Frontenac, when he was not at court, usually established himself at the family estate, where he lived far beyond his means.

"While Frontenac was at St. Fargeau," the princess recalled, "he kept open table, and many of my people went to dine with him, for he affected to hold court, and acted as if everybody owed duty to him. He praised everything that belonged to himself, and never came to sup or dine with me without speaking of some *ragout* or some new sweetmeat that had been served up on his table, ascribing it all to the excellence of the officers of his kitchen. The very meat that he ate, according to him, had a different taste on his board than on any other. As for his silver plate, it was always of good workmanship, and his dress was always of patterns invented by himself. When he had new clothes, he paraded them like a child. One day he brought me some to look at, and left them on my dressing table. We were then at Chambord. His Royal Highness [her father] came into the room, and must have thought it odd to see breeches and doublets in such a place.

"Frontenac took everybody who came to St. Fargeau to see his stables; and all who wished to gain his good graces were obliged to admire his horses, which were very indifferent. In short, this is his way in everything."

Frontenac's relations with La Grande Mademoiselle were rarely close or warm. If he was not quarreling with his wife—who had become estranged from the princess—it was with the princess. Once, accompanying the king and the queen to a play, she saw that Frontenac had arrived before her and taken the best seat. "I confess," she wrote, "I was so angry that I could find no pleasure in the play."

For all his brusqueness and vanity, Frontenac had the reputation of being a splendid commander. In 1669 a Venetian embassy came to France to solicit aid against the Turks, who for more than two years had been attacking Candia, the principal city of their possession on Crete. They offered to place their own army under a French commander, and asked the great Marshal Turenne to name a French general to lead it. At once Turenne chose Frontenac. Delighted to be so honored by the first soldier of Europe, the count immediately took charge at Candia. Though the city was doomed and finally fell, the siege had cost the Turks losses of 180,000 soldiers. Such severe casualties were attributed to Frontenac's skillful handling of Candia's defenses, and he became a national hero. Even his estranged wife, Anne, was constrained to swallow her pride and congratulate the ogre of her life on his great defensive stand.

Three years later King Louis, who had all but forgotten General Frontenac, alone with his horses on his country estate, suddenly remembered his service on Crete. During the past ten years, assisted by his great minister Jean Baptiste Colbert, Louis had hoped to recover New France from the turpitude into which it had sunk. The Iroquois had become hostile once more, and although they struck only at small parties—especially at friendly Indians coming down the St. Lawrence with canoes loaded with furs—they had refrained from attacking the colony in force. Both king and minister had been watching with increasing alarm the slow, fumbling, but steady growth of the English colonies to the south. Colbert was particularly concerned, for he had a great dream of a stupendous and powerful New France stretching west from Québec, and thence south down the wondrous Mississippi Valley to the mouth of the Father of Waters itself. He had imparted this glorious vision to his master, and Louis had become deeply attached to the possibility.

But now the English colonies, whom both men had hoped would remain attached solely to their agrarian policies of cultivating the land they had steadily acquired from the Indians—either by legal purchase or outright trickery—and planting tobacco, corn, or other agricultural commodities according to the fertility and climate of the particular colony involved, had recently, with their Dutch allies, begun to interfere in the prosperous fur trade that was New France's sole support, apart from the largesse of the king.

Moreover, Louis' well-known ambition to seize the hegemony of Europe had aroused the fear of many of the other kingdoms, with Britain doing its utmost to create a coalition to oppose him. If they—again with the Dutch—should decide to bribe and goad the Five Nations back onto the warpath with secret instructions to intercept and confiscate all convoys of fur-laden canoes heading east for Montréal from the northern waterways, putting to a hideous demise all those who resisted them, they not only would enrich themselves but also make the Anglo-Dutch masters of the fur trade, thus shattering Colbert's great dream and leaving Louis's favorite colony the dreadful choice between starving or freezing to death.

What was needed, both king and counseler agreed, to prevent such a melancholy end to the North American experiment, was a new governor, to replace the present Sieur de Corcelle. He must be a man of proven bravery and ability, an *onontio* of iron will and familiarity with Canada, who would cow the Iroquois and restore to France the golden prosperity of the fur trade.

Momentarily they may have thought of one or two of the numerous silken courtiers available at Versailles. If so, they immediately dismissed such a choice as an invitation to calamity. There was only one man: irate, unlovable, conceited, able; in defeat, unthinkable; in victory, unbearable.

Louis de Buade, Count Frontenac.

MEANWHILE, THE salacious-minded court at Versailles was indulging in the most delightful gossip about Frontenac. According to the Duc de Saint-Simon: "Frontenac is a man of excellent parts, living much in society, and completely ruined. He found it hard to bear the imperious temper of his wife, and he was given the government of Canada to deliver him from her, and afford him some means of living." Derisive songs with bawdy lyrics arose to the effect that the king had become enamored of Madame de Montespan, who had once smiled with favor on Frontenac, and Louis had decided to promote and transfer the count to remove him from his and her presence.

Of all this polite mockery Louis de Buade was well aware. He had already received for the second time the frosty congratulations of his unadmiring wife—so comfortable in her elegant apartment so close to Versailles and so happy amid her circle of so influential and affluent friends—and she was not in the least dismayed or discomfited when in June 1672, as the prospective savior of New France, he embarked alone upon a ship headed for Canada and new adventures.

WHEN FRONTENAC FIRST gazed upon the gulf of the St. Lawrence River—some 90 miles wide—he was indeed impressed; but after he had traversed the great stream about 350 miles to its midway point, and seen to his left opening before him the enormous mile-wide basin of Québec, and gazed upward to the towering rocks reaching to a height of some 350 feet on which the forlorn little city of Québec was perched, he was indeed so impressed that he immediately wrote to the king and Colbert:

"I never saw anything more superb than the position of this town. It could not be better situated as the future capital of a great empire!"

ALTHOUGH LOUIS DE BUADE would never revise his original opinion of Québec as the future capital of a great empire, he would have, within a few days, amended it closer to the reality of a cluster of little settlements strung out for three hundred miles along the northern shores of the St. Lawrence River. Sailing upriver, he had passed Tadoussac, St. Denis, Malbaie, and St. Paul's Bay, almost identical in appearance: each consisted of a small group of wooden-walled, high-roofed houses built close to the banks of the great stream flowing downriver to the sea. Higher still—about 180 miles more—were Three Rivers and Montréal, both hardly different in construction and location.

Around each settlement—except Québec, with its line of cliffs stretching west to Cape Diamond—were a few acres of virgin forest laboriously cleared and planted with corn or vegetables. Fields running down to the river were divided by split-rail fences, within which small herds of cattle grazed—most, except for a few cows and the younger bulls, to be slain in the fall before the brutal Canadian winter could freeze them all to death, then butchered and preserved with salt. The spared livestock were sheltered in communal barns among the villages, all stocked with ample feed of hay to keep them alive during six or seven months of bitter winter. In each settlement there existed a white-washed stone-walled church, together with a few riverside ware-houses built of sturdy rough-hewn timber, and at the riverfront a small wharf. Thus New France, the little colony along the great river, founded by the legendary Samuel de Champlain and carefully nur-tured for a century by successive kings of France. The last of these— the all-powerful Louis XIV, the Sun King—had, by a policy of peo-pling the colony with young and single men and women sent across three thousand miles of ocean as pioneers, raised the population of New France to a total of about twenty thousand French in September 1672, when Count Louis Frontenac arrived in New France.

NOT LONG AFTER Frontenac's arrival the vast sums of money that King Louis had begun to pour into this colony that was so close to his heart seemed to be beginning to take effect. In Québec, recently ar-rived colonists could be seen strolling in safety along streets of both the Lower Town and the Upper Town, none of them in fear of those sudden, shrieking Indian attacks that had once been the daily concern of pioneers such as Champlain and Jacques Cartier. New houses were being erected, a small fishing vessel was under construction at a slip-way beside the river, a brewery had been built and begun to produce beer, and there was talk of finding a hardy variety of grape resistant to the Canadian winter for producing wine. At Three Rivers, ninety miles upstream, a primitive iron mine was being exploited for its ore. New farms were appearing in the freshly cleared settlements along the river, but as yet no large-scale attempts at agricultural development— a project close to the king's heart—had been attempted.

Even so, all of these improvements in lifestyle and comfortable liv-ing did not rival the *habitants'* approval of the new governor's deter-mination to make the colony's defenses against the marauding Indi-ans impregnable. Because of it, there was widespread relief when even the dreaded Iroquois sent representatives to meet the new *onontio* and to report to their tribesman on what they thought of his character.

Thus there were crowds of colonists at the wharf of the Lower Town gazing in curiosity at the delegation of Mohawks arriving in canoes and unarmed, this last the first observation made by Count Frontenac as he greeted them, his sunken, shrewd soldier's eyes alert for the first sign of a surprise attack.

They were tall, daubed with war paint, naked except for a breech-cloth, their heads semishaven, their impassive gaze fastened on the *onontio* who stood before them.

They were impressed by his direct glance, his strong nose, his belligerent chin, and his bold air of confidence. They were astonished as he strode confidently among them accompanied by a mixed-breed interpreter, surprised when he admired their colorful headdresses and sampled the rank tobacco they offered him, cutting it with a knife on a small board they always carried for that purpose. Frontenac could be either charming or commanding at will, but here among these savage warriors who could be terrible enemies he was the soul of courtesy and friendship, so much so that the Mohawk braves returned to their long houses full of admiration for the new war chief at Québec.

"There has never been an *onontio* like him," the Mohawk sachem reported. "He dresses very plainly, does not wear a wig, and is said to be a man of savage temper. We were told he is a brave and cunning leader of soldiers. Certainly he walks and holds himself like a warrior. True, he has almost no soldiers in this country of ours, but we counsel patience for the time being. It would be unwise to make an enemy of this *onontio* before we know what he plans to do."

Ferocious savages that they were, these Iroquois had the warrior's true instinct of wariness: not to take a possible enemy for granted, or to act on a notion of what he would do, but rather on what he had the capacity to do. Count Frontenac always understood such an attitude to be the basic wisdom of warfare, so he was pleased to see the Iroquois nodding to each other thoughtfully as they clambered back into their canoes.

CHAPTER 11

Frontenac and the Fur Trade

LOUIS DE BUADE, Count Frontenac, took charge in New France with all the ungentle fury of a tropical hurricane. A man of glittering courts and dismal camps, of splendid cathedrals and rollicking barrack rooms, of colorful parades and melancholy battlefields, he would never have allowed himself to revise his estimate of Québec as the future capital of a great empire, for he saw immediately with his military eye that the little wooden town atop the great cliffs could easily be held by a bare company of brave soldiers in the face of an entire army.

He was not overjoyed, however, with the dinginess of his quarters and headquarters inside the shabby, two-story wooden structure with the grand name of Château St. Louis. He was perhaps even more displeased with the discomfort of his travels on the St. Lawrence to visit the settlements on its northern shores. It did not seem to him at all proper that a lieutenant general of the king should be compelled to crouch on a sheet of bark on the bottom of a so-called canoe—but actually a dugout carved from a birch tree—fearing to move his head in any direction without overturning this fragile vessel so unbecoming to the dignity of a high officer of His Majesty the king of France. To replace such a pathetic means of travel by water was among the first defects of the colony that he planned to correct. Another was his bold decision to invoke in New France the antiquated social systems of the three estates: clergy, nobles, and commons.

This he did on October 23, 1672, in the Church of the Jesuits graciously loaned to him with the secret ulterior motive of laying him under an obligation to them, and even decorating it for the occasion. But the black-robed sons of St. Ignatius would soon be among his chief enemies, so that he opposed them as fiercely as he cultivated the friendship of the Recollet friars, if only because they were rivals of the Jesuits.

When the governor-general arose to speak to the throng inside the church—all eagerly waiting to hear him justify his reputation as an orator—he well knew that he was addressing a double audience: the representatives of the three estates present before him, and the king and his minister three thousand miles away. He observed that he had not called them to assemble before him because he doubted their loyalty, but to give them an opportunity to express their devotion to a monarch, the terror of whose irresistible arms was rivaled only by the charms of his person and the benignity of his rule. "The Holy Scriptures command us," he said, "to obey our sovereign, and teach us that no pretext or reason can dispense us from this obedience." In a glowing eulogy of Louis XIV he declared that loyalty to him was not only a duty but also an inestimable privilege and added: "The true means of gaining his favor and his support is for us to unite with one heart in laboring for the progress of Canada."

Then he administered the oath of loyalty, and the assembly was dissolved. Frontenac next devoted his energies to framing a constitution for the city of Québec, again referring to it as the future capital of a great empire. It is very doubtful if moderns can appreciate the boldness of these measures, accustomed as most of us are to the great liberties of true democracies. But in Québec at that moment there was a gentleman—Intendant Talon—who knew full well with how little favor the king whom the count had been exalting would look upon such social heresies. Through bitter experience he had learned that Louis' unvarying policy was either the quiet neutralizing or ruthless suppression of even the faintest challenge to his autocracy.

The dispatches in which Frontenac announced to his masters what he had done, and why he did it, were not supposed to be read for some time by either the king or his minister, for the governor had quickly realized that the cold Canadian climate was in fact his ally. From mid-September until April the St. Lawrence River was frozen solid, and no ship could either enter or depart from the colony with important messages to be read on either side of the Atlantic. But in due time the answer from Colbert, master of the courteous rebuke, was placed before the count. Colbert wrote:

"Your assembling of the inhabitants to take the oath of fidelity, and your division of them into three estates, may have had a good effect for the moment; but it is well for you to observe that you are always to follow, in the government of Canada, the forms in use here; and since our kings have long regarded it as good for their service not to convoke the states-general of the kingdom, in order, perhaps, to abolish insensibly this ancient usage, you, on your part, should very rarely, or, to speak more currently, never, give a corporate form to the inhabitants of Canada. You should even, as the colony strengthens, suppress gradually the office of the syndic, who presents petitions in the name of the inhabitants; for it is well that each should speak for himself, and no one for all."

In this reply the very soul of French colonial rule in America was made plain. It was a government of honest and high intentions but of arbitrary means. Frontenac, just as full of noble purpose and as sincerely desiring the prosperity and happiness of the colony, in his municipal government, three estates, and meetings of ordinary citizens, had rashly set himself against the prevailing style of the king. He had to obey—and he did. If he had not, he would have been recalled in disgrace. Had he been permitted to continue what he had begun, it could not have been other than good for the colony.

FRONTENAC, AFTER THAT polite rebuke of Colbert's and the deep sense of failure that succeeded it, was now a changed man. His zeal for the colony remained unabated, but his high purpose seemed to have been dissipated by the series of violent quarrels that he had with the church, Bishop Laval, Intendant Talon, the Jesuits, the fur traders—in fact, with anyone who had the audacity to criticize or question his policies. This may have been because two other influences had seized control of his ambition, for Lieutenant General Louis de Buade, Count Frontenac, was no simple soldier, bluff, brave but utterly insensitive to anything but the imperatives of his training. His was a penetrating and cultivated mind, the product of extensive travel, wide experience, and intuitive observation.

The first and most powerful influence was that he had sunk so deeply in debt that he was a ruined man financially, and he meant to recover his fortunes. His desire for the colony to prosper was also joined by a determination that he should enjoy much of that prosperity himself. Second, his temper had become so uncontrollable that he could not endure a rival; opposition maddened him, and when he became thwarted, or crossed or challenged, it was said, his passion was such that he actually foamed at the mouth.

Both these mercenary goals were at the bottom of Frontenac's battle with Bishop François Laval, the colony's chief ecclesiastic. His Excellency had already provoked a running battle with Frontenac over the brandy trade, from which the governor-general undoubtedly prospered. But when Laval actually persuaded a priest to denounce the king himself for having licensed the traffic in spirits that he—Laval—

considered to be a sin, Frontenac's rage burst all bounds. He not only accused the bishop of attempting to subvert the state but also sneered at his moral theology as being fit only to govern a nursery.

In another tirade against the Jesuits, he accused their superior of trying to make his society "masters of all spiritual matters, which, as you know, is a powerful lever for moving everything else." He complained that they had spies all over the colony, in the countryside as well as in the villages and towns. He accused them of "abusing the confessional," perhaps the greatest charge that can be leveled against an ecclesiastic, and one that must be delated to Rome. Frontenac also accused his favorite whipping boys of intruding in family quarrels, setting husbands against wives and parents against children. He referred to his instructions from the king and his minister to civilize the Indians by teaching them the French language and inducing them to be assimilated by the white men. Instead, he charged, they contented themselves with teaching their converts the doctrines and rites of the Church, while allowing them to retain the food, dress, and customs of barbarism.

"The Jesuits," he wrote to Paris, "will not civilize the Indians, because they wish to keep them in perpetual wardship. They think more of beaver skins than of souls, and their missions are pure mockeries."

Thus wrote one of the angry old men of history, and one who stood alone in support of the king's intentions—which he almost alone actually understood—but who also might have provoked a storm of controversy that could have done serious injury to the Canadian Church if this fiery apostle of orthodox monarchy had not been distracted elsewhere in another crusade against evil arising from the activities of an unscrupulous crown official reaping enormous and illegal personal profits from the great fur trade, lifeblood of New France.

AFTER THE DISCOVERY of the New World by Columbus in 1492, the great powers of Europe—Britain, Spain-Portugal, France, and to a lesser degree Holland—had begun to plant their colonies across the Atlantic. They did so guided by an economic theory known as mercantilism, and because of this their colonies were on the Roman model, strictly organized, regulated, and directed from the national capitals. They sought to obtain a favorable balance of trade, and also by the extensive traffic across the seas, to train a steady source of seamen to man their navies in time of war.

But the chief function of these colonies was to produce the raw materials required by the mother countries to convert into finished products—clothing, tools, kitchen utensils, naval stores, grains, and so on—and these very articles were then to be in great part shipped back to the colonies and sold at outrageous prices. Forbidden to buy from other suppliers, the colonists often sought to reduce the costs by smuggling; and if they did and were caught, they were ruthlessly prosecuted. On the other side of the coin of mercantilism was the fact that the price of the colonies' raw materials was fixed by its mercantilist buyers at a rate so low that it barely paid for shipping costs. Thus the Atlantic Ocean had become a veritable one-way street, with the colonists compelled to sell low and buy high. Inevitably, of course, the colonies rebelled: the first group along the North American seaboard becoming the United States of America, to be followed everywhere in South and Central America and in the Caribbean.

New France was France's only colony, and its sole means of support—apart from the limited largesse of the king—was the fur trade in the pelts of millions of aquatic small animals such as beavers and muskrats swarming in the lakes, rivers, and ponds of Canada.

The fur trade was a monopoly of the French monarch under which the highest bidders for these valuable furs and skins became the French government's recognized agents, or farmers, as they were called. They were responsible for the export of all the "peltry" of Canada: the most valuable beavers or fox to clothe or adorn the persons of the upper classes of Europe; or the skins of deer, muskrats, or moose to be made into the work clothes of the lower classes. No one else but these farmers were allowed to participate in the fur trade, excepting, of course, the Indians who shot or trapped and then cured the peltry. Because of this monopoly the agents could fix the prices they would pay the Indians—usually in gay trading trinkets, or tools of iron such as axes or cooking utensils—as low as possible, while collecting a commission of 10 percent.

Now beginning to interfere in this monopoly in Canada there appeared a new type of Canadian called the *coureurs de bois*—that is, the bush ranger, who despised the settled life of a father of a family or owner of a farm, and sought instead the freedom of the forests. There they could live the carefree life of an Indian brave and also trade with him for his furs and to sell them at a much higher price among the English and Dutch colonists on the southern side of the St. Lawrence. The money they earned, of course, would be spent mostly for beer and brandy in the gambling halls of Québec, Three Rivers, or Montréal.

Thus the number of *coureurs de bois* rapidly increased, and the colony's lands remained undeveloped for agriculture. There were two types: first was the one who, instead of awaiting the Indians at Montréal or Three Rivers, went out into the wilds himself either in a canoe or on foot with a pack on his back, a musket in his hand, and buckskins on his body. Most frequently, this type of bush ranger still had close ties to a settlement and might even have left a wife and family behind him, providing for them with what furs he could sell across the river. The second group comprised a very different type of white man, who spurned civilized ways altogether to join a band of roving savages, adopting their weapons, customs, and costumes and becoming even fiercer, wilder, and crueler than his new companions.

The king had expected the authorities in New France to exercise rigid control of the fur traffic, but actually they were powerless to prevent this steady flow of furs southward to New England or New York. Consequently Boston, Albany, and other English towns began to flourish, while the towns of New France found themselves sinking into a poverty caused by the languishing fur trade.

King Louis became incensed to learn of this dwindling source of income, not only because of its loss but also because of the defection of brave, strong, and able young men whom he had hoped would become the fathers and husbands who would form the nucleus of a sturdy class of peasants like those of France. So he issued orders to Frontenac to suppress both classes—especially those who had "gone native"—and to demand their submission to the king's orders to gain his pardon, or if they defied him, to execute them.

IT IS POSSIBLE that there dwelt in the old soldier's heart of Count Frontenac a certain admiration—even sympathy—for these brave and daring men, and that these draconic orders of King Louis did not encourage him to launch a crusade against the *coureurs de bois*. Certainly he would arrest those of whom he had information, and probably do his utmost to persuade them to beg the king's pardon. But *execute* them? *All* of them? Perhaps not. Certainly he had no use for the bush rangers who "went native," and would not waste words trying to persuade them to make their submission. But he still did not exactly yearn to play the role of a wrathful revenger of wrongs done to a merciful monarch whom he sincerely admired.

That was, until a threat to the fur trade far more subtle and destructive than the individual peccadilloes of the bush rangers: an actual conspiracy to rob the king's fur traffic by an unscrupulous crown official aroused his anger to the extent that he vowed to bring him first—and not some simple forest-rover—to the gallows.

※   ※   ※

WHEN JEAN BAPTISTE TALON, the first intendant of New France named by King Louis in 1665, who had returned to France in 1672, came back for his second tour as intendant in 1669, he brought with him an officer named François Marie Perrot and Talon's niece, who had married him. Perrot, anxious to trade upon the influence of her uncle, discovered that there was an excellent opening in Montréal. The priests of St. Sulpice who were feudal owners of the town had the right of appointing their own governor. At the urging of Talon, Perrot received the post, with the reservation that it was revocable at the priests' will. The new governor, probably again at the instance of his uncle-in-law, begged another commission from the king. This, of course, would always take precedence over any other. To get rid of Perrot, the fathers of St. Sulpice would have to receive the royal consent.

Perrot, ambitious and greedy as well as clever and audacious, found himself in excellent position to make money. Not, of course, by legal means, for he was also unscrupulous. Not just a few hundred livres, either, or whatever he was earning as governor of Montréal; for this short, dumpy man with heavy jowls and doglike pouches under his small, shrewd eyes was eager to cut a fine figure in New France. The fact that the colony's chief source of income was the lucrative fur trade, strictly scrutinized and regulated from Paris, did not frighten him, not even that it was risky and also dangerous.

Perrot quickly—probably through his relative Talon—learned all he needed to know about the fur trade. The tribes of the upper lakes and waterways and all neighboring regions brought down their furs every summer to the annual fair at Montréal. It would be a simple thing, Perrot thought, to preempt this monopoly of the little city of which he was the governor by introducing another terminal so many safe miles above it. He soon found it on a little island in the St. Lawrence that still bears his name, and built a storehouse there.

Next he put it in charge of a retired soldier named Lieutenant Brucy, a dishonorable scoundrel like himself. Then he supplied Brucy with a stock of trading items favored by the Indians: knives, fishhooks, iron pots and kettles, and for their squaws and children gay articles such as colored beads and caps. Settlers who knew Governor Perrot were surprised that he was able to provide Brucy with so many trading articles, for he was known to earn only a modest income from the fathers of St. Sulpice. But those days were soon behind Perrot, for both he and Brucy were now able to accumulate a considerable fortune.

Brucy's routine was to stop the Indians on their way downriver with their canoes loaded with furs to obtain what may be called "the pick of the peltry" in exchange for the merchandise provided by

Perrot. Thus the profits he made for himself and his master were greater than for the traders downriver, and in that proportion were depleting the colony's income from the fur traffic.

The Indians were also pleased to trade with Brucy, preferring to deal with him at his island on the river because it saved them a trip downriver to Montréal, or even lower, to Three Rivers or Québec.

It was at about this time that King Louis issued his wrathful edict condemning the bush rangers and outlawing them, and which also declared that they must come into Québec and make their submission to Governor Frontenac, leaving the forest and accepting a settled life. If they did not, and were captured, they would immediately and without a trial be subject to execution.

It was probably inevitable that the sly Perrot would make himself the protector of these outlaws, so he deliberately ignored the royal edict, and instead had begun to connive at the desertion of his soldiers, who escaped to the woods to become bush rangers and to commence trading with the Indians for their furs. All furs thus obtained—either by deserted soldiers or veteran forest rovers—were to be sold to Perrot; and if they grumbled that his prices were the lowest anywhere, he had only to mention the king's edict.

Frontenac probably could have easily handled the problem of the bush rangers if he had been back in France. Just send out a sheriff with a few musketeers to bring them in, and then pay an executioner to take them to the gallows. But in the vast and untracked forests of New France, a bush ranger or two would be mighty difficult to discover, let alone to apprehend; and many of them might even join forces with the hostile tribes. Moreover, Frontenac had no soldiers to speak of, only his bodyguard of twenty men, of whom he had consistently complained to the minister as a pack of sullen, scowling brutes spoiled by the soft life of Paris, yearning to return to its bright lights, bistros, and brothels. Four or five Canadian bush rangers, he well knew, could handle the whole detachment.

So instead of force, he tried the law—even though ineffective as it usually is in an enormous, unsettled, and wild country. He sent orders to the judge in Montréal to arrest any bush ranger who entered the city and detain all who were already inside it. Any bush ranger who submitted to the king's edict and asked his pardon would be freed; those who defied it would be hanged.

Frontenac knew that even in fair weather it would take about two weeks to cover the 185 miles to Montréal on foot. When the river was frozen and the cold winds were biting, it could be a grueling, snowshoe journey of three weeks or more. He was also aware that any *habi-*

tant in any weather seeing a messenger hurrying upriver would immediately guess the purpose of his mission and hasten to warn the unsuspecting bush rangers. These outlaws—again akin to Robin Hood's merrymen—were much admired by the *habitants* tied to the land and their families; and there also might have been in the soldier's heart of Louis de Buade some of the small sympathy he could always feel for a brave and daring man. Nevertheless, even if he would take no pleasure in arresting them, he would uphold the king's edict.

By this time Perrot thought himself secure. Relying on his commission from the king, his protection from Talon, as well as the friendship of many of the chief inhabitants of Montréal, he had entered upon the immemorial mistake of the criminal who thinks himself untouchable. Instead of detaining any bush rangers inside "his city," he ordered an accomplice named Carion to warn them and send them fleeing for the sanctuary of the forests. Returning to confront the judge and those notables, Perrot flew into a feigned fury, imprisoning the judge who was his inferior and covering his "friends" with vituperation. But then his clever criminal mind began to misfunction, for he had overlooked two difficulties: Talon was not there, and neither was Frontenac's messenger, who had quietly slipped away and was even then hurrying back to Québec to report.

When Count Frontenac was informed of Perrot's treachery, he, too, flew into a rage, which was in no way pretended, and—as his enemies always insisted—he actually began to foam at the mouth.

"Mutiny!" he bellowed. "Mutiny and rebellion! By God, if it's Perrot who wants the rope—not the scum who follow him—I'll give it to him."

With scarcely a soldier of his own to carry out the edicts of the king, and with no faith in his skimpy bodyguard, he still had a plan to deprive the rebellious governor of Montréal of his minions the bush rangers. He had already petitioned the minister for a galley to which he planned to enchain every bush ranger taken captive, thus supplying the king's agent in New France with a means of transportation suitable to his dignity, while dispensing with those wretched canoes and also giving to all the *habitants* along the St. Lawrence ample warning of the fate of those who violated the king's edicts.

But then he recovered his composure, and this turned his active and perceptive mind in another direction. Here indeed was the opportunity to kill two birds with one stone! One of them—Perrot—had flaunted the king's edict and must be punished; the other—still Perrot—had been making great and illicit profits from robbing the king's property, while he, Frontenac, the superior of Perrot and faithful governor of the entire colony, had been making none. Thus Perrot, the double-dealer, was guilty on these two counts and must feel the rope. So would this Lieutenant Carion, who—Frontenac's messenger had reported—had actually spread the alarm among the bush rangers and had been harboring two of the most notorious in his house. A different judge thereupon sent a constable there to arrest them, but Carion threatened him and helped the culprits escape. Perrot arrived and praised Carion for what he had done and warned the judge that he would put him in jail if he ever again attempted to arrest any of "his men."

Frontenac realized that Perrot was a resourceful scoundrel and that he himself had limited means to apprehend him, especially with all those bush rangers at his back. Nevertheless, he doubted that the governor of Montréal would openly defy the king of France. So he sent three soldiers under a Lieutenant Bizard to Montréal to seize Carion and bring him to Québec. It was a delicate mission, for the arrest was to be made in Perrot's dominion; and either a courtesy call by the official making the arrest must be made, or a letter explaining what would happen should be delivered. Bizard, forgetting the letter, did make the arrest and took Carion prisoner, preparing to hustle him down to Québec.

But before he could depart, Carion's wife hastened to Perrot and told him that the governor had seized her husband. In a frenzy of outrage, Perrot, followed by a sergeant and three or four soldiers, intercepted Bizard. The sergeant leveled his halberd and pressed its point against Bizard's breast. Perrot, choking with passion, demanded, "How dare you arrest an officer of my government without my leave?" Bizard's reply was that he was in Montréal on orders of the governor of New France, hoping thus to cow Perrot; but when he handed him Frontenac's letter that he had been unable to deliver, Perrot seized it, threw it in Bizard's face, and shouted, "Take it back to your master, and tell him to teach you your business better another time!" Bizard protested, but Perrot, now choleric and choking, nevertheless threw him into prison. He was followed a few days later by Le Ber, the chief merchant of Montréal, who had signed an attestation of the scene he had witnessed.

This might have sent Perrot into a paroxysm of anger, had he not begun to feel alarmed at what might happen to him could his defiance of the king be proved. His situation was now desperate, and he knew it. But he also knew that apart from the king, he held the best cards. He was informed by his spies in Québec that Frontenac had at his command only those unsoldierly ruffians of his bodyguard and could never have subdued Perrot's private army: bush rangers, disbanded soldiers and forest rovers, the best fighters in Canada. Not even a muster of militia would have helped the governor, for these were mostly unwarlike peasants for whom muster day was a social event with music, dancing, and picnic tables loaded with delicacies, with sweetmeats and chocolate for the children and beer from the new brewery for the men—after a half hour of leisurely drill.

This, Perrot reasoned, could lead to civil war, with the wrath of the king falling on both parties. At the same moment, it is possible that Count Frontenac was also brooding over unhappy thoughts with the identical unwelcome solution. So he wrote to Perrot, inviting him to come to Québec and to explain his conduct. It was not an imperious message, merely a friendly, courteous invitation.

Perrot showed it to his friend Abbé Salignac de Fenelon, one of the priests of St. Sulpice who had conferred the commission of governor of Montréal on Perrot. Fenelon saw nothing suspicious or sinister in it, eager as a priest to play the role of peacemaker, and advised Perrot to accept. It being midwinter, both men strapped on their snowshoes and walked 180 miles down the frozen St. Lawrence to reach Québec, where Fenelon availed himself of the hospitality of the Jesuits, and Perrot walked gingerly to the Upper Town and into the Château St. Louis, the home and headquarters of Louis de Buade, Count Frontenac, governor of New France.

THE MOMENT THAT François Marie Perrot walked into the presence of Count Frontenac he may have gotten the sinking feeling that he had accepted an invitation to an assassination banquet; for Louis de Buade had no intentions—now that he had Perrot in his power—of allowing him to return to Montréal. He did not, however, intend to harm him.

Relieved, taking this restraint as a sign of weakness, Perrot proved himself to be just as stubborn and imperious as the count himself. Apparently the petty despotism that he had enjoyed at Montréal during the past few years had given him delusions of grandeur, and thus the interview was as brief as it was stormy—ending when a deflated former governor of Montréal accepted residence in the prison at Québec, with guards watching him day and night. Meanwhile, Frontenac replaced Perrot at Montréal by one La Nouguere, a retired officer whom he knew he could trust. Under La Nouguere, Perrot's partner Brucy was arrested, tried, and imprisoned; and with that a hunt began for his *coureurs de bois*. Among others the two whom Carion had set free were captured, and one of them hanged in full view of Perrot's prison cell.

Thus what today might well be called "The Big Fur Fiddle That Failed" came to an end with the result that the fur traffic that had been reduced by the Perrot-Brucy peculations resumed its normal volume.

Pleased with this fortuitous and final result of his own watchfulness, Frontenac had Perrot removed from the cell he had occupied from January to November and shipped him back to France along with Fenelon, who had followed the former governor of Montréal as a fitting subject for the fulminations of Frontenac. An immense mass of papers accompanied them to Versailles, for the edification of the king and his minister, and the final disenchantment of both the embarrassed *abbé* and disgraced former petty tyrant of Montréal.

King Louis wrote Frontenac a calm and dignified conclusion of the entire episode, declaring: "I have seen and carefully examined all that you have sent touching M. Perrot; and, after having also seen all the papers given by him in his defence, I have condemned his action in imprisoning an officer of your guard. To punish him, I have had him placed for a short time in the Bastille, that he may learn to be more circumspect in the discharge of his duty, and that his example may serve as a warning to others. . . . After keeping him there a few days, I shall send him back to his government, ordering him first to see you and make apology to you for all that has passed."

Fenelon did not escape so easily, for he was ordered never to return to Canada, the vast and wild colony he had learned to love so deeply.

CHAPTER 12

James II, King; William III, Usurper

IT IS DIFFICULT to explain the causes of King William's War, as the English colonists in America called the War of the Grand Alliance, because it was so much a part of what has become known as the "Drawn Battle" in Europe between advancing Protestantism and resisting Catholicism. But it must be explained to show how a member of an ancient Dutch family that was almost a thousand years old at the time of these events of the second half of the seventeenth century could find himself on the throne of Britain.

This family became known as the Princes of Orange (Nassau), and it became a practice to give to all its firstborn males the customary name of William. This particular William was born in 1650, just after the death of his father. The child grew up under differing circumstances. At first he had lived in the tumbledown castle of Nassau-Dillenburg, the eldest son in a large penny-pinching family of impoverished German aristocrats. But then—as though the Fairy Princess had waved her wand over his head—the death of a cousin invested him with vast estates and the title of prince, but only on the proviso that he become a Catholic.

In this there was no difficulty. William had in fact been baptized a Catholic. But his father had turned Lutheran, because, as his neighbors sarcastically observed, "the Catholic Church owned little of value in Nassau-Dillenburg." But Count Nassau was hardly a man to allow a second change of religion to stand in his son's path, so he returned to the ancient Church. At eleven, then, William of Orange who was called prince was also fabulously wealthy.

But he was not so well endowed physically, being dwarfish and sullen, with a strong aquiline nose and the long, flowing, auburn hair and creamy complexion so peculiar to the Dutch. He was not, however, very popular with his friends. As he grew to youth and manhood, to gain their approval he loaded them down with gifts, as well as other people who became partners in his sexual vices. The first of these was a man of good family named Bentinck, and next an extremely beautiful boy named Keppel.

Still, because of his obvious intelligence, he caught the eye of Emperor Charles V, who had also been King Charles I of Spain, who invited him to his court and fixed on him—probably mistakenly for a Catholic sovereign—as a bright youngster who might one day administer the Netherlands, still under Spanish rule. He also hoped that William would befriend his own son and heir, Philip, because they were both about sixteen years old. But William's affable pose did not attract or deceive the deadly serious Philip, who, William realized, would one day be the most powerful ruler in the known world. In a word, they despised each other. Philip detested heretics, and William tried to pretend that he was still a Catholic, which he was not. The two princes—both rivals for the emperor's affection and goodwill—mistrusted each other forever after. Philip, for all his scowling intensity, could turn a wounding phrase. Thus William, having twice become a Catholic and a Protestant, changed his faith as easily as he changed his shirt. Would he do it again? Indeed he would, for William eventually became the leader of the Dutch revolt against King Philip II of Spain, a turnabout that deeply distressed the Emperor Charles.

William of Orange had now definitely decided that the Protestant card in the "Drawn Battle" was the one to play. Gazing across the English Channel at what is now known as the United Kingdom, it was becoming clear to him that England's powerful navy, the gift of both Charles I and his son James II—both excellent sailors but incompetent soldiers—was making the island kingdom the dominant Atlantic power. Better still, William's first cousin Mary Stuart—daughter of James, duke of York, who would, as James II, succeed his brother Charles II—was available as a wife, and if she was not quite an idiot she was at least a simpleton who would interfere in neither his plans nor his vices.

King Charles II approved the match because his brother James had become a Catholic and was the heir to the British throne upon his—Charles's—death. This, Charles thought correctly, would save the Stuart dynasty by counteracting his brother James's conversion. Charles was also well aware that by the time James became king, Britain would be about three-quarters Protestant.

In 1685 James II became the legitimate king of England. Almost at once the policy of the *nouveau riche* families became a quiet drive to take over the government and to destroy whatever power remained in the crown and thus serve their own selfish interests. Actually, the monarchy had been so weakened by the religious quarrel that it was now reduced almost to futility. Nevertheless, if the rich Protestants, through their two great committees—the House of Commons and the House of Lords—could ensure the presence of a puppet on the throne of England, they would have achieved all they sought.

All they needed was to depose James II, replacing him with someone *called* king. There he was, across the English Channel, waiting for their summons: the prince of Orange.

Not having been nicknamed William the Sly for nothing, he began quietly gathering his forces, secretly seeking huge loans from Dutch bankers whom he would repay with interest by the taxes he would impose when he became king. There were, of course, many of Henry VIII's "New Men" ennobled and enriched by him as a reward for having served him in his struggle with the ancient Church. His spoliation of its vast lands, splendid specimens of architecture from every age and for every function, together with the unrivaled wealth to be accumulated from the steady expropriation of the bejeweled vessels of gold and silver used in the service of the altar, had not been entirely for his own enjoyment, nor even to be exhausted in rewarding these faithful servants. Much of it was transferred to the Church of England founded by him, even though through the centuries all this plunder was brought or built by the pence of the poor and the pounds of their masters. Thus the New Men, either nobles or prelates, King Charles reasoned, might be willing to accept James the Catholic as their king—for a brief period at most—knowing full well that his Protestant daughter Mary was just one heartbeat away from ascending to the throne herself.

To William, Mary's outstanding attraction was that she had been reared as a Protestant even though her father, James, had become a Catholic. So William quietly proposed to King Charles II that he marry his niece Mary. Charles was delighted, for this would enable him to keep a foot in both camps, and also counteract his brother James's Catholicism by placing his Protestant daughter next in line for the crown.

To impress those powerful British lords who were considering him as the primary candidate, William the Sly concocted a monstrous calumny. As a boy at the court of King Louis of France, he maintained many years after his final embrace of Protestantism and full rebellion against his legitimate sovereign, that the king had confided in him his intention to massacre all Protestants within his realm. Hearing this, he said, he had been horrified, but had disclosed the plot to no one, waiting for the right moment to reveal it.

That time had come, he now declared. That a powerful monarch notorious neither for cruelty nor slaughter should confide such a state secret to a mere page was even less credible than the story of the plot itself. That he should have remained silent for half a lifetime when disclosure would have been of decisive importance is even less likely. However, these were fanatical days—either side was always willing to believe some monstrous calumny of the other. William the Sly's fanatical followers were only too eager to do just that, and this is why, because of his feigned unwillingness to discuss the story, the nickname of another much older William of Orange called "the Silent" before his assassination has supplanted "the Sly" in history.

WILLIAM'S ARMY, made up of Protestant mercenaries from the kingdom of Western Europe, landed unopposed in Devonshire, across the channel. Most of its officers were French Huguenots, and the finest fighting force was the Dutch Blue Guards. James had an equally large army to protect himself, and might have done so had he not been betrayed. The Judas was John Churchill, later the duke of Marlborough—and an ancestor of Winston Churchill—whose career had been made by King James. There was nothing for the legitimate king of Britain to do but flee, while William of Orange marched on London. There, in a compact between himself and the aristocracy, he and his wife were proclaimed cosovereigns, so that the reign of the usurper prince of Orange might now be known as that of "William and Mary."

William, of course, was himself a distant fourth in line to become the king of Britain, and his obedient wife had dutifully removed herself from any impediment in his path, if, in truth, she had ever been capable of either protest or complaint.

James had not surrendered, however. In France he was promised help from King Louis XIV. It came, but it was meager. It is quite unbelievable for anyone with even a trace of military experience to read an account of the so-called Battle of the Boyne River in Ireland in 1690, which pitted James—supposedly assisted by Louis—against William: both probably among the most inept generals in military history.

Thousands of Irish Catholic recruits—bold, brawny, and belligerent—flocked to James's standard. In his camps they were supposed to be furnished arms from a stand of twenty thousand muskets, only one in twenty of which could be fired.

Artillery was close to nonexistent. On the first march northward something like five thousand foot soldiers and eight hundred or nine hundred horses were supported by exactly *two* guns. When the siege of Derry began there were under its walls about ten thousand men depending on three field pieces, two small mortars, and two twelve-pounders to knock down walls twenty-four feet high and eight or nine feet thick. One of James's colonels reported that "in all his regiment there are only seven muskets; the others have little sticks three feet long; a few have pikes, but without iron on them." Among a group of Irish mutineers a court-martial condemned them to draw lots to see who would be shot, but when the unlucky man had been selected, nowhere could be found a firearm that would fire!

This was *war*? This was *combat*? This is the "great victory" that the little general with the diminutive body never stopped talking about until his dying day, which came in 1702, when he fell from his horse and perished.

James was hardly better. Still confident on his familiar element of water, he had challenged his absent Usurper's fleet on the channel and been decisively defeated by the very British Royal Navy he had done so much to create.

THUS BEGAN THE War of the Grand Alliance in the Western Islands, where the Reformation completely crushed the Catholic Church, with no hope of a renaissance until the beginning of this century with the appearance in England of French and Irish immigrants, all of whom were Catholics.

In the long and complicated annals of monarchy there is no record anywhere that an ordinary man or woman can become a legitimate sovereign through his or her spouse, either of whom might actually possess the one and only possible credential: the right of birth. Not even because of a physical deficiency can this be done, as it was in the case of a simpleton such as Mary Stuart, the eldest daughter of the rightful monarch: King James II. If this claimant is what we call today "retarded" or "slow," she or he is therefore unfit to rule; and a search for a legitimate claimant must have been begun. But one did in fact exist and for some time had been the true and actual king, until evicted by a *coup d'état*, and he was living in France and still available.

But the powerful Protestant nobles of Britain who wanted to rule through their coreligionist William of Orange, and thus acquire even greater wealth and power, sidestepped this "minor difficulty" by what their rubber-stamp Houses of Lords and Commons called "parliamentary title" to the throne, rather than through right of birth, as it was and still is everywhere else. This right was supposedly to be shared by the usurper William with his childless and childlike wife Mary so that the reign of "William and Mary," in what lapdog historians still call "the Glorious Revolution of 1688," would insure that henceforth none but a Protestant would wear the crown of Britain.

If it is suggested that there *was* a precedent for a dual monarchy in the joint reign of Ferdinand and Isabella of Spain, that is true. But in that instance, each was of royal blood and a sovereign in his or her own right, who were married before each inherited a throne: Isabella that of Castile, Ferdinand that of Aragon.

IN NORTH AMERICA, of course, the backlash of the War of the Grand Alliance was called by those English colonists fighting their French counterparts "King William's War," though it is evident from the literature of the time that these combatants had no notion that the king whose honor they were supposedly defending was an illegitimate sovereign.

WHEN JAMES STUART, duke of York, cautioned his older brother Charles II, king of Britain, about his lax security precautions, the lighthearted Charles chuckled and said, "Don't worry, Jamie—they'll never kill me to make you king."

In that exchange is told the whole story of these kingly brothers, so different in almost everything they did: except in battle, or on a throne—or in bed with an obliging lady. Charles II was outwardly Protestant but inwardly Catholic, and as he lay dying he received the last rites of the ancient church from Father Hudleston, the very same priest who had saved his life after the Battle of Worcester. Charles was also lighthearted and lazy, although well liked; but James was dour and—among many Catholics still surviving in Britain—disliked. Both were tall and strong, scions of the Bourbon Dynasty, and as swarthy as their cousin King Louis XIV of France.

Even after Charles died in his bed, there were not too many people who wished to see his crown on his brother's head. Nor did anyone ever believe that the dashing young Duke of Monmouth, Charles's only "son," was really legitimate. If he had been, that would have canceled James out—and the history of Britain might have been less bloody and treacherous. For if the vice of the French is said to be lechery, the vice of the English is *known* to be treachery. So when the young duke rose in rebellion, King James II wisely moved quickly against him. Monmouth would not have made a good king, but then, practically no one—even among the surviving Catholics—believed that James would either. Actually, it wasn't James himself who put down Monmouth—executing him after he was captured—but rather John

Churchill, the rising military star of Europe and the ancestor of another such luminary, Winston Churchill. For this feat, James made Churchill a lieutenant general.

In his younger days James had been a soldier of fortune, commanding in the armies of other than English kings—and had acquired quite an admirable reputation. His war memoirs—surprisingly well written—also showed that he had been a fine soldier, a development not to have been expected of a boy who had had such a miserable childhood and youth: in civil war, exile, poverty, tragedy, and fitful fortune. The tragedy, of course, was in the death of his father—King Charles I—defeated in battle and beheaded by that miserable, hymn-singing swine Oliver Cromwell. That single, stunning blow may have been enough to make of him an introvert. His brother Charles II simply forgot it, glad enough to welcome the crown back among the Stuarts. Also, his mother—Queen Henrietta Maria—had been forbidden by those powerful new men to raise her second son in her Catholic faith, and that had been another blow.

A third was that his first wife, Anne Hyde, daughter of the earl of Clarendon and a truly devout Catholic, was also ordered to bring up their two daughters in a fanatical Protestant mode that made most sincere Anglicans blush. Thwarted in her plans for her children, Anne turned to proselytizing her husband, which really was not necessary because he was already a thinking, if not a practicing, Catholic. But because he was the heir to the throne, he was duty bound to stay in the Anglican Church. Outwardly, he did stay, and he allowed his daughters Mary and Anne to remain Protestant as well. But he himself was eventually received into the Catholic Church as early as 1668 or 1669, but quietly, until it became an open secret; and in 1685, upon the death of his brother Charles II, the crown passed to him.

Openly and actively, King James began what might have been a copy of the Catholic Counter-Reformation in Europe. He greatly expanded the army, appointing Catholic officers to the new regiments, much to the annoyance of a hitherto agreeable Parliament. So James prorogued it in November of his ascension year. It never convened again in his reign. In 1686, having appointed several judges to the King's Bench, that worthy tribunal ruled that the king had the power to dispense individuals from the Test Act oath, thus permitting Catholics to hold high office again. James also suspended his outspoken enemy the bishop of London from his office.

All that was needed to assure a Catholic succession to the throne was a male heir, or for one of the Stuart sisters to renounce her Protestantism, which James—having been long ago rebuffed on that score—

did not bother to attempt. But then, his first wife died, and James married the beautiful Italian princess, Mary-Beatrice of Modena. Her first pregnancy was not successful, but in her second one she brought forth a healthy baby boy, who was indeed the son of King James II and who would succeed him as his heir, King James III.

Unfortunately, the sometimes infuriatingly stupid James did everything wrong in repudiating the Anglican attempt to disqualify the new heir. Required by law and custom to fill the delivery room with witnesses to the birth of his son and heir, he selected none but Catholics—giving the Anglicans the chance to say that he lied. They said that the baby boy brought into the delivery room in a warming pan was not a Stuart. Poor James, he had not the wit to ask, since no Anglican was present, how did they know that he lied; and that no true newborn Stuart male could fit into a warming pan without cutting off a few of his limbs.

But even if James possessed the throne and its power, the Anglicans had the public's ear, and so—as they say in America—the protagonists split along party lines. So what was needed now was a Protestant champion, and little William of Orange was quickly interviewed and found to be wanting—wanting with all his heart and soul to become the king of Britain.

One after another, all the nobles and knights of the realm who were made by James began to desert the Catholic cause. But the greatest of these Judases was John Churchill—who might have still been a colonel but for James—because his was also perhaps the finest military mind in all of Europe, and the one upon which James completely depended; his was the most devastating defection. Churchill was no more interested in Protestantism than were the rest of the turncoats, and he knew as much about religion as a pig knows about Sunday. Yet he was fairly certain of which way the wind was blowing and would dearly like it to remain at his back.

King James II sensed that change in direction, too. Of course, he would rather fight than flee, except that he was nearing sixty and much to old to overcome the overwhelming odds against him. Moreover, he might have dreaded the thought of provoking another civil war that might bathe Britain in blood, and end for him as it had ended for his beloved father.

In his flight, King James II was captured by "a band of self-appointed frontier guards," much to William's annoyance. It was no part of his plan to harm his wife's father at all. Moreover, William would not like to enter history as a regicide, like the now universally detested Cromwell. So James was permitted to escape a second time, again taking refuge in France as the guest of his first cousin and good friend Louis XIV, a good Catholic who was also the dedicated enemy of the little Usurper from Holland.

James had also seen to it that his wife and especially his son made it to France in safety. If anything had happened to either or both of them, civil war would have been a certainty. Still, poor Queen Mary of Modena had to hide behind the buttress of a parish church, awaiting dark and a small boat to take her and her baby across the Channel. James joined them there. En route in his own small boat, he dropped the Great Seal in the Thames.

CHAPTER 13

The Martyrs of New France

EVEN MORE FEROCIOUS than the dreadful massacre at La Chine was the animosity the Iroquois bore against the Jesuit missionaries of New France. It would seem inexplicable, except that being allies of the English to the south, they might have been urged especially against them because these sons of St. Ignatius of Loyola—founder of the Society of Jesus—had been the leaders of the Catholic Counter-Reformation in Europe, during which so many former Catholic strongholds had been recovered and the anti-Catholic movement begun by Martin Luther had been halted, and in some countries even reversed.

Certainly the warriors of the Five Nations could tell a Jesuit from a Recollet, because the cassocks of the former were black and those of the latter gray. Thus, on the morning of August 2, 1642, they knew that they would find Jesuits among the twelve Huron canoes moving slowly along the northern shore of the St. Lawrence known as the Lake of St. Peter. Distributed among them were about forty men, mostly Indians of the Huron tribe and four Frenchmen, among them a young Jesuit missionary, Isaac Jogues. Born at Orléans in 1607, Jogues was then thirty-five, which is to say that after a novitiate of thirteen years or more, he had been ordained a priest of the Society of Jesus and assigned to the missions of New France. Probably he had not been in holy orders for more than three or four years. His oval face and fair complexion, together with his refined features and modest, reflective nature, suggested an unusually sensitive human being devoted to serving "the greater Glory of God." He was also a finished scholar, and might have earned a literary reputation had he not chosen to serve his Maker in the green hell of Canada with its horrible history of massacre, bloodshed, scalping, torture, and cannibalism among its savages, to whom Jogues had hopefully come as the agent of the Risen Christ.

Jogues's slight frame did not suggest any great physical strength—

though all his movements were quick, and in running he had yet to be caught from behind by any Indian—but at the moment he seemed to be reflecting on his satisfaction with the good works he had recently had the pleasure to effect among the tribes of the Great Lakes. During the last autumn (1641) with Father Charles Raymbault, he had traveled as far west as the Sault Sainte Marie to preach sermons to two thousand Ojibwas and other Algonquins who had assembled there to hear him and his companion speak of Jesus Christ and the healing powers of His religion.

He was now on his return from an even more dangerous errand. The Huron mission to which he had been assigned was in a state of near decay. It was short of almost every need: clothing for its priests, vessels for the altars, writing materials, bread and wine for the Holy Eucharist—and much, much more. During the present summer of 1642 Jogues and others had descended to Three Rivers and Québec with canoes full of Huron pelts. These they had exchanged for the supplies, and were now en route back to the mission.

Also in the little flotilla were a few Huron converts, and the Christian chief Eustache Ahatsistari. There were a few other novice Hurons preparing for baptism, but most of those in the party were heathens in canoes laden with the materials bought by their furs.

There were two other young Frenchmen—René Goupil and Guillaume Couture, *donnés* of the mission, that is, laymen who from religious motives and without pay had attached themselves to the Jesuits. Goupil had formerly entered the novitiate at Paris but had been forced to leave because of bad health. Sailing to Canada, he had offered his services to the mission and was accepted—though assigned to the humblest duties, although he later became an attendant at the hospital. His friend Couture was a man of vigor and intelligence—and equally unselfish. Both were with Jogues in the foremost canoes, while the fourth Frenchman was with the unconverted Hurons.

The convoy had reached the western end of Lake of St. Peter, where it was dotted with numerous islands. Close on their right was the forest, its shallow shore filled with a thick growth of tall bullrushes. To avoid the swift current, they kept close inshore, where primeval silence reigned, broken only by the splashing of the paddles, the high, keening cry of waterfowl flying in thick V's, bound for the warmer lakes and rivers of the south. It was a charming scene, and the Frenchmen were delighted by it. Not the Hurons; they glanced around them in quick, fearful, darting movements—and suddenly out of the bullrushes burst an armada of Iroquois war canoes filled with hideously painted braves, whooping and screeching and paddling furiously down on the Huron flotilla. They filled the air with visible arrows and the crackling fire of muskets, together with the chilling whine of invisible bullets.

To the rear the terrified heathen Hurons at once leaped erect—abandoning their canoes loaded with loot for the Iroquois—and fled into the forests. For a time the four Frenchmen at the head of the Christian Hurons gave battle, but when they saw another fleet of war canoes speeding toward them from opposite shores and islands—their paddles flashing in the sun, screeching and whooping, their arrows whistling, bullets whining—they lost heart, and those who could flee joined the other Hurons in the forest.

At the head of the Huron flotilla, Goupil was seized amid triumphant yells from his assailants, and several Huron converts were also captured. Jogues quickly hid in the bullrushes, and might have escaped, until he saw Goupil struggling in the clutches of the Iroquois and knew that he could not abandon him. Rising and with an incredible calm that quieted his screeching enemies, he walked toward them and surrendered. A few of them had been detailed to guard the prisoners, while the rest pursued the fugitives into the woods. Again tempted to flee, Jogues struggled to master his anguish, and took comfort from the act of solacing the captive converts by baptizing them with handfuls of water scooped from the lake.

Couture had eluded capture. But when he, too, realized that he could not abandon his companion in Christ to the dreadful mercies of the Iroquois, he turned and came slowly out of the sheltering forest. Five Mohawks—for such they were—ran at him, and one of them pointed his musket at him (they rarely took careful aim by squinting along the barrel)—but his firearm misfired. Without thinking, Couture fired his own weapon, and laid the savage dead. Springing at him with fierce and angry yells, the four remaining savages hurled themselves upon him, threw him to the ground—stripping him of his clothing, tearing out his fingernails with their teeth, gnawing at the fingers with the famished fury of starving dogs—pausing only long enough for one of them to draw his knife and plunge it through one of his victim's hands.

Sickened at what he saw, Jogues broke free of his guards and rushed to his friend to throw his arms protectively about his neck, turning as though to defend him. Momentarily, the savages paused with the same hesitance they had shown at his astonishingly calm surrender, but then, as though shamed by their own compassion, they sprang on the defenseless Jesuit with vengeful yells, dragging him away from Couture, beating him senseless with their fists and war clubs. When he revived, they lacerated his fingers with their teeth, as they had done with Couture. Then they fell on Goupil with the same ferocity, easing only after they had tired of the sport, and turned to helping their companions relieve the captive Hurons of their weapons. None of them was harmed at the moment, however, probably because of the distraction caused by the torture of the Jesuits.

In all, there were twenty-two captives, although three Hurons had been killed in the fight. The Mohawks, who numbered about seventy, had lost only the brave killed by Couture. Quickly hustling their prisoners into their own canoes, they transferred their plunder into their own boats and embarked onto the lake, but not until after they had murdered an old Huron whom Jogues had just baptized with his mangled hands. From there they paddled southward under a burning August sun to the site of where the town of Sorel now stands at the mouth of the Richelieu—and there they encamped. The next day they moved farther southward, up the Richelieu and Lake Champlain, and thence by way of beautiful Lake George to the three Mohawk towns.

There was no more torture for eight days, for the pain and torment of their wounds, alone almost unendurable, were as nothing in comparison to the clouds of biting mosquitoes that settled on their bloody, suppurating flesh, leaving them without peace or sleep, and had also introduced into their veins the alternating chills and fires of malaria with its thirst, nausea, and bone-cracking ague.

They had barely recovered from these afflictions when a large Iroquois war party of about two hundred braves arrived at their camp on a small island near the southern end of Lake Champlain. Perceiving their comrades' booty, and their clutch of prisoners who might soon furnish the flesh for a feast, they seized their war clubs and thorny thick sticks to form two facing lines of warriors climbing a path up a rocky hill. Through this their prisoners would be forced to run in one of the favorite mass tortures of the North American Indians, known as "running the gantlet." This was a double line of facing braves armed with war clubs and thick sticks or even clubbed muskets through which their naked prisoners were forced to run, struck at from start to finish, beaten to their knees or tripped and sent sprawling, staggering erect seemingly bleeding from every pore, their ears filled with the piercing yells and mad screeching of their tormentors.

Not one of the captives passed through this satanic street without receiving more bruises and shedding more blood, and slight, small-boned Isaac Jogues, whom the savages regarded as the chief man among the captives, had deliberately chosen him to be the last in line. Swift runner that he was, he was clubbed and beaten with such furious fervor that he fell unconscious halfway through the gantlet, drenched in blood and half dead. As a reward, his hands were again mangled, while the Huron sachem Eustache was singled out for additional tortures even more atrocious. That night, children and young braves and squaws assembled chanting and singing around their exhausted prisoners, lacerating their bruises and wounds and pulling hairs from their heads and beards.

Arriving by canoe at the point where, more than a century later, the English colonists would locate and built Fort William Henry, and the gentle Marquis Montcalm, among the New World's finest soldiers, would conquer it, they began their march for the closest Iroquois town. Each of the prisoners was made to carry his share of the Mohawk plunder, even Jogues, though he was by far the weakest of them all, yet his load was the heaviest.

At last they reached a palisaded town standing on a hill above the Mohawk River. This was Osseruenon, their hometown. Here the dreadful deviltry of running the gantlet was repeated, much to the whooping delight of both young and old. Here also two captive Hurons were burned alive. Through this "narrow road of Paradise," as Jogues called it, the captives were forced to run in single file. Couture was in front, behind him about ten Hurons, then Goupil, then the last of the Hurons—and Jogues again last. Throughout their passage they were saluted with yells and screeches, and a drumbeat of blows. One Mohawk bigger than all the others struck Jogues so hard it knocked the wind out of him and momentarily stretched him on the ground, unconscious. But the warning cries from his faithful comrades revived him, and so, lest he be killed where he lay, he staggered erect and stumbled off like a drunken man.

Inside the town they were all placed on a high scaffold of bark erected in the middle of a square of beaten earth. Here the children gathered, laughing and hooting beneath them, each endeavoring to impress their parents with their originality or ingenuity in causing pain. The three Frenchmen had suffered the most and were frightfully disfigured. Goupil was streaming blood, and his naked body was so bruised that he appeared to be a two-legged leopard. But the tumult ceased when the chief sachem of the town appeared, crying, "Come, my children, let us caress these Frenchmen!"

With a great shout, the ecstatic throng—all bearing knives down to the smallest little girl—began to climb the scaffold. A Christian Algonquin woman who was a prisoner among them was ordered to cut off Jogues's left thumb, which she did lest she die on the spot; and the same was done to Goupil, a clamshell being used because it was duller and ragged-edged and so would cause the most pain. In every way these excited savages, who had descended from the scaffold, dancing and chanting around it, strove to exact the most pleasure from the suffering of their victims, always seeking the greatest variety of torments, but none so final that it would kill and thus put an end to their entertainment.

At night the captives were taken down from the scaffold and placed in one of the longhouses, each of them stretched naked upon his back with their limbs extended—and their wrists bound to stakes driven into the earth. It is possible—but certainly not known for sure—that cries of ecstasy might have issued from the bruised and broken lips of the Jesuits, and also some of the Christian Hurons, for the "X" formation formed by their tormented bodies was an exact replica of Christ on the cross, leading them to imagine that they would follow Him there. But then the children—again trying to impress their parents with their inventiveness in torture—amused themselves by covering their victims' naked flesh with live coals and red-hot ashes, which they, being bound, could not shake off.

In the morning they were again placed on the scaffold, and the delight and delectation of the previous day repeated for two more days. Then they were taken to the next town, where Jogues was hung by his wrists from a bar on two upright poles, with the tips of his toes just touching the ground, in which stretching agony he remained for a quarter hour until—almost fainting—he was delivered by a Mohawk who, on a sudden impulse of pity, freed him from his bonds.

A sudden burst of shouting and whooping outside the palisade announced the capture of four fresh Hurons, who were also escorted to the scaffold. Jogues, ever eager for converts, caught an ear of green corn tossed among them for food. Seeing it covered with raindrops, he used them to baptize two of the newcomers. The others received the sacrament of baptism the next day with water from a brook they crossed.

Couture, meanwhile, though he had killed an Iroquois, had shown by his bravery and great stoicism under torture that he was worthy of adoption, so he was given to one of their families to replace an elderly brave who had just died. This was like a gift of life for the hardy Jesuit *donné*, though he kept clear of his former companions lest he arouse suspicion.

Less fortunate than he, Goupil and Jogues calmly awaited martyr-dom. They had seen a trio of Hurons burned to death and expected to follow them. A council was held to discuss their fate, but so many dissensions arose that in the end nothing was done. Nothing—until Goupil unwisely made the sign of the cross on the forehead of a child, grandson of the old Indian in whose lodge they lived. He had been told by the Calvinist Dutch that the sign of the cross was the Devil's device and would be harmful. The old man thought Goupil was casting an evil spell on his grandson, and consulted two young braves on what was to be done with his shamanist guest.

Goupil and Jogues knew nothing of this as they left their squalid lodge clad in tattered animal skins, strolling together in the forest in prayer, mutually exhorting each other not to be dissuaded by fear of pain or death in their mission to convert the savages of Canada. On their return to town, they encountered the two young Mohawks consulted by the aged grandfather. They joined the two Jesuits, walking with them back to town, but showing by their sullen and glowering silence that they bore them no love.

Suddenly one of them stopped and turned. Drawing a tomahawk from beneath his blanket, he plunged it into Goupil's head. He sank to the ground, murmuring the name of Christ. Jogues went on his knees, lowering his head—as though awaiting the blow. But he was ordered to get up and go home. He obeyed, but not until after he knelt again to give absolution to his still-breathing companion, and to watch in utter heartbreak to see his now lifeless body dragged through the streets amid derisive hoots and howls of contempt.

Jogues arose the next morning from a night of anguish, aware that with Couture adopted and Goupil dead, he was alone among the Iroquois. Still, he went forth to retrieve his friend's remains.

"Where are you going so fast?" the old Indian who had betrayed him demanded. "Do you not see those fierce young braves, who are watching to kill you?" Jogues said nothing, but the old man asked another Mohawk to accompany the Jesuit as his protector.

In tears, Isaac Jogues, assisted by the Indian, found the corpse of René Goupil. It had been flung into a stream at the bottom of a ravine. Stripped naked, it had been gnawed by dogs. Dragging it from the water, he covered it with stones to prevent other predators from mutilating it further, and also to mark where it lay. He returned to town, determined to come back the next day and secretly bury it. But during the night a violent storm broke, and when he went back to the ravine he found it a raging torrent in which both body and stone marker had been swept away.

It was early October, but the winter had already begun, for there was a thin film of ice on the rocks in the stream. Removing his bearpaw sandals, hiking up his animal skins, Jogues entered the freezing water, taking soundings first with his feet and then with his stick—but he found no resistance except among rocks. Leaving the water, he searched the rocks, the thicket, the forest—but found nothing. Crouching in misery on the banks of the stream, his tears mingled with its waters, while his wails and groans as he chanted the service of the dead counterpointed its steady roar.

But it was not the storm or the stream that had thwarted Jogues in his search for his friend's remains. Early in the following spring, when the ice and snow had begun to melt, Mohawk children told him that the body had been sighted in a lonely little cove farther downstream—probably flung there by his murderer. There he found Goupil's bones, gathering them up tenderly—weeping again to see how they had been gnawed clean by foxes and birds, and polished by the water. Finding a hollow tree, he hid the bones there, hoping to return to give them a Christian burial in consecrated ground.

But he did not.

IT HAD SOON BECOME clear to Isaac Jogues that his life among the Mohawks after the murder of René Goupil was not worth a polliwog's tail. For some time he lived in momentary expectation of the tomahawk in his own brain. Many of the braves—especially the younger ones, whose eagerness to prove themselves as warriors made them that much fiercer—had the utmost contempt for him, treating him like a squaw good enough for nothing but to fetch firewood, plant corn, cook food, and take care of the children. Actually, Isaac was profoundly thankful for this neglect, for under its welcome cover he could catechize the little ones, and sometimes also be asked to speak to their elders out of his vast knowledge of such things as the sun, moon, planets, and stars, and the rhythmic cycle of the seasons. This they understood, but when he shifted from astronomy to theology—his true purpose—they grew bored and hostile again. When he spoke of the Crucified Christ, his Master and Savior of Mankind, they laughed aloud in scorn and mocked his devotion to such a God who would surrender His life so tamely. Then, to their unique astonishment, this pathetic slave would leap erect to rebuke them in their own tongue. On these occasions he spoke—like Christ—"as one having authority."

Gradually the hopelessness of his life might have worn him down, except for those ever-present sanctuaries of prayer and hope. Even so, existence became not a joy but a burden, and he prayed to die: a martyr's death, of course. War parties were constantly going into the forest, returning loaded with loot and prisoners, shouting for a victory feast he knew he could not avoid, and would be compelled to watch as his countrymen and their Indian allies were mangled, burned, and devoured.

At last Isaac Jogues began to dream of escape and a return to France, where he could recover his health and return to Canada to renew the missionary life he had at first embraced. Thus, at the end of July in 1643, he accompanied a party of Mohawks to a fishing place on the Hudson about twenty miles below Albany. There he heard that another war party had returned to Osseruenon and had there burned two Hurons alive. Jogues was conscience-stricken. If he had remained in Osseruenon he might have been able to give these heathens absolution and baptism. So he begged the old woman who had been placed in charge of him to send him back there the first chance she got. Soon after, a canoe went upriver, and she sent him with it. Reaching the Dutch village of Rensselaerswyck—a community of about a hundred settlers who were farmer tenants of Van Rensselaer, the patroon or lord of the manor—the Iroquois went ashore and took Jogues with them.

In Fort Orange Jogues met Dominie Megapolensis, a Dutch Calvinist minister who had written a short history of the Mohawks. He had heard of Jogues, and was prepared to salute him as a fellow scholar until he beheld what was nothing less than the deliberately cruel wreckage of a human being. He was horrified. Jogues, who could not forget about the Dutchman who had told the Indian who killed Goupil that the sign of the cross was a device of the Devil, was astonished and gratified at the kind and gentle treatment of him by the dominie's congregation. They had heard of him, and, like their pastor, were stunned by the marks of extensive torture they perceived on his body, and the perpetual dread they had marked in his eyes. They were also on excellent terms with their Indian neighbors and had sometimes intermarried among them. Having heard of Jogues, they—to their great honor—had made attempts to gain his release through a ransom of considerable value in goods: but to no effect.

Jogues now heard that the warriors of his village were enraged against him for having disappeared and were sending out a war party to seize and burn him, and one to strike at a small French fort at the mouth of the Richelieu River. At once he asked for paper and, writing a warning in a jargon of Latin, French, and Huron, gave it to a messenger to deliver to the commander. When the war party arrived at the Richelieu and cunningly asked for a parley aimed at disarming the commander, he turned his cannon on them. They fled in terror, abandoning baggage and guns. Reaching Osseruenon, they cursed the name of their late guest and accused him of betraying them! Such ignoble anger amused the Jesuit, as well as several of the principal Dutchmen who advised Jogues never to go back.

Instead, one of them, named Van Curler—who had made the attempt to ransom Jogues—offered him a berth on a small Dutch vessel on the Hudson opposite the settlement. It would take him to either Bordeau or Rochelle. Jogues thanked him with great warmth, but then, to Van Curler's astonishment, asked for a night in which to pray to God for an answer.

Jogues twisted and turned, first in hope, then in anxiety, then in fear that self-preservation would persuade him in the wrong direction of flight. His first real fear was for his friend Couture should he escape to France. But he also suspected that now that he was regarded as the Great Betrayer of the gentle, solicitous Iroquois, their wrath would be diverted to Couture. Of his friend's ability to flee once he understood his predicament he had no doubt.

So he accepted Van Curler's offer, crossing the river by rowboat to the sailing ship, where Dutch sailors kindly hid him in the hold. He remained there in foul, stifling air for two days, after which he was transferred to a garret in the house of a selfish old man. Food was sent to him, most of which was appropriated by his host, and Jogues nearly starved. Six weeks later the Indians accepted a large ransom from his Dutch friends, and Jogues was free to continue south to Manhattan—now New York City—where the Dutch director-general, Kieft, received him with a kindness not quite customary with him, replacing the Jesuit's tattered animal skins with a suit of Dutch cloth. He also gave him passage in another small sea vessel just about to sail.

The long voyage was rough, wet, and cold, for Jogues had no cabin, spending the days in prayer seated on a coil of rope, and the nights sleeping on the deck, often drenched by cold waves breaking over the ship's side.

At Falmouth in Britain the captain and all the crew went ashore for a carousel, leaving Jogues on board alone. Soon a boatful of cutthroats came alongside, clambering topside to threaten Jogues with a pistol, robbing him of his hat and coat and whatever else aboard that was portable or valuable. To his great gratitude some sailors from a French ship in the harbor came to his rescue, and he soon crossed the English Channel to Brittany in a small coal vessel. From there he was set ashore the next day at a point in open country north of Brest.

There, seeing a small peasant cottage, he knocked on the door and asked the way to the nearest Catholic church. The peasant and his wife invited him inside to share their supper, an invitation he gratefully accepted—for he had had little to eat for days and was famished. Then he left for the church. In time for the evening Mass, he approached the altar with a beating heart, kneeling at the communion rail to receive the sacrament of Holy Eucharist that had been denied him for so long.

Returning to the cottage in a state of joyous exaltation, he noticed that his hosts were gazing in dismay at his terribly mangled and mutilated hands. When he explained what had happened to him, they almost fell upon their knees in combined horror and veneration. Their two young daughters—similarly struck—begged him to take all they possessed: a handful of sous. Their father, rushing in joy to his neighbor's home, informed him of the character of his guest and described his passion at the hands of the savages. Next, a trader from Rennes rode a horse to the door, inviting Jogues to mount it for the ride to the Jesuit college in that town.

On January 5, 1644, Isaac Jogues dismounted and knocked at the college door. The porter answered it, taken aback at the sight of what appeared to be a bedraggled old beggar in a soiled old woolen nightcap. Jogues asked to see the rector, but the porter, made overbearing by his lofty station, replied coldly that the rector was busy in the sacristy. So Jogues humbly begged him to say that a man at the door had news of Canada. At that time the missions of Canada were an undertaking of paramount interest among the Jesuits, and above all to those of France, as well as to most of the houses of the Society of Jesus in Catholic Europe.

A letter from Jogues had been written during his captivity, and had already arrived in France, as had also the Jesuit *Relation* of 1643, which contained a lengthy report of his capture and subsequent ordeal. In all probability the agony of Father Isaac Jogues had been a subject of constant discussion among the houses of the French sons of St. Ignatius.

The father rector was vesting for Mass when the porter informed him that a poor man from Canada had asked for him. He postponed the Mass and went to meet him at the door. Jogues, without revealing who he was, silently handed him a letter from Director-General Kieft explaining who the bearer was. Without reading it, the rector began questioning Jogues about Canada, asking him if he had known Father Jogues.

"I knew him very well," the visitor replied.

"The Iroquois have taken him?" he inquired fearfully. "Is he dead? Have they murdered him?"

"No," Jogues answered, "he is alive and at liberty—and I am he."

Then he fell on his knees to ask his superior's blessing.

And that night in the Jesuit College of Rennes was one of great thanksgiving and jubilation.

JOGUES SOON BECAME A subject of curiosity and reverence. He was summoned to Paris, where the queen, Anne of Austria, asked that he be brought to her. When the mangled and mutilated slave of the cruel Mohawks was conducted into her presence, she wept and kissed his horrible hands, while the ladies and titled women of Versailles gathered around him in open admiration.

It has been said—probably with truth—that these well-intentioned honors were received politely but with little enthusiasm by this modest and single-minded servant of God, who, having been rescued, could think of nothing else but returning to Canada to take up again the work of converting those savages who had so cruelly tortured him.

They would have gnashed their teeth in furious frustration to learn that they had inflicted upon Jogues an injury worse than the most ingenious torturer among them could have imagined, for a Catholic priest with any inhibiting bodily deformity is barred from saying Mass: the central act of his life and the cause of his vocation. If the Iroquois had known or even suspected such a unique though unwitting triumph, they would have celebrated indeed, for their cruel teeth and knives would have robbed him of the chief consolation of his life. But Pope Urban VIII had heard of Jogues's suffering and disabilities and had restored to him this great privilege; and with the arrival of the spring of 1645, this dauntless servant of God sailed once again for Canada.

BEFORE HE DID, however, another son of St. Ignatius fell into the clutches of the Mohawks. His name was Father Joseph Bressani, born in Rome, where he entered the Society of Jesus. In the spring of 1644 he set out on a mission to the Hurons, but his party was captured by Iroquois. Months later his provincial received the following letter:

"I do not know if your Paternity will recognize the handwriting of one whom you once knew so well. The letter is soiled and ill-written because the writer has only one finger of his right hand entire, and cannot prevent the blood from his wounds, which are still open, from staining the paper. His ink is gunpowder mixed with water, and his table is the earth."

Thereafter Bressani described an ordeal that began with the quartering, roasting, and consumption of one of his Indians and reached its peak of ferocity in a Mohawk village on the upper Hudson. The priest's captors began the sport by splitting his hand with a knife between the little finger and the ring finger. Then they beat him with sticks until he was covered with blood. Next, as a spectacle to a crowd of four hundred Iroquois, he was placed atop a bark torture-scaffold, where he was stripped naked and forced to sing. Perhaps here also, though Bressani does not say, the children burned the soles of his feet through the scaffold's crevices, as was customary. But the young Iroquois did order him to dance, jabbing him with sharpened sticks and pulling hairs from his head and beard.

"Sing!" ordered one, and another: "Hold your tongue!" If he obeyed the first, the second burned him with a firebrand, or vice versa. "I will eat one of your hands," one child would scream, and another: "I will eat one of your feet."*

Every night for a week, a chief went through the village crying, "Come, my children, come and caress our prisoners!"

Upon this summons, the torture would commence. Bressani would be stripped again, burned with live coals and hot stones, forced to walk on hot coals. Now a fingernail would be burned off, now a knuckle—and now a finger gnawed to the bone by human teeth. Never were the Iroquois extravagant with their torture. Always they reserved a little for another night, careful not to endanger the life of this source of so much pleasure. At about two o'clock each morning, after the fun had grown stale, Bressani would be left on the ground, fastened to four stakes and covered with a bit of deerskin.

But there were other villages to be entertained, and soon Bressani was forced on an exhausting march of several days to another Iroquois dwelling place. Here the catalog of horrors was repeated, augmented by such novelties as hanging him by the feet with chains and spreading food for dogs on his naked flesh so that the hounds might gnash him as they ate. At last Father Bressani was such a ruin that even the Iroquois were revolted by the sight of him. "I could not have believed," he wrote to his provincial, "that a man was so hard to kill."

At length the Iroquois fed him, assuring him that they were fatten-

---

*Dominie Megapolensis, the Dutch Calvinist minister at Fort Orange who was so kind and generous to the fugitive Isaac Jogues, presents in his *Short History of the Mohawks* an interesting aside on the Iroquois practice of cannibalism. "The common people," he wrote, "eat the arms, buttocks and trunk; but the chiefs eat the head and the heart."

ing him for his execution. But in solemn council they decided to give him to an old woman who had lost a son. She, finding him useless, sold him for ransom to the Dutch at Albany. Eventually, though maimed and disfigured for life, Bressani recovered his health and made a successful missionary trip to the Hurons.

Such incidents, however, were isolated deviations from the general custom of butchering and burning captives. More often, stoicism was only a goad to more fiendish torments. In 1642 an Algonquin taunted his torturers with this boast: "Look at me. You cannot make me wince. If you were in my place, you would screech like babies." The Iroquois—men, women, and children—at once plied their knives and firebrands with demonic fury, turning his body into a charred and tattered wreck, after which they hacked him slowly to pieces, tore out his heart, and ate it squatting on top of his bloody remains.

Thus the "noble savage" of whom his apologist—perfumed and posturing Jean-Jacques Rousseau—could write with such perverse admiration. Or those kind and loving Quakers of Philadelphia, actual rulers of Pennsylvania who declined to help their countrymen being slaughtered, burned, and eaten by similar savages on the western frontiers, but whom the Society of Friends dared not rescue on the grounds of a religious abhorrence of violence; but would send money instead with the quaint proviso that it not be used to kill anyone. Next, of course, during the Holocaust of World War II, our own modern liberals avoiding military service on the plea of such disabilities as thick toenails or empty soul-cases while the new Antichrist—Adolf Hitler—convulses the world and sends six million innocent Jews to their death. No, do not weep for the passing of such wolves in human form. Listen instead to the great historian Francis Parkman, who lived among the Iroquois and knew them well, and who could say that though they were the most able, political, and formidable of savages, they were savages still. Women ordered to burn their husbands or to watch their babies being roasted over slow fires—often being forced to eat their flesh—would find it difficult to understand that the Indians were only acting in the context of their customs and their folkways.

"They are not men, they are wolves!" a Frenchwoman said, sobbing after describing how her baby was burned before her eyes.

Human wolves that they were, they would have devoured New France had they possessed the slightest understanding of military art or of that discipline that is the chief mark of civilization. But the Iroquois could only make forays or raids. A battle was won or lost in an instant's rush. Stealth and surprise comprised their tactics. A siege was to them an incomprehensible bore, to maneuver in the open a madness. Even so, skulking in the forests by day, coming yelling out of the dark by night, the Iroquois struck terror into the hearts of the French and came close to achieving their ferocious objective: the extermination of their enemies.

Gradually, however, the warpath wore them out. Their victories had exhausted them, their villages were silent, and by the year 1660 the Iroquois could count only twenty-two hundred warriors, of whom more than half were adopted prisoners from the Hurons, Eries, neutrals, and various Algonquin tribes.

Nevertheless, until the very last chapter of the history of New France the Iroquois were to remain a threat to Canadian security. Goaded by the British, they dashed themselves again and again against the French and their Indians. And then, after the Peace of Paris had made Canada a colony of the British crown, they became, as loyal allies of the English, the bloody scourge of American revolutionists to the south.

WHY ISAAC JOGUES in 1644 should have returned to Canada and to his mission to the Mohawks could only be explained by the unlikelihood of peace among the Iroquois, the Hurons, and the Algonguins, and between these three with New France. But it had happened after Governor Champfleur, the commandant at Three Rivers, had called for a great peace council between these three principal tribes and the French. There was much speechmaking, widespread exchange of gifts and of wampums, until, after feasting that lasted for a week, a general peace was agreed upon.

It was into this atmosphere that Father Isaac Jogues arrived on his second visit to New France, but the truce was of short duration, broken by the Mohawks in their attacks on the French and their Indian allies of the lower St. Lawrence. Father Jogues was not surprised. No white man—with the possible exception of his friend Couture, still living among the Iroquois—knew their language and their character as well as he did. That is why he was sent to join Couture in an effort to mend the broken peace.

His errand was half political, half religious; for on the first obligation he came as a bearer of gifts and messages of friendship from Governor Champfleur; on the other, as a Jesuit missionary he was to found a new mission, its altar vessels, vestments, portable baptismal founts, and other articles of worship blessed in advance and given the sadly prophetic name Mission of the Martyrs.

Jogues, of course, had not asked for permission to return to the wilderness of his sworn enemies, he had expected to be reassigned to the missions—and he was. For two years after his return he had been at Montréal, baptizing and catechizing, probably on the order of his superior there who knew full well what the Mohawks would do to him now that they were again on the warpath. Obedient to the end, Jogues still felt a presentiment that his death was near, writing to a friend: "I shall go and I shall not return." From an Algonquin convert he received wise advice: to go as a civilian and to exchange his long black cassock—the uniform of Ignatius Loyola—for a short coat, a civilian's doublet, and hose.

On August 24, 1646, Jogues set out on his mission to the Mohawks accompanied by a young French *donné* and three or four Hurons. Making their way through the forests toward the Mohawk towns, they encountered other Indians, who warned them that the Iroquois were having a change of heart. With this, the frightened Hurons withdrew. But the gentle Jogues pressed on. The *donné* at his side was only slightly less determined. Both continued on, wondering what had occasioned this radical reversal among the Mohawks.

What they did not suspect was that on a previous visit to the Mohawks, Jogues on his departure had left with them a small locked chest. Distrustful as ever, they suspected that some evil spirit dwelt therein. Jogues therefore opened it to show them that it contained only a few harmless personal necessities, closing and locking it again and leaving it in their care.

Of all the Indian tribes in North America, none was more suspicious or superstitious than the Iroquois, and so in Osseruenon the Huron prisoners there sought to ingratiate themselves with their enemies by vilifying their friends the French. They said they were sorcerers and evil spirits who could cause drought, famine, and many similar catastrophes. At once Mohawk suspicions of Jogues's locked box were redoubled. They became convinced that it contained malignant forces, such as those now spreading a mysterious illness in town, plus the plague of caterpillars eating their corn—all of which was attributed to Jesuit black magic, or some local evil *okies* or *oktons*—that is, Indian supernatural beings.

Not everyone agreed, and three chief families or clans in Osseruenon—the Bear, the Tortoise, and the Wolf—were divided in their opinions. While the Bear raged in fury against the French and howled for war, the less belligerent Tortoise and Wolf dissented and staunchly stood by the treaty. The loudest, angriest voices reached the most ears, and thus the chiefs of the Bears chanted their war songs to attract adherents from the two other clans, and with two frenzied war bands went back on the warpath.

Unfortunately for Jogues, his habit of quiet contemplation, which had betrayed him before, rose again to afflict him as he and Lalande encountered one of these bands in the forest between Lake George and the Mohawk River. At once the Indians seized them, stripped them, and led them in triumph back to their town. There the usual crowd of chanting, jeering savages surrounded the gentle Jesuit. One of them cut thin strips from his arms and back, crying, "Let us see if this white flesh is the flesh of an *oki*."

Jogues, of course, knew what an *oki* was, and so he replied, "I am a man like yourselves, but I do not fear death or torture. I do not know why you would kill me. I come here to confirm the peace and show you the way to heaven, and you treat me like a dog."

A great shout rose from the crowd, and the warrior who cut flesh from Jogues's body cried, "You shall die tomorrow. Take courage, we shall not burn you. We shall strike you both with a hatchet, and place your hands on the palisade, that your brothers may see you when we take them prisoners."

That night of October 18, 1646, Jogues sat in a lodge in great pain from his wounds and bruises, when a Mohawk entered and invited him to a feast. To refuse would have been an insult, so he arose and followed him. Jogues bent his head to enter when an unseen brave standing beside the entrance struck him with his hatchet. An Iroquois whom the French called Le Berger bravely held out his arm to deflect the blow, but it cut straight through it, sinking into the brain of the missionary, who fell at the feet of his murderer—his head severed from his body.

Lalande was similarly slain next morning, and his head also chopped off. Both bodies of the Frenchmen were thrown into the Mohawk, and their dripping heads stuck up on the points of the palisade.

Of the dead martyr, Francis Parkman, the unbiased son of Protestant and anti-Catholic New England, could write: "Thus died Isaac Jogues,* one of the purest examples of Catholic virtue this Western continent has seen. The priests, his associates, praise his humility, and

---

*Canonized in 1930 by Pope Pius XI along with his companions René Goupil and John Lalande, all tortured and murdered by Iroquois at their Indian village of Osseruenon, now Auriesville, New York.

tell us that it reached the point of self-contempt—a crowning virtue in their eyes; that he regarded himself as nothing, and lived solely to do the will of God as uttered by the lips of his Superiors. They add, that, when left to the guidance of his own judgment, his self-distrust made him very slow of decision, but that when acting under orders, he knew neither hesitation nor fear. With all his gentleness, he had a certain warmth or vivacity of temperament; and we have seen how, during his first captivity, while humbly submitting to every caprice of his tyrants and appearing to rejoice in abasement, a derisive word against his Faith would change the lamb into the lion, and the lips that seemed so tame would speak in sharp, bold tones of menace and reproof."

CHAPTER 14

Canada the Quarrelsome

IT WAS AN UNHAPPY day for New France when Intendant Talon returned to his homeland after his second tour of duty in Québec. He had been for the harassed and hotheaded Governor Frontenac like an ocean of calm and a sanctuary of peace, as well as a fountain of many innovations that the unabashed Frontenac did not hesitate to claim as his own.

Talon was a practical and careful thinker, and his plans for the colony were based upon a deep desire for it to prosper. He accepted the widely held belief that New France could survive on the fur trade alone. But it also had to be more versatile and self-supporting through the introduction of other sources of wealth. This was economic heresy for Canada, dependent as it had always been on the king's largesse, but Frontenac accepted it because it dovetailed with his expanding vision of a great empire.

Talon believed that there was a need for development of agriculture and better methods of obtaining it. He had planned and built a modest shipyard to provide vessels for fishing and trading, and had even planned to open trade with the West Indies, exchanging fish and lumber for sugar and molasses. One necessity of organized agriculture would be the various grains, to be followed by the mills to turn out flour and cereals for home consumption. Perhaps his most original insight was to propose and produce a brewery to counter the crusade of Bishop Laval and the Jesuits against the brandy trade.

The brewery idea was perhaps Talon's most intuitive contribution to a spirit of amity that might squelch the bitter battle over the brandy trade raging between Bishop Laval as the church, and Governor Frontenac as the state. It was a potent argument against the generally accepted assertion that if the French didn't supply the Indians' thirst for brandy, they would be debauched by British rum. Moreover, British rum unchallenged by French brandy—which, indeed, the Indians preferred—would remove the savages from the guidance of Holy Mother Church and relinquish them to the spiritual debasement of Protestant Calvinism. The vast majority of the French in Canada—led by Frontenac and Talon—believed that brandy-and-baptism were a lesser evil than rum-and rebellion.

Probably the most furious and outspoken enemy of the brandy traffic was Father Étienne de Carheil, a Norman of noble birth who had spent thirty-six years in Canada, twenty of them as missionary to the Hurons at Michilimackinac, when he wrote his all-inclusive denunciation of what might be called The Four Evil Callings, published in 1702, long after Frontenac was dead. No one was more debauched by brandy, he wrote, than those soldiers whose "pretended service to the King is reduced to these four pursuits." The first was in keeping a tavern where the Indians could trade furs for brandy; the second was in being sent by their commandants from one post to another selling brandy; the third was in making their fort a place where women of pleasure were more welcome than beaver skins; and the fourth was inveterate gambling, presumably while consuming the fiery nectar themselves.

For years Bishop Laval had been writing in the same caustic style, but with much more force and passion as he described how Indians, if there were not enough brandy available for everyone to get drunk, would pool it and draw lots so that at least a few of them could lose their senses and maim and murder their sober friends; or how a drunken Indian with a knife or tomahawk in his hands was the most dangerous creature in the forests; how if a group of them had come into possession of a keg of brandy they would drink themselves to death; and of how all manner of abominations would be committed upon women and children by braves gone mad under the influence of liquor.

In the end, this explosive and divisive controversy was never settled amicably, and was actually acerbated by the arrival in Canada of Jacques Duchesneau, the intendant replacing the gifted Talon. Duchesneau almost immediately sided with Bishop Laval and the church, having decided to detest Frontenac on sight. Duchesneau's absolute lack of familiarity with the brandy question did inadvertently have a favorable effect on the subject; in his unwavering support of Laval it elicited from Colbert, if not a final decision, at least the last word: "We would run the risk if we yielded to his [Duchesneau's] opinion, not only the risk of losing this commerce but [also] of forcing the savages to do business with the English and the Dutch who are heretics; and it would thus become impossible for us to keep them favorably disposed toward the one, pure, and true religion."

THE DISPUTE OVER BRANDY was probably the most divisive of all the quarrels between the church, as represented by Bishop Laval, and the state, in the person of Count Frontenac. This was the fundamental disagreement between the two disputants, concealed as it was beneath so many other lesser quarrels and disagreements. Thus Laval, stern and uncompromising, sometimes gentle to those in need, often motivated by a messianic complex; and his rival Frontenac, fiery and unbending, immovable in his conviction that he was defending the rights of the king.

Laval did not fear debate; he had succeeded in conflict with three prior governors and believed himself about to vanquish a fourth. Frontenac loved a challenge with a passion, and was in no way intimidated by the rosary wound around His Excellency's waist, and especially not by the glittering pectoral cross at his breast. On the whole, Frontenac was the better debater, quicker on his feet and in repartee. He had entered this last dispute, which actually had been begun by his mortal enemy Intendant Duchesneau, by recording in the register of the Council of Québec the formal declaration that the rank of governor was superior to intendant; and then he began his farewell philippic, intended to refute Laval's assertion that the governor rarely ridiculed or criticized anyone who was not a partisan of the bishop and the Jesuits.

Frontenac had earlier written to the minister, "Nearly all the disorders in New France spring from the ambition of the ecclesiastics, who want to join to their spiritual authority an absolute power over things temporal, and who persecute all who do not submit entirely to them." Then he unburdened himself of a long litany of complaints.

The Jesuits: These black-robed sons of St. Ignatius were among the governor's chief enemies. His litany of complaints to the minister—who probably passed many of them on to King Louis—were full of criticisms of these learned but perhaps too subtle casuists. "Another thing that displeased me," he wrote, "and this is the complete dependence of the Bishop and the seminary priests on the Jesuits, for they never do the least thing without their order; so that they [the Jesuits] are masters in spiritual matters, which, as you know, is a powerful lever for moving everything else." He also accused them of having spies in town and the countryside, that they abused the confessional (a most severe charge, which, if pressed, must actually be delated to

Rome), meddled in families, set husbands against wives and parents against children, and all, as they say, for the greater glory of God. Then he anointed himself as the only protector of the king's authority in the colony.

Bishop François Laval: he denounced the chief ecclesiastic in the colony for declaring that King Louis had exceeded his powers by licensing the trade in brandy (from which Frontenac certainly had profited), which he, the bishop, considered to be a sin, and had assigned a priest to preach a sermon against it. "I was tempted several times," Frontenac wrote, "to leave the church with my guards and interrupt the sermon; but I contented myself with telling the Bishop and the superior of the Jesuits, after it was over, that I was very much surprised at what I had heard. . . . they greatly blamed the preacher and disavowed him. . . . I told them . . . if the thing happened again, I would put the preacher in a place where he would learn how to speak."

Continuing, he maintained that the intendant and the councillors were completely under their control and did not dare decide any question against them; that they had spies everywhere, even in his own house; that the bishop told him he could excommunicate even a governor, if he chose; that the missionaries in the Indian villages said that they are the equals of *onontio* and told their converts that all would go wrong till the priests had the government of Canada; that directly or indirectly they meddled in all civil affairs; that they traded even with the English of New York; that, what with Jesuits, Sulpitians, the bishop, and the seminary at Québec, they held two-thirds of the good lands of Canada; that, in view of the poverty of the country, their revenues were enormous; that, in short, their object was mastery, and that they used all means to compass it.

This was indeed Frontenac's last peroration, his final indictment of his enemies—the intendant, the church, and the bishop—his sad farewell to the little colony along the great river that he had served to the last degree of his strength and affection.

DURING 1675 FRONTENAC spent much of his time supervising construction of a heavy, stone-walled fort at the outlet of vast Lake Ontario into the St. Lawrence River. With typical vanity he named it Fort Frontenac, entrusting it to the care of a young and intelligent Frenchman named Robert de La Salle. Half explorer and half trader, it was his honesty above all that impressed Frontenac, who wrote to him, "Garrison the place with whatever men you can find. I have not troops to spare for the task. But make sure that the fort to which I have given my own name is strongly held at all times."

It was Frontenac's hope that the new fort would at least be able to protect the fur-harvesting tribes of the upper lakes and waterways as they paddled to the fair at Montréal with their canoes loaded with skins.

In that same year of 1675 the bitter quarrels and squabbles that had characterized the governor-general's relations with the party of the religion that he professed as ardently as they did were renewed and intensified by the arrival of Jacques Duchesneau, the replacement for Talon.

Duchesneau, a vain and arrogant man with a fondness for the intrigue that would enrich him personally and increase his worth in the eyes of the king and his minister, had almost immediately allied himself with the bishop and the church. As a result, during the next five or six years these disputes and quarrels—from the brandy trade to the order of precedence at religious ceremonies or state functions, the mutual distrust between the count and the Jesuits, the presidency of the council—all these and many new complaints invented by Duchesneau grew more bitter and divisive, increasing in volume and a tone of mutual hatred that so infuriated the king that his rebukes to them all became sharper and more threatening.

Indeed, it was fortunate for New France that the horrible raids and massacres encouraged among the Iroquois by their English and Dutch allies had become less and less frequent, thus diminishing their own fears that the colony and they themselves would perish in a terrible bloodbath among the ruins of burning warehouses and the smoke and flames of blazing cabins—their ears filled with the howls and shrieks of the maddened savages dancing around their funeral pyres.

No one—not even the doughty Count Frontenac—was aware that this blissful interlude of peace was not in answer to their prayers to the Lord on high, but rather to the distraction among the English and Dutch settlers by similar horrible episodes in King Philip's War, joined by the healthy reluctance of the Five Nations to heed the Anglo-Dutch rather than the wrath of the greatest Onontio they had ever known.

By 1681 the enmity between the camps of Frontenac and Duchesneau had degenerated into a comic-opera war that had filled the lowly *habitants* of New France and even fugitive bush-rangers with a disgust for these so-called leaders who had the well-being—and even the safety—of the colony in their care. Indeed, though lowborn themselves, they had more dignity than these supposed dignitaries. Nor were they edified to see Count Frontenac—a man most of them admired—chasing one of Duchesneau's sons who had mocked him with an obscene gesture out of his office, lifting his cane as though to brain him, but deciding to pull the sleeve off his doublet instead. He had also become so irritable that he began to imprison those who displeased him or supported the intendant, even as his own followers began to win heated arguments with their walking sticks.

When Duchesneau ordered Midgeon, bailiff of Montréal, to arrest some of Perrot's bush rangers, Perrot at once arrested the bailiff and sent a sergeant and two soldiers to enter his house with instructions to badger the family as frequently as possible. Also in retaliation, one member of the bush ranger's family walked all night in the bedroom of the bailiff's wife. Another time the bailiff invited two friends to dine with him: the famous Le Moyne d'Iberville and one Bouthier, agent of a commercial house at Rochelle in France. As conversation turned to the profits from the fur trade made by Perrot, a follower of that unworthy governor overheard them and reported it to his master. At once Perrot appeared at a window and struck Bouthier over the head with his cane, drawing his sword to pursue him while he fled for safety, clambering over the wall of the nearby seminary. Its superintendent, Dollier de Casson, quickly dressed the frightened fugitive in a priest's hat and cassock, and in that disguise he escaped. Perrot was obviously now a misfit who delighted in disorder, antagonizing everyone by once again locking up the count's guardsmen, or crawling around in the dark to eavesdrop at windows—actually chasing a derisive trader at the point of his sword. Then he was seen mixing water with brandy to sell to unsuspecting Indians. With one of them he bartered his hat, coat, sword, shoes, stockings, and the ribbons of his office, boasting of the bargain of thirty pistoles he had made, while the happily drunk savage staggered around Montréal dressed as the governor.

There is no doubt that such incredibly undignified antics were being reported to Versailles by unknown witnesses to such infantile foibles and *gaucheries* of the supposedly sophisticated officers of the colony. What made them particularly repulsive was that the year 1681 had become a period of distress and despair, rather than the blessed respite from strife and danger it should have been, when the leaders of both camps should have buried the hatchet, as the Indians would do after they had sickened of murder and mayhem. Instead of joining together to take advantage of this fortunate lull in Indian raids and massacres by strengthening the fortifications of their colony, building forts and fortified houses, and fostering trade with friendly Indians, they preferred to schedule meetings that were nothing less than calls to combat, when they would spend whole days shouting at one another, pounding tables, and pointing fingers, while spending much of their free time composing those memorials and complaints that had become the special hair shirt of the king and his minister.

Inevitably the ax fell: In that same bad year of 1681 Intendant Duchesneau and Count Frontenac were both recalled.

IT IS NOT INTENDED in these pages to portray Louis de Buade, Count Frontenac, as an irritable old man, full of wrath for those who challenged or thwarted him, a gentle saint in the mold of Francis of Assisi with those who supported him. No man alive has ever been thus: half devil, half angel. Nor did he pass all his time in office in debates and quarrels. Many of them, such as about the brandy trade, were not of his provocation. Every governor sent to New France had to deal with an uncompromising prelate such as François Laval over a problem no European of authority ever before had to face. Where in their experience had they ever met men who actually killed for the "firewater" they coveted so pitifully, who sold their ancestral lands for it, who at their maddest maimed or murdered their own wives and children for this fiery nectar that made them forget—only to awake in horrible remorse to remember what they had done under its influence? That is why all those thoughtful rulers that the kings of France sent to the little colony along the great river were at first puzzled by a problem they had never before encountered, and then angered by some interfering prelate who in his zeal for the salvation of souls also incurred the displeasure of the governors.

The experience of one of them—Baron Dubois d'Avaugour, a bluff old soldier of forty years' service and the second governor-general— suffices to explain the predicament of Church and State in this insoluble problem, for the credentials of both were impeccable. In essence the situation was much akin to Abraham Lincoln's parable of the wolf and the shepherd: the shepherd saw the wolf as the murderer of his sheep; the wolf saw the shepherd as the denier of his dinner. Thus when Baron d'Avaugour arrived in New France in 1661 he had been appalled to hear about the awful consequences from the Indian craving for strong drink. Because the brandy trade was a source of income for the crown, he, being an officer of the Crown, had no quarrel with it. But Bishop Laval, Jesus Christ's agent on earth, did indeed. Through his efforts it was banned; and two weeks after the governor's arrival, two men were shot and another flogged for selling brandy to Indians. D'Avaugour did not interfere.

But then a woman was condemned to prison for the same offense, and a humane and good-natured Jesuit named Lalemant, moved by compassion, took her case to the governor. At once the crusty old general exploded: "You and your brethren were the first to cry out against the trade, and now you want to save the traders from punishment. I will no longer be the sport of your contradictions. Since it's not a crime for this woman, it shall not be a crime for anybody."

And there it stood, and might still stand today, were there alive many Indians possessed by that same fatal fascination for firewater. Moreover, d'Avaugour's dilemma was the despair of every other chief magistrate charged with the government of Canada, and especially Count Frontenac.

Most surprising of all, among so many of the higher-class Canadians possessing either wealth or authority, most of them were not unhappy to see the sails of the ship carrying Frontenac back to France vanish beneath the horizon. But among the Indians—even the Iroquois—and the humble *habitants* there was a general but unexpressed mood of regret. For all the tempestuous count's rages and explosions, the records show that there were indeed prolonged periods of untroubled peace, when the wheels of government whirled quietly and surely, although it is not always the calm sea that is remembered, but the wild and angry one so easily recalled. Frontenac, when not provoked, had an even-handed approach to his office, and it is possible that no white man of that age had ever equaled or even challenged him in the art of dealing with red men.

It has been best described by Francis Parkman, the great historian of *France and England in North America:*

> There seems to have been a sympathetic relation between him and them. He conformed to their ways, borrowed their rhetoric, flattered them on occasion with great address, and yet constantly maintained towards them an attitude of paternal superiority. When they were concerned, his native haughtiness always took a form which commanded respect without exciting anger. He would not address them as *brothers,* but only as *children;* and even the Iroquois, arrogant as they were, accepted the new relation. In their eyes Frontenac was by far the greatest of all the "Onontios," or governors of Canada. They admired the prompt and fiery soldier who played with their children, and gave beads and trinkets to their wives; who read their secret thoughts and never feared them, but smiled on them when their hearts were true, or frowned and threatened them when they did amiss. The other tribes, allies of the French, were of the same mind; and their respect for their Great Father seems not to have been permanently impaired by his occasional practice of bullying them for purposes of extortion.

It is possible that Frontenac had a secret sympathy for those *coureurs de bois* he pursued so relentlessly on the king's command, in particular those he could recruit from rival fur traders. Men everywhere who have been accustomed to danger and the triumph of survival do indeed possess this unspoken fraternity, especially—like policemen and criminals—if they have both been enemies of the hunt. Frontenac was like that. He could not have cared a fig that the high-born of Canada were rejoicing to see him go, for he knew in his valiant heart that the simple *habitants* deeply regretted his departure, realizing that without him any new and sudden menace might overwhelm them.

CHAPTER 15

The Sun King and the War
of the Grand Alliance

IN 1680 KING LOUIS XIV of France—shaken by the failure of his colony of New France to fulfill his vision of a great French-speaking empire in the New World—had begun to shift his energies toward what would ultimately become an attempt to dominate the continent of Europe. By then France's population was approaching nineteen million, three times the number of people in Britain or Spain, and nearly eight times as many as in the United Provinces, as Holland was then called.

It seemed then that the glory of the Sun King would rise to that inevitable zenith when its brilliance would dazzle the world. Indeed, Louis was already expanding his armed forces at an alarming rate. His minister of war—François-Michel Le Tellier, Marquis de Louvois—had already created the most powerful army in Europe, while the financial and administrative genius of his favorite minister, the tireless, selfless, and devoted Jean-Baptiste Colbert, had provided what seemed to be an inexhaustible war chest, while placing in the hands of his master one of the three powerful navies on the Atlantic Ocean. After the Royal British Navy withdrew from Tangier in 1684, the French sailed unchallenged in the Mediterranean Sea.

Unlike those of Holland and Spain, France's economy was not dependent on overseas commerce. Moreover, Anglo-Dutch attempts to place unbearable economic pressure on the French had distinctly failed.

Small wonder then that France's growing and undisguised expansionist policies should arouse widespread fears among the powers of the Continent. Emperor Leopold, having defeated the Turks, was strengthening his position in Central Europe to prevent French encroachment there; while Germany's Protestant princes—notably Frederick William of Brandenburg—had begun to align themselves with

William of Orange; and in Britain the Protestant aristocracy was maneuvering to evict King James II, who, having become a Catholic, was therefore both their enemy and the friend of King Louis of France.

Louis's revocation of the Edict of Nantes, granting religious freedom to the Huguenots, as the French Calvinists were called, had been a grievous error, for it enabled William the Sly to establish an anti-French coalition (League of Augsburg; July 9, 1686). Two years later King Louis provoked the league into preparing for war by claiming the Palatinate and meddling in the election of the bishop of Cologne. Simultaneously in Britain, the *coup d'état*, that is, an illegal act of unconstitutional force by which a legitimate sovereign is overthrown, that drove King James II of Britain from his throne, replaced him with this same William, a Dutchman who had not the barest shred of legal right to it, and was not himself a king or even of royal blood.

Of this small difficulty, as we have seen, the British Protestant peers, many of them descendants of the New Men enriched and ennobled by King Henry VIII as a reward for helping him in his successful struggle against the Catholic Church, could hardly have cared less. What they wanted was someone they could *call* king, not an actual active ruler who might not submit to their will. So William joined the British in their diplomatic struggle to create a military coalition against France. In the end, Britain, Holland, and the German states were arrayed against France alone, and if these Protestant powers hoped to block the expansionist ambitions of Catholic France, they also wanted to thwart Louis's attempt to put the Catholic James back on the British throne that was his by right of birth—the sole and only credential of monarchy.

The cause of this inconclusive struggle of nine years' duration was religious: an advancing Protestantism colliding with a resurgent Catholicism, just like the earlier Thirty Years' War (1618–1648), although not nearly as bloody but in which King Gustavus Adolphus of Sweden, the Protestant champion, and Albrecht von Wallenstien, duke of Friedland, the Catholic war chief, were distinguished generals indeed. Not so the uninspired siege warfare of the War of the Grand Alliance as it was fought in the Netherlands, which became an alternating rhythm of defeat and retreat for both sides because of the military incompetence of William of Orange and the naval ineptitude of King Louis of France. It is doubtful that few officers below the ranks of general or admiral and certainly no common soldiers or sailors actually knew why the war was being fought, and when it was ended by the Peace of Ryswick, France had received a small increase in land and

Britain had made a comparable improvement at sea. William was much the less capable of the two, and has gone into military history as the leader "who never won a battle or lost an army," meaning, of course, that he never risked as much as a hangnail, or heard a shot fired in anger.

But there is no doubt that William, being Dutch and by then definitely Protestant, had been of great service in Britain's diplomatic campaign to form a military coalition against France. Eventually this united Protestant front–Britain, Holland, and German states–was achieved, and the War of the Grand Alliance was begun. William of Orange's reward for such assistance was nothing less than the crown of Britain, illegally wrested from James II.

But it was as religious in its origin as the dreadful bloodbath known as the Thirty Years' War had been. The Catholic king of France sought not only to extend his power and influence but also to regain the British throne that by right belonged to his Catholic friend and cousin James II, while the Protestant powers fought to block Catholic French expansion and to maintain the British crown as a Protestant possession in perpetuity–rightfully, or not; legally, or not.

CHAPTER 16

Frontenac Returns—
Renews Border War

In 1688—THE YEAR OF the eruption of the War of the Grand Alliance in the Netherlands—King Louis of France began to think once again of his colony in the New World. He was, of course, still the Sun King— still the brilliant author of the glories of his palace at Versailles.

On three evenings a week, it had been his pleasure to assemble his entire court to stroll with him through the vast suite of apartments now known as the Halls of Abundance, of Venus, of Diana, of Mars, of Mercury, and of Apollo. Everywhere there was beauty, a brilliant reign of splendor never before achieved within the confines of a single structure, to say nothing of the gorgeous gardens, cascading waterfalls, bubbling fountains, and mirrorlike lakes in parks where the king's deer gamboled among undulating green lawns and groves of trees. The magnificence of the palace's interior was still breathtaking: again beauty everywhere, paintings of the great Italian masters; statues of silver and gold, the work of the world's finest sculptors; marble busts and statues, frescoes, mosaics, tapestries, and marvels of ceramic art— urns, vases, and jardinieres, many of them bearing the coat of arms of the kings and nobles of France, or of battle scenes from the shining victories of French arms. Here also were the great names of France: dukes and princes, generals and admirals, diplomats and architects, a veritable cavalcade of history as expressed in every art form unfolding before one's eyes. Here as well strolled the courtly throngs, given to feasting, dancing, gambling, promenading, conversing, a moving, colorful mass of bowing, curtseying nobles or the current geniuses of arts and letters, composers and conductors, all swathed in silks and satins. Here was a society unrivaled in its many excellences, a court to which no other kingdom or palace could compare.

For many years the king was always present at these evenings, gracious and affable, mingling with his courtiers, pausing to discuss a rare vintage with a winemaker or the drawings of a famous architect; but lately he no longer shared their amusements but had grown graver, and was more often conferring with his cabinet ministers on some pressing object of administration, or discussing with his generals and admirals the progress of the war in the Netherlands. His volume of correspondence was also a heavy weight upon his mind, and he almost hated to open a letter from Canada's governor Denonville, filled with the customary laments, complaints, and recitals of failure. The most recent jeremiad, like the whine of an alley cat, caused him to remember that New France was perhaps too much for Denonville and that a new and experienced governor might be needed.

Of course! Frontenac! He was still present at court, low on funds, but loyal and uncomplaining like a faithful hound. Immediately King Louis sent for him, resolving to restore him to the command from which he had so precipitously removed him seven years ago. For excellent reasons, of course—for a monarch cannot err—and he now informed this loyal old war dog standing before him that he had learned that the charges against him were without foundation. If he had lifted his cane, it had not been to brain someone; or if he had torn off someone's coat sleeve, he must have had ample provocation.

"I send you back to Canada," the king said, "where I am sure that you will serve me as well as you did before—and I ask nothing more of you."

Nodding, Count Frontenac knelt before his sovereign and kissed his ring—rising again as Louis thanked him and dismissed him. To return to Canada as its governor again was not an attractive prospect to a man in his seventieth year. He would be alone with only a few wretched soldiers to support him in what would be a most uneven battle against two enemies—the Anglo-Dutch colonists and their Iroquois allies—with a force not even the equal of one of them alone. On that point His Majesty had been most adamant: no more troops for New France.

Nevertheless, the audacious old count accepted the assignment, hastening to Rochelle, where two ships of the French Royal Navy were waiting for him. Embarking in one of them, he sailed once more for the New World, unaware that his ship and another bearing Callieres, governor of Montréal, toward Paris with a scheme to conquer New York, had passed in the night. At Versailles, Callieres quickly learned that the king could spare no forces for Canada, nor money or supplies. So the plan laid before him became a model of boldness and thrift. Callieres argued that New York could be conquered with the forces then in Canada: a thousand regulars and six hundred Canadian militia, supported by two warships. He told the king that the blow must be struck at once to take the English by surprise.

The attacking force would move down Lake Champlain and Lake George in *bateaux* and canoes, cross to the Hudson River, and capture Albany, seizing all available river craft to descend the Hudson to the town at its mouth. Callieres estimated that New York then was a place of about two hundred houses and perhaps four hundred fighting men. The two warships would cruise outside the harbor, awaiting the arrival of the little French army, when they would join the attack with a naval bombardment. Callieres maintained that the entire operation could be ended within a month, so that by the end of October King Louis would be the master of northeastern America.

Callieres' recital of the many benefits arising from a successful conclusion of the operation brought a gleam of interest into the dark eyes of the king. First, said Callieres, the Iroquois, deprived of English arms and ammunition, would be helpless against the French; English ambitions to cross the western mountains would be blocked forever; the king would acquire a watery means of access to New France incomparably superior to the St. Lawrence, and navigable all year round; and eventually all New England would be isolated, and open to conquest in the future.

King Louis accepted the plan with modifications intended to improve it, but actually complicating and weakening it. His participation in the planning showed almost immediately to Callieres that he had no real knowledge of field operations and was especially ignorant of the vast distances of travel in the wildernesses and wild waterways of the New World, as well as the endless difficulties of troop movement and navigation. Once the brutal Canadian winter had seized the land in its iron grasp there was really very little hope of bringing an enemy to battle. As a forestate of such delay the two warships scheduled to support the operation required more than a month to fit them for sea. Sailing against headwinds, they were fifty-two days in reaching Chedabucto, at the eastern end of Nova Scotia. From there Frontenac and Callieres had to board a merchant ship to reach Québec and begin to plan for the expedition. Moreover, Frontenac wrote a letter to the naval commander at Chedabucto informing him of the upcoming operation and ordering him to sail to New York to participate in it. It did not reach that naval base until September 12, 1689, and by then the ice floes were forming in the Gulf of St. Lawrence and the entire enterprise was ruined.

It was not, of course, the fault of either Frontenac or Callieres, but it did demonstrate the folly of inviting an autocratic monarch to participate in the actual planning of an operation. They seldom understood that armies do not move obediently on paper maps but on earth, where they must contend with all the trials and tribulations of weather, climate, supply, arms and ammunition, transportation, and the proper time and place to give battle.

Frontenac, however, aware that the weather alone placed the New York operation out of reach, was nevertheless determined to mount some sort of offensive against the English—and perhaps, if it achieved early success, against the Iroquois as well. He had gone personally to La Chine to view for himself the ferocity of the Iroquois massacre there and to promise the dismayed and disheartened people of New France that the Five Nations would pay dearly for atrocities that would never be forgotten. So he decided to go on the offensive of his own accord, and by striking a series of sharp, rapid blows against the English, make it known to both friend and foe that the great *onontio* was back.

To do this he formed three war parties of picked men—those same hardy, valiant *coureurs de bois* who had so mortified the king—one at Montréal, one at Three Rivers, and one at Québec. The first would strike Albany, the largest target; the second, ravage the border settlements of New Hampshire; and the third, carry the torch to those of Maine.

Montréal's was the largest force and the first to be ready to march. It consisted of 210 men, of whom 96 were Indian converts. Recruited from the two mission villages of Saut St. Louis and the Mountain of Montréal, they were Catholic Iroquois whom the priests had persuaded to leave their native villages and settle in Canada, much to the indignation of their former heathen brethren and to the dismay of the English colonists, alarmed to find once-friendly allies changing into formidable foes. These Iroquois would not, of course, move against their former comrades, for blood is indeed thicker than holy water; but to lift the hatchet and the scalping knife was now a pleasure. The French of the parties were mostly bush rangers. They had shared the general demoralization in the colony caused by the La Chine massacre, and under the cautious Denonville had become somewhat mutinous and lawless. But under true commanders and disciplinarians there were no better bush fighters.

Chief of the Montréal was Jacques Le Moyne de Sainte-Hélène, the brave son of the famous Charles Le Moyne, with D'Aillebout de Mantet as his second-in-command, supported by the redoubtable Le Moyne d'Iberville, Le Moyne de Bienville, Repentigny de Montesson, and Le Ber du Chesne, as well as other members of the Canadian *noblesse* formed in the New World by King Louis. All were hardened by ordeal, trained in audacity by adventure, skilled in Indian warfare—and thirsting for revenge.

The Indians had painted themselves for the warpath. Their faces were hideous with vermilion, blue or ocher stripes, horizontal bars, or waves. Some had smeared their faces jet black with red rings around their eyes like gaudy owls; others were red with black rings. One man had painted his shaven head completely black, for he was in mourning for his father, a high sachem of the Caughnawagas. All wore red or blue blankets belted at the waist. Their leader was the Christian chief of the Saut St. Louis, whom the French called Le Grand Agnie, or the Great Mohawk, and the Dutch called Kryn.

It was in the depth of the winter of 1690 when they began their march, striding on snowshoes over the vast white corridor of the frozen St. Lawrence. Each man moved with the hood of his blanket coat over his head, a musket in his mittened hand, a tomahawk, a knife, a tobacco pouch and a bullet pouch at his belt, a pack strapped to his shoulders, and his precious, inseparable pipe safely hung about his neck in a waterproof case. Indian sledges piled high with baggage, blankets, and provisions were dragged over the snow.

Floundering in snowdrifts as they moved, they passed through silent forests, pelted by falling snow from the boughs above them. Reaching the frozen Richelieu, they took four or five days to emerge on the windswept ice of Lake Champlain. Here a whistling snowstorm struck and they pitched camp. Cutting saplings, they roofed them with bark and huddled together for warmth beneath this frail protection. Sainte-Hélène decided it would be a good time to hold a council. He sent for the Great Mohawk. He came, squatting alongside the Frenchman Indian style. He asked: "Where does the great *onontio* send us, my brother?"

"Albany!" Sainte-Hélène replied, filling his pipe and lighting it.

"Albany!" the Indian repeated in dismay. "How long is it since French grew so bold? There are two hundred soldiers there."

"We have as many."

"But they have walls to stop our bullets, and we have only our blankets to stop theirs."

Sainte-Hélène nodded noncommittally, blowing smoke from his pipe. He had been about to retort that they had come to New York to reclaim the honor that had perished at the massacre of La Chine, but decided instead not to give this sarcastic sachem the opportunity for a second wounding gibe. Instead he said, "We will speak of it another time, my brother," and the Great Mohawk arose with a smirk, shaking his head dubiously.

At once the trek was renewed, neither the French nor the Indians having come to any agreement. After continuing for eight days, during which the weather seemed to be gradually abating, they reached the Hudson River. Here they came upon a crossroads: one path leading toward Albany, the other to Schenectady. Still silent, although Sainte-Hélène by then had obviously changed his mind, they all followed the trail to Schenectady.

Now the march became a horrible ordeal. A partial thaw had turned both woods and streams and swamps into a clinging mixture of mingled ice, water, mud, and melting snow, so that soon their clothing was covered with a wet and soaking gray paste. Inevitably grains of this horrid slime entered their mouths, turning the pemmican they chewed upon as they marched to a near-choking cud of dried meat and dirt. At such a painful pace it took nine more days to cover only forty miles, and then the weather changed again—for the worse.

A sudden snowstorm changed day into dusk. It raged around them like a wailing white sorceress. It came pelting at them in flakes as big as bottle caps; and then, changing, swirled around them in waves of tiny white pellets that might have been sleet or the congealed snow from the trees, blinding them as they stumbled over roots or snaked around boulders, clinging to these with one hand while with the other they sought to protect their weapons from the mud or melting snow that would enter their muzzles and foul their powder. Sometimes the snow fell straight down upon them in sheets, or came billowing and smoking through the forest, beating against their faces or gathering within their hoods in patches, where it melted on their necks and went trickling cold down their backs. About them in the hollows the sheltered great trees stood sheathed in snow, as though they were sentinels in an arboreal cemetery, but atop the hills and ridges the oaks and elms and beeches were blown a bare wet black or gray. On the twenty-third day after they had left Montréal they reached the Mohawk River. Schenectady was only six miles away.

THE SNOWSTORM THAT HAD engulfed Sainte-Hélène's brave and hardy band—though they were upon a barbarous and murderous mission—had struck earlier at Schenectady, the farthest outpost of the colony of New York. It had once been Dutch, but now it was English, like the colony of New Jersey. Westward lay the forests of the Mohawk, while roughly fifteen miles to the southeast stood the capital once known as Orange but now called Albany, after one of the titles of James, duke of York, now the fugitive King James II of Britain.

The village was protected by an oblong wooden palisade that had two gates: the eastern one toward Albany, and the western toward the Mohawk. A blockhouse near the Albany gate was occupied by about eight or nine militiamen on loan from Connecticut under a Lieutenant Talmadge. About thirty friendly Mohawks were inside the village on a visit. At this time—the eighth of February 1690—all of Schenectady's Dutch inhabitants were in a state of discord. The revolution in Britain that had crowned their opportunist little countryman, the so-called prince of Orange, had produced a revolution in New York.

A Dutch rebel named Jacob Leisler had seized Fort William and was struggling to lead an uprising of his countrymen to recover control of the colony. But the citadel of Albany was still held by the anti-Leisler or conservative party under Mayor Peter Schuyler.

Almost to a man the Schenectady Dutch were partisans of Leisler and had threatened to kill Schuyler, as well as Magistrate John Sander Glen, a brave supporter of the mayor who lived in Schenectady. Lieutenant Talmadge and his militiamen had received similar threats. There were probably about fifty or more householders in Schenectady; with their wives and children, two hundred or more human beings. Each householder had his own cabin, and these, with the little Dutch Reformed Church often used as a council house, were the only buildings in the village.

While the thickening storm whipped and wailed about the tiny, huddling village, Magistrate Glen had called a meeting of householders to warn them that a large war party of French and Indians was marching toward Schenectady to avenge the massacre at La Chine. He had been informed of the danger by the friendly Mohawks, who also told him and Lieutenant Talmadge standing beside him at the table that the redoubtable Count Frontenac was back in Québec. Thus the faces of Glen and Talmadge were grave as they watched the householders enter the council house one by one or in pairs, snorting through their noses as they brushed the snow from their coats and stamped their feet on the beaten earth of the church floor before taking their places on rude wooden benches.

Yet they were perspiring, for the heat flowing from an oak-log fire in a huge fireplace inside a sidewall, combined with the warmth of their bodies, had made the chamber almost stiflingly hot. Glen at once invited his guests to shuck their coats, which they did with shouts of approval. But when he informed them of his reasons for assembling them there, he was greeted with cries of derision and ridicule.

"Py Godt," a red-faced, bald-headed, sweating householder shouted, rising to his feet, "King Villiam's var iss King Villiam's Var—nodt mine."

Shouts of support arose from the Dutch. They stomped their feet and knocked their pipes against their benches.

"He iss right!" one of them yelled. "Adam Vrooman iss right. Vy should ve fight the Vrench?"

Magistrate Glen gazed sourly through the blue pipe smoke drifting up to the ceiling, carefully studying the sturdy, stolid men seated before him. Twenty-six years! he thought wryly. New York has been English since 1664, and these damn Dutchmen still act as though it belongs to Holland.

"Good householders," he said patiently, "King William is your sovereign. You must fight his enemies."

Vrooman waved his pipe excitedly, winking broadly as he shouted, "You mean ve iss going to invade Ganada?"

An explosion of laughter reverberated around the room, and Glen waited until it had subsided before he shook his head and said, again patiently: "No, I do not. I mean the French are coming here. The Mohawks have informed Albany that a war party has set out from Montréal. Canadians and Indians. Perhaps as many as three hundred of them."

"Here?" Vrooman repeated dubiously, waving his pipe once more. "*Schnectady?* Dis leedle blace? Vat for dey vant here ven dey gan gapture Albany? Den dey gan go down der Hudson und take New York!" He grimaced and shook his round, bald head in open contempt.

"Hey, Adam," a comrade cried, "maybe dey vants your vife"—and the laughter began again.

Glen waited for it to subside. He was a wise man, and a man of courage, steadfastly loyal to the English government in Albany. He knew that these stubborn villagers resented this. Only a year before, he had faced them down when they had sided with the rebel Jacob Leisler, unmoved even when they threatened to kill him. He wondered if Vrooman and his friends weren't being stubborn just to pay him back for supporting the Albany Convention. After the laughter faded into snickering and then silence, he stared hard at Vrooman and said: "They aren't strong enough to take Albany, and they're certainly not strong enough to capture it and then take New York. But they are strong enough to massacre all of you." He paused dramatically. "Yourselves, your women and your children . . ." He paused again before saying with a snarl: "Do you take Frontenac for a fool?" Turning to Talmadge, he asked: "How many men do you have, Lieutenant?"

Talmadge started. He had been thinking of his pregnant young wife, almost at her term. "N-nine, s-sir," he stammered, and Glen swung on Vrooman, and the others eyeing them dubiously. "Did you hear that? Nine men and one officer to stop three hundred bloodthirsty Canadians and Indians. Can't you see you're in mortal danger?"

They shook their heads doggedly, and Vrooman spoke for all of them when he muttered: "Dey von't come here. Ve is so var away from zivilization dey don't even know ve iss alive."

"My God, men!" the magistrate cried, his voice rising in incredulous dismay. "You must arm yourselves! Prepare for the worst! It could come any moment. Even tonight!" There was no reply, and Glen began to plead with them. "Won't you at least bar your gates and post sentinels?"

Again they shook their heads. "Dey von't come here," Vrooman repeated with infuriating assurance, pointing toward the door and the wind whistling outside. "Dere iss anudder storm becomink. Dere iss already too much snow. Dey vould die in der forest."

Murmurs of assent followed Vrooman's words. Some of his fellow householders began reaching for their coats. Glen arose, his eyes cold with suppressed rage. "All right, then," he said softly, in a tone of such ominous certitude that the least excitable among them began to blink in apprehension. "Let the blood of your own be upon your own heads."

Their faces sullen, scowling at the magistrate's words, the Dutchmen got to their feet. They knocked out their pipes, grinding the smoldering tobacco into the earthen floor. One of them broke up the fire. Then, struggling into their coats, they began to leave.

Outside, two groups of boys were having a snow fight. They crouched behind the snowmen they had built to either side of the open Mohawk gate, hurling their snowballs at each other. Magistrate John Sander Glen watched them with a sinking heart. He saw that they had crowned their snowmen with empty bird's nests for helmets, and put sticks for muskets under their shoulders.

"Dere, Meinheer Magistrate," Adam Vrooman said with a derisive sneer, "dere iss your sentinels."

"No one?" Sainte-Hélène asked in surprise, and the Canadian nodded: "None." Sainte-Hélène and the Great Mohawk exchanged smiles, and the Indian sachem said softly: "We will take many easy scalps, my brother."

IN KEEPING WITH the single, unfailing tactic of wilderness warfare, it had been the purpose of the French and Mohawk coleaders to postpone the attack until two o'clock in the morning, when all the villagers—fathers, mothers, children, and infants—were soundly asleep and the raging storm had risen to its shrieking height. But the attackers had reached the limit of human endurance. They dared not make fires, and they knew that they must move to the assault without delay lest they freeze where they stood and perish of inanition.

On that same eighth of February, Indian scouts sent ahead by Sainte-Hélène had found an Iroquois hut occupied by four terrified squaws. They took them captive, sending another scout to the rear to inform Sainte-Hélène of their good fortune. Soon the hut was thronged with half-dead braves and bush rangers, warming their numbed hands in front of a fire and stomping the chill from their feet. There were so many of them that the heat of the bodies contributed to the warmth of the cabin—magnifying as well the stench of their unwashed flesh—while all around them vacant tepees were similarly occupied. At about four in the afternoon they emerged into the storm again while the Great Mohawk harangued them to cleanse in blood the many wrongs done them by these innocent Dutch householders—peasants all—whom they would shortly be murdering, torturing, and eating.

Just before they resumed their march, a bush ranger named Gignieres, who had gone on a reconnoitering party with nine red men, returned to report that he had come in sight of Schenectady and had neither seen nor heard anyone.

Guided by the terrified squaws, they went sliding over the Mohawk ice, stumbling through the drifts and blinded by the swirling snow sweeping down the darkened valley of the frozen stream. At about eleven o'clock they stumbled to a halt, gazing half in fear, half in desperation, at the snow-plastered stakes of the swaying palisade. At that moment, if an enemy had appeared before them—as one of the participants in the massacre admitted later—they would have surrendered to him without protest.

But something—perhaps the very absence of a guard or the incredible sight of nothing more menacing than those silent snowmen with their bird's-nest helmets and their ridiculous mock muskets—sent the blood of battle coursing through their veins, and they stood quietly at attention while Sainte-Hélène ordered Iberville to find the Albany gate and bar it against the escape of fugitives. But he missed it in the dark; and after he returned—in two bands, one led by Sainte-Hélène, the other by Mantet—the war party passed through the gate in dead silence, one moving noiselessly to the left, the other to the right until the two leaders met at the farther end—whereupon Sainte-Hélène lifted to his lips the little silver whistle hanging about his neck and blew.

FROM EVERY THROAT—white or copper—came the screech, the shriek, the war whoop, and the "wa-wa-wah-wah" of the Indians beating the palms of their hands against their mouths—after which the cabin doors were burst inward with hatchets and musket butts and the dreadful work of massacre was begun.

For some—particularly the women and children—there was only the fleetingly horrible sight of the bush ranger in buckskin or the Indian in war paint, both with uplifted tomahawks, and then the obliterating blade in the brain. Others were less fortunate, particularly those who fell into the hands of the Indians quickly tearing stakes from the unguarded palisade for use as posts to which their captives could be tied and the savage sport of torture commenced. Neither women nor children were spared, for as Peter Schuyler, who had arrived the next day at Schenectady with a war party, reported: "No pen can write and no tongue express the cruelties that were committed."

It could not have been otherwise, for there was little resistance, except at the blockhouse, where Talmadge and his militia fought bravely, holding on until the doors were forced open and all inside either killed or seized for the torture stake, while their fort itself was set on fire. Once the Indians realized that Schenectady had very few true defenders, their zest for battle seemed to nourish their thirst for the blood of innocent women and children. Sainte-Hélène had given orders that the life of Peter Tassemaker, the village dominie or Calvinist minister, must be spared because it was believed that valuable information might be obtained from him. But the French chief was ignored, because by then the blood of the painted red men was truly aroused, and they hunted Tassemaker down like a wounded stag, hacking him to pieces—pausing only to set his home on fire and roast the edible portions of his body in the flames.

Poor Adam Vrooman, who had made such sport of Magistrate Glen, provoking from him the horribly accurate prophecy "let the blood of your own be upon your own heads," seemed at first destined to be another victim of both bush ranger and red man. Having seen his wife shot and his child brained against a doorpost, Vrooman turned upon his assailants in a maniacal fury, fighting them with clubbed musket and so showering them with their own blood that they withdrew in combined consternation and admiration, granting him—as was occasionally their custom—the life that he had so dearly defended.

Others, either more agile or just fortunate, successfully passed through the Albany gate that the attacking French and Indians had unwisely left open behind them, thus unwittingly presenting their prey with an escape hatch to safety. Many fled through the storm to seek shelter at Albany or in houses along the way.

Meanwhile, all over the village the screams and the shrieks continued—whether from the assailant or assailed could never be distinguished—as the flames of burning cabins, church, and palisade flickered on the figures of mothers kneeling in snow or ashes, their babies clasped to their breasts, pleading for mercy from these merciless, howling, human wolves.

Only after two hours did the massacre and pillage cease, and then simply because both ranger and red man were exhausted. In all, sixty persons had been murdered outright, of whom thirty-eight were men and boys, ten were women, and twelve were children. Among the victors, only two had been killed. The number of villagers captured was between eighty and ninety. None of the thirty Mohawk visitors was harmed, but were instead treated kindly and told that the war party had no quarrel with them, but only with the Dutch and the English.

Once the carnage had ended and the flames subsided among the ruins, the exhausted conquerors of helpless little Schenectady sank like their victims into red-stained snow and blood-caked ashes, while others were posted as sentinels or as guards of both the booty and the prisoners.

In the morning a small party crossed the river to the house of Magistrate Glen. It stood above the Mohawk on rising ground, a loopholed and palisaded fortress now defended by Glen at the head of his servants and tenants. Finding the gates closed, the French asked for a parley, informing Glen that he had nothing to fear from them, for they were under orders to harm nothing of his—not even a chicken.

After they had obeyed his request to lay down their arms, he allowed them to enter. Urging him to return to the village with them, he complied on the condition that one of their number be held as a hostage by his followers. At that point Iberville, accompanied by the Great Mohawk, appeared at his gates.

Drawing a commission from Frontenac from his coat, the French officer explained that he had been especially charged to pay a debt to

Glen owed him by the French for his action in saving the lives of French prisoners in the hands of the Mohawks. Glen and his family, Iberville explained, especially his wife, had shown these freed men the utmost kindness.

Arriving at the village, Glen was led before the crowd of miserable prisoners in French hands, and told that not only were his own life and property safe, but that of all his kindred as well. As canny as he was fearless, Glen stretched this exemption to its utmost, so much so that the sarcastic Great Mohawk complained that everybody in the neighborhood seemed related to Glen. Pretending not to hear, Glen returned to his home, where he awaited the rescue party from Albany that he was certain would soon appear.

So were the French and Indians, and they prepared for an immediate exit. Those cabins that had not already been burned were now consigned to the flames, except for one where a French officer lay wounded, another belonging to Glen, and several more that might or might not have belonged to his ubiquitous relatives. By noon of February 9, 1690, the village of Schenectady was no more than a heap of smoking ashes in the snow.

Without delay, the French and the Indians withdrew laden with their booty piled on sledges drawn by thirty or forty captured horses. About sixty survivors—mostly old men, women, and children—were left behind in the care of the Mohawk visitors who had joined Glen in begging that they be spared, to which plea Sainte-Hélène quickly agreed. For these fortunate villagers—and Glen and his people as well—there was nothing now to be done but to await the arrival from Albany of a rescue party.

GLEN WAS CONFIDENT of succor because he had learned from a Mohawk visitor that a Dutchman named Simon Schermerhorn, awakened by screams and war whoops, had thrown himself upon a horse and galloped out the Albany gate. Both French and Indians had fired at him but only wounded him—and he escaped, arriving in Albany the next morning in time to give the alarm.

At once Mayor Peter Schuyler—"Quider," as the Indians called him—summoned all soldiers and able-bodied inhabitants to arms, ordering cannons fired to arouse the countryside while a party of horsemen rode off to Schenectady, followed by some friendly Mohawks. The Mohawks had promised to carry the dreadful news to their three towns on the river above; but when they reached the raped and ruined village they were so frightened by what they beheld that they refused to go farther. Thus two vital days were lost before the Mohawk towns were alerted, although much time was recovered by troops of braves armed with tomahawk and musket who came hastening down on snowshoes to pursue the fleeing French.

Fifty youths from Albany similarly armed soon joined them, and the sizable posse thus formed emboldened the pursuers, although it appeared that they would never overtake their enemies, moving with their horses at top speed over the ice of Lake Champlain. Unwisely, however, the French and their Indians paused to kill, roast, and eat most of their stolen steeds, a mistake that slowed them considerably, for a party of Sainte-Hélène's stragglers, fatigued from the battle, was run down by a band of fleet-footed Mohawks, who fell upon them and killed or captured about fifteen of them just as they came almost within sight of Montréal.

Peter Schuyler, who had joined the posse and taken command, interviewed a trio of these terrified captives, who informed him that Frontenac was preparing a crushing spring campaign against Albany. This was not true, although it was a common tactic of the French when taken prisoner, but Schuyler seems to have believed them, appealing to Massachusetts for help.

"Dear neighbors and friends," he wrote later, "we must acquaint you that nevir poor People in the world was in a worse Condition than we are at Present, no Governour nor Command, no money to forward any expedition, and scarce men enough to maintain the Citty. We have here plainly laid the case before you, and doubt not but you will so much take it to heart, and make all Readinesse in the Spring to invade Canida by water."

Even the Mohawks—never completely reliable in the face of common danger—agreed that a major operation against the French was necessary. Their elders came down to Albany to condole with their Dutch and English allies on the Schenectady disaster.

"We are come," their orator exclaimed, "with tears in our eyes, to lament the murders committed at Schenectady by the perfidious French. *Onontio* comes to our country to speak of peace, but war is at his heart. He has broken our house at both ends, once among the Senecas to the west and once here; but we hope to be revenged. Brethren, our covenant with you is a silver chain that cannot rust or break. We are of the race of the bear; and the bear does not yield, so long as there is a drop of blood in his body. Let us all be bears. We will go together with an army to ruin the country of the French. Therefore send in all haste to New England. Let them be ready with ships and great guns to attack by water while we attack by land."

Schuyler, outwardly attentive, was not so sure inwardly, for the Iroquois were among the most fickle of Indians. Yet he did decide to believe the orator, even though he knew full well that though their speechmaking might be among their most civil achievements, it was rarely either a promise or a pledge. Yet he moved quickly to send commissioners to the several governments of New England, proposing a combined assault upon Québec.

NEW ENGLAND NEEDED no encouragement to punish Frontenac and New France, for her colonies were tasting some of the same hell broth that had been brewed for Schenectady, and the war party that had ravished that star-crossed village had been but the first of three sent south by Frontenac to remind the Anglo-Dutch of the horror of La Chine perpetrated by their Iroquois allies. For as much as these two races might disclaim any enmity against their neighbors above the St. Lawrence, while the French had never concealed their leadership of their own savage allies, the truth was that the greedy, grasping Dutch traders were the first to sell arms to the Indians, though they seldom used them themselves; while the sons of Perfidious Albion—affecting an amity they did not feel—were content to remain apart from the battlefields onto which they directed—but never led—their own howling human wolves.

Thus Frontenac's second war party was sent against the English borders. This troop, commanded by François Hertel, consisted of twenty-four Frenchmen, twenty Abenakis of the Sokoki band, and five Algonquins. They left Three Rivers on January 28, 1690, and after two months of indescribably severe hardship and suffering—exceeding even the horrible ordeal of Sainte-Hélène's much larger punitive expedition—they approached the little settlement of Salmon Falls, on the Maine–New Hampshire border.

Bursting into the unsuspecting hamlet with howls and shrieks, Hertel's band destroyed almost all of its buildings and killed nearly half of its inhabitants. Some of those captured were turned over to the Indians for torture, until Hertel ordered all forty-nine French and Indians to march northward in hopes of meeting Frontenac's third war party. In late May they converged, so that the combined forces now totaled four hundred to five hundred men.

At Casco Bay, where the city of Portland now stands, they tried to take the fort by a customary surprise night attack, but were repulsed. After an English sortie out of the fort was annihilated, with only a few survivors retreating to safety, Hertel ordered what might have been the first attempt in King William's War to take a citadel by siege tactics. Surrounding the fort, the French and Indians began digging trenches for concealment and safety, and when they reached its walls, the English cause became hopeless.

Promised quarter, the garrison surrendered, marching out to lay down their arms as required—only to be overwhelmed by the Indians. Try as the French officers might, and they did try, knowing full well that the enraged red men could not be restrained, even though they struck them with the flat of their swords, many an Englishman perished in the ensuing massacre. Quite a few survived, however, only to be carried off as prisoners. But a good number of these fortunate men were ransomed by the French missionaries and Catholic laymen, a policy adopted early in the war by the French government.

These were not the first raids along the Maine and New Hampshire coasts, for many of the Abenaki Indians of the region—under the influence of the French and their tireless missionaries—had migrated to Canada, taking up the tomahawk and the torch in the interest of New France. These were purely Indian attacks, having no military value or leadership from white men. Even so, the English colonies of northeastern North America were aroused by Frontenac's raids. A joint expedition of 750 men and as many Iroquois as could be persuaded to join were to be led up the Champlain Valley against Montréal. Fitz-John Winthrop of Connecticut was to command the operation. He had never been known as a fiery leader, and his only credentials seem to have been a pleasant personality and the fact that he was the grandson of John Winthrop, the first governor of Massachusetts. This attack was to be coordinated with Sir William Phips's amphibious assault on Québec from the St. Lawrence River.

At the very outset the attack on Montréal fizzled. As was customary, disputes between the men of both colonies arose, while the "milishy" of New York began to sulk, eventually quarreling with each other. There were no boats or canoes available—a monstrous oversight in a waterborne operation—simply because no one understood that in the lateness of the season it would be difficult to reach the northern regions, where the mighty canoe birch—clearly regarded as the best material for boatmaking—grew in profusion. In the area in which they had pitched camp there were only elms, the bark of which was not only the worst, but also could not be peeled in cold weather. These difficulties, multiplied by a spreading fear of a smallpox epidemic, ruined an enterprise that had been mismanaged from the beginning.

Still, Winthrop—perhaps embarrassed that Massachusetts and Sir William Phips would be left to conquer Canada alone—authorized Captain John Schuyler of New York, grandfather of General Philip

Schuyler of the Revolution, to lead a raid of revenge into Canada. Schuyler departed the Wood Creek camp with a band of 29 Dutchmen and 120 of their Indian allies. Passing Lake Champlain, they descended the Richelieu to Chambly. From there they burst suddenly upon the little French settlement of La Prairie, a few miles upstream from Montréal, only a short time after Frontenac had withdrawn most of his troops from its garrison. The others were in the fields with the inhabitants reaping wheat when Schuyler attacked.

As he certainly must have expected, the Indians got out of control, as they always did when they scented fresh blood and easy scalps. Before he could stop them they had killed or captured 25 French, including 4 women. Perhaps to clear himself of the shame of murdering women, he ordered his red men to assault a nearby fort, but they refused—again as they always did. They also slaughtered about 150 cattle, dining royally on fresh meat all the way back to Wood Creek. It was not indeed a skirmish of which the English could be proud, but it did suggest to Frontenac and New France that they could strike back.

From La Prairie until the end of the war, savage combat of the wilderness variety was to ravage both sides of the St. Lawrence. In 1691 Frontenac was to put a price of ten crowns on the scalp of an Englishman. This was soon lowered, however, and a higher price was paid in the ransom of a captive under the humane policy already in place.

Scalp-taking, however, because a scalp was much easier to carry than the burden of a live prisoner, continued to flourish—both north and south of the great river. Soon the officials responsible for certifying the crown of a human being's head began to suspect that a mysterious increase in scalps could be explained by the fact that many of them had been "doctored." A bit of judicious cutting and trimming was all that was necessary to make it look genuine. Indeed, in the Illinois country the Indians had found that the head of a buffalo, properly scraped and plucked, could deceive even the most suspicious officer. Scalping, of course, was normally done on a dead or badly wounded enemy—civilian or no, and of either sex—but if upon a still-living person in haste or imperfectly, was not unfailingly fatal.

CHAPTER 17

Heroines of Both Frontiers

BRAVERY WAS NOT uncommon in women of the colonies north and south of the St. Lawrence. The most famous of these was Madelon of Vercheres, the fourteen-year-old daughter of the *seigneur* of the fort there. This was in a strong position on the south bank of the St. Lawrence, about twenty miles below Montréal. On the morning of October 22, 1692, all the inhabitants were at work in the fields, with no one left in the fort except two soldiers, Madelon's two younger brothers, twelve and ten, an old man of eighty, and the rest women and children. The *seigneur*, a former officer of the famous regiment of Carignan, was on duty at Québec—and Madelon, whom he admired with all his heart and soul, was in command at Vercheres. With a hired man named Laviolette, she was at the landing place on the river, not far from the fort gate. Suddenly she heard musket fire in the fields, and then Laviolette shouting, "Run, *mademoiselle*, run! Here come the Iroquois!"

"I ran for the fort," she told her astonished father upon his return, "commending myself to the Holy Virgin. The Iroquois who chased after me, seeing that they could not catch me alive before I reached the gate, stopped and fired at me. The bullets whistled about my ears, and made the time seem very long.

"As soon as I was near enough to be heard, I cried out, 'To arms! To arms!' hoping that somebody would come out and help me. But it was of no use. The two soldiers in the fort were so scared that they had hidden in the blockhouse. At the gate, I found two women crying for their husbands, who had just been killed."

Madelon made them go inside the fort, quickly following them and barring the gate before hastening to inspect the defenses of the blockhouse. Almost immediately she found two fallen-down palisades by which the attackers might easily gain entrance. She ordered them set up again, helping the soldiers to do so. Then she checked the blockhouse where the ammunition was stored, and there—to her fright and amazement—she found the two soldiers, one cowering in a corner and the other with a lighted match in his hand.

"What are you going to do with that match?" she asked. He replied with wildly rolling eyes, "Light the powder and blow us all up!" Now infuriated, Madelon snapped: "You are a miserable coward, get out of here!" He slunk away and Madelon tore off her bonnet, donned a soldier's cap, seized a musket, and told her startled brothers, "Let us fight to the death. We are fighting for our country and our religion. Remember that our father has taught you that gentlemen are born to shed their blood for the service of God and king."

They nodded, starry-eyed. Soon they and those two reluctant soldiers who heard her noble words took up firing positions at the loopholes. Their bullets reawakened the enemy's reluctance to attack a fortified position, and they spent their time instead in butchering unarmed people caught unawares in the fields. Madelon ordered a cannon to be fired as though signaling for a sortie, and also to warn other soldiers out hunting. Now the terrified women and children inside the fort began weeping and screaming. She turned on them in a rage, ordering them to stop lest the enemy take heart.

Suddenly she saw a canoe loaded with a family named Fontaine approaching the landing place. They had not been noticed by the Iroquois, but Madelon still feared that they would be detected and slaughtered. She ordered the soldiers to rescue them, but they hung back in terror. Telling Laviolette to stand guard at the gate, she hurried to the dock to lead the Fontaines to safety. Guessing that the enemy would mistake her party for reinforcements, she led them boldly to the gate and inside the fort. Once safe, she ordered all who were armed to fire on anyone they saw outside. As darkness fell and a strong northeast wind began to blow, Madelon thought that the Iroquois might try to gain the fort under cover of darkness and the wailing wind.

So, as she told her father with amazing good humor, "I assembled all my troops, that is to say, six persons," and told them: "God has saved us today from the hands of our enemies, but we must take care not to fall into their snares tonight." With that she stationed all "her troops" at critical loopholes, arming everyone—even the eighty-year-old man—with a musket. Throughout that terrifying night with its whistling, moaning winds—and with snow now added—she kept "her troops" calling to one another, "All's well," from the fort to the blockhouse, and the blockhouse to the fort—so that the Iroquois were

completely deceived, as they later confessed to M. de Callieres, governor of Montréal.

At last the faint and rosy light of dawn began to climb the sky to
their right, like a gentle zephyr blowing away their fears. "Everybody
took courage," she told her father, but then, sniffing: "Except for
Mademoiselle Marguerite, wife of the Sieur Fontaine, who, being very
timid, as all Parisian women are, asked her husband to carry her to another fort. . . ." He answered: "I will never abandon this fort while
Mademoiselle Madelon is here." And so was passed a full week of
danger, as much from the fears of "the garrison" as from the presence
of the skulking Iroquois, who eventually gave up in disgust when they
saw Lieutenant de la Monnerie arriving at the head of forty men dispatched from Montréal by de Callieres.

One of them cried, "We are Frenchmen. It is la Monnerie, who
comes to bring you help." Ordering the gate to be opened, Madelon de
Vercheres—like Joan d'Arc raising the siege of Orléans—came striding
out to come to attention and salute their saviors.

"Monsieur," she said to la Monnerie, "I surrender my arms to you."

"Mademoiselle," he responded gallantly, in true, storybook French
style, "they are in good hands."

FIVE YEARS LATER—in the spring of 1697, with the end of the War of
the Grand Alliance only a few months away—a party of Frontenac's
Abenaki allies struck at the Massachusetts village of Haverhill, where
Hannah Dustan—another frontier woman of remarkable courage and
resourcefulness—lay nursing her week-old eighth child. With her was
a neighbor, Mary Neff. Her husband had just taken the seven other
children with him to work in nearby fields. Hearing the war whoops,
he ordered them to run to the nearest fortified house, a mile or more
distant. Then, snatching his musket, he flung himself on his horse and
galloped toward his own house to save his wife and newborn baby. He
was too late—the Indian war party was already there. Dustan now
thought of saving his other children. They were by then out of sight,
but he knew the location of the house to which they were running, the
oldest probably carrying the youngest in their arms.

Dismounting, he knelt to begin firing on the painted marauders,
keeping them at bay until he was sure that the other children were beyond capture. Meanwhile, to his great sorrow, he saw that his house
had been set ablaze and that the savages were carrying off his wife,
her neighbor Mary Neff, and the infant. He saw also that there were
too many of them for him to attack and that he must hasten to the side

of the other children, by then safely inside the fortified house. With tears in his eyes, he rejoined them.

Before departing the blazing Dustan home, the Indians had seized the squalling newborn boy, killing him by dashing his brains against a tree. Then they dragged Hannah and Mary Neff into the forest, rejoining other members of the raiding party who also had captive whites from Haverhill in their clutches. Some of these—too old or too sick to make the journey north—were quickly tomahawked and scalped, and the rest—with Hannah and Mary—divided among their captors.

Hannah and Mary fell into the hands of an Abenaki family of two warriors, three squaws, and seven children, heading north toward their village, 250 miles distant. An English boy captured at Worcester was also a prisoner. So on the Indians began to amuse themselves by describing to Hannah and Mary the tortures that would be inflicted upon them when they reached their destination, among them to be stripped naked and forced to run the gantlet and clubbed almost to death as they did, after which they would be burned alive.

Hannah Dustan did not despair. Almost immediately she decided to attempt to escape, explaining in English to both Mary and the boy, who agreed to join her. Halfway to the Abenaki village and lying down in feigned sleep in the depths of the snowbound forest, Hannah and the other two waited until they were certain their captors were asleep, whereupon they crept softly toward them. Seizing the tomahawks lying among them, they all struck at once. Again and again they struck, till blood spurted among them and their dying screams frightened off an old squaw who sprang to her feet and ran screeching into the woods, followed by a small boy whom they purposely left unharmed.

Hannah Dustan calmly waited until the rosy rays of dawn filtered through the trees, whereupon she scalped them all, and the three of them made their way back to their settlement, carrying the grisly trophies as proof of their exploit.

Such was a settler's wife—a mostly dreadful compound of both brutality and bravery—on both sides of the great river.

BEGINNING IN January 1692, French-and-Indian war parties struck at the British borders with sudden, swift savagery. First to hear the war whoop was the little hamlet of York on the Maine coast, where at least half a hundred settlers were slain and many more captured, although only a few months later an attempted raid on Wells was repulsed.

Two years later Oyster River, now Durham, New Hampshire, was attacked while the men were away in the fields, and many women and children were massacred. A branch of this war party split off from the main body a few days later and murdered about twenty settlers in the region of Groton, Massachusetts.

Apparently the fort at Pemaquid—also in Maine—had become a thorn in Frontenac's flesh. For half a dozen years it had existed as a meeting ground between those Abenaki Indians who had migrated to Canada, and the garrison of British soldiers. Moreover, it had also become a trading post for contraband furs that were diverted to British merchants to the south. Most irritating of all, Fort Pemaquid had been so sturdily built and so well armed with seven or eight cannons handled by about 150 regular soldiers, who also carried muskets, that Frontenac realized there were no Indians in all of Canada who would attempt to conquer it.

But then the council of safety in New England, with customary obtuseness, ordered half of the garrison withdrawn, after which the remaining troops were again halved. Lieutenant James Weems now had only about fifteen soldiers to command, most of whom were unfamiliar with artillery. In 1696 Frontenac decided that Pemaquid was ripe for conquest.

Thus two French warships, about a hundred mission Indians accompanied by Father Thury, a seminary priest at Québec, and supported by naval gunfire, descended on the fort. This last was decisive, and on the following morning Lieutenant Weems pulled down his flag and asked for quarter. Although it was generally believed that there was a massacre of both civilians and soldiers as well, in fact no one was butchered or tortured, chiefly because the French sachems had wisely stove in the fort's supply of rum. Before departing, the French burned the fort, thus leaving the long New England frontier exposed to the torch and the tomahawk.

For years to come until the end of the war, British settlers in New England seldom went into the fields to work or harvest their grain without being armed. This in itself was a discouragement, but the difficulty of storming a garrison house was even more daunting for the Indian allies of the French.

ON JULY 4, 1696, Count Frontenac, at the head of about twenty-two hundred men—French and Indians—set out on his last campaign to break forever the power of the Iroquois. His objective was the town of Onondaga—home of the tribe of that name and also the headquarters of the Five Nations. Though seventy-six years of age and enfeebled by a lifetime of battle—sixty-one years of combat, to be exact—he nevertheless took the field himself at the head of his forces. A swarm of Indian canoes led the way, followed by two battalions of French regulars in *bateaux*—their white coats and black gaiters brilliant against the sunlit waters—followed by more *bateaux* carrying cannons and mortars, shells and rockets, and other supplies, then Frontenac himself, surrounded by his brilliantly uniformed staff and guard.

On the nineteenth they reached Fort Frontenac—recaptured and restored—and then, poling, hauling, and paddling against the currents and rapids of the St. Lawrence, they crossed to the southern shore of Lake Ontario, where all aboard grew tense and nervous, for they well knew how rogue winds could churn up waves fully as huge and as disastrous as those of the open ocean—and thence to the mouth of the Oswego River and up it to Lake Onondaga.

Here—at the falls of the Oswego—fifty war-painted Indians howling and singing seized the count's great bark canoe upon their shoulders to bear him over the portage. Doubtless Onondaga scouts hastened homeward to report the approach of this magnificent forest armada. Hanging on Frontenac's flanks, they flitted through the woods ahead of him, while he was lifted from the canoe and carried in an armchair lashed to two stout carrying poles. Thus did the crusty old count take to the field.

As night fell, the entire army crouched inside a makeshift temporary fort, which held their canoes and *bateaux* and stores as well, and perceived a ruddy glow rising above the southern forest, which told them that the town of Onondaga had been set afire. Upon this vision, a great shout broke from their throats, and Count Frontenac perhaps permitted himself a small smile, to realize that, though he had only a few more years to live, he had at last achieved his paramount objective of shattering the power of the Iroquois.

The next day, as though to set a seal upon his triumph, the count's army held the burned and abandoned capital, although the disappointment of the Indians and the bush rangers in buckskin was great when they found that their enemies had escaped and that their rising thirst for blood would not be quenched. Only a few Onondagas could be found, among them a withered old man of about eighty caught hiding in a hollow tree. Frontenac would have spared him, but his thwarted Indian allies insisted on amusing themselves by tying him to a stake and torturing him. To their amazement, he did not whimper.

With his last breaths the old stoic berated his tormentors. "I thank you," he cried contemptuously, "but you ought to have finished me as you began, and killed me with fire! Learn from me, you dogs of Frenchmen, how to endure pain; and you, you dogs of dogs, you Indian allies, think what you will do when you are burned like me!" The new governor, Vaudreuil, found in the agony of the defiant old man more pleasure than his savage afflictors, laughing uproariously because as he was burned to death he made such funny faces!

SOON AFTER, King William's War came to an end. Far, far away in Paris and London, the fourteenth Louis and the third William had terminated the War of the Grand Alliance; Louis because even that powerful prince could not afford to fight all Europe, William because the sting of his own personal defeats on the field of battle was to be removed by halfhearted recognition of his right to rule Britain.

William had cared even less than Louis for the New World fighting flaring up on the fringe of the larger conflagration. But that attitude was to be gradually reversed. Britain was to be concerned more and more—and France less and less—for their colonies in America. England was also to become almost exclusively engaged in gaining mastery of the seas, while France was to turn foolishly away from her coasts on the English Channel, the Atlantic, and the Mediterranean to concentrate upon her land frontiers. Meanwhile, in 1698, a year after the signing of the Peace of Ryswick occurred, Count Frontenac's valiant heart ceased to beat. That very summer he had marched once more against the dreaded Iroquois, but in November he took to his bed in his chamber in the Château St. Louis. He died there, in his seventy-eighth year, full of composure and in the bosom of his Church; and New France went into deep mourning.

Perhaps it was understood that something more than a governor of Canada had breathed his last. An era was also perishing. Cartier, LaSalle, Champlain, Jogues, Breboeuf, Joliet, Marquette, all those bright and shining names that ennoble the history of France in the New World, all these had come before the fiery count from the Pyrenees, and now Frontenac was also dead.

Soldiers and explorers and martyrs were to be replaced by peculating intendants, vain and petty governors, and worldly clergy. It was almost as though the death of Frontenac had been concurrent with the death of the dreams of Louis XIV. All the glory and dominion that the Sun King sought had been his throughout most of the seventeenth century. Now the eighteenth was at hand, and with it disaster for Louis and for France.

CHAPTER 18

Sir William Phips Wins and Loses

WHEN COUNT FRONTENAC formed his three war parties and sent them against the colonies of New York and New England, it was his intention to revive the diminishing ardor of the *habitants* of New France—still stunned and frightened by the La Chine massacre—as well as to demonstrate to the triumphant Iroquois that they could no longer depend on instant aid from the English, while encouraging the friendly Abenakis to renew their attacks on the enemy's border settlements. Frontenac also expected that deliberate, bloody retaliation for La Chine would remind the British that border warfare was a two-way street, and instill in them a more conciliatory attitude toward their less populous but more martial Canadian neighbors.

But this was not to be. Even as the count's bush rangers and war-painted Indians slipped like silent ghosts through swirling fogs and blinding snowstorms, their snowshoes hissing on frozen lakes and streams, the governments of New England and New York with surprising speed hastened to embrace an Iroquois proposal for a combined onslaught on Canada. Early in May 1690, a congress of their delegates had gathered in New York City to formulate plans for a counterattack. Four hundred fighting men were to be furnished by the colony of that name, while Massachusetts, Plymouth, and Connecticut were to raise a joint force of 355 militia. Later, the Iroquois who had suggested the operation added their not-always-reliable pledge to join the expedition with at least 1,500 warriors.

This formidable force was to rendezvous at Albany, and thereafter advance upon Montréal by way of Lake Champlain. Mutual jealousies that always acted like an abrasive hair shirt upon the martial ambitions of the several British colonies made it difficult to agree upon a commander. Finally, the timid Fitz-John Winthrop of Connecticut was given the command.

While Montréal was attacked by land, the delegates at New York agreed, Québec was to be assaulted and captured in a collective amphibious invasion of the northern colonies led by Massachusetts. This was no minor objective, as the salty descendants of these seagoing colonies were well aware. Massachusetts was particularly dubious about its prospects: both because of the costs involved, and the difficulty in traversing the deep and swift St. Lawrence in the face of an advancing winter. Those veterans who had actually seen Québec could shiver at the thought of conquering the bristling little citadel atop its perch among those soaring cliffs.

Moreover, Massachusetts had no money, and was already engaged in mounting a less daunting, distant, and expensive enterprise. During the past winter her commerce had suffered grievously at the hands of French corsairs issuing from the sanctuary of Port Royal in Acadia, and also from hostile Indians supposedly supplied there by their French allies. If anything, rather than risk a severe—even disastrous—setback at Québec, as their delegates explained to their neighbors, they would rather attack and capture French Acadia's finest port and turn it to the advantage of all the English-speaking colonies of northeastern America.

To do this, Massachusetts already had seven ships manned by 288 sailors impressed for the operation, and 400 to 500 militia drafted for the assault. All that was needed was a proper commander familiar with both elements of land and sea. This would be that rugged, dauntless son of New England, Sir William Phips.

THE AMBITION OF William Phips was nearly as great as his immense body, while his prowess with his hamlike fists was at least the equal of the other two. Born in 1650 at a rude border settlement in Massachusetts on the Kennebec River and later called Woolwich, Phips was one of twenty-six children, all of the same mother. His parents were poor and probably illiterate, and Phips until he was eighteen was sent out by them to earn his living as a shepherd. Such a life did not exactly conform to his high hopes for the future, so he left his sheep behind him and walked to Boston, where he learned the trade of a ship's carpenter.

Having laboriously begun to climb the ladder of success, he fairly flew up it upon meeting a rich widow beyond him in years, in property, in wealth, and in station. At this point he learned to read and write, being either self-taught or more likely tutored through the generosity of his helpmeet. He may have received no more than a first-grade education, but just enough, as he informed his wife, to be able to command someday a king's ship and own a "fair brick house on the Green Lane in North Boston," a quarter then occupied by those high-born residents ultimately to be known as the "Boston Brahmins."

William Phips was as good as his words on both these points, though fortune did not smile upon him for several years. Reverse succeeded reverse, continuing even after the Good Fairy who was his wife passed on to her reward. But the pressure of continued failure seemed to inspire in him the decisiveness of a gambler ready to risk all on a single throw. He would outfit a ship of his own and sail the West Indian seas in search of a Spanish treasure ship wrecked there and sunk fifty years ago. Full of this project, he went to England, where—probably for no better reasons than the impressions made by his enormous size and his almost insufferable self-confidence—he gained a hearing from investors willing to back him and actually induced the Admiralty to give him a frigate.

Sailing into the West Indies, he began a long but fruitless search, though he did profit from adventures that eventually made of him a capable and daring sea captain. As he came about to return to London, this being the epoch of piracy, and the West Indies then being their home, his crew mutinied. They were tired of a vain and toilsome search, and they approached him on his quarterdeck armed with cutlasses, demanding that he "go on the account"—that is, turn buccaneer. With a frightening roar he fell upon them with his fists alone, instantly decking the ringleaders and driving the others to the sanctuary of the ship's rail, where they fell to their knees and begged for mercy.

Not long after, another, far more formidable mutiny arose, and this time, wisely reminding the mutineers of the outcome of their earlier conspiracy, he strode among them quietly with great courage and address, quelling them by his presence alone and holding them to their duties until he reached Jamaica and exchanged the entire crew for more reliable seamen.

Even so, the frigate loaned to him had turned out to be as leaky as a floating honeycomb. Although Phips, by nature of his former career as a ship's carpenter, was able to keep it afloat, he returned to London to report an unsuccessful voyage. But then Phips—with a native cunning seeming to bely what he usually achieved through physical strength alone—seems to have gained information from an unknown source almost certain to lead to a sunken galleon. He inspired such confidence that the duke of Abemarle, with other aristocrats and gentlemen, provided him with another ship rigged for treasure-hunting and dispatched him once again to those fabled seas of instant riches. This time he found the wreck, raised it, and took from it in gold, silver, and jewels a trove valued at three hundred thousand pounds sterling.

Sailing back to London, this crew also conspired against him, preparing to seize the ship and divide its wealth among themselves. Phips, not a stupid man though a greedy one, accepted reality and promised that each of them should have a share in the bonanza, even if it came from his own abundant portion. On arriving in England he kept this pledge so well that, after redeeming it, only sixteen thousand pounds sterling was left for him. Nevertheless, this was ample fortune for the former shepherd from the Kennebec River cabin, and enough to realize his dream of that "fair brick house on the Green Lane in North Boston." To his surprise and gratification, he came back to Boston a rich man and a knight, arriving there just in time to take command of the operation against Port Royal.

SAILING FROM Nantasket at the end of April 1690, Phips reached Port Royal on May 11, landed his troops, and summoned Governor Meneval to surrender his fort. With seventy half-starved and sullen soldiers available to repel the invaders and the rickety fort apparently ready to collapse upon itself, Meneval hauled down his flag.

Before he did, he had first prudently stipulated that private property must be respected, that the church should not be harmed, and that the troops be allowed to return to Québec or to France. To these customary courtesies extended to an enemy who offers no resistance, Sir William readily agreed.

But then Phips changed his mind, having been informed that during the parley that followed Meneval's surrender, a quantity of goods belonging to King Louis and local merchants was supposedly found in the woods. Sir William flew into a rage, claiming that by this action the agreement between him and Meneval had been violated, and used this as his pretext for plundering the merchants, imprisoning the troops, and desecrating the church. "We cut down the cross," one of Phips's henchmen wrote gleefully, "rifled their church, pulled down their high altar, and broke their images." By this peremptory resort to such barbarism, with no cooling-off period ordained or any pretense of another parley with the defeated governor arranged, there is much credence to the claim that it was Phips—not Meneval—who had deliberately planted the "stolen goods" in the woods where a search party would—at Phips's direction—quickly discover them.

The house of the two priests—Petit and Trouvé—serving the Catholic church at Port Royal was also pillaged, and all the settlers commanded to swear their allegiance to the British crown if they wished to secure their life, liberty, and property, which most of them did. There was, of course, lawful loot such as twenty-one pieces of artillery and a sum of money, both belonging to King Louis, while smaller articles were taken from the merchants and those who refused to take the oath, all of which was packed in hogsheads and carried aboard the ships. Who received it is not known, although the rapaciousness of Sir William Phips was very well known indeed. The French Jesuit writer Charlevoix says in his *History of New France* that Phips robbed Meneval of all his money. Meneval himself reported that he had given his money to Phips for safekeeping, but that Phips would return neither the money nor various other articles he had entrusted to his conqueror. These included "six silver spoons, six silver forks, one silver cup in the shape of a gondola, a pair of pistols, three new wigs, a gray vest, four pair of silk garters, two dozen of shirts, six vests of dimity, four night caps with lace edgings, all my table service of fine tin, all my kitchen linen," and many other items that were also not returned, according to Meneval.

While the hapless governor was counting his household articles, his despoiler—whose credo must have been "to the victor belongs the spoils"—was busy through a Captain Alden taking possession of all the poorly manned or abandoned posts in Acadia, which would eventually be called Nova Scotia. This effortless seizure of a vast island—together with the capture of Port Royal—Sir William Phips intended to present to the government of Massachusetts as the first gift of his conquering sword, unaware that the little Puritan commonwealth had neither the men nor the money to maintain it.

SIR WILLIAM WAS delighted with the hero's reception that he received upon his arrival in Boston on May 30—only nineteen days since he had landed at Port Royal—bringing with him those men he had promised to protect but who were now his prisoners: Meneval and his tearful wife, the two priests, and fifty-nine dispirited French soldiers.

The governor and the priests were confined to a house in Boston under guard, while Meneval mournfully petitioned the governor and council for redress of his grievances, sadly concluding, ". . . but, as they have little authority and stand in fear of Phips, who is supported by the rabble, to which he himself once belonged, and of which he is now the chief, they could do nothing for me." This is not quite true, for the council went on record requiring Phips to restore to Meneval all his possessions. Phips ignored it, until Governor Bradstreet wrote to him commanding him to obey the council's order. Sir William reluctantly complied, giving up some money and the worst part of the clothing, keeping the rest for himself. Unless Governor Meneval also possessed the physique of a giant, it is doubtful if any of the clothing fitted Sir William.

Moreover, when the commander of a fort yields without resistance, making certain stipulations agreed to by his conquerer—to wit, money, household articles, and clothing entrusted to the conqueror for safekeeping—it is safe to say that the conquered commander was no hero, but that the conqueror who received but refused to return this "booty" was indeed either a robber or a pirate.

IT IS ONE OF THE many cardinal mysteries of military history that so many cowards want to command, and so many clowns seek military glory through that most improbable agency of "bloodless victory."

In the annals of American arms the chief exponent of the second impossible art—to conquer without pain—was General George McClellan, famous—or rather, infamous—in the American Civil War for training the powerful Army of the Potomac that he never actually used and that the caustic Abe Lincoln once described as "McClellan's bodyguard."

Sir William Phips was of this second variety. By his voice alone he had conquered a tumbledown French fort commanded by a timid bureaucrat leading seventy starving, sullen soldiers. As a result, he was hailed as a hero throughout the colonies of New York and New England, and given command of an amphibious force to carry out the water-borne assault upon Québec; while a second force, under Major Peter Schuyler, who was also mayor of Albany, was to make an overland march and strike at Montréal.

The triumphant Phips returned from Port Royal to find Boston throbbing with preparation for a much bigger venture: the capture of Québec.

England had been asked to supply arms, while Massachusetts got ready the ships and men. Even though the Bay Colony's funds were short, it was believed that the plunder of Canada's capital city would more than offset outlays for the expedition. Accordingly, thirty-six ships of all sizes were assembled, and a call for volunteers was issued. After enlistments failed to produce the desired number of men, the colony calmly impressed the rest.

In all, the expeditionary force was to number twenty-two hundred sailors and soldiers—if raw farmers and fishermen may be so designated. At their head was Sir William Phips. Beneath him was John Walley—"Major" Walley, now—one of the colony's most respectable citizens and therefore, by the standards of a merchant republic, eminently qualified to command men in battle.

But vain considerations for the arts of war would have seemed a contradiction to the race chosen by the God of Battles. These citizen-soldiers of New Jerusalem—all these Jonathons and Sauls and Calebs, these Abrahams and Israels and Jedidiahs—could they possibly fail in the holy war against the idolators of the North? Was the New Jerusalem not to be the instrument of God's vengeful wrath upon the New Canaan? Certainly it was, and to suggest that the Almighty's own purpose might be thwarted was to utter a blasphemy. Just to be sure, however, the populace was exhorted to do penance, a day of fasting was ordained, and the Lord was imprecated to look with favor upon the instruments of his will.

Meanwhile, the reply from England had come, and the answer was no. King William was too busy with James II in Ireland at that moment. Nevertheless, the expeditions sailed. Phips had already waited too long to begin operations, and he left Nantasket on August 9, 1690.

Contrary winds delayed Phips for three more weeks, and it was well into October before he arrived. During that time, Frontenac had fortified Québec. Entering the basin with the city on the cliff before him, Phips also contemplated a bristling fort. Still, he had taken one French fortress simply by raising his voice—so he summoned Frontenac to surrender.

This time the white silk flag with its pale gold lilies continued to float bravely on the breezes above Québec. Phips's emissary, a young subaltern, was received on the strand of the Lower Town. He was blindfolded and led hither and thither while an immense hubbub was made around him to create the impression of enormous martial activity. Then he was ushered into Frontenac's presence and the blindfold was removed.

The youth blinked in dismay. The old count had arrayed himself in all his silks and decorations. Around him stood his officers, resplendent in perukes and powder, in gold lace and in silver, in glittering sword hilts and flashing buckles. It might have seemed to that startled subaltern that all of the gorgeous society of Versailles had been transplanted to the mud banks of the St. Lawrence. Nevertheless, he recovered his composure and handed an interpreter the surrender demand. It is quite likely that the annals of warfare between civilized societies have never—before or since—recorded a summons to surrender in such insulting, lying, bragging, boorish, demanding, threatening, gas-conading, and bombastic language. The reading of it by an interpreter consumed at least a quarter hour, during which an unbroken silence reigned among Frontenac and his officers. When it was finished, the subaltern drew his watch from his pocket and handed it to the governor. Frontenac could not, or pretended he could not, see the hour. The messenger then told him that it was ten o'clock and that he must have his answer by eleven.

At that point a great cry of indignation broke from the throats of these officers of a polite society. General Valrenne called out that Phips was nothing but a pirate and that his man ought to be hanged. Frontenac shook his head slowly, struggling to contain himself before addressing the envoy in the most courteous tones:

"I will not keep you waiting so long. Tell your general that I do not recognize King William; and that the Prince of Orange, who so styles himself, is a usurper, who has violated the most sacred laws of blood in attempting to dethrone his father-in-law. I know no king of England but King James. Your general ought not to be surprised at the hostilities which he says that the French have carried on in the colony of Massachusetts; for as the king my master had taken the king of England under his protection, and is about to replace him on his throne by force of arms, he might have expected that His Majesty would order me to make war on a people who have rebelled against their lawful sovereign."

Then, turning with a smile to the officers gathered about him, he continued: "Even if your general offered me conditions a little more gracious, and if I had a mind to accept them, does he suppose that these brave gentlemen would give their consent, and advise me to trust a man who broke his agreement with the governor of Port Royal, or a rebel who has failed in his duty to his king, and forgotten all the favors he had received from him, to follow a prince who pretends to be the liberator of England and the defender of the faith, and yet destroys the laws and privileges of the kingdom and overthrows its religion? The divine justice which your general invokes in his letter will not fail to punish such acts severely."

Another great silence ensued, during which the youthful messenger seemed astonished and badly shaken until, recovering his composure, he asked if the governor would give him his answer in writing.

"No," Frontenac replied, "I will answer your general only by the mouths of my cannon, that he may learn that a man like me is not to be summoned after this fashion. Let him do his best, and I will do mine."

Then he dismissed Phips's emissary abruptly, and he was again blindfolded, led over the barricades, and sent back to his fleet by the boat that brought him.

SIR WILLIAM PHIPS during his many adventures at sea had indeed given proof of his personal courage, but during the six-week voyage from Nantasket to Québec his steady frown and hermit-like retreat to his cabin suggested that in abandoning his sheep he had indeed exceeded his capacity to command. Moreover, an enterprise so large as an amphibious invasion of a clifftop fortress above a deep and swift-flowing river was something rather more daunting than a simple search for sunken treasure. Once Sir William's fleet had glided into the huge basin of Québec below the city's soaring cliffs, his frown grew deeper and his appearances on deck fewer.

Emerging from his solitude only to call councils of war, he immediately scheduled another when he heard Frontenac's reply. He was not so perceptive as to understand that councils-of-war are rarely if ever ordered by resolute commanders. Instead they provide the fainthearted among his subordinates with an opportunity to counsel retreat, which may also serve as an excuse for their timid chief, should he be defeated. Sir William was unusually silent at this latest council, so that Major John Walley, the commander of the land troops, had no difficulty in taking the lead and outlining a practical plan for victory.

At Walley's urging it was decided to land at Beauport, a town just below Québec but separated from it by the St. Charles River, which emptied into the St. Lawrence.

Major Walley would take his men up the St. Charles to a ford, cross, and strike at the rear of Québec. The smaller ships would sail up as far as the ford to give fire support. Once the British soldiers had begun attacking Québec's rear, Phips and the heavier ships would bombard the city from the basin. Neither Phips nor Walley seems to have known that Frontenac had constructed a line of fortifications behind the city. Nor did they pay much attention to French prisoners who told them of a place a mile or two above Québec where a little-known path led upward to the heights. Seven decades later a red-haired British general named Wolfe would scrutinize similar information a little bit closer.

Daylight was fading as the council of war reached its conclusions. At nightfall the colonists heard the peal of fifes and the roll of drums from atop the cliff. The British asked a prisoner named Granville what it meant.

"Ma foi, messieurs," he answered, smiling, "you have lost the game. It is the governor of Montréal with the people from the country above. There is nothing for you now but to pack and go home."

It was true. Québec had been reinforced just in time. Between seven hundred and eight hundred men—regular soldiers and unruly *coureurs de bois*—had come downriver to enter the city, shouting and singing, to swell the garrison to three thousand armed men and to make Sir William's slim chances of success even narrower.

Nevertheless, the assault went forward. Walley took some thirteen hundred militia ashore at Beauport. They were met by a delaying force of three hundred sharpshooters under Sainte-Hélène. Slowly, taking causalties, Walley's men drove the Canadians back. They gained the St. Charles and made camp for the night. In the morning they would rendezvous with the fireships and move upriver.

Unfortunately, the impatient Sir William had gone into action. With neither Walley nor the smaller ships as yet on the St. Charles, he had opened fire on Québec. Actually, it was Frontenac who had opened fire on him. From the Château St. Louis perched on the brink of the cliff, the fiery old count had watched the biggest British ships leave their moorings and sail into position under the town—and he fired the first shot in a furious cannonading that reverberated in one long re-echoing crash around the basin of Québec. The British ships spat flames and shot and the cliff belched back with fire and ball. Next day, the duel was resumed. But now the British Crown's failure to provide adequate ammunition, yoked to the colony's faith in God rather than in gunnery practice, began to tell.

The French were superior in shot and in skill. Eighteen- and twenty-four-pounders aimed personally by Sainte-Hélène and his brother, Maricourt, battered the enemy's biggest ships. One cut off Phips's flagstaff, and the Cross of St. George fluttered into the river, to be rescued as a prize by Canadian boatmen. Infuriated, the colonists turned their guns on a banner of the Holy Family floating from the spire of the cathedral. They missed it, and the jubilant French—whose priests and nuns had not neglected to impetrate the Virgin for direct hits—promptly proclaimed a miracle. However, as Parkman dryly observed, "the miracle would have been greater if they had hit it."

His ship riddled and listing, Sir William retired from the combat. He had attacked prematurely, he had exhausted the slender supplies of ammunition needed for the moment when Walley pressed his attack from the rear—and he had, in effect, lost the entire battle. Walley, to his credit, tried to persevere in an impossible situation. Though his small fireships never appeared, probably because their masters also owned them and were loath to risk them under Frontenac's cannons, he still attempted to press on to the ford. But he never crossed the St. Charles. Frontenac, with battalions of regulars, militia, and Indians, crossed it instead to oppose Walley's frozen troops. A series of inconclusive actions was fought in which the New Englanders suffered more and in which the gallant Sainte-Hélène received his mortal wound.

Four days after they had landed at Beauport, the British withdrew to their boats. Phips sailed behind the Isle of Orléans, which lies inside the basin of Québec, to repair his ships out of range of the city. Then he turned their prows for Boston, and his sails had hardly vanished from the St. Lawrence before the solemn notes of the "Te Deum" resounded in the nave of the cathedral at Québec.

NEW ENGLAND WAS virtually clothed in sackcloth and ashes when the crestfallen Sir William Phips returned in late November. Some of his ships and men did not appear until February, while some were never heard from again. Massachusetts had not only been humbled in its pride, it also had been dealt a severe financial blow. Soldiers and sailors clamoring for pay had to be placated by the first paper money issued in the English-speaking world. Actually a bill to be acceptable as legal tender for taxes,* it quickly depreciated, adding to the distress of the colony. Finally, the Puritans had been seared in their souls. They searched their consciences for the sin that had brought down upon them such a terrible manifestation of the Lord's displeasure; but they might better have listened to the observation of an opponent who was later to become more distinguished with pen than with sword.

"They fought vigorously," wrote Baron La Hontan, "though as ill-disciplined as men gathered together at random could be; for they did not lack courage, and, if they failed, it was by reason of their entire ignorance of discipline, and because they were exhausted by the fatigues of the voyage."

Almost every word of that paragraph is descriptive of the weaknesses that were forever to plague the Americans as a military nation: Brave, though ill-trained; not only ignorant of the chief military virtue, discipline, but also unappreciative of the debilitating effects that a

---

*These "bills of credit" explain the American custom of calling a dollar note a dollar "bill."

long march or a prolonged sea voyage can have upon troops. In a word, scornful of war as an art to be learned, like, say, statesmanship, but regarding it something that comes as naturally as running or jumping or the instinct for gain. From the defeat before Québec to the sacrifice of ill-prepared troops during the early days of the Korean War 260 years later, this valiant and vigorous race, so obsessed with a passion for training that it presently regards it as necessary for every bit of trivia or commonplace from playing cards to weening a baby away from diapers, would continue to regard military training with disinterest and distrust. A people prizing liberty will naturally resist the restrictions of military life; but a race cherishing independence should be willing to grudge a few months of training to defend it.

Much of this reluctance was due to the perfidious system of drafting unwilling soldiers and sailors, an obtuse, counterproductive policy that never crippled the U.S. Marine Corps, where the word "draftee" continues to be a curse word. But the appearance during the Persian Gulf War of an all-volunteer armed forces was a blessed event that has since been hobbled by starry-eyed American liberals—with their Liberation Lizzy mentality—who, just like the Russian Communists, have no comprehension of human nature, and as a consequence have introduced females into the armed forces and are now clamoring for them to be sent into combat zones.*

However, unfortunately for the American concept of warfare, as well as for the colonists themselves, the kind of combat that *is* as natural as running or jumping was to return to the frontiers in all its screeching horror. Frontenac had already written to King Louis:

"Now that the king has triumphed by land and sea, will he think that a few squadrons of his navy would be ill employed in punishing the insolence of these genuine old parliamentarians of Boston, and crushing them in their den and the British of New York as well? By mastering these two towns, we shall secure the whole sea-coast, besides the fisheries of the Grand Bank, which is no slight matter: and

---

*Permit the author a single digression on this subject: In World War II the chief German ace, Erich Hartmann, shot down no less than 352 enemy planes. Our chief ace, Richard Bong, had 40 kills. What would happen to an American female fighter pilot challenging either one of these superior gentlemen of the skies? Obviously, she would lose her life, and the U.S. Air Force would lose not only the time and money wasted in training her as well, but also an aircraft valued at $36 million.

this would be the true, and perhaps the only way of bringing the wars of Canada to an end; for, when the British are conquered, we can easily reduce the Iroquois to complete submission."

Although Louis was at that moment too busy upon the Continent to consent to Frontenac's proposal, the Sun King was not averse to a resumption of raids against the British borders in the New World. Frontenac again sent out his war parties, and the frontier was again aflame from the Connecticut to the Kennebec.

Occasionally, the colonists—particularly in New York—countered with raids of their own during the half-dozen years while King William's war sputtered toward its conclusion. Most of the attacks, however, were made by the French and their Abenaki allies.

PART IV

War of the Spanish Succession, 1701–1714 (Queen Anne's War)

CHAPTER 19

Anne Succeeds William

THERE IS NO DOUBT that without the defection of John Churchill with five thousand veteran troops—the man whom James II had made by promoting him to lieutenant general—William of Orange would never have been able to drive the legitimate King James from the British throne that the little usurper from Holland coveted more than salvation itself.

Those powerful men—both Whigs and Tories—who put that crown on William's head had not the slightest intention of allowing him to rule as the sovereign of the (puzzled) English, (reluctant) Welsh, (unhappy) Scots, and (hostile) Irish. As this study has observed, they wanted someone *called* king who would do their bidding so that both the political power and the great wealth that would flow from it would be in their hands. These men had put it about that James had abdicated. But had he, or had he merely departed—like a thief in the night, in a small boat bound for France—in the way that Alfonso XIII had departed Spain in 1931, without signing anything away? No. Neither did James II. Until his dying day he considered himself the legitimate king of England, and his son to be his heir by the sacred right of birth and to be called James III. With the arrival of the man who called himself William III—by right of the impeccable credentials of his simpleminded wife, Mary, oldest daughter of James—William sat on the throne of Great Britain. But was his a lawful government? Doubts about this have persisted to this day, many of them raised by Winston Churchill, in his study of his great ancestor the duke of Marlborough. These were:

> Was the throne vacant? Could the throne ever be vacant? Was there a contract between the king and the people, which James had broken? Had he abdicated by flight, or merely departed? Could he be deposed by Parliament? Arising from all this, should William become regent,

governing in the name of the absent James? Should Mary become queen in her own right? Had she not, in view of the virtual demise of the crown, in fact already become queen? Or should William be made sole king, or should William and Mary reign jointly? And if Mary died, should Anne forthwith succeed, or should William continue to reign alone as long as he lived?

William had no love for Britain or for its people. He would have much preferred to live in Holland, but he stayed where he was because Britain was much more populous, wealthier, and more skilled in war than the United Provinces, and he needed all these resources to continue as the Protestant champion and to bring down Louis.

But this was not to be. It has been well said that a cat may look at a king; but what about a much smaller, more insignificant little creature such as a mole, who actually dethroned a king? Really? Aye, really and truly, for it was one of those minuscule moles that delight in digging those tiny tunnels in the earth, into one of which the horse bearing William of Orange stuck its foot, stumbling so violently that he threw his dainty little rider and so ended his days in the year 1702, just as he was preparing to move against his mortal enemy Louis of France. As Winston Churchill observed: "A *queer, unnatural** interlude in English history had reached its end."

To which Anne Stuart, daughter of King James II, might have said "Amen" as she gravely mounted the steps to the throne of England.

BUT IT MAY BE THAT William actually outwitted these powerful men who thought that they had created a first-class stooge. Certainly he had had no intention of being any reigning wife's consort; nor was he willing to step aside for her sister Anne, should his wife predecease him—as she did in 1694 at age of thirty-two—because he wanted *Mary*, the legitimate sovereign, to be *his* consort. It was much more tactful—this time at the urging of the same kingmakers, who had had second thoughts about William—to set up the joint reign that was agreed upon as the so-called but unconstitutional "parliamentary title" supposedly, but illegally, authorized by both houses.

William was delighted by this underhanded device, for he would lose nothing because of it, for Mary had come quickly and unwaveringly under his spell the moment he—not she—sat on the throne of England. And yet, at her wedding eleven years earlier—in 1677—she had wept uncontrollably. Did she really dislike him that much? Most

*Italics are the author's.

people did, for William the Sly was a hard, cold, miserable man. He had no real friends, except for those sycophants who shared his vices and whom he loaded with rewarding gifts. But perhaps Mary wept because before she gave him her hand she had learned that he not only did not love her but also was actually a lover of men. So he would have no heirs and she would have no children.

In its simplest terms, this sparrow-man, this simulacrum of a warrior who was among the fiercest haters of history, wanted the crown of Britain because he thought of it as the source of the troops, supplies, and money that he would need to destroy his mortal enemy: King Louis XIV of France. It was not the French nation, of course, it was Louis—his personal *bête noire* and also his first cousin once removed, and Mary's as well.

Queen Anne had despised her diminutive brother-in-law since he married her older sister Mary and thus made himself king of England. He had no right to be the sovereign, but Mary did. Sweet, simple-minded Mary had inherited that right from her father, King James II, by all the sacred rights of blood. William had no such claim, and Anne not only had hated him for twenty-five years, she also had despised him not only because he was more than a foot shorter than she was but also because he had deceived her sister, who longed to bear children but had found after her marriage to him that he was not going to be helpful in their procreation.

But Anne had them. In all, Anne Stuart had had seventeen pregnancies: at least one born alive, but most stillborn—but no survivors now that she was queen. And her sister Mary, of whom she had been so fond, had died still resenting her sister Anne because she could become pregnant so easily. Anne did not feel that way about Mary, and had been happy with her husband, Prince George of Denmark. She had disliked her cousin Prince George of Hanover, who had come to London especially to see her—that is, to look her over to judge if she would qualify as his wife. But he was taken sharply aback upon meeting the tall princess, and George did not like the idea of his wife looking down on him, nor did he want to enter into a marriage with a family the head of which was a Catholic and whose wife, Anne Hyde, was a commoner; so he went home in a huff, snob that he was.

Princess Anne shed no tears when she gazed for the last time on the scowling, pudgy face of Prince George of Hanover, as he departed Windsor Castle in the royal coach, his back arched like a petulant hedgehog's, bound for the London docks and the ship that would take him back to France. He was more than satisfied to return unpledged to his comfortable little Electorate of Hanover, where he was the First

Frog in a mighty small pond; where, if his writ may not have traveled very far, it did travel deep; in fact, deeper than Hell itself.

The first of these Hanoverian kings was George I, the second elector of Hanover, born in 1660. At twenty-one he married his sixteen-year-old cousin Sophia Dorothea of Zelle. Charming, vivacious, and witty, she fell in love, at age twenty-six, with one of her courtiers, Count Königsmark. In 1693, Königsmark vanished, presumably murdered. A year later George divorced Sophia and imprisoned her in a castle in which she spent the last thirty-two years of her life, her children taken from her by her former husband. In 1698 George took possession of his Hanoverian throne and seemed moderately happy. But then in 1714 Queen Anne of Britain died. Despite her seventeen pregnancies she had left no heir, and the Whig leaders of Britain demanded that George, as a grandson of James I, was the rightful heir to Queen Anne, who had indeed so named him in her will, and must accept the throne of Britain. With great reluctance, George complied.

George reigned for thirteen years, always a German prince, uncaring to learn either the customs or the language of his subjects. When he conversed with his ministers, who spoke no German, it was in a kind of imperfect Latin. Lord Chesterfield described him thus: "George the First was an honest, dull, German gentleman as unfit as unwilling to act the part of a King, which is to shine and to oppress, lazy and inactive even in his pleasures, which were therefore lowly and sensual . . . [he preferred] the company of wags and buffoons. Even his mistress, the Duchess of Kendal, with whom he passed most of his time, and who had all influence over him, was very little above an idiot. Importunity alone could make him act, and then only to get rid of it. His views and affections were singly confined to the narrow compass of his Electorate; England was too big for him." Chesterfield added: "The King loved pleasure, and was not delicate in his choice of it. No woman came amiss to him if they were willing and very fat. . . . The standard of his Majesty's taste made all those ladies who aspired to his favor, and who were near the suitable size, strain and swell themselves like the frogs in the fable to rival the bulk and dignity of the ox. Some succeeded, and others burst." But vulgar George could not care less. Stubborn and suspicious, stingy and crude, "so cold that he changes everything to ice," after hearing of the death of his former wife, Sophia, he sank into a melancholy from which he never recovered, dying suddenly of apoplexy in 1727.

WHEN ANNE STUART met George of Denmark, she fell immediately in love with him. He was big and handsome in a fair-haired, Scandinavian way; very agreeable, even if he did drink a little too much beer and came so often to her boudoir. George had also shown himself to be a brave soldier. When his brother King Christian of Denmark was captured by the Swedes, George had cut his way through enemy ranks to rescue him.

Besides being tall, Queen Anne was a husky, hearty woman, like her ancestress Mary Queen of Scots, who was also beautiful, but murdered in the end by the Pirate Queen who seems to have inherited her syphilitic father's fondness for cutting off the heads of those who had served the House of Tudor or who seemed to menace it. There was nothing either beautiful or glamorous enough about Anne to have led anyone to die for her in a revolt against William.

But she also might have been similarly infected by some disease of her father. The Dutch writing couple Henri and Barbara Van Der Zee have maintained without proof in their enormously inflated biography of William that James II also had been syphilitic. Because the Europe of the late sixteenth and early seventeenth centuries had been devastated by the disease brought back to the brothels of Barcelona by the sailors of Columbus from the New World, and because many of the blue bloods of Europe were so accustomed to demand "the *debitum*" from any attractive woman they fancied, they were among its first victims. But to suggest without a wisp of proof that James II had been so contaminated seems to indicate that this adulatory Dutch couple was not exactly impartial. Proof of their prejudice resides in the fact that when little James III was born, he had no visible defects that would arise from syphilitic contamination from either of his parents—James II of Britain, or Mary-Beatrice of Modena, a province of Italy—and also by the fact that he grew to full and wholesome manhood, and was possessed of such a high sense of honor that he indignantly refused the offer of his half sister Queen Anne to abdicate in his favor if he would renounce his Catholicism and become a Protestant. To do so—as both of them well knew—might have plunged Britain into another dreadful civil war.

Some psychiatrists have compared Queen Anne's inability to bear a healthy child—only the little duke of Gloucester lived for as long as eleven years—with the "family disease" of porphyria that afflicted all four Hanoverian Georges who ultimately sat on the British throne, and all of whom were quite mad.

After becoming queen, Anne was never as healthy or as high-hearted as she had been as just a princess. Like so many long-term invalids, she had her own diagnosis of what ailed her: "gout in the stomach," which gave her indigestion and "hysterical affections" and an occasional convulsion. She also complained of "gout in the bowels," although this affliction never appears internally, but first attacks the big toe, and then other joints. Believed to have been caused by an excess of fine foods and liquors, it has since been diagnosed as the work of a virus. But Anne was never known as an epicurean, and the real gout she felt in her knee and foot, and later made her need a stick or even two for walking, might also have been a symptom of porphyria. In her final illness she had fits of delirium. As Winston Churchill remarked of Anne, "Her life was repeatedly stabbed by pain, disappointment, and mourning."

Apparently what Queen Anne desperately needed without knowing it was a friend. Her sister Mary had been no help when she came over from France as the junior partner in the Company of Wm. & Mary Ltd.—for limited it surely was, with Mary bearing the credentials, and William wearing the crown. The barren Mary openly resented her sister's amazing fertility—just as the dwarfish little Dutch usurper resented her enormous height—and she had had very little sympathy for the discomfort, pain, and despair that were the suffering Anne's almost daily companions.

The friend that Anne needed would not have been a man—certainly not agreeable old George *Est-il possible*—"It is possible"—with his beery breath and faithful coupling; but rather a woman she could admire, depend upon—even adore. She found her long before Mary became queen. She was Sarah Jenning, with whom she had played as a child when she was eight and Sarah was twelve. Almost uneducated—not exactly a drawback in those days—Sarah was very intelligent and intuitive, and above all beautiful. Eventually Princess Anne found Sarah Jennings the most exciting person in her dull and uneventful life. That was what Sarah wanted, because Sarah Jennings wanted John Churchill more than anything or anybody else in the world. After Sarah noticed Churchill, the rising young soldier noticed Sarah. In 1678 they were married and they rose together: John to become a duke, and Sarah his duchess. Sarah Churchill was born to rule and command, just like her husband—and her incredible ambition was matched by her husband's.

Sarah's own rise was not through a king but through a queen, James's daughter Anne. Sarah—with John away at war so often—began her own ascent by ruling Princess Anne; and then, after the return of her hero husband and the death of the Dutch usurper, by ruling *Queen* Anne and Britain together.

But there was a bad taste in the mouths of some important people.

Not everyone was enchanted by the high station of the duke of Marlborough. (He used that ducal name, now; no longer was he merely General John Churchill.) It was being whispered about that some of his great victories—Ramillies, Blenheim, Malplaquet—benefited Holland and Austria more than Britain, and it was remembered that it was William the Dutchman who had sent him there.

Suddenly his meteoric rise had begun its descent. Queen Anne, who had sought to relieve the stiffness that her regal presence might induce in her good friend Sarah and her brilliant husband, had invented "play names." For themselves Anne and George were Mr. and Mrs. Morley; Sarah and John, Mr. and Mrs. Freeman. Such infantile twaddle could not have enchanted Mrs. Freeman, while Mr. Freeman thankfully remembered battlefield engagements elsewhere. He was not charmed, however, when General Schomberg, William's second-in-command, met him with the greeting "Ach, you are der first three-star deserter I haff effer met." John, whose unusually effective diplomatic skills included a very thick skin, merely smiled.

William and Marlborough had worked well enough together in the wars aimed at breaking the military power of Louis XIV. Though they did not quarrel, they disliked and mistrusted each other—each having been knowingly a traitor. Though Churchill could betray, he was not skilled in the difficult art of treachery. Thus, while in William's pay he did not hesitate to make advances to James II, even though in Holland he had to be surrounded by the Usurper's agents. But when William lay dying he could think of no other general than Churchill to complete the work he had been unable to finish. Even in this estimate he was false; so far from "finishing" the destruction of the Sun King, he had not even been involved in it at the start.

But there is no question that John Churchill had become the Captain of the Age and that the famous Age of Anne was not so much due to the queen herself but to the splendor of his military record, unchallenged until the twentieth century writhed and bled in those two dreadful bloodbaths that were nothing less than the Civil War of the West. Queen Anne did treat her friend Mr. Freeman with splendid generosity, doing her utmost to further the public subscription for his magnificent Palace of Blenheim, named for his greatest victory. Before then, Mrs. Freeman fell from grace, and her handsome, dashing husband, the legendary "Corporal John," who had become really and truly the darling of the troops he commanded—as well as the debonair conqueror of all those who opposed him on the field of battle—also fell, but less precipitously.

❈ ❈ ❈

SARAH'S FALL WAS simply because Sarah's enemies had at last found an unexpected—yet unrivaled—opportunity to bring her low. Anne herself would never have noticed anything untoward when she found a place at court for her poor relation Mrs. Abigail Masham. To Anne it was nothing more than just one of those many acts of kindness by which she might brighten her day or banish the boredom of her queenly commitments.

But Mrs. Masham thought otherwise. Gradually, subtly, quietly, Mrs. Masham ingratiated herself with her relative. She showed the queen some captivating accomplishments: Her fund of court gossip was complete and deliciously salacious, she was devoted to Her Majesty without stint, but best of all, she was the finest tirewoman that Queen Anne had ever had. That is to say, Mrs. Masham, after a few discreetly careful months in Anne's employ, revealed to Her Majesty that until she came to court she had been very much in demand as a hairdresser and lady's maid. Thus Abigail had captured the queen's ear. Between her and the sorority of Sarah's enemies—and there were many, all of them earned—she supplanted the duchess of Marlborough in the queen's affection.

Now thoroughly aroused and beginning to remember Sarah's inability to conceal her contempt for her, and how she had so often smilingly explained it away as "Sarah's style," she stripped Sarah of all her offices and emoluments and removed her husband from command of the army, absolutely uncaring of what such a draconic decision might do to the fortunes of British arms abroad. Told that a rejoicing Louis XIV had said, "The affair of displacing the duke of Marlborough will do all for us we desire," she merely shrugged.

Sarah, naturally enough, was furious and heartbroken. John, upon his return to London, was his usually calm self. Without a word of protest or complaint, Sarah and John left the court and retired to the magnificence of the still uncompleted Blenheim Palace. The duke had had enough glory for a couple of conquerors, and both had more than enough of gold—for they had grown immensely rich in their service of the queen, her father, James II, and her brother-in-law, the detestable (to her) William. It may have been that the Marlboroughs anticipated that their great home would not be finished, that Anne might call a halt to construction of it. But she did not, and the Marlboroughs—Sarah and John, lovers still—were permitted to live happily into old age.

It was Queen Anne who was brokenhearted. She had lost Sarah: beautiful, exciting, dynamic Sarah, the one friend she had sought and found—and adored. Mrs. Masham was no replacement for Sarah, and

Her Majesty also suspected that she was in communication with Robert Harley, earl of Oxford and also Viscount Bolinbroke, once both close friends and heads of government but now bitter enemies. She was intriguing now only for herself—and she did emerge as *Lady* Abigail Hill Masham—but also for her brother, the ever-popular court favorite Jack Hill.

It was not so much the duke of Marlborough whom Anne missed, for she knew that if she needed him he would come, but Sarah! To this rapidly aging woman it was as though all were lost. Ascending the throne, seeing her armies conquering the Sun King's—even the recurring tragedy of all those unborn, stillborn, or dead children, now merely memories, a family of ghosts—even these would not have been as important to her as Sarah had been.

Without the Marlboroughs, Queen Anne surrendered herself to unhappiness. She complained constantly of her "gout." She had become a repulsive figure: huge, fat, in constant pain, her face red and spotted, negligent in her dress, tottering on her pair of sticks for support, her foot buried in poultices and bandages—absolutely uncaring of her appearance.

That was in 1712, when she was forty-seven. By then she had little recollection of marvelous Sarah. She thought of nothing but who should succeed her on the throne. There was her half brother, James III. She knew that he was a true Stuart, not the mythical, "warming pan" baby her father's enemies had concocted to discredit him further. She knew that James III was the true heir, that her sister and she were unwitting usurpers—and that her despicable brother-in-law was certainly one.

But Anne was also a Stuart, a lady, and the product of a deliberately fanatical Protestant childhood and youth, who knew as well that it was her sworn duty to protect and defend the Church of England, and the last thing she would do would be to accept her half brother, the Catholic James III, as the rightful king of Britain (even though he truly was) and thus deliver her kingdom into another frightful civil war. James III's uncompromising refusal had absolved her of any hateful agonizing over such a doleful duty. Besides, the Act of Settlement, which practically made of the British throne an outpost of the Hanoverian dynasty and its German princes, had to be considered.

That thought made her remember Prince George of Hanover, who had come to woo her unable to speak a word of English and who behaved like any Teutonic oaf—before going home in a purple rage. Anne did not like his mother, either—her cousin Electress Sophia—and because she didn't and Sophia was in ill health, then she—Anne—

would do her best not to die before her. Even so, it was being suggested by some of her ministers that George should come back to Britain and take his place in the House of Lords as the duke of Cambridge, and this unauthorized and insolent proposal had been made without consulting her.

Aroused from her unhappy and unhealthy torpor, an infuriated Queen Anne of Britain vowed that none of that gaseous Hanoverian tribe of beer-swilling sauerkraut eaters would ever set foot in England while she lived. Cousin Sophia also exploded in turn upon hearing of this declaration, rushing into her garden with her face reddening angrily as she strode back and forth until she suffered a stroke and sank into a heap—dying just two months before Queen Anne died, turning up her toes with perhaps a small smile in the year 1714 and at age forty-nine.

CHAPTER 20

Borders Aflame Again—
Québec Debacle

FROM A PURELY military standpoint it would seem that the advantage during the two Colonial Wars to come would lie with the French.

Feudal in structure and directed by the strong hand of a centralized government, New France was almost as military as Sparta. Its settlers or *habitants*, as the ordinary French people of Canada are called to this day, were not loosely scattered through the forests, as were their southern neighbors of New England. Rather, they were strung out in *côtes* (riverside settlements), under the leadership of the local *sieur* (leader), on either side of the St. Lawrence. A cannon shot from Montréal or Québec could send them sprinting for the forts. An order from the governor could muster them as militia.

Moreover, the French spent the five-year truce conferred upon America by the Peace of Ryswick in preparing for the second round of battle. New France's seaward flank had been secured by the restoration of Port Royal to the French crown. Now, with the power of the Iroquois broken by Frontenac, the way was clear to pen the English colonies between the Alleghenies and the sea. A fort had been built at Michilimackinac at the point where the waters of Lake Michigan enter Lake Huron, and another was erected at Detroit to command the confluence of Lake Huron and Lake Erie. Eventually there would be a chain of forts stretching westward from Montréal to the Mississippi; then, with the planting of a new French colony at the mouth of the Father of Waters, French lines of communication would reach from the Gulf of St. Lawrence to the Gulf of Mexico.

Such formidable activity did not seem to trouble the English colonists. More commercial than military, fragmented as a whole, and perhaps even looser in its democratic parts, the English society on the Atlantic was quite naturally reengaged in growth and gain. It was, at the beginning of the eighteenth century, a community of some quarter million souls. That was perhaps five times larger than the colony on the St. Lawrence, thanks not so much to greater immigration but to a birth rate that was already the astonishment of Europe.

In the South, tobacco made the Chesapeake aristocrats prosper; in the middle colonies it was land and trade; and in the North, trade alone. In the South and middle—all, except for New York, distant from Canada—there was little fear of French incursions, and little disposition to succor either New York or the North should they recommence. True enough, the South and the middle had Indian troubles, but nothing to compare to the howling hell that could burst on the northern borders upon a fresh outbreak of hostilities between England and France.

And that was to occur after Louis of France had cast his covetous eyes on the crown of Spain.

IN SIMPLIFIED TERMS, the War of the Spanish Succession broke out because King Louis claimed the Spanish throne for his grandson Philip of Anjou. In justice to the French king, however, he was all but forced to make that claim. Had Spain gone to the rival house of Austria, the old French fear of encirclement would have been realized. Nevertheless, England could never allow France to carry on the profitable trade between Spain and her colonies that was not assigned to English and Dutch merchants under cover of Spanish names. And then, after Louis followed up his justifiable claim by a series of unwarranted aggressions, and did exclude English merchants from the Spanish colonial trade, the war began. It was a commercial war to the death. Because King William had died of injuries suffered in that fall from his horse and his sister-in-law Anne now reigned in England, the Americans called it Queen Anne's War.

"I HAVE SENT NO WAR PARTY toward Albany," Philippe de Rigaud, the marquis de Vaudreuil and now the governor of Canada, reported to Paris, "because we must do nothing that might cause a rupture between us and the Iroquois; but we must keep things astir in the direction of Boston, or else the Abenakis will declare for the English."

Thus the political basis of the scalping war that was to befall New England, and also an explanation of why New York was to be spared similar torment during the first half-dozen years of Queen Anne's War.

Before Vaudreuil wrote those lines, New England had already sought to bind the Abenakis to peace. Governor Dudley of Massachusetts realized that the ravages of King William's War had left most border settlements, especially those of Maine, all but defenseless. Open hamlets and villages clustered on the edge of forests—or worse, between the woods and the sea; they were made for surprise. Their chief defenses were the "garrisons," or fortified houses pierced with firing loopholes and having upper stories that, projecting over the lower floor, enabled defenders to fire at attackers crouched below with ax or firebrand. Only a few villages were palisaded. And for some reason the borderers—a breed of men of whom half were industrious and half lazy, most were illiterate and all were hard-drinking—never thought of defending themselves until the war whoop came screeching from the forests, and then the grim trick was to get inside the garrison or the palisaded hamlet before the Abenakis did. As Dudley anticipated, some of them would not quite make it—and so, in June of 1702, a month after the outbreak of war, he summoned all the Abenaki tribes to a meeting at Casco in Maine.

Two of their chief sachems, known as Captain Samuel and Captain Bomazeen, told Dudley that French missionaries had come among them to incite them to the warpath but that they had refused. They were as "firm as mountains" in their friendship for Britain, and their love would endure "as long as the sun and moon." Then they proposed a war dance. Dudley agreed, wisely distributing the chiefs around him, much to the dismay of the Abenakis, who had loaded their muskets and were prepared to kill the British governor—if he would only give them a decent target. Forced to put on a joyous face, they finished the dance, and bound themselves by the Treaty of Casco. Dudley departed, and three days later a party of French and Indians who had come to capture him and his council put in a tardy appearance. A year later the scalping parties were ravaging Maine.

Throughout the late summer of 1703 they burned and killed from Casco to Kittery, beginning with the massacre at Wells. They were to torment these borders intermittently for ten years. In 1712 they came back to Wells to interrupt a wedding and to carry off the bridegroom for ransom. Captain Bomazeen, leader of the party with Captain Nathaniel and one of those two chiefs who had assured Dudley of his enduring love, well knew that a British scalp was worth more untouched than detached. The note that his captive sent his father is eloquent with the pathos of those terrible times:

SIR,—I am in the hands of a great many Indians, with which there is six captains. They say that what they will have for me is 50 pounds, and thirty pounds for Tucker, my fellow prisoner, in good goods, as broadcloth, some provisions, some tobacco pipes, Pomisstone [pumice stone], stockings, and a little of all things. If you will, come to Richmond's island in 5 days at farthest, for here is 200 Indians, and they belong to Canada.

If you do not come in 5 days, you will not see me, for Captain Nathaniel the Indian will not stay no longer, for the Canada Indians is not willing for to sell me. Pray, Sir, don't fail, for they have given me one day, for the days were four at first. Give my kind love to my dear wife. This from your dutiful son till death,

Edisha Plaisted

Eventually Plaisted was restored to his wife's bosom. Meanwhile, the village of Deerfield in western Massachusetts had been sacked. At the close of the year 1704 a war party had sallied from Canada under the partisan leader Hertel de Rouville. They had passed through an ordeal of their own: hooded, muffled figures trudging by day through gloomy, snow-still forests, by night burrowing in the drifts for warmth; gnawing on pemmican or tearing with chattering teeth at the freezing flesh of freshly killed animals; stumbling over snowswept hills or shuffling along the surface of frozen rivers. And then, shivering with cold and insane with hunger, they bided their time in the early morning dark until they could scramble up the snowdrifts piled like a ramp against Deerfield's palisades, vault over the pointed stakes, and sink their tomahawks into the brains of sleeping British. In all, 111 of Deerfield's 293 inhabitants were carried off captives and between 47 and 53 were killed. Many more were wounded, of course, so that fewer than half of the entire community escaped the wrath of Rouville's marauders.

As had happened in the time of Frontenac, the news of Deerfield did more to enrage than to terrify New England. Major Benjamin Church, the crusty old Indian fighter of King Philip's War, was so infuriated that he threw himself on his horse in Tiverton, Rhode Island, and rode all the way to Boston. He arrived with both himself and his horse in a froth and the poor beast staggering. Church had by then grown so stout that he could not pursue Indians into the woods unless accompanied by a sergeant detailed to hoist him over fallen trees. Though fat and frenetic and already sixty-five, Church was nevertheless the only veteran soldier in the colony. Governor Dudley at once agreed to let him lead an expedition of retaliation, giving him the rank of colonel. And, of course, Colonel Church, like Sir William Phips before him, turned his ire against the innocent inhabitants of Acadia.

Though separate from Canada and subordinate to her, Acadia was also accessible by sea. She and her smaller sister of Cape Breton Island would make constant expiation for the sins of the mother colony, inaccessible through forests filled with friendly Indians.

Church wanted to invest Port Royal, but Dudley refused permission. Instead, Church laid waste to Saint-Castin's fort and burned houses at Grand Pré. The chief event in that otherwise minor expedition seems to have occurred when Colonel Church was told that there were some Frenchmen in a hut who refused to come out. "Then knock them on the head!" he bellowed, and it was done.

That was in 1704. Three years later Boston decided to try again at Port Royal. Colonel John March of Newbury was placed in command. March seems to have received his commission by reason of his popularity with the men. Under him was the customary crowd of militia hastily recruited for the adventure, and between the civilian colonel and his "milishy" a fiasco was produced. The only officer of experience, a British engineer named Rednap, lost his temper and vowed that "it was not for him to venture his reputation with such ungovernable and undisciplined men and inconstant officers." Captain Stuckley, commander of a British frigate, agreed, with this lament: "I don't see what good I can do by lying here, when I am almost murdered by mosquitoes."

Colonel March reembarked his force and sailed back to Casco Bay, whereupon Governor Dudley's son, William, wrote home to report how disease and desertions were whittling the expeditionary force and how jealousies and rivalries were dividing the remnant. Dudley reacted like a true democratic politician. He sent March a committee!

Two inexperienced militia officers and a divinity student arrived at Casco, accompanied by a paltry reinforcement of a hundred men, and urged March to return to the attack. He did, with reluctant bad grace, arriving at Port Royal to find the French reinforced. His men went ashore and plunged into a brief fight, of which a chaplain named John Bernard has succinctly written: "A shot brushed my wig, but I was mercifully preserved. We soon drove them out of the orchard, killed a few of them, desperately wounded the privateer captain, and after that we all embarked and returned to Boston as fast as we could."

Colonel March might have been court-martialed, but a sizzling exchange of charges and countercharges among the expedition's leaders made it difficult to select a single scapegoat. However, he did not escape the jeers of his fellow citizens as he walked the streets, and it was some time before children stopped running after him, saying with a hiss:

"Wooden sword!"

THE SWORD OF THAT energetic and tenacious people whom the French called "les Bastonnais" was actually no such child's toy, and it was soon lifted again against the marauders from the North. Exasperated by continuing border outrages, Massachusetts decided to rid herself of this recurrent scourge by conquering Canada itself.

It was then that the perplexed and confused Governor Dudley turned to the adventurous son of a religious Scots family of strict and dedicated Presbyterians to lift them from the horns of their dilemma.

His name was Samuel Vetch.

SAMUAL VETCH HAD already entered American history in 1705, when he helped negotiate an exchange of prisoners between New France and the colonies of New England. He had also carried a letter from Governor Dudley to Governor Vaudreuil of New France proposing a treaty of neutrality between their respective colonies. Vaudreuil liked the idea, but nothing came of it because the French wanted the British excluded from fisheries in the Gulf of St. Lawrence and the Acadian seas; and the British refused because, as they claimed, they had been fishing there since days immemorial, which was not exactly true. Whatever, their emissaries still claimed that nothing would induce the people of New England to accept it. So Vetch had returned to Boston empty-handed, although on his visits to Québec he had seized the opportunity to disguise himself to study its defenses until, as he said, he knew them better than the French.

Such an adventure was typical of this dynamic and daring descendant of Scottish ministers known as Covenanters. His father, grandfather, three uncles, and one of his brothers became fanatic followers of the Presbyterian reformer John Knox as he expounded John Calvin's twin dogmas of predestination and the Bible as the rule of all doctrine. Samuel Vetch had been the lone family dissenter, rejecting the grim joy of denying pleasure to others, and choosing instead the freedom of life upon the sea or the carefree life of a soldier.

Both he and his brother William obtained commissions in the British Army, ending their career there when the Treaty of Ryswick brought the War of the Grand Alliance to its end. Next they became sea captains in the ill-fated Darién Scheme of 1695, which proposed a sea route across the Isthmus of Darién to secure the trade of the East.

William Vetch died at sea, and Samuel sailed instead to New York. Charming, handsome, representing himself as a world traveler, he married a daughter of Robert Livingston, one of the colony's chief men. Livingston's grandson Philip became a successful New York merchant who was also a founder of the present Columbia University and a signer of the Declaration of Independence. With such credentials, the adventurous Vetch decided to remain in New York, where he became active in the Albany Indian trade, and its accompanying smuggling into Montréal. In 1702 he moved to Boston and engaged in the same illegal traffic with Acadia. He was said to have sold guns and ammunition to French and Indians in that vast region. Vetch was charged twice with illegal trade, but with typical mental agility was able to avoid conviction on technicalities. Through his experiences in northern America Samuel Vetch became convinced that the only solution to the scalping war on New England's borders was the conquest of Canada itself.

In Boston at the beginning of Queen Anne's War, Vetch hurled himself into the atmosphere of excitement generated by a popular demand for the conquest of Canada. The bloody massacre at the village of Deerfield in 1704 had finally convinced the General Court of Massachusetts that, contrary to its instincts and past practice, instead of trying to solve the problem of the French and Indian raids itself, it would appeal to the mother country for the troops and ships needed for the conquest of Canada. What was needed was a vigorous representative at the court of Queen Anne—an agent experienced in war on land and sea: persuasive, sophisticated, and intelligent. Who better than the late arrival from New York, Captain Samuel Vetch? A more vigorous agent in the colony's plan of conquest could not be desired. Moreover, he not only conformed to the General Court's notion of what was needed in such a representative, he was also impetuous, energetic, daring, astute—and full of ambition.

In 1708 he sailed for Britain to plead New England's case. En route he expanded his plan to include the capture of Newfoundland and the expulsion of the Spanish from Florida. Then he wrote: "Her Majesty shall be sole empress of the vast North American continent."

Queen Anne, however, could be quite content with Canada alone, and Vetch returned to Boston in 1709 empowered to execute a campaign that was to end with himself installed as governor of the conquered province. Montréal was to be attacked by land and Québec by water. New York with 800 men, New Jersey with 200, Pennsylvania with 150, and Connecticut with 350 were to furnish a total of 1,500 men to be mustered at Albany by the middle of May. This force, under Colonel Francis Nicholson of New York, was to strike at Montréal by way of the Champlain route, while a British squadron bearing five regiments of regular troops—about 3,000 men—and 1,200 militia from Massachusetts, New Hampshire, and Rhode Island sailed up the St. Lawrence to invest Québec.

New York and Connecticut promptly furnished their troops. But New Jersey, far removed from the fires of border warfare, gave no men at all; and Pennsylvania, ruled by pacifist Quakers, supplied only £3,000, with the quaint proviso that the money should not be used to kill people.

Nevertheless, Colonel Nicholson was able to move up the Hudson with a force of 1,500 men. He built a stockade fort where Fort Edward now stands and cut a rough road to Wood Creek, which led to Lake Champlain. Then, while canoes were made and flatboats were brought upriver and dragged to Wood Creek, and after an inconclusive brush with a French force that seemed to return to Montréal as suddenly as it had appeared in New York, Nicholson sat down to await word of the arrival of the British fleet in Boston.

The New England soldiery encamped near Boston Harbor also awaited the British squadron. Each morning they arose and searched the horizon for the welcome sight of sails. Days became weeks and weeks months, and as the New Englanders fidgeted and Captain Vetch wrote imploring letters to Britain, a malignant dysentery broke out in Nicholson's camp far to the west. Men dropped by the scores. The able-bodied were busy tending the sick one day and burying their corpses the next.

At last, as autumn turned that dark green wilderness into a glowing riot of rubies and topazes, the disgusted Nicholson was forced to accept the fact that land operations against Canada were now no longer feasible, and he withdrew to Albany—his men cursing Vetch and swearing that he should be hanged. On October 11 the unfortunate Vetch received a letter from England advising him that the troops promised him had been diverted to Portugal instead.

Though deeply disappointed, the dogged New Englanders did not give up all hope of reprisal, and once again lowered their sights, from Québec to Port Royal. England was again persuaded to provide ships, and in 1710 Massachusetts again rounded up its semidrilled throng of farmers, mechanics, plowboys, clerks, and apprentices. The soldiers of 1709 were asked to enlist again, this time lured by the promise that they might keep the musket supplied them. Once again, when volunteers fell below quotas, the colony calmly drafted the reluctant. Seamen were impressed by the forefathers of that nation that would fight a war to protect its seamen from British press gangs, and the parents of those sturdy provincials who would make mock of the dainties and delicacies in the elaborate war train of Gentleman Johnny Burgoyne did not hesitate to vote twenty sheep, five pigs, one hundred fowls, and one pipe of wine for the table of General Nicholson. A dinner was held at the Green Dragon Tavern in honor of Nicholson, Vetch, and Sir Charles Hobby, the British squadron commander, and on the following morning, September 18, the expedition, numbering about forty ships, large and small, sailed from Boston for Acadia.

Six days later the British threaded the narrow entrance to Port Royal. One ship was driven on rocks and sunk with the loss of twenty-six men, but the others anchored safely in sight of the fort. Without interference from the French garrison under Subercase, the new governor of Acadia, Nicholson began putting his troops ashore. By the following day, September 25, the British had landed four battalions, comprised of four hundred British Marines and about fifteen hundred militia—no slight achievement in an era when transports were always at the mercy of the wind and the tides. They began moving against the fort, two battalions under Vetch attacking from the north, two under Nicholson from the south. The French harried them with cannons and small arms, but the British continued to move forward until they had occupied ground within artillery range of the fort. Then their own artillery was brought up and emplaced. On September 29, after a British bomb ketch had exchanged shots with Subercase's gunners, a French ensign arrived with a note from Port Royal's commander.

Subercase informed Nicholson that the ladies in the fort were distressed by the British cannonade. Would Nicholson be good enough to receive them into his camp? Nicholson would, "for the queen, my royal mistress, hath not sent me hither to make war on women." However, Nicholson detained the French ensign, who had not approached beating drums or allowed himself to be blindfolded—as the rules of war required—and sent a British officer to the fort instead. Subercase thereupon detained the British officer, and sent back a note that said:

> SIR,—You have one of my officers, and I have one of yours; so that now we are equal. However, that hinders me not from believing that once you have given me your word, you will keep it very exactly. On that ground I now write to tell you sir, that to prevent the spilling of both English and French blood, I am ready to hold up both hands for a capitulation that will be honorable to both of us.

The French ladies, therefore, remained within the fort, and on October 1, after a desultory—and probably perfunctory—exchange of shots, Subercase asked for terms. Once more the golden Bourbon lilies came fluttering down the flagstaff, the French soldiers—about 250 men—came marching out with drums rolling, colors flying, and arms reversed; the British troops went marching in, the Union Jack went hurrahing up the pole, the queen's health was drunk—and in the morning the distressed French ladies were treated to a breakfast by the British officers.

For the third time irate New Englanders had responded to Canada's border attacks by seizing the capital of Acadia. This time, however, the city that Nicholson renamed Annapolis Royal in honor of Queen Anne was to remain British. Eventually the entire province of Acadia would fall to the British crown.

However, one more expedition—mightiest of all in Queen Anne's War—was to be mounted against Québec.

THE DUKE OF Marlborough was falling out of favor.

He had been England's man of destiny, this military genius whose name was John Churchill. To him, as to his great descendant Winston Churchill twenty-four decades later, had fallen the charge of leading his country in her hour of need. King Louis had seemed invincible at the opening of the War of the Spanish Succession. The United Provinces of Holland were demoralized, the Empire of Austria was decrepit, and Britain, ruled by a sickly queen, seemed incapable of carrying the revived Grand Alliance to victory over France and Spain. Then Marlborough had appeared. The dread of his enemies and the delight of his men who called him "Corporal John," he had bested Turenne and Louis's other generals in a succession of victories of which the name Blenheim shines the brightest.

But Marlborough also had enemies at home. He was accused of peculations and intrigues. Although he was certainly not innocent of either charge, he was also, if judged by the easy standards of his day, far from being the blackguard his Tory foes described in their regular and rancorous attacks upon his reputation. Still, the Tories realized that they could only chip away at Marlborough's immense prestige. What was needed was a rival hero, a great victory of their own.

If France could be evicted from America, it could be shown that this triumph would be of greater value to Britain than all of Marlborough's victories, already being sneered at as of more benefit to Holland and Austria than to Britain. So the new Whig ministry looked across the sea to America. A force of twelve thousand men was to be raised to assault Québec. The sea command was given to an armchair admiral and woefully incompetent sailor named Sir Hovenden Walker, and the ground forces were to be led by Mrs. Abigail Masham's brother Jack. "Lady" Masham, as she called herself, was that same clever lady's maid who had so artfully insinuated herself into the confidence of Queen Anne that she supplanted the duchess of Marlborough as the new royal favorite. How the duke must have chuckled when he heard that Lady Masham's brother Jack Hill had been given command of the ground troops in the great amphibious assault upon the capital of New France. For it was Lieutenant General Churchill who had made Jack Hill—just as King James II had made Churchill—first making him a colonel to please Queen Anne, and then giving him a brigadier's star.

A man who had never heard a shot fired in anger—or known few moments of hardship—Jack Hill was nonetheless a man of great social grace and a courtier of undeniable charm, always invited to the great social events: regattas and horse races, a levee at Windsor Palace or a solemn investiture at St. Paul's, certainly the opening of a new gambling club—no matter, Jack Hill was always there: smiling, bowing, impeccably dressed as always, for in such important matters Jack was always considered expert.

That a social butterfly and an armchair admiral should be put in command of an operation of such immense importance was not so peculiar as it may seem to a student of modern military history. In the early eighteenth century, however, kings and queens still actually reigned—with their choices instantly approved—unlike modern public-relations sovereigns, designing their own uniforms or exchanging decorations like actors in a play.

Probably the only competent commander in the entire expedition was the colonial general Nicholson, who was again to move against Montréal by Lake Champlain.

Walker and Hill sailed into Boston in June 1711. They had nine ships of war, two bomb ketches, and about sixty transports and supply ships, carrying seven British infantry regiments, six hundred Marines, and artillery. After picking up fifteen hundred colonial militia, they steered for the St. Lawrence.

Although it was only August by the time they had reached it, Admiral Walker was already full of misgivings about the Canadian winter. He could think of nothing but ships stove in by freezing ice and men perishing of cold and hunger. "I must confess the melancholy contemplation of this," he was to write later, "for how dismal must it have been to have beheld the seas and the earth locked up by adamantine frosts, and swoln with high mountains of snow, in a barren and uncultivated region; great numbers of brave men famishing with hunger, and drawing lots who should die first to feed the rest."

However, calamities of a different order were to afflict Walker's fleet. Because of his own poor seamanship, eight transports and two other ships were driven ashore and wrecked during a fog. Perhaps nine hundred soldiers and seamen perished, and a witness has written: "It was lamentable to hear the shrieks of the sinking, drowning, departing souls." Shaken, Walker called a council of war. Both he and Jack Hill were eager for an excuse to withdraw. They found it in the ship captains' report that they could not sail up the St. Lawrence without experienced pilots. Walker was aware that Sir William Phips had done that very thing thirty years earlier; nevertheless, in the face of opposite—and indignant—counsel by such colonials as Samuel Vetch, he sailed back the way he had come.

At the foot of Wood Creek, prepared to enter Lake Champlain, General Nicholson heard the disgraceful news. "Roguery!" he cried, tearing off his wig and hurling it to the ground. "Treachery!" he screamed, stamping on it. Recovering his composure, he ordered his forts burned and marched his force of twenty-three hundred men back to Albany again.

Walker's ordeal was not quite ended. As the nonvictorious British fleet sailed slowly up the Thames, a sailor attempting to steal gunpowder accidentally blew up the flagship, *Edgar*. Five hundred more men were lost. Thus was the shameful conclusion of the most ambitious of all projects to conquer Canada. The commanders sent out to eclipse the glory of the great Marlborough had accepted defeat without unsheathing their swords, the "Te Deum" was again chanted on the cliff above Québec, and the Tories were more than ever eager to end the war.

This they did a year later.

PART V

War of the Austrian Succession,
1740–1748 (King George's War)

CHAPTER 21

The "Milishy" Take Louisbourg

THE TREATY OF UTRECHT, which ended the War of the Spanish Succession, made Britain the mistress of the seas.

Britain, Holland, and Austria had fought to prevent the union of France and Spain under a Bourbon king, but the war ended with a grandson of Louis of France firmly seated on the Spanish throne. Nevertheless, both France and Spain were exhausted. France was forced to cede Acadia, Hudson's Bay, and Newfoundland to Britain, while Spain handed over Gibraltar at the mouth of the Mediterranean, and the sentinel of Minorca inside it. Both France and Spain granted Britain important trade concessions, while Spain, by leasing to Britain the slave trade to Latin America, indicated to what woeful depths her once-proud fleets had sunk.

The British lion had not only obtained its customary share, it also had grown stronger at sea at the expense of its ally—but foremost maritime rival—the Dutch Republic. Holland had supplied only three-eighths of the naval forces, against Britain's five-eighths, but 102,000 soldiers against Britain's 40,000. By accident or design, the Dutch exhausted themselves in an unfamiliar land war while the British Navy grew stronger upon the sea. Queen of the waves she was, wrote the great naval historian Captain A. T. Mahan, "not only in fact, but also in her own consciousness."

Posted now in the Mediterranean, America, and the West Indies, she was prepared to build that far-flung empire that was to dazzle the world for two and a half centuries to come. She was to achieve this because she was conscious of the unique value of sea power, as her rivals in the House of Bourbon were not. Her conscious policy was the destruction of the French and Spanish navies and the strengthening of her own. Ports and harbors and strategic islands, not kingdoms, were the objects of her desire; and she sought them as outlets for trade and as bases for her fleets. She could cross no enemy's land frontier, but she could strike at them all from the sea. Without borders of her own, the sea gave her the world for her neighbor.

That was why, in 1739, Britain declared war on Spain in that prelude to the third round of the Anglo-French war for empire that has gone into history under the comical name of the War of Jenkins's Ear.

WHILE OPENLY ALLIED with Britain, France had made a secret agreement with Spain that said: "Whenever it seems good to both nations alike, the abuses that have crept into commerce, especially through the British, shall be abolished; and if the British make objection, France will ward off their hostility with all its strength by land and sea."

Spain's method of abolishing abuses was to seize British ships and mistreat or impress their crews. This has been described by the West India merchants who petitioned Commons in 1737, claiming:

> For many years past their ships have not only frequently been stopped and searched, but also forcibly and arbitrarily seized upon the high seas, by Spanish ships fitted out to cruise, under the plausible pretext of guarding their own coasts; that the commanders thereof, with their crews, have been inhumanly treated, and their ships carried into some of the Spanish ports and there condemned with their cargoes, in manifest violation of the treaties subsisting between the two crowns; that the remonstrances of His Majesty's ministers at Madrid receive no attention, and that insults and plunder must soon destroy their trade.

To a seafaring race regarding the sea as their lake, such insults were infuriating; and when some of the seamen who had been imprisoned or tortured by their Spanish captors were brought to the bar of the House of Commons to recite their ordeals, the anger of the people— carefully nourished by the war party in Britain—swelled to an outraged roar. One of the sailors who testified was a certain Jenkins, master of a merchant brig. He told the Commons that a Spanish officer had torn off one of his ears and told him to take it back to the king, his master, and to say that he also would have lost his royal ears had he been in Jenkins's place.

To avenge the honor of the dull-witted, money-loving German who sat on the British throne under the style of George II, king of Britain, war was declared on Spain. But the British had only jumped the gun. In a few more months she would be joined by her old allies of Austria and Holland in the War of the Austrian Succession.

❊ ❊ ❊

IT WAS THE new Kingdom of Prussia that began the war.

A mere duchy on the marches of Poland, Prussia had been ruled by the margrave of Brandenburg under the title of king *in* Prussia; but in 1701 the margrave known as Frederick I proclaimed himself king *of* Prussia, that is, of Brandenburg-Prussia. However, this new sovereign state was always to be known as Prussia, and it had demonstrated its military prowess—as well as its hatred of France—in the late War of the Spanish Succession. After Utrecht, Frederick I died, to be succeeded by his twenty-four-year-old son Frederick William.

Energetic, brutal, and uncouth, Frederick William was to infect Prussia with that spirit of merciless militarism that, organizing the German peoples under a single rule, was to make France pay again and again for the sins of the armies of Louis XIV, while giving birth to the twin horrors of global conflicts that convulsed the world in the twentieth century.

Frederick William was obsessed with his army. He stinted every other department of state to finance it. He conscripted all nobles of military age and trained them to command it, and he filled its ranks by direct impressment or slave hunts. His first love was his regiment of giant grenadiers (which he would never risk in battle), and he kidnapped men in countries as far distant as Ireland to supply it. No unusually tall man was safe from Prussia's slave gangs; even Abbé Bastiani was sandbagged while saying Mass in an Italian church and dragged off to Prussia. Tall girls were also enslaved, to mate with the grenadiers.

Although Frederick William's army of eighty thousand men was not formidable in size, it was still dreaded for its discipline. Training was so brutal that men preferred the battlefield to the barracks. Not even Frederick William's own children escaped the inhuman hectoring of this despotic drill sergeant. On one of these fourteen offspring, Karl Frederick, he lavished particular indignities. He made him his steward and threw plates at his head; he thrashed him with a cane in public; he spat in his food to prevent his eating too much; he tried to strangle him with a curtain cord; and then, after taunting him for submitting to such treatment, he imprisoned him for attempting to run away from it. Still not satisfied, the king had his son condemned to death, and when his councillors refused to acquiesce in the sentence, he shot his friend Katte before his son's eyes. At last Frederick William died. On May 31, 1740, while those around him sang the hymn "Naked I Came into the World and Naked I Shall Go," the dying king roused himself sufficiently to mutter: "No, not quite naked; I shall have my uniform on." Then the father of Prussian militarism breathed his last, and the son who would be known as Frederick II and then, deservedly, as the Great, lifted the sword his father had forged and swung it against Austria.

THE AUSTRIAN EMPEROR, Charles VI, also died in 1740, bequeathing his personal dominions to his daughter Maria Theresa. His will had been guaranteed in advance by the chief powers of Europe, but not a sovereign kept his word. Led by young Frederick of Prussia, who almost at once marched into Maria's province of Silesia and seized it, a pack of bejeweled jackals flocked forward to despoil the beautiful young queen. After Frederick came Spain, Bavaria, and then France. Britain, ever anxious to preserve the balance of power as well as George's Hanoverian holdings, rushed to Austria's side. Holland followed. Maria Theresa herself fought back. Appearing before her wild Hungarian nobles with her child in her arms, she appealed for their help; and they clashed their swords together and thundered: "We will die for our king, Maria Theresa!"

The conflict that the colonists called King George's War had begun.

THE FIRST BLOW STRUCK for King George in America came from the new colony that had been named Georgia in his honor.

In the summer of 1740 James Oglethorpe, Georgia's founder, decided to evict the Spanish from the first European settlement in North America: St. Augustine. Then Florida would fall to the Union Jack and the Atlantic seaboard would be British from the Bay of Fundy to the Gulf of Mexico. Certainly Oglethorpe felt himself qualified to lead such an expedition. He had served under the famous Prince Eugen as a boy, and had distinguished himself at the siege of Belgrade. He had distinguished himself perhaps still more during a celebrated drinking bout with a prince of Würtemberg.

When the prince deliberately flicked the dregs of his wineglass into the young ensign's face, Oglethorpe paused momentarily. If he challenged the prince immediately, he might risk being branded as a quarrelsome youth with no respect for noble birth; if he accepted the insult, he would be considered a coward. Smiling evenly, Oglethorpe said: "My prince, that is a good joke; but we do it much better in Britain." Then he threw the contents of his entire glass in the prince's face, much to the approval of an old general, who growled, "That was well done, my prince—for you began it."

Such a man was obviously more than a match for the stiff-necked Spaniards to the south. Having barred all Papists from Georgia,

Oglethorpe desired to disenfranchise the rest of North America as far as Havana. But the Spaniards foiled him. They reinforced St. Augustine from Havana, and Oglethorpe's motley of two thousand British and Indians sailed back to Georgia sunburned and hungry.

Three years later, the commander at St. Augustine, Don Manuel de Monteano, attempted a reverse expedition. He hoped to expel the heretics from the weak colony that stood as a buffer between New Spain and the rich and populous Carolinas. Even Virginia—and thus the entire South—would be annexed to Spain.

Monteano's force was much larger than Oglethorpe's had been. About fifty ships carrying about six thousand men and artillery sailed up to St. Simon's Island off the Georgia coast. Here Oglethorpe had entrenched himself with a few thousand American rangers and wild Highlanders from Scotland, and here he proved himself a more capable commander on defense than on offense. Though outnumbered, he took ship and struck boldly at the Spanish vessels, after which he returned to land, forced Monteano into attacking him piecemeal, destroyed the pieces, and finally frightened the Spaniards off with a bogus letter that—planted on Monteano by an "escaped" Spanish soldier bribed for the occasion—warned of the approach of a huge British fleet.

The first and only land clash of any consequence between Britain and Spain in North America had ended in a stalemate. There was to be no more colonial fighting under the southern sun. Henceforth, the colonial wars would be fought within the familiar gloom of primeval forests or the mistbound coasts of the North.

LOUIS XIV HAD hated to give up Acadia. He had even offered to bar French fishermen from those Newfoundland coasts they had patrolled for more than a century if the British would allow him to keep those lands now called Nova Scotia. But all that he could obtain by way of compromise was the restoration of Cape Breton Island, just a few miles east of Acadia. Even in this, the British ministers at Utrecht were not wise. True enough, the new Tory ministry that had entered power upon the disgrace of Marlborough was anxious to pick, as quickly as possible, the fruits of his victories in the War of the Spanish Succession. But in relinquishing Cape Breton Island they at once destroyed the military value of Acadia.

King Louis saw that the island wilderness was the true guardian of the St. Lawrence, and before he died he caused a port to be fortified to that end, and against the day when war would be resumed and France might attack New England and attempt to recover Acadia.

The new port, which was to grow into a fishing village of four thousand persons, to become a harbor so well-defended and a privateering refuge so secure that it would be called the "Dunkirk of America," was named Louisbourg in the king's honor.

"PERHAPS," AN UNKNOWN but disconsolate *habitant* of Louisbourg was to write, "the British would have let us alone if we had not first insulted them."

The insults were the merciless scalping warfare again unleashed along the New England borders, as well as French attacks on Canseau and Annapolis Royal. The first had fallen, but the second had resisted; and both had shown New England that Acadia was at the mercy of French power based in Louisbourg.

Governor William Shirley of Massachusetts resolved to destroy that power. He swore the General Court to secrecy and proposed that the Bay Colony alone mount an expedition against Louisbourg. After a few days of consideration, the members rejected Shirley's proposal. It would be too expensive for Massachusetts alone. Besides, the ordinary people were up in arms. One of the members of the court had prayed too loud for divine guidance; his entreaties had been overheard, and the sturdy democrats of the North, at once understanding the meaning of the closed doors, were almost as quick to resent it.

Shirley was downcast for about as long as his aggressive and ambitious nature would permit. He prevailed upon the General Court to reconsider. Encouraged by reports of mutiny among the soldiers at the Louisbourg garrison, it was agreed to invite the other colonies as far south as Pennsylvania to join them. As was customary, all but the New Englanders declined. Even Rhode Island, nursing its old grudge against the persecutor of Roger Williams, would eventually fail to provide any men in time for combat. Of the force finally assembled, 3,300 would come from Massachusetts, 516 from Connecticut, and 454 from New Hampshire, of whom 150 were paid by Massachusetts. Some of these men—particularly the hardy borderers from Maine—had fought in the recent war against the Norridgewock Indians; but few, if any, had the sort of experience required for siege warfare against the ramparts and casemented batteries of a fortified town.

"Fortified towns are hard nuts to crack," Benjamin Franklin had written to his brother in Boston, "and your teeth are not accustomed to it. But some seem to think that forts are as easy taken as snuff."

Indubitably good advice, but it came, unfortunately, from a man then sojourning among those Quakers whom the Puritans had once persecuted as waverers from the True Path, and whom they now detested as purring hypocrites who would not hesitate to trick the Delaware out of huge tracts of land, but would not, on the excuse of their pacifism, have the courage to evict them—rather hiring the bloodthirsty Iroquois to carry out that unpleasant contradiction of their tenets. Counsel from colonies remiss in their duty to both God and king was certainly not to be heeded. Furthermore, tough nut or no, Louisbourg and its Papists had already been consigned to the jaws of the Lord.

What Cotton Mather once called "the wheel of prayer" was whirring night and day. The very man whom Governor Shirley had appointed to lead the expedition was known to be a pious man of God. William Pepperrell, a highly successful merchant as well as a man of extreme good sense—though no military experience, as he would himself declare—counted many clergymen among his friends. With him at the very moment Shirley appointed him a lieutenant general was none other than George Whitefield, that squint-eyed breather of fire whose archangelic voice had summoned New England to its Great Awakening. At the moment that revivalist frenzy seemed to be subsiding, and another of Pepperrell's clerical friends was already complaining, "The heavenly shower [is] over; from fighting the devil they must turn to fighting the French."

Pepperrell himself would have preferred to continue with the devil, for he was aware that his forces included not an officer of experience, not even an engineer. Nevertheless, he was persuaded to accept. Whitefield, meanwhile, was persuaded to supply a motto. He offered *Nil desperandum Christo duce* (Despair not in Christ the leader). Old Parson Moody, he of the iron lungs and marathon sermons, also joined the crusade against the Antichrist. He brought along an ax to hew down his abominable altars.

Such was the crusading character of the expedition, and it would be a grave mistake for descendants of these crusaders to stand three centuries off and belittle or deride them. It has, of course, become fashionable to do so, perhaps because the very virility and hardihood of these forebears revolts a generation less robust and convinced that trial and adversity are not so much the schools of manhood but rather social sins to be erased and replaced by comfort and convenience from cradle to the coffin. But the fact is that these Puritans were truly exalted. If they were fanatic, they were also fervent; if they seem naive, they were really idealists; and if they were violent, it was—to their mind—in the cause of the highest virtue.

Somehow the *Nil desperandum* of Parson Whitehead is considered amusing by those sons of Puritanism who, having lost the faith of their fathers, would now like to get rid of their fathers as well. True, there is irony in a Protestant preaching a crusade against Catholics and using all the paraphernalia of True Faith to do it. But in a little trading republic as united and fervent in its faith and institutions then as Christendom had been seven centuries earlier, Whitehead's slogan was just as powerful and compelling as the cry of *Deus vult!* (God wills it!), which swept Europe into the First Crusade.

Nor is Parson Moody to be smiled at by his more refined descendants. His ax was to him as real an instrument of God's wrath as the mace of the Crusader before him. He was convinced, not just that the Lord was on his side, but that he was on the Lord's side. His attitude may have been what is today called a "psychological fact," but whether or not God truly exists, whether or not He was truly for Protestants against the Papists, or vice versa, as the French in Louisbourg also thought, it was this conviction that had brought Parson Moody and General Pepperrell and ninety ships and forty-two hundred raw recruits to Louisbourg on the morning of April 28, 1745.

The French, being a wise and practical race, refrained from laughing and prepared to defend themselves.

To enter Louisbourg basin would have been suicide. Even the warships of the British squadron that had joined the colonists would not have attempted it. Instead, they blockaded the port.

To the east or the right of the town itself was a small entrance barely a half mile wide. Commanding this was the "Island Battery," mounted on a rocky island to the west or left of the entrance. Directly ahead of the entrance on the basin's north shore was the "Grand Battery." Ships attempting to force the harbor would be raked port and prow. So General Pepperrell sagely decided to put his troops ashore at Flat Point, three miles west of the town.

Chevalier Duchambon, governor of Louisbourg, sent 120 men to repulse them. Although Duchambon had 560 regulars and 1,400 militia, he probably did not send a larger force because he could not rely on rough and untried conscripts of soldiers ready to mutiny over pay and rations. So a Captain Morpain led his handful of defenders to Flat Point. They dug in, awaiting the British rowing toward them. Suddenly the British veered away, as though they dared not risk the surf boiling over Flat Point's rocky coast. Captain Morpain relaxed. He began to flatter himself on a bloodless repulse. But then, to his dismay, he saw that more British boats had been lowered away and that the reinforced body was rowing madly for Freshwater Cove, another two miles to the west.

Morpain and his French soldiers went flying up the coast. But they were too late. The invaders were already ashore. Turning, they fell upon the French, killed six and captured six, and routed the rest against only two of their own men wounded. More and more boats came bobbing through the surf, and soon General Pepperrell had a firm beachhead.

Louisbourg had been flanked.

ON MAY 2 Captain William Vaughan, a bold though sometimes rash man, led four hundred troops through the hills to the northwest of the town. His men saluted Louisbourg with three rousing cheers, and the inhabitants, surprised by the ragged and disorderly appearance of this crowd of colonists, were also startled by their vigor. Then Vaughan marched to the hills to the rear of the Grand Battery and put a supply of naval stores to the torch. Thick, oily coils of smoke swirled skyward, to the dismay of the occupants of Louisbourg—and to the unseemly fright of the troops holding the Grand Battery.

Imagining that Vaughan had come to attack them, they hastily spiked their guns, threw gunpowder into the well, and withdrew to the town in boats—leaving thirty of the king's good cannons to fall into the hands of Vaughan, who quickly occupied the battery in their absence. Soon a squad of soldier-mechanics had drilled out the cannons' spiked touchholes, and, in the words of the *habitant* of Louisbourg, "The enemy saluted us with our own cannon, and made a terrific fire, smashing everything within range."

The ragged rabble the ignorant civilian Pepperrell commanded was amazingly constant and cheerful. They had built an encampment near Freshwater Cove, making tepees by stretching old sails over poles, or building sod huts with spruce boughs for roofs. They had unloaded boats by wading up to the waist through ice-cold surf, and at night they threw themselves down, dripping wet, on soggy ground, discharging the mists and chills of the thaw.

Next, in tatters and sometimes barefoot, they began dragging Pepperrell's cannons eastward toward Louisbourg. The first attempt to move a gun through the intervening marsh resulted in the loss of the piece, which vanished in the slime. Sledges of timber sixteen by five feet were then made; cannons were placed on top of them, and teams of two hundred men harnessed in breast straps and rope traces, sloshing through knee-deep mud and mush, began hauling them over the marsh. But this could only be done under cover of night or thick fog. Toiling "under almost incredible hardships," as Pepperrell was to write in admiration, they got the guns in place.

Battery after battery was planted under the strangely languorous nose of Chevalier Duchambon. Louisbourg was hammered from the west, northwest, north, and northeast. In all, the bellowing of five new batteries had been added to the cannonade issuing from the captured Grand Battery. Still Duchambon sent forth no sallies to destroy the guns that were destroying him. Perhaps he still feared mutiny, although mutiny would seem less dangerous than the torrents of balls that were shredding Louisbourg's walls and forcing a terrified citizenry to take refuge within stifling casements.

It may also have been that Duchambon was aware that the New England army was in dire straits. Their food supply was low, ammunition was running out, Louisbourg's cannons and the accurate small-arms fire of the French soldiers had whittled their ranks, and dysentery and fever had ravaged the remainder. In all, Pepperrell had only twenty-one hundred men fit for duty. The disadvantages that always work against the besiegers in siege warfare were beginning to work in Duchambon's favor. And if the promised reinforcements arrived, he might still be saved.

SHE WAS THE *Vigilant*, carrying 64 guns and 560 men and munitions and stores for the relief of Louisbourg. The marquis de la Maisonfort commanded her. He was confident that the guns of the Island Battery would hold off any English warships while allowing him to enter the harbor.

On May 19 the *Vigilant* came upon a small British cruiser. The little Britisher attacked! *Vigilant* replied with broadsides. The cruiser fled, still firing; *Vigilant* pursued, and found that she had been led straight into the massed guns of a British squadron. Maisonfort and his men fought gallantly, but after eighty men were lost, the French commander was forced to strike his colors.

British seapower had saved Pepperrell's army and doomed the French. "We were victims devoted to appease the wrath of Heaven," wrote the *habitant*, "which turned our own arms into weapons for our enemies."

Nevertheless, Duchambon would not know that he was doomed until after the British had also incurred the heavenly wrath.

THE IMPETUOUS CAPTAIN Vaughan was certain that the Island Battery was the key to Louisbourg. Capture it, and British troops could enter the harbor while Pepperrell's men stormed the town from the land. Vaughan proposed this before news of *Vigilant*'s fall reached Pepperrell.

After midnight of May 23, about three hundred men clambered into boats beached off the Grand Battery. It was a dark night, and they hoped to gain the Island Battery undetected. They used paddles to make no noise. A rising wind also covered their approach. The leading boats reached the island's breakers, drove boldly through them, and scrambled ashore—still unseen.

And then they began to cheer!

"Hip-hip, hooray! Hip-hip, hooray! Hip-hip, hooray!"

Only the high-hearted military amateurs of the British colonies could have entered battle as though expecting a typical "milishy meeting," with refreshments, rum, beer, or cider—after a leisurely half-hour drill.

Yankee-doodle keep it up
Yankee-doodle dandy
Mind the music and the step—
And with the girls be handy!

It is possible—even probable—that for a few long, disbelieving moments the French gunners and musketeers inside their impregnable Island Battery could not really believe what they were hearing. But then, recovering quickly, the Island Battery "blazed with cannon, swivels, and small arms." A withering fire plunged into these foolish commandos, and into the following boats piling up on the shore. The British fought back bravely. They even succeeded in placing a dozen scaling ladders against the walls of the fort, but with daybreak it was hopeless to fight on. Those who did not escape surrendered, to the number of 119. In all, British losses were 189, or more than half of the attacking force.

The only pitched battle had ended in a British defeat, although Louisbourg was already undone. The town's fate was sealed when Pepperrell more wisely decided to mount another battery on Lighthouse Point, across the harbor entrance from Island Battery. The lighthouse guns gradually reduced the island to impotence. All was in readiness for a final land-sea assault jointly commanded by General Pepperrell and Commodore Peter Warren, commander of the British squadron. It was to commence on June 15. On that day Captain Joseph Sherburn, at the advance battery, wrote in his diary: "By 12 o'clock we had got all our platforms laid, embrazures mended, guns in order, shot in place, cartridges ready, dined, gunners quartered, matches lighted to return their favours, when we heard their drums beat a parley; and soon appeared a flag of truce, which I received midway between our battery and their walls. . . ."

Duchambon was asking for terms. Two days later Louisbourg was occupied by the British. "Never was a town more mal'd with cannon and shells," Pepperrell wrote to Governor Shirley, "neither have I red in History of any troops behaving with greater courage."

He was right. The disorderly rabble had taken a fortified city with the bold precision of troops trained in siege warfare. Pepperrell's New Englanders had won the only outstanding engagement of King George's War. True, there would be skirmishes to follow, and a French fleet more powerful than the British one that Admiral Walker and Jack Hill had led to disaster and disgrace in the last war was to encounter ordeals even more dreadful and to achieve as little in its attempt to re-take Louisbourg and succor Canada.

Even if it had done so, its success would have been superfluous, for much to the indignant disgust of *les Bastonnais,* the Peace of Aix-la-Chapelle, which ended the War of the Austrian Succession in 1748, had returned Louisbourg to the French crown.

CHAPTER 22

George II—British Colonies Explode

THE GEORGE IN "King George's War" that a new generation of British colonists in America was serving in the War of the Austrian Succession was not quite the murderous bully and vulgar lover of fat women that his father—George I—had been; and there actually were a few good or decent things that could be said about him. First, he seems actually to have loved his wife; second, he was undoubtedly brave, having at age twenty-five led a cavalry charge at the Battle of Oudenarde. Unhorsed, he continued to fight on foot. Third, when he was sixty, he did practically the same thing at the Battle of Dettengen; fourth, he tried fairly hard to be a conscientious king of Britain, as his father had never done, saying kind words to the people and not constantly making unfavorable comparisons between them and the doltish clods of Hanover.

In a positive sense, George II of Hanover was—like his father, son, and grandson, all of whom became kings of Britain—quite mad.

It is likely that among these four Georges, the second one was the least attractive physically. He was a small, strutting man with a deep purplish-red face and a backward-slanting forehead almost as extreme as a ski slope. Short and plump with the puffy, gargoylelike features of the typical Hanoverian monarch, he was nevertheless surprisingly neat, dapper, and orderly, although somewhat neurotically exact and concise in his records, which he always imagined were being "cooked" by some disloyal nobleman. Although he spoke English—something his father had never even attempted—it was with a heavy Teutonic accent.

One of the best descriptions of George II comes from Lord Chesterfield, who knew him for forty years but who was no more kind to him than he had been to his father. "He had not better parts than his father, but much stronger animal spirits, which made him produce or communicate himself more. Everything in his composition was little, and he had himself all the weaknesses of a little mind, without any of the virtues—or even the vices—of a great one. He loved to act the king but mistook the part. . . . Avarice, meanest of passions, was his ruling one; and I never knew him deviate into any generous action."

It is possible that the Second George—being so thoroughly hated by his father—was inclined to imitate him in a decidedly love-hate relationship. He knew that his mother—who had been the lover of the Swedish von Königsmark—was for her infidelity locked up in a prison for the rest of her life, with her children taken from her and her paramour quietly murdered. It has also been suggested that Königsmark had not met with foul play but rather had been kidnapped and deported to America. Certainly no one ever knew what happened to him, except that the court knew to a man that George I of England, elector of Hanover, had always been thorough.

His son was rather more absentminded, if not intentionally so. At the first meeting of his council, the archbishop of Canterbury handed King George II his father's will. With a vague nod he put it "in his pocket and it was seen no more"—just like Königsmark. That was in 1727, when George was forty-four and had ascended the throne. When he was much younger—in 1705—he had married Caroline of Anspach, a princess lower than he in station but much above him in maturity and intellect. She also seems to have been warm-hearted, "a rare thing as times go," a contemporary remarked. Caroline took an interest in politics and also in handling the king like a manager with a prizefighter. Thus almost all his ideas first issued from his wife's mouth. Caroline was not in the least upset by George's fascination for his mistresses—which was customary and accepted among royalty in those days—wanting only an occasional copulation herself just to keep the queenly franchise, and a steady issue of children. Actually, mistresses then were like fixtures of the royal household: a valet, majordomo, or page, as well as a symbol of the master's sexual prowess.

For some strange reason she shared George's hatred for their son, Frederick Louis, Prince of Wales. After all, George's own father had borne him nothing but enmity. Why should the present George duplicate it? Perhaps because Frederick Louis was small, frail, and ugly, his face the perfection of all those repulsive Hanoverian features: the low, receding forehead, the bulging eyes with their baggy eyelids, the thick, long nose and pouting mouth above a flabby, swinging chin. Yet listen to his father: "My dear firstborn is the greatest beast in the world, and I most heartily wish he were out of it." And from his mother!: "Fred is a nauseous beast and he cares for nobody but his nauseous little self!"

Although George spoke guttural English, he still yearned to live in Hanover, to which he constantly repaired, leaving Caroline to rule as queen. On his return it was clear to Caroline that his disdain for the British had been nourished both by his dislike of them and his fondness for things Hanoverian: polkas, Lutheranism, beer, sauerbraten mitt kaduffelglaze, oompah bands, large-breasted, obliging barmaids—and two thousand years of German humor.

His declaration of detestation for the customs of his subjects, frequently repeated, was: "No British cook could dress a dinner, no British confectioner set out a dessert, no British player could act, no British coachman drive, no British jockey ride, nor were any British horses fit to be ridden or drive. No Briton could enter a room and no British woman dress herself." Though he pretended to have a love for the arts, when Hogarth dedicated a painting to him, he cried aloud in his angry German accent: "Damn der Bainters, und der Boets, too!"

George's besetting sin was avarice. A miser, he was always counting and recounting his money, leaving vacancies at court unfilled to save money. He did give Queen Caroline a gift of a matched team of huge Hanoverian horses but used them mostly for himself, and charged Caroline for their fodder. Yet, to his great prime minister, Sir Robert Walpole, whom he admired for his financial acumen, he did give a diamond. On closer examination, Sir Robert saw that it was cracked.

It is possible that George and Caroline detested their son because he had written *Histoire de Prince Tiki,* a biting caricature of his parents. This vengeful expression of his own enmity toward his mother and father might have led his father to evict Frederick and his new wife, Princess Augusta of Saxe-Gotha, from Kensington Palace, vowing never to speak to him again. He kept his word. But sometimes, at unexpected meetings between king and queen and prince and princess, Caroline would allow Frederick to hold her hand, but would not look at or speak to him. In revenge, the despised Prince of Wales joined his father's political opposition and made open allies of such degenerates as Sir Francis Dashwood, whose libertine cronies met semiannually at his splendid estate for week-long sexual orgies. At each get-together the high point was customarily reached when a coach filled with prostitutes dressed in nun's habits came clattering up the drive, the occupants bursting out both doors but not yet in the proper uniform for the sport that would soon begin. Greeted with glad cries of welcome, they were stripped for their own freedom of movement—and then "raped."

Even when George's beloved Caroline lay dying, George forbade

his son from visiting her; and when she did gasp her last after an ex-
cruciating ten-day agony, this cruel epitaph for the reign of herself and
her husband was posted on a placard at the Exchange, declaring:

O Death where is thy sting—
To take the Queen and leave the King?

DURING THE FIRST five or six decades of the century, the Anglo-French
struggle for possession of Canada continued to be a succession of skirmishes and raids, sea fights and massacres. No really decisive battle
was fought until the defeat and death of General Edward Braddock at
the hands of the French during the Battle of the Monongahela River.
At the same time—again between the French and the British—something like a population contest was being resolved heavily in favor of
Britain.

During the preceding century of the 1600s King Louis XIV of
France, through his energetic and dedicated servant in Canada—Intendant Jean-Baptiste Talon—had sought to populate New France by
inducing many men and women of the sturdy peasant classes to immigrate there from France. All this was financed by Louis from his
own personal fortune, and always among *unmarried* candidates for
immigration. This, together with the brutal winter above the mighty
St. Lawrence River, ultimately defeated his attempt, much to the regret
of Louis; for to have raised his beloved colony's population from a
miserable handful of 2,500 under the great Sieur Samuel de Champlain to an ultimate peak of 25,000 at the end of the seventeenth century was at best a very meager success. It did continue to rise, but very
slowly, so that by the time of the eruption of the Seven Years' War
(1756–1763), in all of New France there were a mere 80,000 colonials,
and of these only 55,000 in the vicinity of the St. Lawrence, the remainder in the Great Lakes region and down the Mississippi to the colony
of Louisiana.

Conversely, during the same period and by the time of this last and
fourth colonial war, the population of the thirteen British colonies
south of the great river totaled 1.25 million people. This was an overwhelming population advantage of a trifle fewer than sixteen to one. If
it came to a fight—and it did—not even the martial superiority of New
France, organized as it was along military lines, could survive against
such fearsome odds. But what has not been generally recognized is
that the very first wave of British immigration was among decent,
hardworking, God-fearing Bretons fleeing religious persecution of

every variety and motivated in the main by a minority refusing to accept a faith foisted on them by a majority using the tactics of a police state.

The second wave of British immigration, however, in no way resembled the first. Usually, and mostly never through faults of their own, these immigrants were the dregs of a British society numbering about 10 million souls, almost evenly divided between the haves—nobility, gentry, professionals, freeholders of land, merchants, craftsmen, and petty officials—and the have-nots—laborers, paupers, clerks, apprentices, servants, soldiers and sailors, criminals, homeless, and prostitutes. Forty-seven percent of the population belonged to the upper classes and 53 percent to the lower. Of these unfortunates it has been estimated that among them were 50,000 beggars, 80,000 criminals, 10,000 vagrants, 100,000 prostitutes, 10,000 rogues, and 1,041,000 on parish relief. The remainder of the lower classes lived a cruelly hard and generally short life. They worked from six in the morning until eight at night for a pittance that barely sustained them. They had no holidays except Christmas and Easter, or public hanging days when rich and poor, exploiter and exploited, rubbed elbows in glee at the sight of those wretches kicking and jerking at the end of a rope because they had stolen a handkerchief or a loaf of bread. Orphans, legitimate or otherwise, abounded. They were sent to workhouses or to parish orphanages, where, it was estimated, only seven out of a hundred of them survived their third birthday.

Of this population—half happy, half despairing—there was no need or purpose for any of the upper classes to immigrate to America, but among those of the lower still young and healthy enough to endure a long sea voyage, the tales they heard of the freedom and opportunity in the New World and of the colonies' crying need for cheap labor made their hearts leap with that stranger joy of hope. And land! They could own their own *land!* At first this vision was just that: a dream. How could a young maid who hated her mistress, and whose only affordable solace was in gin and animal rut, possibly save enough money to finance a transatlantic trip? Eventually, however, the growing demand for labor in the colonies produced the system of indentured slaves that made the dream possible to attain.

It was based on the ancient custom of apprenticeship. Agents paid for the passage of men and women, who contracted themselves to work for a specified number of years to pay off the costs of their voyage.

Such a system—like bounties for military enlistment—lent itself to abuse. Crimps and "spirits"—for "spiriting away"—abounded "like birds of prey along the Thames, eager in their search for such artisans, mechanics, husbandmen, and laborers" whom they could sell to a merchant for shipment to America. Tavernowners and innkeepers found such kidnapping a profitable sideline, for a drunken or sleeping patron was an easy victim. One crimp boasted that he had been spiriting people away for twelve years at the rate of five hundred a year. He would pay twenty-five shillings for a likely candidate and immediately sell him or her to a merchant or shipmaster for fifty. Not all of these spirits were as depraved as the imaginary ones mothers used to frighten their children into obedience, and many of them helped young men and women to immigrate against the wishes of their parents or employers.

These may indeed have been "the poorest, idlest, and worst of mankind, the refuse of Great Britain," but they did supply the colonies' demand for labor, and most of them prospered alongside those first arrivals whose purpose and means of immigration might have been nobler. Here, indeed, is a study in sociology, proof that it is poverty and exploitation, not choice or heredity, that produce the so-called dregs of humanity. Through indenture—crimps and spirits included—tens of thousands of British poor were able to make their way to the New World, where they became known as indentured "servants," the word "slaves" being used only to describe black bondsmen.

At the end of their service they were free and provided with enough money and clothing to make a new start in life. In some colonies they received land at the end of their terms. In North Carolina fifty acres of land and three barrels of Indian corn plus two suits of clothing worth five pounds were provided. Kind masters might allow the most industrious of their indentured servants to go free before the expired term, or at least allow them to grow their own crops and keep their own livestock while still indentured. Conversely, a cruel master, just like a cruel slaveowner, could make the term of indenture a sacrament of hell, as many letters back home suggest.

There is no doubt that not all of those who arrived on the shores of America were prodigies of morality and industry. The crimp's net was as likely to catch a criminal as a law-abiding citizen, and old Mother England did not hesitate to empty her jails for transportation of hardened criminals to the New World, thus transferring the expense of caring for them and the risk of being murdered, raped, or robbed by them to their beloved cousins across the sea.

Three or four times a year the convicts to be so transported were marched in irons from Newgate Prison through the streets of London to Blackfriars in a form of entertainment almost as popular as hanging day. Hooting, jeering mobs gathered to either side of the street to form a gantlet of derisive contempt, to which the felons responded with appropriately pungent obscenity and blasphemy. They could be—and often were—an unwelcome trial to the colonists, yet many of them did establish themselves as respectable citizens. It is therefore possible that some of those staid and superpatriotic Daughters and Sons of the American Revolution, so proud of their heritage, may discover on tracing their ancestry back to its beginnings that they have descended from a pickpocket or a prostitute.

PART VI

Seven Years' War, 1756–1763
(French and Indian War)

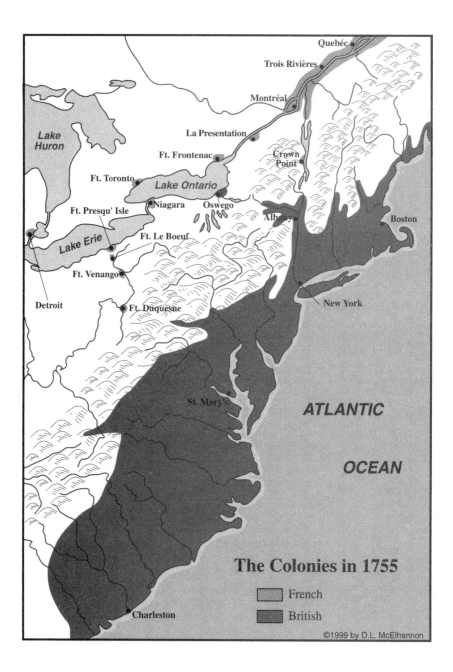

Québéc

Trois Rivières

Montréal

Lake
Huron

La Presentation

Ft. Frontenac

Crown
Point

Ft. Toronto

Lake Ontario

Ft. Presqu' Isle

Niagara

Oswego

Albany

Boston

Lake Erie

Ft. Le Boeuf

Ft. Venango

Detroit

Ft. Duquesne

New York

St. Mary's

ATLANTIC

OCEAN

The Colonies in 1755

French

British

Charleston

©1999 by D.L. McElhannon

CHAPTER 23

George Washington

ALTHOUGH MUCH HAS been made of George Washington's supposedly patrician forebears, the truth is that if the Washingtons—or Wessingtons—could boast of a family tree stretching back five centuries in Britain, they were neither high nor low: of the landed gentry, but not the nobility; yet above the common people. After Henry VIII they were steady Anglicans and loyal Royalists, Cavalier adherents of King Charles I in the Civil War ending in his execution and the triumph of Oliver Cromwell—the dictatorial "Lord Protector" and one of the most detestable human beings in military history: a hymn-singing, sword-swinging swine if ever there was one.

Many of these despoiled Cavaliers fled to the friendly shores of Virginia, there helping to establish what was nothing less than a feudal society. It was a social pyramid rising from the broad base of black slaves in the fields upward through indentured servants and other poor whites—all unlettered—higher to the despised though literate merchants and mechanics, and thence to the farmers and smaller planters, most of whom struggled and schemed to climb to the apex of the structure, where the grandees owning thousands—sometimes millions—of acres of land resided and ruled in almost regal splendor.

In such a society democracy did not flourish. There were few settled municipalities in this vast, sparsely populated province, unlike the northern colonies—especially those of New England—with their town meetings, where men might legislate for themselves, or sit together in the numerous taverns and discuss over a glass of wine or a mug of punch how men weak individually might unite against the grasping strong.

In Virginia the grandees had no difficulty controlling both the House of Burgesses or the Anglican Church. The only restraint upon their power was the royal governor, a true despot transplanted from the mother country who ruled with a council of his own choosing. But the governor, so often interested in enriching himself, could be persuaded. Such a society was most attractive to those blue bloods fleeing the bloody wrath of the regicidal Cromwell, so that between 1640 and 1670 Virginia's population rose from fifteen thousand to seventy thousand.

Among these arrivals was John Washington, who came to the Old Dominion in 1658 on a commercial venture and decided to stay. He was followed by a brother, Augustine (the family was fond of naming its sons John, Lawrence, or Augustine), and then a sister, Martha. Eager to join the ranks of those seigneurial families at the apex of the pyramid, John began to accumulate land and slaves. So did his son Lawrence, and his grandson Augustine, the father of George Washington.

Augustine had married Jane Butler, who had four children, including two sons—Lawrence and Augustine—who survived him. On Jane's death in 1730, he married Mary Ball, a woman in her mid-twenties who, though barely able to write her name, was nevertheless self-willed and given to a perverse pleasure of reminding her husband of her common origin. Mary bore seven children, the first of whom was George, born on February 22, 1732. When George was three, the family moved to a plantation on Little Hunting Creek on the south bank of the Potomac. Later they took up residence at Ferry Farm on the north bank of the Rappahannock near Fredericksburg. Here Augustine died in 1743.

Because seven of his nine children survived infancy, something of a record in those days, his progeny were far too numerous for him to bestow any great legacy on each of them. So the bulk of his possessions went to Jane Butler's sons—Lawrence and Augustine—both of whom had been educated in Britain. Lawrence received the estate on Little Hunting Creek, and Augustine an older one, on the Lower Potomac. George was given Ferry Farm, a few parcels of land elsewhere, and ten slaves. He was eleven, and until he came of legal age, his mother was his guardian—meaning she controlled the family finances.

Mary Washington took her guardianship seriously, seeing at once that there was simply no money to educate young George abroad like his older half brothers, or even to attend William & Mary College in Virginia. Uneducated herself, she set no store by such patrician fopperies, and kept George at Ferry Farm to help with its management. So his schooling was local and brief, and may not have equaled Abraham Lincoln's pathetic total of twelve months in a classroom. Of classical learning, then, George had none, spelling badly, knowing nothing of syntax, and yet, where he could, he found books to educate himself.

Thus he read *Don Quixote* and *Tristram Shandy*, and developed a handsome, cursive handwriting, picked up a smattering of science and mathematics, and became a good draftsman. But the literary work that had the utmost influence upon his life was a little pamphlet titled *The Rules of Conduct and Politeness.*

It was composed in 1595 by the Jesuit fathers of La Fleche in France, intended for the sons of the French nobility and ruling classes. It is a surprising document, for of its 110 maxims only 1 concerns God, 1 conscience, and 2 kindliness, while no less than 21 are devoted to cleanliness and 57 to politeness. But this, after all, is nothing less than the customary pragmatism of the sons of Ignatius Loyola, with their policy of adapting to the customs and social mores of their environment.

The success of this little book was enormous, being translated into Latin, German, English, and Bohemian. By the time it had reached George, the name of its authors had disappeared, and luckily so, for it is doubtful that the feudal lords of Virginia, most of whom were anti-Catholic Freemasons, would have allowed circulation of a work by such formidable foes of their secret society. Young George treasured these admonitions, committing many of them to memory, for they clearly marked out the path he should follow to make himself amenable to the seigneurs of Virginia. Here were rules for proper table manners, dress, comportment in the presence of the mighty, sympathy for the unfortunate, modesty, moderation, pity for the guilty, fidelity, generosity, and prudence, together with reverence for the Almighty, respect for parents, and a resolve to be guided always by "that little spark of celestial fire called conscience."

To say that young George scrupulously obeyed all these admonitions would be to suggest that he became a combination of Machiavelli, Little Lord Fauntleroy, Lord Chesterfield, and the Second Person of the Holy Trinity—but he tried to. As a result he was most welcome at the estate of his half brother Lawrence, who took an interest in him. Lawrence upon his return to Virginia from London had served briefly in an unsuccessful British expedition against Cartagena in what is now Colombia. His admiration for his commander, Admiral Vernon, was so great that he named his plantation Mount Vernon. There he prospered, becoming adjutant general of the Virginia militia and a member of the House of Burgesses. His fortune and influence rose even higher upon his marriage to Anne Fairfax, daughter of the colonel of that name who owned Belvoir, a nearby estate. Colonel Fairfax was also a member of the governor's council and a cousin of Lord

Fairfax, possessor of nearly six million acres of land. So young George found himself welcome not only at Mount Vernon but at Belvoir as well, and even Lord Fairfax's home at Greenway Court. In a word, George learned to ingratiate himself with the First Families of Virginia, not by any exceptional wit or charm, which he did not possess, but by the quiet manners of a perfect gentleman, while keeping his own counsel and his mouth shut.

Even so, at age fourteen he encountered a crisis: his mother did not know what to do with him, whether to encourage him to follow the life of an obscure poor relative on Ferry Farm's infertile acres or take up the life of a land surveyor, at which he appeared adept. But then Lawrence suggested the sea. Mary Washington was skeptical, writing for advice to her half brother Joseph Ball. His reply was a vigorous negative: British ships were floating hells, George could not be promoted without influence in London, it would be better to apprentice him to a tinker than send him off to sea. Mary agreed, and decided to permit George to continue to live at Ferry Farm while following a surveyor's craft.

This he did with great success, for he possessed a natural eye for land and the constitution and strength of a horse, able to spend long hours in the saddle riding through the wilderness and in every kind of weather, his long legs encased in those protective cowhide chaps that, a century later, would be identified with the western cowboy. He was much in demand and his earnings were high; he was able to accumulate more than fourteen hundred acres of land before he was twenty-one. By then Washington had matured physically. He stood at least six feet tall, perhaps two or three inches taller.* His shoulders were strong and sloping, his torso thick, and his hips lean. His arms were long and muscular, his hair reddish-brown, and his eyes a light blue, which, in rare moments of rage, could blaze with anger, or go cold and hard when challenged or displeased. Although his features were regular, his nose was long with a slight leftward twist at the end, and his

---

*In later years George Washington wrote that he was 6 feet tall. The error in attributing to him great height probably occurred when Dr. James Craik measured him and reported that he was 6 feet 3-1/4 inches tall. But Craik measured him from the top of his head to his toe, rather than to his heel, thus adding 3-1/4 inches to his height.

However, Charles Wilson Peale's portrait of Washington after his death does indeed suggest a very tall man, and it is possible that Washington might have grown a few inches more after he was measured at 6 feet.

cheeks were pitted with the livid scars of the smallpox that afflicted him in Barbados, where he had gone with Lawrence when his half brother sought to alleviate his pulmonary tuberculosis in balmier weather.

During his surveying travels he stopped frequently at inns or taverns for rest or refreshment and became known as a good companion.

Though not witty, he had a good sense of humor, quick to laugh at a good joke or join a ribald chorus, ready to play billiards or card games such as whist or loo, usually losing but always carefully marking the amounts in his notebook. He liked a glass—developing an iron head for wine or rum—and was extremely fond of pretty lasses.

It is probable that Washington accepted the young southern bachelor's dichotomy of "good girl to court with, bad girl to play with," for the evidence seems to suggest that, like most of his peers, he was not averse to seeking surcease among girls who were, if not bad, at least obliging. On the first axiom, however, he seemed not so successful, either because of those uncomely scars on his cheeks, or the perpetually serious air he had adopted from his *Rules of Conduct and Politeness,* or because he seems to have treated genteel ladies as though they were the younger sisters of the Blessed Virgin Mary.

Yet behind those blue eyes so expressive of his moods, there seemed to be a screen, a shutter shielding a boundless ambition, not so much to rise into the First Families of Virginia alongside his half brothers, but to shine with military glory.

WHEN THIS SECRET passion for the profession of arms first possessed George Washington is not exactly known. In his teens he had fenced with Jacob van Braam, a retired Dutch soldier who may have enchanted him with tales of warfare, or he might have felt a kinship for his great-grandfather John Washington, a colonel of Virginia militia who led a punitive campaign against the Indians with such success that in admiration they called him Conocontarius (Destroyer of Villages). All that is known is that after he left his half brother Lawrence still suffering from pulmonary illness in Barbados in December 1751, returning to Virginia, he rode almost at once to Williamsburg to present Lawrence's letters to Robert Dinwiddie, the new governor of the colony.

Dinwiddie was a canny Scots merchant who had made a fortune in West Indies trade and was now, through his high office, intent upon increasing it through acquisition of land in the Ohio Valley. He invited his solemn young guest to dine with him and quickly became favorably impressed by him. What they discussed is also not known, but in the spring of 1752, learning that Virginia was to be divided into two military districts for the training of militia, Washington wrote to Dinwiddie, asking to be made the adjutant of one of them. The request was granted, and in December of that year Washington was commissioned major in command of the southern district, with an annual salary of £100. It was quite a plum for a young man not yet twenty-one, even though it was for the southern rather than the northern district, which he desired. But this difficulty was quickly overcome, probably through the influence of his distant relative Colonel Fairfax on the governor's council. Next, Washington found a deputy to carry out his military duties for half the salary. Such sinecures were common enough in both Britain and the colonies, but for this young man to have moved so quickly to obtain one suggests a sophistication not quite conforming to Parson Weems's cloying confection of the Perfect Little Prig or that bewigged fussy old woman in men's clothing whom Gilbert Stuart's wretched portrait of the Father of His Country has preserved for posterity—most notably on the one-dollar bill.

Another false image was created that year after Washington's induction into the Masonic Order in Fredericksburg. Washington the Ardent Mason simply never existed, nor does the mistaken belief among the Masons of France and Spain that Freemasonry in Britain and her colonies shared their political activism. In truth, Washington seldom attended Masonic meetings, and there is no proof that the order shaped his convictions or helped him to rise in the world. Rather, his twin benefactors were his half brother Lawrence and Governor Dinwiddie. It was therefore a great shock to George when Lawrence returned to Mount Vernon in 1752, only to die of his affliction that July. It was as though George had lost a loving and wise father, ending an affectionate and almost adoring relationship never to be replaced by the attitude of a dutiful but not overly fond son, which he showed to his importunate mother. To fulfill his ambition, George Washington must now depend on Dinwiddie alone.

IN 1752 IT APPEARED that Washington's military ambitions would be confined to training militia, when and if he deigned to appear at any of their meetings. This was because the Treaty of Aix-la-Chapelle in 1748 seemed to have ended the Anglo-French struggle for worldwide colonial supremacy. Both nations were exhausted, and their rulers—George II and Louis XV—weary of the dreadful costs of war. No war, no glory. Yet, the greed of the commercial upper classes of both nations had not been satisfied. When the French moved to rearm, the

British did likewise. The prospect of a renewal of hostilities by these two leading powers—hostile in race as well as religion—stupefied the rest of Europe. As Voltaire would write upon the outbreak of the Seven Years' War: "These two nations have gone to war over a few acres of snow in Canada, and, in it they have spent a great deal more than Canada is worth."

In the spring of 1752 the French had begun to make attempts to link their vast possessions along the St. Lawrence River in Canada with those to the south in what would become known as Louisiana by entering the disputed valley of the Ohio. If successful, they would contain the thirteen British colonies in America between the Allegheny Mountains and the sea. Even though the French numbered only 80,000 in North America, of whom about 55,000 were in New France, as opposed to about 1,250,000 British colonists, by the nature of their militarist society, and through their Indian allies and the assistance of a powerful French fleet blockading the Atlantic coast, they might just conquer the thirteen colonies; and the eastern seaboard, from being British and Protestant, would become French and Catholic.

Such, in effect, was the dire prophecy of impending disaster that Robert Dinwiddie transmitted to his superiors in London once he learned that a body of French troops from Québec had landed on the south shore of Lake Erie. They built a fort at Presque Isle, now Erie, Pennsylvania, and another to the south, called Fort Le Boeuf—on territory sacred to the British crown! Dinwiddie's alarm was not without personal and commercial considerations. He was a member of the Ohio Company, formed in 1747 by leading Virginians—including Lawrence Washington and sundry Lees and Fairfaxes—to settle and exploit the Ohio Valley. The project had been approved in London, and when Lord Holderness, the secretary of state for the colonies, learned that the French had invaded "our province of Virginia," he ordered Dinwiddie to evict them, if necessary "by force of arms." Meeting with his council on October 22, 1753, the governor decided to send a message to the commander of the French troops in the area, demanding that they be withdrawn. Learning of the decision, probably from Colonel Fairfax, Major George Washington asked to be appointed as the bearer of the message. His request was granted, and on November 14 Washington and his party of horses, baggage, four hostlers and orderlies, the frontiersman Christopher Gist, and Jacob van Braam, a retired Dutch soldier and also young Washington's dueling partner who said he could speak French, set out for the Ohio country.

It was a difficult journey over unfamiliar terrain and in the cold rains of a dying autumn that would soon be succeeded by the iron hand of a western winter. But on December 4, Washington's command rode out of the dripping woods at Venango.

The French officers there greeted Washington with flawless courtesy. They also tried to lure his Indians to their side. Failing in this, they suavely refused the young Virginian's message and sent him up French Creek to Fort Le Boeuf to their superior officer, Legardeur de St. Pierre. At Le Boeuf, Washington presented Dinwiddie's demand that the French leave the Ohio country. It was politely refused by St. Pierre. "He told me," Washington wrote later, "that the country belonged to [the French]; that no Englishman had a right to trade upon those waters; and that he had orders to make every person prisoner who attempted it on the Ohio, or the waters of it."

On December 16, bearing St. Pierre's reply, Washington and his party started downriver for Venango. They hurried, plying their paddles furiously, for the creek had begun to freeze. Leaving Venango, Washington discovered that his horses, which had been quartered there, were too feeble to carry riders. They dismounted and began to walk. Snow was falling regularly. The temperatures fell. Some of the men were so frostbitten they had to be left in a temporary shack. Washington pressed on grimly, eager to get the French answer to Dinwiddie as soon as possible. If he delayed, he might be snowed in until spring, when the French would be already on the move. Eventually the young major struck out on foot with his guide.

"I took my necessary papers, pulled off my clothes, and tied myself up in a match coat. Then with gun in hand and pack at my back I set out with Mr. Gist, fitted in the same manner."

They were shot at—and missed—by a false Indian guide. Attempting to cross the Allegheny by a log raft, Washington was thrown into the icy water, only saving himself by throwing one long arm across the raft. But both men could not pole through the current to either shore, and they waded ashore on a little island, spending the night sheeted in ice. In the morning, to their inexpressible joy, they beheld the treacherous river locked in a silent white vise of ice. They crossed, and on January 16, 1754—exactly one month after his departure from Fort Le Boeuf—George Washington placed the French refusal in Governor Dinwiddie's hand.

At age twenty-one the Father of America had already entered his nation's history.

CHAPTER 24

Defeat and Death of Braddock

AS YET, NEITHER Britain nor France had found it convenient to make a formal declaration of hostilities, and the Seven Years' War that was to engulf Europe was yet nineteen months away. Nevertheless, both countries seemed content to allow their colonists in the New World to continue to strike at each other in what was nothing less than a head start on the fourth and final round in the great Anglo-French war for colonial empire.

Again, the early advantage seemed to lie with the French. Their decisiveness in strengthening Fort Duquesne—indeed, the very speed with which they could move as well—had so impressed the wavering western Indians that they came to the side of the lilies of France almost in a single body. Already flanked in the South by both the Spanish in Florida and the French in Louisiana, the thirteen British colonies were now also hemmed in by the French in the West and the North. With the sea at their backs and faced by the western mountains like great impassable stone forts to their front, and divided and disorganized, they at last decided to act.

A congress was convened at Albany and an Indian agent, William Johnson, was sent to the Iroquois to persuade the Five Nations to remain loyal to the British. No abler man than Johnson could have been sent. Admired, often loved by the Iroquois, he alone seemed to understand them or could make himself understood by them. But the reply given by one of their orators at the council fire at Onondaga chilled even Johnson's heart.

"We don't know what you Christians, British and French, intend," said one of the sachems. "We are so hemmed in by you both that we have hardly a hunting place left. In a little while, if we find a bear in a tree, there will immediately appear an owner of the land to claim the property and hinder us from killing it, by which we live. We are so perplexed between you that we hardly know what to say or think."

Johnson at last induced the Iroquois to send sachems to Albany to make a treaty with the colonies. Chiefly because of him, the Five Nations agreed to accept a chain belt of wampum as a pledge of friendship. But the truer state of their minds was expressed by the haughty sachem Hendrick in replying to the British charge that the French were trying to take western lands from the red men.

"The governor of Virginia and the governor of Canada are quarreling about lands that belong to us," he said, "and their quarrel may end in our destruction." Drawing attention to the fact that not even Albany, on the very frontier with France, had been fortified, Hendrick continued: "You desire us to speak from the bottom of our hearts, and we shall do it. Look at the French: they are men; they are fortifying everywhere. But you are all like women, bare and open, without fortifications."

Hendrick's contempt was justified; even the colonial delegates assembling for the Albany congress knew that the time had come to bury their differences and unite in the face of the common danger. Unfortunately, neither the colonies nor the crown could sink *their* mutual distrust, and the famous plan for union laid before the congress by Benjamin Franklin was rejected by the Crown because it gave too much power to the colonies, and by the colonies because it gave too much power to the Crown. Neither side was willing to relinquish governmental functions to the central council proposed by Franklin.

With no concrete action taken at Albany, the colonies floundered along while the French war parties roamed the northern borders and the garrison at Fort Duquesne grew stronger. At last the mother country, alarmed by the letters with which Governor Dinwiddie had been bombarding London, decided to come to the aid of her distracted daughters.

ROBERT DINWIDDIE WAS an energetic and resourceful man. He saw at once that the forks of land (modern Pittsburgh) where the confluence of the Allegheny and Monongahela Rivers formed the great Ohio were the keys to the West. Washington had written: "The land in the forks I think extremely well situated for a fort, as it has the absolute command of both rivers. The land at the point is twenty or twenty-five feet above the common surface of the water; and a considerable bottom of flat, well-timbered land all around it, very convenient for building."

Eager to fortify the forks before the French could do the same, Dinwiddie soon found, like all royal governors before and after him, that the colonies were hopelessly divided and that his own House of

Burgesses was extremely jealous of its prerogatives. They made him a frugal grant of funds and placed it in the hands of a committee of their own. His appeal for assistance to the other colonies was either ignored or rejected, except for North Carolina, which also had claims to western lands. Still, in February 1754 he was able to send a party of backwoodsmen to the Ohio forks under orders to build a fort there. Meanwhile, he bickered with the Burgesses for more funds while busily rounding up companies of British regulars, which he joined to half the Virginia militia of three hundred men and sent this force under George Washington, now a lieutenant colonel at twenty-two, moving westward to garrison the completed fort. But before he could get the other half of the militia moving, the French, demonstrating their capacity for swift movement, came bobbing down the Allegheny, seized the British fort by summons, demolished it, and replaced it with a stronger one of their own.

Fort Duquesne now held the West for France.

LIEUTENANT COLONEL WASHINGTON was just across the Alleghenies—perhaps 110 miles southeast of Duquesne—when he heard of the disaster. Immediately he began pushing northwest to establish a forward base for the arrival of reinforcements and artillery. On May 28, 1754, halfway to Duquesne, he surprised an advance party of French.

Jumonville de Villiers, the French leader, was slain in the first volley. After Washington's Indians had brained and scalped the wounded, there were ten French dead, one wounded, and twenty-one captured, against Washington's losses of one wounded. It had been the youthful commander's first fight, and he was elated at the near-perfect result. In fact, his biggest difficulty came in keeping his fierce ally Half King from killing and scalping his prisoners. Half King swore that he would be avenged on the French for killing, boiling, and eating his father.

But Washington dissuaded him, after which the young Virginian withdrew ten miles to a place called Great Meadows. Here he threw up a ramshackle stockade aptly named Fort Necessity. Meanwhile, all Canada and later France seethed with rage over the "murder" of Villiers by "the cruel Vasington [sic]." The dead man's brother, Sieur Coulon de Villiers, came marching hotly from Montréal to avenge *"l'assassinat."* On July 3 his nine hundred men clashed with Washington's four hundred at Fort Necessity.

The French quickly drove the English into rain-filled trenches and then carefully shot down every horse, cow, or dog within the fort. In a half hour the British realized that their transportation and meat were gone. By nightfall it was obvious that they were beaten, and the disconsolate young Washington, certain that a glorious career had ended before it had barely begun, sent his old comrade Jacob van Braam out into the night to ask for terms.

The French were generous. They could not have known that van Braam had mistaken the French word for assassination for the word for death, and they were pleased that Washington was willing to acknowledge his crime of murdering Jumonville. Unaware of a concession he would certainly never have made, Washington capitulated. Next day the British were accorded the honors of war.

Drums beating, colors flying, arms reversed, they marched out of the slime of Fort Necessity while the Indians went rushing in to plunder all that had been left behind. Though the British attempted to show a proud face, they were weary and hungry, many of them carried wounded men on their backs, and they had barely enough powder and ball to drive off the hostile Indians who harried them along the sixty miles back to Wills Creek. A heartbreaking march had begun, and the youth who led it never forgot the day it started.

It was the Fourth of July.

GEORGE WASHINGTON did not return to a hero's welcome in Virginia. Although his friends among the Burgesses stood by him, it was widely bruited about both in the province and the mother country that he had admitted to "murder" to save his life. Washington indignantly denied the charge, trying to explain that he spoke no French and had relied on Braam's supposed skill in that language. But now he knew that his Dutch friend was at the least exaggerating. Moreover, if he were guilty of murder, why was he not punished by Villiers? Obviously the term *"l'assassinat"* was of a political nature, and all Villiers wanted was an admission that a French officer had been slain on French soil. Furthermore, his friends argued, the young commander's reputation for integrity and bravery was so unassailable that he could not possibly be accused of cowardice.

Doubtless, but the stigma did not disappear, and when in the autumn of 1754 Governor Horatio Sharpe of Maryland—a former British officer—was commissioned to lead a force of a thousand regulars against Fort Duquesne, Dinwiddie dissolved the Virginia militia and offered Washington a captaincy in this force. Disgusted, certain that British officers of the same rank would insist upon being senior to him, the young colonel resigned. Although this campaign never materialized, he still headed north, for Mount Vernon. There it is possible that he sought surcease from his disappointment among the ladies of pleasure in Alexandria. So it may be inferred from letters to him from companions-in-arms, such as his old friend George Mercer, writing from South Carolina to complain that the ladies there lacked "those enticing, heaving, throbbing, alluring plump breasts common with our northern belles."

Washington did not disagree.

ALTHOUGH THE DEATH of Jumonville de Villiers and the fight at Fort Necessity were the sparks that set battlefields blazing worldwide, France and Britain did not renew their hostilities until 1756. In the meantime, they allowed their colonies in the New World to strike at each other in a sort of prelude to this fourth and final round in the great conflict for colonial supremacy—each side providing battle fleets and regiments of regulars to ensure victory. Thus while France in 1755 prepared to send a fleet carrying three thousand soldiers to the New World, Britain countered by ordering Major General Edward Braddock to sail for Virginia with two regiments and to take command of all regular and colonial forces in America. Braddock arrived in February of 1755.

His arrival excited the passion for glory slumbering in the breast of George Washington, and he informed Braddock of his desire to join the expedition forming against Fort Duquesne. He asked for a regular's rank of major, thus hoping to outrank those disdainful British captains who refused to serve under colonials. Washington was still naively unaware of the need for powerful friends in the mother country to obtain such rank at age twenty-three, or of the necessity of buying such a commission. Mentioning neither, he heard nothing until, in desperation, he offered to serve as a volunteer on Braddock's staff. This was immediately and gladly accepted.

IT WAS THE policy of France to purr of peace while preparing for war. While strengthening their garrisons in America, the French also began rebuilding a navy that had sunk to less than half the strength of the British force of two hundred ships. At the ports of Brest and Rochefort, eighteen ships of war had been fitted out to carry the six battalions of Artois, Béarn, Bourgogne, Guienne, Languedoc, and La Reine—three thousand men in all—to the shores of America. With them would go their commander, the German veteran Baron Dieskau, who had served under the great Marshal Saxe, as well as Canada's new governor, Pierre François Rigaud, marquis de Vaudreuil, son of that Philippe de Vaudreuil who had been an early governor of Canada, and now, by virtue of his overvalued experience as governor of little Louisiana, as well as his own unflagging faith in his very modest abilities, about to conquer a continent for the crown.

Britain, of course, had learned of the French preparations. For too long the British lion had listened to the French lullaby. This news, together with Dinwiddie's alarms, roused even the inept government of the fussy duke of Newcastle. Besides two five-hundred-man regiments already sent to America, where they would be expanded to seven hundred each by local recruitment, a fleet under Admiral Edward Boscawen was ordered to intercept the French force sailing in the same direction.

Boscawen stationed his squadron off the mouth of the St. Lawrence. But a fog that had scattered the French fleet also permitted all but two to elude Boscawen and arrive safely at Québec and Louisbourg. The other two—*Alcide* and *Lis*—were attacked by Boscawen on June 8, 1755.

According to Captain Hocquart of *Alcide*, he was between Boscawen's flagship and the *Dunkirk*, commanded by Captain Howe. Calling out, "Are we at peace, or war?," he heard Howe reply in French, *"La paix, la paix."* Hocquart then asked the admiral's name, and learning that it was Boscawen, he said, "I know him. He is a friend of mine." Hocquart said he was about to give his own name when smoke and fire leaped from *Dunkirk*'s gunports and British broadsides raked his decks. Hocquart fought back, but both *Alcide* and *Lis* were overpowered, and eight companies of the battalions of Languedoc and La Reine were taken prisoner.

The two mother countries had at last crossed swords.

EDWARD BRADDOCK was short, stout, and choleric. It has been said that he had no wit, but it seems rather that he had wit but no humor. He could say to a young maid named Penny, "You are only a penny now, but I hope on my return you will be two pence," but he was a humorless bulldog when he met his friend Colonel Gumley on the field of honor.

"Braddock," Gumley called cheerfully, "you are a poor dog! Here, take my purse. If you kill me, you will be forced to run away, and then you will not have a shilling to support you." Braddock grimly refused the purse, just as, having been disarmed, he refused to beg for his life.

Invincibly brave, unbearably bullheaded, that was Major General Edward Braddock—and he had not been in America for very long before he had condemned most colonials as a crowd of ignorant sloths, reserving a special wrath for the inhabitants of the middle colonies.

Braddock arrived in Virginia ahead of his troops. Why Virginia was chosen as a base of operations against Fort Duquesne rather than the direct route from Philadelphia is not clear. It has been charged that the Quaker merchant John Hanbury, who traded in Virginia, had persuaded his friend the duke of Newcastle to quarter the expedition in a place where he might profit. It might also have been that the pacific Philadelphians and the stolid Germans of Pennsylvania—who had come to the New World to escape the military excesses of the Old— did not want a large army passing their way. Whatever the reason, Braddock was farther away from his objective than he should have been; and his irascible nature was irritated further when he found the colonials apathetic and unwilling to contribute funds or furnish supplies. For their part, some of the colonists suspected the alarm against France as a trick to encroach upon their liberties. This was not true of either Virginia or New England, whom Braddock commended, but it was fairly characteristic of Maryland and New Jersey, and above all, Pennsylvania—against whom His Majesty's commander raged and ranted.

Braddock had a fourfold plan for eviction of the French. He would personally lead the operation against Duquesne, while another force was to destroy Fort Niagara on Lake Ontario, a third under William Johnson was to reduce the French bastion at Crown Point on Lake Champlain, and a fourth would sail to Acadia to rid that province of the French forever.

All these points were to be attacked at once, neither Braddock nor the governors—who should have known better—seeming to question the feasibility of coordinating complicated operations in a wilderness passable only along its waterways or by painfully cleared roads, and in an age when all forms of transportation were still entirely at the mercy of the weather. Braddock, of course, could only suspect that the way to the forks of the Ohio might be rugged; he could never have known what horrors of military movement lay before him. Young George Washington might have told him, but George was only twenty-three, and though far from shy, certainly not likely to collar such a demigod as Major General Edward Braddock, nor to pick holes in the easy assurances given Braddock by Deputy Quartermaster

General Arthur St. Clair. Moreover, Braddock was openly contemptuous of colonial troops.

Braddock was schooled in the tactics of European warfare that had been evolved since the turn of the century. After the flintlock had replaced the firelock—a hammer striking flint now providing the sparks to explode the charge in the breech—and development of the socket bayonet, infantry tactics had been simplified. Four kinds of infantry—pikemen, musketeers, fusiliers, and grenadiers—were now reduced to one general type of foot soldier armed with bayoneted flintlock. He was drilled incessantly and subjected to a barbarously rigorous discipline* that made him, in effect, a battlefield automaton. He fought in the open against other automatons, also taught to wheel and to dress ranks amid the very smoke and screams of battle, to load and advance, fire and reload—and to drive home the assault with the bayonet under the smoke of the final volley.

A musket's killing range was only a few hundred paces, and firing was not very accurate; in fact, the British fire drill of the period did not include the order "Aim" before the order "Fire!" The object was not so much to riddle the enemy as to frighten him and pin him down for the shock action of the cavalry. Such tactics, adjusted to terrain and weapons, as tactics always are, were almost the opposite of American bush fighting, in which the forests imposed a premium upon dispersion, cover, and accuracy. To say that Braddock could not or would not see this difference is only to say, after all, that he was an ordinarily competent commander not gifted with the insights of genius. New wars are always being fought with the fixations of the old, and Edward Braddock was no exception to that dreary axiom.

In all, Braddock had something over 2,000 men divided among 1,400 British regulars in bright red coats; perhaps 450 Virginia militia—those contemptible "blues" of whom Braddock said "their slothful and languid disposition renders them very unfit for military service"; about 300 axmen assembled to cut the road; and an unknown number of Indians. The red men disgusted Braddock, and one of his officers wrote: "In the day they are in our camp, and in the night they go into their own, where they dance and make a most horrible noise."

Braddock's staff was not the harmonious whole it might have been. Neither Colonel Thomas Dunbar nor Sir Peter Halkett—the regimen-

---

*In 1712 a British guardsman was sentenced to 12,600 lashes and nearly died after receiving the first 1,800.

tal commanders—could abide the youthful and irreverent Captain Robert Orme, who was Braddock's principal aide. Halkett swore that if the army's command ever fell to him he would fire Orme forthwith. Braddock's slender patience wore thinner and thinner at each new delay, and it gave way entirely when it became clear that his 110-mile route to the objective passed through an appalling wilderness.

Virginia was now included in Braddock's endless and wrathful arraignments of the colonists as a pack of dishonest and cowardly rascals, until even the admiring Washington could write: "Instead of blaming the individuals as he ought, he charges all his disappointments to a public supineness and looks upon the country, I believe, as void of both honor and honesty." Young William Shirley, son of the governor of Massachusetts, and Braddock's secretary, wrote home to say: "We have a general most judiciously chosen for being disqualified for the service he is employed in almost every respect."

Meanwhile, as drunkenness, disease, and theft increased among the troops, General Braddock drew up his order of march. He would proceed to Fort Duquesne in six stages. He would lead an advance force of about fifteen hundred men while Colonel Dunbar would follow with the remainder. At the end of May working parties began cutting the road.

THE FRENCH HAD decided not to await the British.

Scouting reports had made it clear that the approaching enemy possessed enough artillery to batter down even the stout log walls of Fort Duquesne. The fort, of course, stood within the triangle of land formed as two rivers joined to become the Ohio. On its right was the swift Allegheny, on the left the deep, slow Monongahela. The British were now across the Monongahela—that is, advancing along its right bank—and were thus already inside the triangle and coming up on Duquesne's left rear.

THE SIEUR DE CONTRECOEUR ordered Captain Daniel Beaujeu to ambush the enemy. Beaujeu proposed the maneuver to the Indians, but they replied, "Do you want to die, my father, and sacrifice us besides?"

"I am determined to meet the British," Beaujeu countered. "What! Will you let your father go alone?"

Stung, the Indians agreed. Under the watchful gaze of a young Pennsylvania captive named James Smith, barrels of powder and ball were broken open and placed outside the fort gates. Howling with glee, the Indians filled their powder horns and pouches. They smeared and streaked themselves in orange and blue, red and yellow, and then, after Beaujeu had dressed himself as a savage, hanging about his neck an officer's gorget as the symbol of his command, they followed him into the woods.

Beaujeu was aware that the terrain would probably force the British to cross and recross the Monongahela. About seven miles from Fort Duquesne lay the second or lower ford, which would allow the enemy to return inside the triangle. It was a place made for ambush, and on July 8 Beaujeu led about 900 men—650 Indians, 100 French, 150 Canadians—stealthily southeast toward it.

EARLY ON THE morning of July 9 General Braddock's force neared the lower ford. The hearts of the men had risen, for the agonies of a nightmare march seemed to lie behind them. Once over the river, only seven miles of easy going lay between them and their objective. Some of the British officers were confidently predicting that they would hear the roar of the French fort being blown up before they reached it.

George Washington was also in high spirits. Though racked with pain and weakened by the disease which had kept him an invalid with Colonel Dunbar's near echelon, he had risen from his pallet on a jolting pack wagon, fastened a pillow to his horse's saddle to ease the agony of riding mounted—and overtaken Braddock so that he, George Washington of Mount Vernon, the first Englishman to lay eyes on the site of Fort Duquesne, might also have the honor of witnessing its fall.

Gradually the column grew tense. The critical point of the entire operation was approaching. Men wet with the waters of the first crossing unconsciously strained their ears for the unwelcome sound of shooting that would mean Lieutenant Colonel Gage's advance force had been ambushed at the ford. Suddenly a murmur of delight rippled through Braddock's army. Colonel Gage presented his compliments to His Excellency, begging to report that he was back on the right side of the Monongahela and that his guns now commanded the lower ford.

Unknown to the British, half of Beaujeu's Indians had strayed away that morning, and he had been unable to prepare his ambuscade. Soon the British main body on the left bank could see the scarlet uniforms of Gage's troops on the other side of the river. They were already at work cutting a passage through the bluff. At 2:00 P.M. it was done, and General Braddock ordered the crossing. It went off flawlessly—in the memory of George Washington, the most stirring sight he had ever seen. Gradually the column resumed marching order, bound for the night's bivouac and the morning's march against Duquesne.

From point to rear guard the column was about two thousand yards long. In front were the guides, with six Virginia light horsemen. Behind them came the engineer, marking the route and blazing trees to be felled to make a road. He had no difficulties, for the woods were open here, and it had been decided that a road twelve feet wide would be sufficient for the guns and wagons. The men could take care of themselves.

Following the engineer were the covering rifles of three hundred soldiers under Gage. Next came the axmen and the pioneers under Sir John Sinclair, and after them a pair of six-pounders with their ammunition wagon and a guard. This was the advance force. Closing behind them was the vanguard under Lieutenant Colonel Ralph Burton, with most of the wagons and some of the artillery. The rear guard, with the reset of the cannons, was under Colonel Halkett. Numerous flanking parties had been thrown out a hundred yards to either side from front to rear, while between them and the marching column the packhorse and cattle, with their drivers, made their way among the trees. To have placed them with the column would have slowed the advance and lengthened the line of marchers.

As often as it has been said that Braddock blundered into ambush, the fact is that he had his security out—fore, aft, and flanks—and that his precautions and organization were of the highest order—judged, of course, by his own standards.

But these came crashing down around him at two-thirty with the sound of firing to the front.

GEORGE WASHINGTON, down once again with "the bloody flux" and what was probably malaria, had been compelled to ride in a covered wagon. Agonizing over the column's slow pace of two miles a day and fearful that such slow progress would give the French time to reinforce Duquesne, he staggered from his wagon to advise Braddock to divide his forces for speed. An advance body of about fifteen hundred men shorn of its wagons and heavy equipment could move swiftly against the fort, while the remainder of the army could follow at a slower pace. Astonishingly enough, Braddock agreed to this violation of the cardinal rule of concentration of forces. He took command of the advance body, while Colonel Thomas Dunbar followed with the second contingent.

Still feverish and weak from dysentery—though pleased by Braddock's decision—Washington returned to his wagon.

✳   ✳   ✳

HARRY GORDON, the engineer, had ridden forward, looking for the guides. They came running back to tell him that they had seen the enemy. Suddenly Gordon saw a man in Indian dress with a gorget around his neck come sprinting through the woods. It was Beaujeu. Behind him were about three hundred French and Indians, also approaching on the run. Beaujeu caught sight of the scarlet coats behind Gordon. He stopped. He waved his arms to right and left and Gordon stiffened in the saddle, to hear the blood-curdling Indian war whoops. Then Beaujeu's men parted and vanished in the woods on either side of the British, and began raking both flanks.

GAGE'S TROOPS HAD wheeled into line almost immediately. Shouting "God save the king!," they discharged volley after volley. They killed Beaujeu and sent his Canadians flying away in fright. Captain Dumas, now in command, thought the battle was lost. "I advanced," he said, "with the assurance that comes from despair." He rallied the Indians, who had not fled. They hid behind trees or fallen trunks, they crouched in gullies or ravines, and thus invisible, they poured a withering fire into the close-packed red coats of the British soldiery.

Soon the British fell silent. In their ears was a frightful cacophony. The endless yelling of the Indians, the screams of their own stricken, the rolling musket fire of the battle—all were picked up and sent reverberating through the encircling gloom of the forest. Rare was the British regular who saw his enemies, and rarer still would be the survivor who would ever forget their fiendish whooping and screeching.

Only the despised Virginians seemed capable of fighting back. A party of them led by Captain Thomas Waggener dashed for a huge fallen tree. They threw themselves down behind it and began picking off red men flitting from cover to cover or darting to the road to scalp a dead or a wounded soldier. But the British regulars mistook their only friends for foes and opened fire on the Virginia rear, killing many colonials and forcing the rest to withdraw.

Now from a hill to the British right came a terrible plunging fire. Demoralized and then terrified, the redcoats fired volley after volley into thin air. They riddled the trees and chipped the rocks. Some of them tried to take cover like the colonials, but their officers would not allow them. They yanked them erect or away from trees and strode among them with bared swords, crying angrily: "Stand and fight!" Back came a pitiful plea: "We would fight if we could see anybody to fight with." And so, rather than disperse, they stood fast; they huddled together, shrinking from the bullets that swept among them, presenting to their merciless tormentors larger and ever larger targets of red.

Suddenly the rumor spread that the French and the Indians were attacking the baggage train in the rear. Gage's men turned and ran. They thundered over St. Clair's working party, abandoned their cannons to the enemy, and came tumbling eastward into the ranks of the British main body even as General Braddock led these soldiers forward.

Now both British regiments were mixed, and confusion reigned unchecked. The towering fury of Braddock riding among them failed to rally this disorganized mass. How could it not have? Braddock beat his men with the flat of his sword rather than allow them to adopt the "cowardly" cover that is the only way to fight in a forest. He refused George Washington's request to allow him to take the colonials against the hill on the right in Indian style. Instead he ordered Burton to storm the height with dressed ranks! Burton obeyed. He rallied a hundred regulars, who followed him until he fell wounded, after which they melted away.

Gage was also wounded, as were Gates, Orme, and William Morris, another Braddock aide, for the carnage among the officers had become dreadful. Mounted, resplendent in laced regimentals, the British commanders were choice targets. Sir Peter Halkett was shot dead. So was young Shirley. Of eighty-six officers, sixty-three were killed or wounded.

Washington himself had four shots through his clothes, and two mounts were shot from under him. Braddock lost four horses, mounted a fifth—and took a musket ball that passed through his right arm and pierced his lung. He fell gasping into the bushes beside the road.

It was then that the retreat that Braddock had ordered became a frenzied rout. The British simply turned and fled for the river in their rear. "They behaved," said George Washington, "with more cowardice than it is possible to conceive . . . they broke and ran as sheep pursued by dogs." They went pelting down the slope of a ravine to their rear, and panting up the other side and onto the river—where some of them were scalped by pursuing Indians even as they plunged into the ford. Washington saw that it was useless to attempt to rally them on the right bank of the Monongahela. Instead, he came to Braddock's side, placed the wounded general in a cart, and conveyed him across the river.

Behind him, howling hideously, the Indians took possession of the field.

"ABOUT SUNDOWN," young James Smith observed in his captivity at Fort Duquesne, "I beheld a small party coming in with about a dozen prisoners, stripped naked, with their hands tied behind their backs and their faces and part of their bodies blacked; these prisoners they burned to death on the bank of the Allegheny River, opposite the fort. I stood on the fort wall until I beheld them begin to burn one of these men; they had him tied to a stake, and kept touching him with fire-brands, red-hot irons, etc., and he screaming in a most doleful manner, the Indians in the meantime yelling like infernal spirits. As this scene appeared too shocking for me to behold, I retired to my lodging, both sore and sorry."

IT HAD NOT BEEN possible to rally the fleeing army on the left bank of the Monongahela either, and it was well for the defeated force that the French had not been able to form their Indians for a second ambush at the upper ford.

Throughout the horrible blackness of the night of July 9, the routed remnants of Braddock's army stumbled steadily southeastward. All along the road back were the sounds of lost horses blundering blindly through the bush, of soldiers cursing as they stumbled over the dying bodies of men who could crawl no longer, or of other wounded crying piteously to be carried away from the dreaded scalping knives of the savages.

Nor was it possible to make a stand when Dunbar's camp was reached, fifty miles back. Here the wagons were burned, cannon and cohorns burst and their shells buried, barrels of gunpowder stove in, and food scattered through the forests. Here, too, the wounded bull-dog Braddock had come to the end of the trail.

He had remained silent throughout the day and night of the tenth, looking up only to say, "Who would have thought it?" Another day passed in giving orders, and then, after another prolonged silence, Braddock added, "We shall better know how to deal with them another time." The next day, cursing his redcoats while praising his officers and "the blues" of Virginia, Edward Braddock died.

Washington buried him with the honors of war. The corpse was lowered into a short, deep trench. It was covered without a marker. To efface the grave from the sight of marauding Indians, the defeated army passed over it on the retreat to Wills Creek.

Pursuing the fleeing British—few of whom paused to succor their pleading, stricken comrades—Beaujeu's savages with knives still bared completed the Massacre at the Monongahela.

CHAPTER 25

Acadian Agony—Western Slaughter

WHILE BRADDOCK WAS MARCHING to his defeat, the colonies were launching the remaining three operations in his fourfold plan to evict the French. Of these, the expedition to Nova Scotia was the most successful.

Although the Acadians, who were the sole inhabitants of Nova Scotia, had taken an oath of allegiance to the British king, the French from Canada had begun to encroach upon those now-British lands. They had built a fort at Beausejour on the isthmus linking Nova Scotia with present-day New Brunswick.

This fort was captured on the lucky chance of a British shell having pierced a French "bombproof" shelter at the moment when its occupants—the officers of Beausejour—were sitting down to breakfast. Six of them were killed, and the British, having only just begun their bombardment, were astonished to see a white flag of surrender waving above Beausejour's ramparts.

Not knowing of the freak accident by which most of the French officers inside the fort were killed by that lucky shot, the British besiegers still did not need to be astounded by the sudden appearance of a white flag of surrender waving over the fort. Through the agency of a French traitor named Thomas Pichon, they had learned that the fort was commanded by Louis de Vergor, probably the most incompetent—and cowardly—officer ever to serve La Belle France in Canada. There is no doubt that Vergor—who might have been illiterate—would have surrendered to a summons, because he valued his life more than his honor; and this evil crony of the thieving Intendant François Bigot in Québec had already been at work with other similarly dishonest officers in stashing away in a safe place a goodly percentage of the fort's portable valuables. He would inadvertently be of even greater service to the enemy when, four years later, he was placed in charge of the detail guarding the heart of the French defenses in Québec.

With Beausejour fallen, the British proceeded with the roundup and expulsion of the Acadians from their centuries-old home. Militia visited settlement after settlement to tear these sturdy though illiterate peasants away from the harvest and march them to such assembly points as the church at Grand Pré, where agents of the Crown such as John Winslow of Massachusetts read proclamations such as:

". . . His Majesty's instructions and commands . . . are that your lands and tenements and cattle and livestock of all kinds are forfeited to the crown, with all your other effects, except money and household goods, and that you yourselves are to be removed from this, his province."

About sixty-five hundred Acadians were thus deported or driven into the wilderness. Their settlements were destroyed, their possessions were seized, and they themselves were herded aboard ships and distributed among the British colonies where, alien in race, language, and religion, they passed a miserable existence. Others entered Canada, only to be cruelly exploited by their fellow Frenchmen. Another group reached Louisiana, where their descendants dwell to this day; and still more, having endured an odyssey of indescribable travail, finally made their way back to their homeland.

Thus the cruel mass deportation which, although defensible on the grounds of military necessity, remains one more crime staining the record of British colonialism in America. It is true that the Acadians were always a Trojan horse inside Nova Scotia. In faith and race more loyal to the French crown than to the British, and maintained in that attitude by their priestly leaders, they were ever ready to rise for France. To prevent this, they were deported. This is the reason, though never the justification, for the heartless uprooting of an entire people; nor does it ever explain why these simple peasants were systematically robbed of all they possessed before being scattered like barren seeds on unfriendly soil.

In the meantime, while Winslow and his comrades carried out a bill of attainder written against an entire province, General William Johnson was moving against Crown Point on Lake Champlain a few miles south of Ticonderoga in New York State.

"I HAVE GIVEN IT THE NAME of Lake George," the toadying William Johnson wrote the Lords of Trade from his fort at the foot of the loveliest lake in America, "not only in honor of His Majesty, but to ascertain his undoubted dominion here."

Unknown to Johnson, that dominion was about to be challenged by Pierre François Rigaud, the marquis de Vaudreuil and the new governor of Canada. He was also the son of one of the first governors of New France, and, like him, just as timid and deceitful. A minor naval officer, he had been governor of tiny Louisiana, and in 1755 he came to Québec to replace Governor Duquesne. Among all the many governors of Canada, he was the only one born in the colony. He had no real military experience, and it would seem that to appoint him as the king's chief officer with authority to overrule the Canadian military was a dreadful mistake typical of the libertine King Louis XV, who had become the timid, pliant creature of Madame de Pompadour, the actual ruler of France.

Vaudreuil might have been appointed to his high post because he was a true Canadian himself and understood and loved the *habitants*. He also understood the Indian tribes, although his single military experience was to accompany a peaceful expedition of Abenaki, whose foul pleasure it was to capture and burn an old brave at the stake. It was said of Vaudreuil that he often recalled that memorable event, relating with great pleasure how the poor old man made such funny faces while he died!

Vaudreuil had hoped to send Baron Dieskau and his newly arrived battalions against the British outpost of Oswego at Lake Ontario. However, papers of General Braddock found on the Monongahela battlefield gave away the English design against Crown Point, and Dieskau was sent to Lake Champlain instead.

While Johnson lay at his leisure in Fort William Henry, quaffing "fresh lemon-punch and the best of wine" and awaiting reinforcements the colonies would never send, Dieskau moved to surprise him. He led about thirty-five hundred regulars, Canadians and Indians, from Crown Point down to Carillon, the promontory on which Champlain fought his first battle with Indians and where Fort Ticonderoga still stands. At Ticonderoga, Dieskau was given his introduction to the Indians of Legardeur de St. Pierre, the officer who had received Washington at Fort Le Boeuf.

"They drive us crazy from morning till night," wrote the refined baron from Germany. "There is no end to their demands. They have already eaten five oxen and as many hogs, without counting the kegs of brandy they have drunk. In short, one needs the patience of an angel to get on with these devils; and yet one must always force himself to seem pleased with them."

But the Indians did capture a British scout, who gave Dieskau the deliberately falsified information that Johnson had withdrawn to

Albany, and had left a force of five hundred men to guard Fort Lyman, between that city and Lake George. Dieskau resolved to attack Fort Lyman.

With about seven hundred French and six hundred Indians, he descended Champlain to South Bay and began moving overland toward Lyman. But then a mounted messenger from Johnson rode by. He was shot from his horse, and a letter in his pocket revealed that the British were, in fact, still at the foot of Lake George. The Indians persuaded Dieskau to attack Johnson's force. He did, pitting thirteen hundred men against twenty-two hundred holding a fixed position.

En route, Dieskau won what was to be a Pyrrhic victory. Ambushing a force of British and Mohawks and killing the valiant old sachem Hendrick, who had tongue-lashed the Albany congress of a year before, Dieskau also lost St. Pierre. Without him the Indians became unmanageable.

They went screeching out of control when the French commander began the assault of Johnson's fort; and the British, fighting back under the skillful directions of General Phineas Lyman, who took charge after Johnson was wounded, repulsed charge after charge. Baron Dieskau was himself wounded. He sat helpless behind a tree while his forces fled before the British sallying fiercely from the fort. He turned to see an enemy soldier aiming his musket at him. He signed to the man not to shoot. But the soldier did, sending a bullet across Dieskau's hips, leaping on him, and commanding him in French to surrender.

"You rascal!" Dieskau roared. "Why did you fire? You see a man lying in his blood on the ground, and you shoot him!"

"How did I know that you had not got a pistol?" the indignant soldier replied. "I had rather kill the devil than have the devil kill me!"

"You are a Frenchman?"

"Yes, but it is more than ten years since I left Canada."

Dieskau was about to say more, but a few more aroused soldiers fell on him and stripped him of his clothes. But they did take the defeated general to Johnson, who had his wounds dressed and treated him kindly. Unfortunately for Dieskau, a few more chiefs had joined Hendrick in the happy hunting grounds. The infuriated Mohawks came into Johnson's tent and demanded his prisoner. Johnson refused, and they filed out, glancing fiercely at Dieskau.

"What did they want?" Dieskau asked.

"What did they want?" Johnson repeated forcefully. "To burn you, by God, to eat you , and smoke you in their pipes. . . . But never fear. You shall be safe with me, or else they shall kill us both."

Johnson was truer to his word than he was to his purpose of expelling the French from New York. Although wounded, he still could have sent General Lyman to Lake Champlain to follow up the advantage gained at Lake George. But he did not, probably because he was already jealous of Lyman. Contenting himself with strengthening his fort while the French quickly reinforced Ticonderoga, he allowed the opportunity to slip away. A cold and raw November arrived, and with it came mutiny and desertions among the men. At a council of war presided over by Lyman, to whom Johnson was now willing to transfer responsibility, it was voted to withdraw. "Thursday the 27th," a Massachusetts chaplain wrote in his diary, "we set out about ten of the clock, marched in a body, about three thousand, the wagons and baggage in the centre, our [general] much insulted by the way."

Although Johnson might have been "much insulted" at home, he was skillful enough to make himself a hero abroad. He had already flattered the king by renaming Lac St. Sacrement after him, and then he had proceeded to name his stockade there Fort William Henry in honor of one of the king's grandsons, and change Fort Lyman to Fort Edward to compliment another. Then he wrote a long account of the fight at Lake George in which he exaggerated both its value and his own part in it, while neglecting to mention Lyman's name. Mightier with pen than with sword, William Johnson was made a baronet, and Parliament gave him a gift of £5,000.

And Crown Point remained French.

FORT NIAGARA ALSO remained French.

Doughty Governor Shirley of Massachusetts had journeyed to Albany to take command of perhaps the happiest force of provincials yet assembled by the British. There were five hundred men in the regimentals of the Jersey blues and about twice that number in the red of Shirley's and Pepperrell's regiments, which were financed by the king. "I have two Holland shorts, found me by the King," Sergeant James Gray of Pepperrell's wrote to his brother John, "and two pair of shoes and two pair of worsted stocking; a good silver-laced hat (the lace I could sell for four dollars); and my clothes is as fine scarlet broadcloth as ever you did see. . . . one day in every week we must have our hair or our wigs powdered."

That was in Albany, but going up the Mohawk to Oswego, these rainbow troops discovered that war is not always drums, flutes, flags, bugles, and lace hats, but rather mud, mosquitoes, hunger, boredom, and the backbreaking agony of dragging boats from stream to stream or of pushing them through swamps. General Shirley also discovered, after his arrival at the outpost on Lake Ontario, that a trained legal mind does not always grasp the most obvious facts of battle.

Shirley had forgotten about Fort Frontenac.

Staring across Lake Ontario toward that French bastion fifty miles opposite Oswego, the governor realized that if he moved west or to his left to attack Fort Niagara, the French in Frontenac would merely cross the lake to take Oswego and occupy his rear.

At one point Shirley thought of leaving half his force in Oswego to defend it while taking the other half against Niagara. Wisely realizing that this would be rash, he reluctantly acknowledged reality, left part of his men in Oswego to strengthen the garrison, and returned to Albany.

Of General Braddock's fourfold plan, only the minor operation against the Acadians had succeeded; but even this modest achievement was to have the adverse effect of goading on the French and their savage allies as they burst upon borders left wide open by the three defeats.

If the british pioneers' desire to settle land, rather than to rove the woods and rivers like the explorers and *coureurs de bois* of New France, was to prove the ultimate strength of their cause, it was also a near-fatal weakness.

It was impossible for these borders to defend themselves against those savages whose tomahawks now were bared for France. Indeed, the French were aware of this. It was the reason why the savages were hounded on and on, in the belief that they would bury the British outposts in blood and ruin and arrest forever that westward movement threatening to enter the Ohio country and to cut the Canada–Louisiana line.

The very love of independence that had brought these fierce and rebellious Ulster Scots and Irish into the forests had caused them to build their log cabins and raise their buckskin-clad families in little clearings scattered miles apart along an undefended border running six hundred to seven hundred miles, from the middle colonies down to the southern ones. The very fact of their families inhibited defense. Each settler tried to defend his own hearth rather than to form themselves into military units protecting a central community. Each settler also was forced to leave that hearth unguarded for a good part of the day, while he was out hunting or working in the fields. Even the little farms farther east, which had been yesterday's outposts, had barely more than a fortified house in which to take common refuge upon that terrible moment when the flaming arrow sped silently from the encircling forest, and bands of howling Indians burst suddenly from the woods to burn and kill.

To retaliate was even more difficult, for the forests were like a trackless waste into which the marauders could vanish as swiftly as they had appeared. And so the years following Braddock's defeat were ones of terrible travail for them. In Virginia young Colonel George Washington wrote again and again to Governor Dinwiddie of the scenes of horror he had found himself powerless to prevent.

"The supplicating tears of the women and moving petitions of the men melt me into such deadly sorrow, that I solemnly declare, if I know my own mind, I could offer myself a willing sacrifice to the butchering enemy, provided that would contribute to the people's ease."

From Pennsylvania came even more horrifying tales of carnage, for these borderers, living closest to Fort Duquesne, were the ones upon whom the bloody hatchets always fell first and most frequently.

"We are in as bad circumstances as ever any poor Christians were ever in," Adam Hoops wrote to Governor Morris of Pennsylvania, "for the cries of widowers, widows, fatherless and motherless children are enough to pierce the most hardest of hearts. Likewise it's a very sorrowful spectacle to see those that escaped with their lives with not a mouthful to eat, or bed to lie on, or clothes to cover their nakedness, or keep them warm, but all they had consumed into ashes. These deplorable circumstances cry aloud for your Honor's most wise consideration; for it is really very shocking for the husband to see the wife of his bosom her head cut off, and the children's blood drunk like water, by these bloody and cruel savages."

Such petitions, though they could melt the heart of the stern Washington, failed to upset the Quakers who serenely ruled Pennsylvania from their comfortable sanctuary in Philadelphia many miles away. The Quakers believed it was a sin to fight the noble savage. Being sincerely liberal and humane, they also had the broadminded man's fear of seeming narrow; and thus from a tendency not to take their own side, they were pushed, by their pacifism, very close to taking the other side. So the Quaker assemblymen shut their ears to the cries of their afflicted brethren in the West and refused to come to their aid.

Such a stand was not, of course, entirely due to Quaker pacifism or to their hatred of Presbyterianism, which, with a flavoring of Catholicism, was the religion of the border. There was also the Assembly's continuing fight with Governor Morris over its right to tax the estates of the feudal proprietors of Pennsylvania. Each bill the Assembly voted to raise funds for defense of the border included a provision to tax the estates of the Penns, and because Morris could not accept this without disobeying his instructions, he rejected all such bills. The Germans of the middle colonies were also reluctant to help their western brethren. Aloof on their plump and prosperous farms, hating any kind of military service, uncaring if they were ruled by France or Britain, they were in no hurry to pay taxes to defend others.

Nor was Benjamin Franklin, then the leader of the Assembly, willing to relieve the border, at least not until the proprietors allowed themselves to be taxed in true democratic style. Thus the miserable borderers found themselves pinioned on the anvil of religious prejudice, to be battered by the hammer of partisan politics.

Slaughter mounted on slaughter, and still the squabble continued, until, at last, the non-Quaker members of the Assembly took the offensive and addressed a petition to the House that said: "You will forgive us, gentlemen, if we assume characters somewhat higher than that of humble suitors praying for the defense of our lives and properties as a matter of grace or favor on your side. You will permit us to make a positive and immediate demand of it."

This infuriated the Quakers. They took to the streets to denounce the wickedness of war, and told the House that any action inconsistent with their pacifism would be considered "destructive of our religious liberties." They said they would rather "suffer" than pay taxes for such ends. Of course, it was the borderers who were continuing to suffer, and they were dying in droves. Eventually, as the flames of war flickered eastward, the House did pass a militia law. It exempted the Quakers and drafted no one. It merely said that men wanting to serve would find it lawful to do so, to form themselves into companies, elect officers, and, presumably, confer with Governor Morris on a campaign.

Anybody's army, of course, was actually nobody's; and the scourging of the border was not relieved until an accident and the approach of war even onto the placid German borders changed the Assembly's mind.

Governor Morris announced that the Penns, Thomas and Richard, had sent him £5,000 to be used in the defense of the colony, but only on the condition that it be accepted as a gift, and not considered payment of a tax on the Penn estates. The Assembly agreed, struck out the clause in the money bill calling for taxation of the Penns, and the tax to raise funds for border defense became law.

Franklin considered the compromise a defeat. Probably it was, to him, although the bedeviled borderers certainly had a right to prize their lives above his libertarian ideals. However, it would remain for the War of the Revolution to settle the quarrel between feudalism and democracy. All that the Philadelphia squabble was to do was mark the beginning of the end of Quaker rule in Pennsylvania.

It had been made clear that a rational conviction erected into a religious principle can be dangerous to the commonweal. By informing a conclusion such as pacifism with all the inflexible dynamism of a moral absolute, the Quakers had demonstrated that, though certainly not disqualified as citizens, they were at least crippled as rulers.

In the meanwhile, a merciful winter had immobilized the border marauders, and the Seven Years' War, which the colonies of both sides had anticipated, was at last erupting in Europe.

CHAPTER 26

Pitt Takes Charge—
Montcalm Arrives—
Lord Howe Killed

"HENCEFORTH," Frederick the Great said after the Peace of Aix-la-Chapelle, "I would not attack a cat except to defend myself." Eight years later he was attacking Saxony, with the explanation, "After all, it was of small importance whether my enemies called me an aggressor or not as all Europe had already united against me."

This was not quite true. Britain, forsaking her old ally Austria to guarantee the king's Hanoverian lands, was on the side of Frederick's Prussia. Britain and France had already declared war, and France, seeing in Prussia a foe more to be dreaded than her ancient enemy in Austria, came to the support of Maria Theresa. Czarina Catherine of Russia also took up Maria's cause. Catherine had been insulted by Frederick, who called her "the Apostolic Hag," and she brought Sweden with her against her detractor.

Frederick's taunts also had annoyed Maria Theresa, and they had enraged Madame de Pompadour. Pompadour ruled France. From being the mistress of the libertine Louis XV, she had become his procuress—and therefore his master. Frederick had called Pompadour "Mademoiselle Fish" in a biting reference to the favorite's mother, reputed to have been a fishwife. Thus three angry women were allied against the captain of his age, and he was to chastise them more severely with his sword than with his tongue.

Unfortunately for Canada, Pompadour's pique led her to neglect America. She sent a hundred thousand troops to help Maria but could spare only twelve hundred for the New World.

If only half of what the pouting Pompadour had sent to Austria had been sent to Canada instead, the conquest of all North America except

Mexico might have been accomplished for France under the plan devised by Governor Callieres of Montréal and approved by Louis XV. It had envisioned a double-pronged assault on New York City by land and sea. Victorious there, the French could reduce New England, securing for themselves year-round access to the great warm-water rivers of the Northeast. But the troops and ships were simply not available, and Canada had to struggle to maintain itself against the British and their colonies.

However, Canada did get a splendid new war chief: Louis Joseph, Marquis de Montcalm de Saint-Veran. A career officer in the French Army, General Montcalm had served his king since early youth and fought in many campaigns, being frequently wounded. He was forty-four years old when he reached Canada in 1756. A Provençal, he was typically excitable, quick to anger and just as quick to cool; but nevertheless he was an eminently capable commander and a man of complete integrity, an uncommon quality in an age when deserters of the highest rank such as John Churchill could sell themselves to the highest bidder. Indians who had heard of Montcalm's reputation as a soldier were amazed to find him small in stature, but they would soon learn that he was easily the finest general ever to issue orders in New France—and that includes Count Frontenac.

Arriving in Québec with Montcalm were his two finest lieutenants: Brigadier Gaston François Levis and the extraordinarily accomplished aide-de-camp Louis-Antoine de Bougainville, then a mere half-pay captain of dragoons. Levis was to rise to the very highest rank in the French Army—a marshal of France—and would die a duke, thus avoiding the bloody guillotine of the French Revolution scarcely a generation away. His able assistant was Colonel François de Bourlamaque.

All these officers were to be of great assistance to Montcalm, but Bougainville was actually *sui generis*—that is, one of a kind. He had to his credit many astonishing achievements before he died as an admiral of France and a peer as well. After the fall of Canada he transferred to the navy—probably because of the asthma that was his lifetime thorn-in-the-flesh—and became a famous explorer, the unsung predecessor of Captain Cook in the South Seas. It was Bougainville who brought back to Europe the huge red jungle flower that bears his name. While still in his twenties he wrote a book on integral calculus that brought him election to the British Royal Society, an unusual achievement for a soldier-admiral. He also had served as a diplomat in the retinue of the French ambassador to Britain, learning to know the British and their language.

Physically, Bougainville probably deserved the Indians' low estimate of him as a person: short, plump, almost fat, he was nevertheless lighthearted and learned, with a brilliant, inquiring mind. He and Montcalm became close friends, Bougainville eventually living with the general, where he kept a diary that became the single most engaging and reliable source of information on the struggle for Canada. He also wrote many letters home, which for their absolute frankness and revealing anecdotes were even better reading.

Neither so gifted nor so loyal as any of these officers was Pierre François de Rigaud, marquis de Vaudreuil. Vaudreuil had come to Québec in 1755 to replace Governor Duquesne. Pleasant and pleasing when he sought some advantage, mild-mannered and affable, but also intensely vain and egotistical, he could easily be led astray by his ballooning ambition, or else, to satisfy his insane jealousy of anyone who rivaled him in the affection of the king, gleefully swallow any calumny upon his character. Closely associated with the evil Intendant François Bigot and his gang of thieves, Vaudreuil seems to have become willingly their pawn, deliberately misinforming the colonial minister about their honesty and reliability while blackening the name of Montcalm.

In contradiction of the division of government in Canada between a civil administrator called the intendant and a governor who had always also been a high-ranking military officer—the eminently workable arrangement provided by the great minister Colbert—Vaudreuil in some way had obtained from the libertine King Louis XV the authority to countermand any order or policy of General Montcalm and to treat him as a subordinate. Eventually, on his own insistence, Montcalm made himself independent of this novel provision, even though to do so made his position a difficult one. Skilled in deceit and the arts of character assassination, Vaudreuil continued to bombard Versailles with lying letters; and at the end, when the very life of the colony of New France was at stake, he countermanded all of Montcalm's wise military provisions so that James Wolfe was unknowingly made the beneficiary of one of the great betrayals of military history.

This, of course, is no ordinary accusation; and yet it can be sustained as this narrative of the four-war Anglo-French struggle for possession of Canada comes to its conclusion.

OPPOSING MONTCALM WAS the new British commander, John Campbell, the fourth earl of Loudon, A Scottish peer who replaced Governor Shirley, the former governor of Massachusetts who had fallen victim of a cabal organized by his great friend Sir William Johnson. Shirley had befriended Johnson earlier, recommending him for the command of the 1755 Crown Point expedition, which earned Johnson his baronetcy and the gift of £5,000 from Parliament. In gratitude, Johnson prevailed upon the lieutenant governors of New York and New Jersey to dump his benefactor—which they did with great gusto. Shirley had hoped that his assistant General James Abercromby—known as "Nannycromby" by his unadoring troops—would be his successor; but Abercromby was as incredibly lacking in military competence as he was in both money and influence.

Loudon left Britain aboard a ship so loaded with his personal traveling requirements—cases of port, many uniforms, swords and horses, as well as sixteen servants and his latest mistress—that his reputation as a competent commander among the local yokels of New York went into a deep dive into oblivion, replaced by an unabashed admiration of his lifestyle. His Lordship established a headquarters such as had never before been seen in America, and would not again be challenged until the arrival of Gentleman Johnny Burgoyne on the banks of the good old Hudson.

Struggling with his companions to survive until Christmas week of 1756, Loudon sat still while Montcalm destroyed Oswego, thereby swinging shut the western gate and also—in a shock greater than the defeat and death of Braddock—containing the thirteen British colonies between the mountains and the sea.

Too busy preparing for the jolly season of Christmas, Loudon remained sedentary. Though it was a struggle, the earl and his friends managed to last until Christmas Week of 1756, providing a festive table groaning with select goodies washed down by fifty-two dozen bottles of fine wine, some of them fortified, not to mention the spirits consumed in their punch.

AKIN TO BRADDOCK in his contempt for the colonials, Loudon was also of the same irascible temper. He was not, however, as energetic. Having arrived in New York in 1756, he did not move until the spring of 1757.

Then he sailed against Louisbourg, found it defended by a mighty French fleet, and sailed back to New York in disgust. Meanwhile, his unsuccessful expedition had left Fort William Henry exposed to the French in Ticonderoga. On August 1 Montcalm left that fort with about seventy-five hundred men. He sailed down Lake George. For the last time the French and their Indian allies took the watery road to the British. In swarms of canoes and hundreds of *bateaux*, with oar, sail, and paddle, while Canadians in buckskins and French regulars in white coats mingled with naked savages streaked like rainbows, the twin perfections of civility and barbarism glided down King George's beautiful lake to fall upon his fort at the foot.

Fort William Henry fought back valiantly, but it never received the reinforcements it needed. Using European siege tactics, Montcalm worked his artillery ever closer to the British position, at last compelling its surrender after his guns were within point-blank range. And then his Indians went screeching out of control, rushing inside the helpless fort to slaughter the sick and wounded in their beds. A French missionary named Roubaud witnessed the butchery and wrote: "I saw one of these barbarians come out of the casemates with a human head in his hand, from which the blood ran in streams, and which he paraded as if he had got the finest prize in the world."

Nor could Montcalm curb the frenzied Indians as the British began to depart for home. The Indians fell whooping on the rear of the New Hampshire regiment and dragged off eighty men. Montcalm rushed among them, crying, "Kill me, but spare the British!" The massacre continued. In all, fifty prisoners were killed, and perhaps two hundred more carried captive to Canada. There, many of them were ransomed by the French, who also bought back the clothes the Indians had torn from the backs of their terrified captives.

Nevertheless, the massacre was a bloody breach of honor. Montcalm's only excuse for not using his own troops to restrain the Indians was that to do so would have lost the red men as allies. This he would not do, and the Indians and their grisly trophies were still with him when he burned Fort William Henry and withdrew to Montréal.

SINCE 1754, British disaster had followed upon defeat, and the drums rolled a dirge of adversity: Fort Necessity, Braddock on the Monongahela, the border scourge, Crown Point, Oswego, the failure at Louisbourg, and now the destruction of Fort William Henry left only little Fort Edward standing between Albany and the Hudson high road to New York City. Should the French follow it, they would cut the colonies in two.

European reversals had also staggered Britain and her ally Frederick of Prussia. The duke of Cumberland had been brought to promise to disband his Hanoverian army, and the great Frederick had gone down in a defeat that enabled a Russian army to sweep into Prussia and commit atrocities that would shame an Iroquois. By October of 1757 it appeared that Frederick was lost. Yet he rallied in the year's last two months to crush the French at Rossbach and rout the Austrians at

Leuthen. The tide was turning, and in London an event occurred that prompted Frederick to say: "Britain has long been in labor, and at last she has brought forth a man."

THE MAN WAS William Pitt, son of a governor of the great industrial state of Madras in British-ruled India. Pitt's first—and perhaps his wisest and most fruitful move personally—was to marry into the powerful Grenville family. A superb orator, he made his reputation in the House of Commons by attacking the government of Sir Robert Walpole. Pitt also showed himself to be incorruptible, shattering all tradition while serving as paymaster from 1745 to 1754 without making a penny for himself. Thus armed, golden-voiced but scorning gold, he increased his hold on the mood of the people by repudiating all parliamentary alliances and earned for himself the invaluable sobriquet of the Great Commoner. Great he was indeed, but common he was not. Rather he was Britain's first imperialist and would inevitably emerge as the true founder of that vast empire upon which until World War II "the sun had never set." Implacable, arrogant, ruthless, contemptuous of small minds and petty ambitions, he was a superb organizer and eventually the savior of his country.

Unknown to William Pitt, the country and people he loved so passionately and intended to save was actually two Britains, not just one. The first Britain of the eighteenth century was one of those sugary myths of which its people had become so fond. It was the fable of all that was noble and exquisite and yet so charmingly simple. Lords of the manor secure in their stately Georgian mansions of antique brick or gray Cotswold stone wisely dispensed justice among their loyal, sturdy yeomen. From the hands of local craftsmen came *objets d'art* lovingly tooled or executed: Chippendale furniture; fine linens or silver service of the table beautifully wrought; delicate, sparkling crystal; fine china riotous in design; paintings from Rome or Venice—whatever might enhance the quality of life or delight the local squire with its beauty. In these villages or county towns there also existed a self-sufficient economy in which proud villagers made most of their own clothing, as well as their own tools and farm implements for maintaining the lord's estate. They also baked their own bread and brewed their own beer, slaughtering their own cattle and curing their flesh. In these happily fabulous times when only the squires sent to London and other big cities for their furniture, clothing, wine, and books, even the dogs lived without fear or want.

But then there was a second Britain, of the great cities: a truer Britain, unvarnished and unembellished, unsanitary and salacious.

Here the narrow, cobbled streets stank of the urine and excrement hurled in hatred from upper-story windows, falling among the droppings of the great dray horses plodding with lowered heads through heaps of nauseous garbage that turned the throughways into obstacle courses. Surging through these noisome streets were the crowds of noisy, mindless poor, their pallid faces spotted with mud flung upon them by the horses' hoofs, their hair lank and uncut, their bodies unwashed and itching—often crawling with the hordes of insects issuing from the earthen floors they shared with them, and with pigs and rats as well.

Saturday nights were real-life reenactments of Hogarth's *Gin Lane*—those brutal canvases crammed with misery and stark despair—always producing drunken brawls without number, amid the screeching of police whistles and the clanging bells of the hospital wagons. Actually, in mid-eighteenth-century Britain a drastic rise in duties on gin, beer, and whiskey did effect an appreciable reduction in street brawling. Up until then, so many people in the great cities were dying of starvation or of injuries received in drunken fights that the kingdom's population would have declined steadily but for the growing birth rate of the countryside.

But along with this improvement there occurred a corresponding increase in crime, rising perhaps from the growing despair of the unwashed condemned to exist in poverty and destitution. To cure this widespread malaise, a commission formed to curb crime produced a cure that was worse than the cause. A draconian code imposed the death sentence for no less than two hundred minor offenses, ranging from horse stealing to shoplifting up to the value of five shillings, to stealing a single handkerchief. Fortunately, the juries were more compassionate than the judges, so that as many as five of six convicts escaped the gallows. Still, execution centers such as Tyburn—the place where Henry VIII and the Pirate Queen imposed the incredibly barbaric capital punishment of drawing and quartering* on those

---

*Drawing and quartering was the ancient penalty for the capital crime of treason, the victim being drawn naked through the streets behind a horse and cart, mounted on a platform, where his heart was torn from his body and burned before his eyes, after which it was cut into quarters, which were flung to the four winds. Henry applied this punishment to his subjects who would not accept his Anglican faith, claiming that by remaining in communion with the Papacy they were denying his sovereignty and continuing their allegiance "to a foreign power."

Catholics who refused to renounce their faith—provided most cities with the most popular and cheap entertainment available.

Highway travel at midcentury was also riskier than falling victim to the numerous "press gangs" that furnished the British Navy with reluctant seamen. Highwaymen such as the notorious—but immensely popular—Dick Turpin and Jack Sheppard were numerous, and the wretched system of cart tracks dignified as thoroughfares were like chains of ambush for the masked, pistol-packing gentry who patronized them. Until a true hard-packed road system was financed by toll and gate fees, an important official document would take days to reach a minister enjoying life on his country estate, and many more as he hastened back to London to address an impasse.

Even the British armed forces suffered more in these lawless and unhappy times than they ever did in battle on land or sea. At the outset of the Seven Years' War the British Navy sank to an incredible low of 20,000 hands, when, in the War of 1812 as a sea mammoth of 600 ships, she needed no less than 150,000 sailors to stay afloat. In the same period the British Army was reduced to 18,000 soldiers, plus the garrisons of Minorca and Gibraltar.

This, then, was the unhappy and fearful kingdom that William Pitt sought to save. For nine months British arms had marched to a dreadful, dolorous litany of defeat and retreat until the Great Commoner was finally granted the powers he needed. But he labored against fearful odds. Newcastle was jealous of him and denied him a parliamentary majority. Little George II had hated him for years because of his bitingly sarcastic references to the Battle of Dettingen, where George had actually conducted himself with great bravery. The duke of Cumberland, inept and bungling son of the king and commander in chief of the army, opposed Pitt's military plans and sabotaged his every attempt to staff the armed forces with competent officers. In April 1757, two years after the defeat and death of Edward Braddock at the Battle of the Monongahela River in North America, a military disaster so shocking to the British that it might have been compared to the triumph of Evil over Good at Armageddon (Hebrew Megiddo), Pitt was dismissed because of it and for eleven weeks Britain had no government.

Thereafter the drumbeat of military reversal was like a death rattle. First had come the disastrous siege of Cartagena in the Caribbean in July 1740, after which from the coast of France to the Continent of Europe to the gloomy forests of North America came the roll call of military reversal. Fort William Henry . . . Louisbourg . . . Rochefort on the

French coast . . . the Continent, where butter-fingered Cumberland signed the Convention of Klosterzeven, thus making a gift of the province of Hanover, the apple of his father's eye. . . . Even Frederick the Great, in spite of his victories over the French and the Austrians, appeared to be encircled and doomed to defeat.

Britain seemed to be on the crest of a rising, roaring, irreversible tidal wave of military misfortune. Above it, however, barely audible at first, but then gaining momentum like the Car of Juggernaut, came the clamor of the British public for the return of William Pitt. He had been confidently expecting a recall, but from the government of the duke of Devonshire, not the people at large. But then he saw, at last and instantly, where the true source of his strength lay, and he said to Devonshire without a trace of gloat or gasconade: "I know that I can save this country and that no one else can."

And he did.

Oddly enough, he slipped easily into harness with his mortal enemy Newcastle, becoming secretary of state and the leader of the House of Commons, in full command of foreign policy and the war. "I will borrow the duke's majorities," he remarked cynically, leaving Newcastle to attend to the dirty—but necessary—business of twisting arms, political jobbery, bribery, intrigue, and patronage. Through these unlovely though efficient arts—and the indomitable purpose of Pitt to destroy France as she stood in his path en route to creating an empire that would rival even those of Rome and Spain—the customarily lethargic British colonies in North America were energized and inflamed.

Pitt saw at once that the three keys to the North American continent were Fort Duquesne, Ticonderoga, and Louisbourg-Québec, and he prepared separate expeditions for each.

All three operations were scheduled for 1758.

BY THE BEGINNING of 1758 the marquis de Montcalm and the marquis de Vaudreuil had learned to distrust and despise one another. Vaudreuil was jealous of Montcalm's military prowess and pretended—as George IV of Britain was to do with Wellington—that they were won by him. Montcalm was disgusted by Vaudreuil's tolerance—through either vanity or venality—of the thieving, evil Intendant Bigot.

François Bigot might have been a scrofulous caricature of the unfaithful steward. He was exceeded in his rapaciousness only by his protégé and chief agent, the butcher's boy Joseph Cadet. Between them Bigot and Cadet robbed the king of millions and millions of livres. As intendant, Bigot was all-powerful in matters of trade, and he could raise and lower prices to his personal profit. With Cadet and other confederates he introduced duty-free goods into the colony and sold them to the king at enormous profits, he charged the king's troops for the hire of boats and wagons owned by the king, and he sold furs cheaply to his associates when by the king's order he was to auction them to the highest bidder.

Few thieves have been more brazen or more florid than this pair. The very warehouse they owned was known as La Friponne (The Cheat). They appropriated the beautiful young wives of their subordinates as mistresses, and dazzled the colony with the brilliance of their dress and equipage and the opulence of their homes. Perhaps the clearest insight into the dedicated dishonesty of Bigot is his instructions to the toadying Duchambon de Vergor, the false commandment at the old French fort at Beausejour. "Profit by your place, my dear Vergor," he wrote. "Clip and cut, and rob the king—you are free to do what you please—so that you can come soon to join me in France and buy an estate near me." Vergor had followed instructions greedily, with one result that Beausejour was so far from prepared when the English appeared before it in 1755 that it hauled down its colors before the besiegers had actually gotten the siege started.

Thus, as Montcalm knew, all of New France was being corrupted and weakened by the grafting immorality of Bigot and his myrmidons, and the vacillations of the vainglorious Vaudreuil. The dry rot of bureaucratic feudalism—which works from the top down—had already set in. By 1758 Louisbourg, the most formidable French bastion in America, had also been exposed to the same debilitating contract-jobbing begun at Beausejour by the swine Vergor.

ON THE MORNING of June 1, Louisbourg's southeastern horizon was fringed with the sails of the British. A fleet of 22 ships of the line, 15 frigates, and 120 transports under Admiral Boscawen had arrived with Major General Jeffrey Amherst and 12,000 soldiers, of whom only 500 were colonials.

Inside Louisbourg were about 3,200 French regulars, besides a body of armed inhabitants and some Indians. Five ships of the line and seven frigates lay inside the harbor. However, the fortifications were not completed, and ramparts made with bad mortar had already begun to fall down. Breaches in the wall were stuffed with fascines. But the chevalier de Drucour, governor of Louisbourg, was an able soldier who was determined to fight.

Colonel James Wolfe was perhaps more eager for battle. His reckless gallantry at Rochefort had already amazed his colleagues and impressed William Pitt, and now he was to lead the assault on Freshwater Cove. This was the crescent-shaped beach that William Pepperrell's colonials had seized to begin their successful siege of thirteen years ago, and Amherst was going to try to duplicate that maneuver—with the added diversion of a double feint at Flat Point and White Point, closer to the town.

About a thousand white-coated Frenchmen held the beaches from White Point to Freshwater Cove. Wolfe had perhaps more than that. After a few days of high surf and fog, they went over the side into their landing boats and pulled for the little quarter-mile beach lying between two piles of rocks.

The French opened up. Volleys of grape and musketry raked the British. Wolfe raised his hand to withdraw, but three boatloads of light infantry either missed his signal or ignored it. They rowed on, driving through the surf and landing among the leftward rocks. They leaped ashore. Wolfe saw them and ordered his other boats to follow. Another party, of ten men, hurdled the rocks and ran up the beach. French fire cut down half of them. Now other boats battled through the breakers. Some were hurled upon the rocks and stove in; others were broached or overturned, emptying their occupants into the surf. Infantrymen and grenadiers weighted with cartridges went down. Some arose without their muskets; others never got up. But the assault was going forward against a nearby French battery, and Colonel James Wolfe, his long, lank, red locks tied neatly behind his head, only a cane in his hand, was leaping among the rocks, urging his men forward and calling upon others to come into line.

Now another division of British came ashore to Wolfe's right, and the French, fearing to be cut off from Louisbourg, broke and ran for the woods. Once again Louisbourg had been flanked, and now the reduction of the fort was begun in steps almost identical to those of Pepperrell's campaign.

Amherst made his camp between Freshwater Cove and Flat Point, brought his guns and supplies ashore, and prepared to work his trenches and batteries forward within range of the fort. The French again abandoned the Grand Battery on the north shore of the harbor—although this time they left it useless to the British—and Colonel Wolfe took twelve hundred men around to Lighthouse Point, just opposite the Island Battery. Once more British cannons pounded the island's guns into silence, while Amherst's siege works snaked closer and closer to Louisbourg. The British guns roared night and day. Louisbourg's rotten walls crumbled and collapsed, sighed and fell apart.

"There is not a house in the place that has not felt the effects of this formidable artillery," a French officer wrote in his diary. "From yesterday morning till seven o'clock this evening we reckon that a thousand or twelve hundred bombs, great and small, have been thrown into the town, accompanied all the time by the fire of forty pieces of cannon, served with an activity not often seen. The hospital and the houses around it, which also serve as hospitals, are attacked with cannons and mortars. The surgeon trembles as he amputates a limb amid cries of *"Gare la bombe!"* [Watch out for the bomb!] and leaves his patient in the midst of the operation, lest he should share his fate. The sick and wounded, stretched on mattresses, utter cries of pain, which do not cease till a shot or the bursting of a shell ends them."

On June 26 the last of the French guns before the town were silenced and the walls so breached as to admit an assault. At that point Drucour asked for terms. Amherst and Boscawen were stern. Their master in London desired an end to the French in the New World. There would be no honors of war so that men allowed to depart with their arms sloped might one day return with muskets leveled. No, the garrison must surrender as prisoners of war.

Drucour refused. He would fight on, and he sent his reply by messenger. The courier had hardly departed before Intendant Prevost came to Drucour, beseeching him to spare the town and its inhabitants from further ruin and misery. He warned of the dangers of exposing the people and their possessions to an assault by storm. Drucour submitted. He sent another messenger to recall the first one, and notified the British that he accepted their terms.

For the last time in history the golden lilies fluttered down the flagstaff at Louisbourg. In Britain there was great rejoicing at the news of the victory. Cannon were fired, and the captured flags of Louisbourg were hung in St. Paul's. Throughout New England bells were rung and bonfires lighted from Boston to Newport.

Most ominous for New France, the tall, thin, nervous redhead who had been foremost in the battle sailed home to Britain on fire for the final thrust up to Québec.

PITT HAD RECALLED Loudon and allowed the American command to devolve upon the next in line, Major General James Abercromby. Pitt thought of Abercromby only less disdainfully than he had thought of Loudon, but even the Great Commoner could not ignore certain influences at court. Moreover, Pitt was hopeful that the real commander of the expedition against Ticonderoga would be Abercromby's junior, Brigadier Lord Augustus Howe.

Howe was the older brother of two other Howes—Richard and William—who were to appear ten years later in American history as an admiral and a general of British arms, respectively. Like his brother William, who had been with Amherst at Louisbourg, Augustus was an excellent soldier. Moreover, he was one British commander who respected the colonials. He had been trained by Captain Robert Rogers, and he insisted that the 6,350 regulars, as well as 9,000 colonials, whom Abercromby was to lead against Ticonderoga, learn to live and fight as the rangers did.

"You would laugh to see the droll figure we all make," one of his officers wrote home. "Regulars as well as provincials have cut their coats so as to scarcely reach their waists. No officer or private is allowed to carry more than one blanket and a bearskin. A small portmanteau is allowed each officer. No women follow the camp to wash our linen. Lord Howe has already shown an example by going to the brook and washing his own."

Howe also gave an example at "officers' mess." He had his staff sit on logs around a large dish full of pork and peas. Pulling a sheath containing a knife and fork from his pocket, he began to cut the meat. His staff looked away in horrified embarrassment, and Howe inquired: "Is it possible, gentlemen, that you have come on this campaign without providing yourselves with what is necessary?" Whereupon he gave them each a sheath like his own and they also fell to like a private.

On July 5 the Ticonderoga force embarked from the ruins of Fort William Henry upon the shining surface of Lake George. Rogers and his rangers led the way in whaleboats. Colonel Gage—the veteran of the Monongahela who would remain in American history for yet another war—was behind with the light infantry, and then Howe with the main body.

The following day the army began landing on the western shore of the lake. It was intended to march around the rapids of Lake George's outlet as they ran northeast and then turned west to Ticonderoga. In this way the British could attack the French fort from the rear.

Lord Howe and Major Israel Putnam went forward to reconnoiter. They encountered a party of about 350 French whom Montcalm had sent down to harass the British. A sharp fight began, and Lord Augustus Howe fell dead, shot through the chest. With one shot the French had saved themselves.

"In Lord Howe the soul of General Abercromby's army seemed to expire," Major Thomas Mante wrote. "From the unhappy moment the general was deprived of his advice, neither order nor discipline was observed, and a strange kind of infatuation usurped the place of resolution."

Worse, from wavering and hesitating, Abercromby moved to the conviction that he must do something—anything—and he attacked Montcalm exactly where that astute Frenchman expected him.

Montcalm had deduced that Ticonderoga was not to be attacked from the front, and he had ordered a huge breastwork constructed on a ridge behind the fort. Even officers had stripped to the waist to join the throng of axmen bringing thousands of trees crashing down. When completed, the breastwork stood eight to nine feet high. Firing platforms were provided behind it, and the entire line was zigzagged so that the front could be swept with flanking fire. On the sloping ground in front of the breastwork the French also built an abatis. An entire forest was felled, with the trunks pointing inward to the breastwork and the sharpened boughs of the treetops outward, toward the approaching British. When they did arrive they were startled to behold a flattened forest bristling toward them and behind that a massive breastwork crowning a hilltop.

And this is what Abercromby attacked. He had the cannons to batter down the breastwork, but he could not wait for them to be brought up from Lake George. He might have occupied Mount Defiance overlooking the redoubt and sent a plunging fire into it, or he might have left a holding force in front of Montcalm while marching through the woods to occupy the road to Crown Point in his rear. If he had turned the French line thus, he could have starved Montcalm into submission, for the French had only a week's provisions. But Abercromby, outnumbering Montcalm fifteen thousand to four thousand, possessing the initiative as well as all the beans and bullets he required while operating at the end of a shorter and menaced supply line, chose to storm a fixed position!

The result was disaster. The British fought bravely, and so did the French. "God save the king!" roared the British in their shortened red coats, and the French in white cried out *"Vive le roi!"* and *"Vive notre général!"* Seven times Abercromby pressed the assault, and each time his men were repulsed in blood and agony. At last he ordered a retreat. Two thousand dead, wounded, and missing had been sacrificed to his foolish conviction that men in the open with muskets can overwhelm men behind breastworks with muskets and cannon.

The second phase of Pitt's threefold campaign had failed. The outraged British soldiery fell back, cursing their commander as "Mrs. Nanny Cromby," while behind them their scholarly conqueror celebrated his victory by erecting a cross inscribed with the Latin poem he had composed attributing the triumph to the Almighty.

Rarely if ever do the defeated declare that God was on their side; and yet those retreating British colonials soon to call themselves Americans might also have claimed divine intervention. In the death of Lord Howe that "special Providence" that the cynical Bismarck, a century later, assigned to "fools, drunkards and the United States of America" already may have been at work. If Augustus Howe had lived it is possible, not so much that Ticonderoga would have fallen, but that the War of the American Revolution might have had a different result, and the history of the world followed a different course.

But Howe had died, and it was his brother William who would oppose that George Washington even then marching west again to Fort Duquesne.

DURING A BRIEF and earlier administration, William Pitt had introduced Scottish Highlanders into the British Army. These wild and kilted warriors—dreadful with their five-foot-long claymore swords and the banshee wail of their bagpipes—had only just been overwhelmed in the Stuart rising of "the Forty-five." But they were always ready to raise the Stuart banners again, and the French were always willing to finance them. Rather than fight them at home, the sagacious Pitt decided to use them to fight the French abroad.

Two regiments had been sent to America. One of them had fought valiantly at Ticonderoga. A handful of them, led by Captain John Campbell, had rushed through the French abatis, scaled the breastwork, jumped down—and been bayoneted there. Another regiment was part of the force of fifteen hundred regulars and forty-eight hundred colonials whom Brigadier John Forbes was leading against Duquesne.

This time the route was the direct one, from Philadelphia. Unfortunately for Forbes, the rigor of a wilderness journey over a rude road his army cut as it marched was too much for him to endure. He became violently ill. Sometimes he could not move, and at other times he moved only on a hammock slung between two horses. Command fell upon Lieutenant Colonel Henri Bouquet, an extremely able Swiss soldier of fortune and a man whom young Colonel Washington deeply admired. Moving by slow stages, establishing depots at regular points, the army crossed Pennsylvania.

On the fourteenth of September the British were only about a mile from the fort. Major Grant of the Highlanders received permission from Bouquet to go forward to reconnoiter. He took about eight hundred men, many of them provincials. By dark he had occupied a height overlooking Duquesne, half a mile away. Next day, he foolishly divided his forces.

He sent two hundred Virginians to the rear to guard his baggage, posted a hundred Pennsylvanias on his right toward the Allegheny, dispatched a company of Highlanders to his left toward the Monongahela, and then ordered another company of Scots into the plain in front of them. They were to take prisoners and burn the French outbuildings. It was early morning, Grant wrote later, and then, "In order to put on a good countenance, and convince our men they had no reason to be afraid, I gave directions to our drums to beat the reveille."

The effect was to arouse the French and Indians in Duquesne. Screeching and yelling, they came pouring out of the fort and fell upon the Highlanders on the plain. The Scots fought back. But then their commander was killed and they broke and fled, in their ears a fiendish whooping even more appalling than their own battle yells, and in their backs the tomahawks. Only the gallant intervention of the Virginians, who held off the entire French force at the loss of two-thirds of their own, saved Grant's command. As it was, he lost close to three hundred killed, wounded, or captured, and he himself was taken prisoner.

It was a melancholy beginning, and the rest of the Highlanders ground their teeth and wept with rage as they passed over the battleground two months later and saw the heads of their fallen comrades stuck up on poles and their kilts flounced around them in insulting suggestion of petticoats. But then the ground shook and a roar came from the direction of Duquesne.

The French were blowing up the fort!

Unknown to Forbes, the supplies destined for Duquesne had been captured by the British. Lieutenant Colonel John Bradstreet had executed one of the most brilliant strokes of the campaign of 1758. He had sailed up the Mohawk River at the head of three thousand men, reached Oswego, crossed Lake Ontario, and taken and destroyed Fort Frontenac. New France shuddered under a blow second only to the fall of Louisbourg. Her supply line to the west was severed, and Duquesne lay at the mercy of the advancing British.

Explosion upon explosion shook the cold November rain from the trees while Forbes's army hurried forward and the eyes of his Highlanders shone with the prospect of revenge. But Duquesne was a pile of ruins. George Washington, who had been first to the forks of the Ohio, gazed with a consummate satisfaction upon the deserted confluence of the two rivers.

The French were gone, five hundred of them, up the Allegheny or overland to Fort Le Boeuf. It was now the turn of the British to fortify the forks, to build a bastion named Fort Pitt, which would, one day, still in honor of the great British statesman, be the city of Pittsburgh.

The west had been won for Britain. New France was cut in two. Canada was flanked on the west by Fort Pitt and Oswego and on the east by Louisbourg. Winter was here, now, and there would be no news of fresh disaster to chill the hearts of the colonists along the St. Lawrence.

But in the spring or the summer, as many of them feared, they would see the white sails of the British creeping up the river to Québec.

CHAPTER 27

Washington: Patriot, Planter, Politician

COLONEL GEORGE WASHINGTON returned to Williamsburg hailed as a hero. No matter that Braddock was defeated and dead or that only the Acadian campaign out of the fourfold plan of conquest had succeeded, the Virginians under their youthful commander had alone stood up to the enemy, and but for them and their leader, total disaster might have befallen the British in this sorry Battle of the Monongahela. An exaggeration, yes, but this was the attitude of Dinwiddie down through the jubilant members of the House of Burgesses, who voted Washington £300 in recompense for his losses during the campaign, while the governor placed him in command of a new regiment of one thousand men to serve on the frontier.

George Washington spent three years on the border, protecting settlers there against the incursions of the Indians unleashed by the French at Duquesne, learning much about wilderness warfare while suffering anew under the onslaught of his twin afflictions of malaria and dysentery, plus a new source of pain from the deterioration of his teeth. Throughout this ordeal he steadily sought a commission in the British Army, and even though he had a staunch ally in Governor Dinwiddie, his campaign for royal rank was never successful. His friendship with the governor also cooled, chiefly through Washington's youthful arrogance and his alliance with those members of the House of Burgesses who were hostile to Dinwiddie.

Nevertheless, Washington had had the satisfaction of gazing upon the destruction of Duquesne. In November of 1758 he was with General John Forbes when he led the final expedition against the French. Approaching the fort with an overwhelming force, he found that its commander, with only five hundred men to defend it, had blown it up. Thus on November 25 George Washington had gazed in satisfaction upon the ashes and charred timbers of the fortification that had been for so long one of the objectives of his young life. Another—a commission of field rank in the British Army—was denied, for Washington shortly thereafter resigned from the Virginia militia.

During four years in uniform, George Washington had shown himself prone to all the arrogant vices of a young man in high command. He had quarreled with his benefactor, Dinwiddie, and played politics in Williamsburg while dissembling to British generals in hopes of receiving that commission. His hasty and rash attack in which Jumonville had died had triggered the greatest of colonial wars, and he had been rudely chastised for this at Fort Necessity. Only his self-possession at the Monongahela had rescued him from the reputation of a bungler, and yet he had shown by his unrivaled physical and moral courage, by a steadfastness in adversity that always redeemed his habit of complaint, joined to an astonishing durability and determination in hardship, ill health, and filthy weather, which, along with a simple dignity endearing him to his officers and the stern but fair discipline that made him beloved of his men, that here indeed was a chief. With this reputation to sustain him, he retired to a planter's life in Mount Vernon.

ALTHOUGH LAWRENCE WASHINGTON in his will had confirmed the arrangements made by his father—that his half brother George would receive Mount Vernon—he also provided that his wife, Anne Fairfax Washington, would have the use of the estate for life. However, Anne quickly remarried and ceded this right or usufruct to George upon annual payment of fifteen thousand pounds of tobacco. Upon her death in 1761 that payment ended, and George held the property free and clear.

Washington enjoyed life as a planter, and was on good terms with his neighbor George William Fairfax and the vivacious Sally. She sought to cure the dysentery that still tormented him by prescribing a diet for him. It was not successful, yet Washington's frequent rides downriver to Belvoir to consult with Sally soon brought him under her spell. She flirted with him, discreetly, especially after her husband departed for London, and Washington fell in love with her. He wrote her letters that were models of how, in a hideously involuted style, a man hopelessly infatuated tries to say something he knows he shouldn't say—and to his friend's wife.

Fortunately, Sally was only amused, holding him at arm's length by means of a kind of coy coquetry that embarrassed him. Perhaps she suspected, as George certainly knew, granting the mores of the day, that such a liaison could only end in the tragedy of a duel. At the same time that Washington was writing these missives he was actively courting Martha Dandridge Custis, a wealthy widow. Finding Sally inaccessible—and perhaps finding the prospect of great wealth pleasing and irresistible—he married Martha.

Martha Custis Washington was a delightful little dumpling. Barely literate, only five feet tall, plump, with a hooked nose and large baby blue eyes, if taller and shapelier she would still not have been sexually exciting. But she was very sweet and very gentle—and also very rich. The fortune she had inherited upon the death of her merchant husband, Daniel Parke Custis, upon her marriage to Washington went to him in accordance with the law and made him one of the wealthiest men in Virginia.

Having been elected to the House of Burgesses in 1765 and re-elected four years later, Washington was now not only a man of great possessions but also of political power. His happiness was real, even though he sired no children, probably because of his own sterility, inasmuch as Martha had borne four in her previous marriage, of whom a boy and a girl survived. Washington took these stepchildren to his heart, and was to them a loving and a caring father.

He now occupied himself with expanding his estate so that he soon presided over more than seven thousand acres, while his work force of a hundred slaves was greatly expanded by purchase and propagation. He was a good businessman, shrewd but honest, and also an agricultural innovator, shifting from the tobacco that so swiftly exhausted land to the farming of food crops, experimenting with varying degrees of success with grains and fibers. Under the relaxing influence of a happy marriage, his health improved remarkably, and he was eventually as robust and hardy as the high-hearted youth who had survived the ordeals of the Venango mission.

In his political life George Washington gradually came to be considered one of the outstanding members of the House of Burgesses. He shared the convictions of most of its members: perpetuation of the feudal status quo in the province, opposition to Parliament's harsher and harsher taxing measures. Although not a gifted orator in the manner of Patrick Henry or Richard Henry Lee, or a thinker of the perception of James Madison or Thomas Jefferson, he was nevertheless forthright and forceful. To him the Stamp Act was a "direful attack" upon colonial liberty. When Britain in 1768 prohibited white settlements beyond the Appalachian divide, ostensibly to protect the Indians, Washington bitterly attacked the decision as actually a measure to contain the colonies.

Charged by his critics with a venal ulterior motive—that is, his holdings behind that line—he replied that these were long-term investments, and no matter what the cabinet might decree, its line would eventually be breached—as it was. His dislike of the British, planted in him by those arrogant regular captains who refused to serve under him, then nourished by his failure to obtain a royal commission, was made to bloom by the London merchants who overcharged him for goods that were often of poor quality. Thus, with his friend George Mason, he was a leading author of Virginia's nonimportation agreement.

After King George III lifted the royal rod to chastise Boston, "that nest of sedition," and Massachusetts as well with his Coercive Acts, Washington rose from his seat in fury to ask: "Shall we, after this, whine and cry for relief, when we have already tried it in vain? Or shall we supinely sit and see one province after another fall a prey to despotism?"

From Lexington and Concord came the fiery reply, and so it was that when the Second Continental Congress convened on May 10, 1775, among those Virginia delegates who rode north to cross their Rubicon at the Potomac River, wearing his old blue uniform, was George Washington of Mount Vernon.

CHAPTER 28

"Clip and Cut, and Rob the King"

IN EARLY 1753 an engineer named Franquet was sent from France to Canada to supervise the strengthening of the fort at Louisbourg and to inspect all the defenses of New France. Intendant François Bigot, who met him at Québec, chose this journey as the excuse for one of his famous progresses to Montréal, supposedly to confer there with the city's governor, and also to show M. Franquet the various forts and fortified houses along the north bank of the St. Lawrence. Not surprisingly, this official journey of inspection, and for the alleged purpose of conferring with an inferior official, which would require no more than a few clerks and copyists to accompany him and the engineer, was immediately transformed into an enormous *voyage de plaisir*, requiring some twenty or more sleighs and sledges, together with the necessary horses, all to transport some twenty guests and their effects for 180 miles and back—all costs to be charged to His Majesty, King Louis XV.

Invitations to these galas of Bigot's were extended only to a favored few and were highly prized by those who received them. Especially happy with hers was the beautiful and witty Madame Pean, wife of the chevalier of that name, who had obligingly assigned all the pleasures of his boudoir to his charming host the intendant. The Chevalier de Pean received no invitation, yet moved a little higher in the esteem of his benefactor.

Because these *voyages de plaisir* were great favorites of the humble *habitants* of Québec, a sizable crowd had gathered outside the intendant's palace to say a merry farewell to the *monsieur* and his guests. The cavalcade of sleighs began on February 8, 1753. It was a cold day, and powdery white snowflakes were falling upon the snow-packed courtyard outside the intendant's palace. Vapor puffs shot from the mouths of the gaily uniformed sentinels on guard duty there. From time to time the sentinels propped their muskets against the palace wall to beat their mittened hands together for warmth.

By twos and fours, citizens of the city began to emerge from the palace. They had been dancing in the hall provided by the bounteous intendant. Although they were never allowed to join Bigot's dinner guests on the floor of his private dance hall, they were permitted to watch them from the gallery. They did not begrudge Bigot this, but rather were grateful to him for giving them their own *plaisance*.

Seeing the silently falling snow, the emerging *habitants* cried out in childish delight. They paused to watch a party of workmen loading sleighs with baggage. Larger sledges were already packed with bedding, blankets, table services, cooking utensils, dressed meats, wines and brandy, cheeses, chocolates, and other delicacies. Curious, the Québecois walked toward them, their boots making crunching noises on the hard-packed snow.

"Careful, there, good people," shouted a thickset man, the intendant's chief steward. "Those are the belongings of Monsieur Bigot's guests."

"Aha!" one of them yelled, as though accusingly. "Is the intendant going on another of his famous excursions to Montréal? *Un voyage de plaisir?*"

"Indeed he is," the steward replied, stamping his feet.

"How many guests this time?"

"Twenty or thirty."

"Aha! And is the lovely Madame de Pean among them?"

A great shout of laughter rose from the crowd, and the steward shook his cane at them angrily. "Off with you, *vous canaille* [you rabble]. Monsieur should hear how you reward his generosity."

"Don't forget the cards, *monsieur*," someone yelled.

"Or the perfume or the wine," cried another, and then, in the falsetto, trembling tone of a fallen woman, "Oh, *monsieur*, it was ze wine. I do not do theese wizout ze wine!"

Now the laughter turned mocking and ribald, even as the first man to ask a question laid an inquisitive hand on the bedding in a sledge, his voice changing to one of gravity: "Surely this is not sufficient for our gracious intendant?"

Still laughing, jeering at the infuriated steward, the crowd broke up and began to drift away—pelting each other with snowballs—and the steward turned to vent his wrath on the workmen: "You there—get these sledges with the food and things harnessed and sent on ahead. And you, Lieutenant," he said to a young officer of the guards, "Monsieur Bigot desires you to commandeer the *habitants* along the way to clear the snowdrifts and beat the roads smooth with their oxen."

"And what if they desire payment?"

"They'll be paid," the steward said, grunting. "Paid so well that the cost of hiring a horse for Montréal and back will cost the king what he paid for it."

The lieutenant snickered. "Clip and cut, and rob the king—it is the way of life in Canada, eh, monsieur?"

"Never mind that!" the steward snapped, staring glumly at the thickening snow, now swirling and whipping in sheets. "And be sure that the horses are harnessed to the sleighs in the morning."

The lieutenant's words were true enough. The colony of New France had indeed become the land of Clip-and-Cut, although it was not until the advent of the new intendant, François Bigot, in 1749, that the corruption of officials such as afflicts any colony of monarchy became, under the hand of this ugly, pimply-faced son of an untitled though noble Bordeaux family, organized and led in the cause of embezzlement.

In the dual government of Canada the governor, representing the king and also commanding the military, and the intendant, in charge of trade, finance, justice, and all other departments of civil administration, usually quarreled, but the governor was still the chief. However, with the almost simultaneous arrival in Québec of Intendant Bigot and Governor Pierre François Rigaud de Vaudreuil, the government operation became one of perfect harmony. That in itself should have been a warning to the king and his ministers in Versailles. Why harmony, rather than a fruitful tension? Why? To rob the king, of course—and any other person or institution of great wealth.

It has been said that François Bigot was "born in the bosom of magistracy," meaning that his father and grandfather had been important members of the Parlement of Bordeaux. They had been his untiring instructors in the arts of government and legislation. They had also been high-minded and honorable men. Their descendant François was not. His political skills, though great, were for but one purpose: exploitation.

At a first meeting his scrofulous features tended to repel a stranger; but when to this repulsive face was joined the charm of such easy and agreeable manners that the stranger soon—having rebuked himself mentally for such a cruel, unfriendly judgment—came under his spell. In spite of imperfect health, Bigot was a tireless worker and an indefatigable pursuer of pleasure and prestige. His achievements were so many and so varied that less gifted friends were actually embarrassed

in his presence. He always sought to put them at their ease. Successful in both business and politics, with great official experience, he
was also energetic, good-natured, free-handed, and eager to oblige.
Friends in need never found him ungenerous, but rather ever ready to
open his purse without interest or strict limitation on the length of a
loan. As a result he had many friends and admirers, few of whom even
suspected that much of this largesse had once been the king's. He was
also a social butterfly, fond of frolics and dances and regattas, and lav-
ish in entertainment.

Bigot was enormously popular, not only with his guests but also
with his stewards, cooks, servants, and winemasters, who followed
the party in sleighs of their own. Each sleigh contained one or two
couples, not all of whom were united in Holy Matrimony. Bigot and
the beautiful Madame de Pean were alone in the leading sleigh. Moving briskly along, the procession, with its hissing steel runners, passed
at full trot down St. Vallier Street, the snorting of the horses mingling
with the farewell shouts of an admiring crowd gathered to either side
of the road. Just before dusk Bigot's happy revelers stopped at Pointe-
aux-Trembles, where all piled out of their conveyances to find lodging
for the night. Afterward they gathered around their bountiful friend to
sup with him.

In the morning Bigot regaled his friends with tea, coffee, and chocolate while the militia captain hastened to harness fresh horses to the
sleds. Setting out again, the caravan clattered into Cap-Sante, stopping
for two hours at the house of another militia captain for a hearty
breakfast, and also to warm themselves. In the afternoon they reached
Ste. Anne de la Perade, where they partook of a splendid supper provided by Bigot in his private lodgings, where many corks were
popped and much Canadian brandy imbibed. Next morning brought
them to Three Rivers, where Franquet's traveling companion—
Madame Marin, whose husband was in Montréal—insisted on stopping to see her sister, the wife of Montréal's governor Rigaud, brother
of the colony's governor. Being ill, Madame Rigaud was unable to receive all her visitors in bed, so they repaired to the governor's dining
room, where an ample dinner awaited them. Later they returned to
Madame Rigaud's bedchamber for coffee, conversation, and cards.
Both Franquet and Madame Rigaud's sister begged off further revelry
on the plea of exhaustion, both retiring to the bedroom prepared for
them.

Isle-au-Castor was the next stopping place. Being called to supper
as they sat down to cards, all were surprised and delighted by the ap-

pearance of Governor Rigaud, who had come up from Montréal. With him were four of his officers, among them the chevalier de Pean and Lieutenant Colonel Michel Marin, who had been made commander of Duquesne's expedition to the Ohio River. Everywhere embraces and glad cries of greeting were exchanged, especially between Madame Marin and her husband, Lieutenant Colonel Marin. Somewhat glumly, M. Franquet spent a lonely evening directing the servants to remove the partitions from the main compartments so all could join in a much larger room for another excellent supper and the customary game of cards.

Reaching Montréal the following night, all but the residents of the city were lodged at the Intendency, the official residence of the hospitable Bigot, who, as usual, provided another succulent meal for all. In the morning they roved the city, visiting friends, and calling upon persons of consequence, such as the naval commissary Varin; the king's storekeeper Martel; and Antoine Penisseault and François Maurin—profiteers all, and soon to exchange their fame for an unwelcome notoriety.

During the next few days a succession of fetes followed, including the blessing of three flags to be carried to the Ohio River by the militia of Colonel Marin. Not to be outdone by the tirelessly beneficent François Bigot, Governor Rigaud arranged for a magnificent dinner and a splendid supper, to which all the quality folk of Montréal were invited. Nevertheless, it was not quite possible to outdo the intendant when challenged. During the week before Lent at least forty guests supped at his table every evening, and dances, masquerades, and cards followed, with unrestrained gaiety everywhere. While torches flamed and candles flickered, the music of the quadrilles excited the dancers to faster and faster rhythms.

Gambling was almost always the chief feature of Bigot's entertainments, and for some unknown reason it seemed that the stakes grew deeper as the flames of the Seven Years' War spread wider and wider, eventually engulfing at least seven of the foremost kingdoms of Europe. Bigot himself played desperately, seated at the tables and glancing to neither right nor left, seemingly hypnotized by the clicking, rolling balls or the sound of the baccarat dealer's voice. Usually he lost; early in 1758 his losses amounted to 204,000 francs, a stunning financial blow, but one he knew how to recoup. So did those sophisticated gentlemen who had accompanied Governor Rigaud to Isle-au-Castor.

No one entertained more lavishly than the intendant. He also delighted in being identified as among the leaders of what may be called the First Families of Canada. Socializing—and with it not only the theater or those fantastic *voyages de plaisir* up or down the frozen great river, but also, of course, wine and brandy—may have been the antidotes for the brutal winters and the ever-present fear of the Iroquois. Yet, the principal Canadian families were so social and so related by intermarriage that, together with the civil and military officers of the colonial establishment, they formed an exclusive society much akin to the corresponding Cavaliers of Virginia. Actually aristocratic rather than democratic with a grace and an ease rare in republics, they astonished visitors from France to find such an accomplished and glittering small social circle flourishing inside an enormous wilderness surrounded and constantly menaced by tribes of savage cannibals.

Membership in this exclusive society was not always easy to obtain, but then, as the European war claimed its victims, the recall of military officers or the patriotism of fathers and sons reduced its ranks; and thus the doors of the finest homes, once open only to "the best" in the colony and closed to all others, began to swing wider to admit unworthy candidates for admission whose only credentials were their bank accounts swollen by peculation.

Chief among these was butcher's boy Joseph Cadet.

SON OF A Québec butcher, Joseph Cadet went to sea as a pilot's boy at the age of thirteen. Quickly recoiling from the dangers of a sailor's life, he next became a cowherd, finally following his father to the butcher's block. Here he prospered, and here he also met François Bigot, who, recognizing a kindred spirit, obtained for him in 1756 the appointment of commissary-general, a move that for both these unscrupulous profiteers swung wide the doors of embezzlement. During the next two years, one after another, Bigot and other associates of Cadet—Pean, Maurin, Corpron, and Pennisseault—sold to the king for about 23 million francs provisions that had cost them 11 million, leaving them a net profit of 12 million. There was no proof that Bigot shared in Cadet's profits, but neither is there any evidence that he did not. Furthermore, Bigot had other sources of wealth.

As intendant, it was part of his function to see that the king's storehouses for the supply of regular troops, militia, and Indians were kept well stocked. With Breard, the naval comptroller, Bigot next formed a partnership with Gradis and Son at Bordeaux. Then Bigot wrote the colonial minister to state that there were already enough stores in Canada to last three years, and it would be more advantageous for the king to buy stores in the colony rather than to buy them in France and run the risk of losing them at sea. Gradis and Son then shipped stores to Canada in great quantities, while Breard or his agent declared at the customhouse that they belonged to the king and thus escaped duty on them. Using fictitious names, and as the occasion arose, they were then sold to the king at huge profits. Frequently they were also sold to some favored speculator or merchant, who in turn sold them to the king's storekeeper.

Often goods passed through several successive buyers until the price rose to double or triple the first cost, Intendant Bigot and his partners sharing the profits with friends and allies. Because they would allow no one else to sell to the king, they established a monopoly that was of great profit to those who held it. Sometime before the war, Bigot set up a warehouse under the name of Claverie on land belonging to the king. It was not far from his own palace. Here the goods shipped from Bordeaux were received, to be sold at retail to the *habitants*, and wholesale to the king and favored merchants. This was the establishment popularly known as La Friponne (The Cheat). Soon there was another Friponne opened in Montréal.

Now from the perfervid brain of François Bigot there began to issue an astonishing variety of fraudulent schemes. Thus, as intendant it was his duty to sell the king's huge fortune in furs to the highest bidder at public auction. Instead, he sold them quietly and at a low price to his own confederates. It was also his duty to provide transportation for troops, along with other munitions, provisions, and stores. Here he touched nothing, except the ships and boats he hired or bought and rented or sold to the king at high prices.

Yet, for all of Bigot's clever manipulations, he was still only the second-greatest thief in Canada. His partner Joseph Cadet was the true Ali Baba, and from his post as commissary-general he reaped a golden harvest that made him the richest man in New France, but still—alas!—only the second in ugliness behind Bigot.

Yet Cadet needed the assistance of Bigot when Cadet embarked upon his greatest raid upon the Royal Treasury. Having bought for 600,000 francs a great quantity of stores belonging to the king, he sold them back to His Majesty for 1.4 million francs! He eclipsed even this coup when he bought stores for the post at Miramichi for 889,544 francs and sold these, too, to the king—for 1,614,354 francs.

A man of oafish personality and insatiable greed, Cadet was not a clever swindler in the silky-smooth style of François Bigot, but rather an unimaginative knave in the traditional style of the crooked entrepreneur who reaps his stolen profit with fertilizing showers of gifts and favors to venal clerks, post commanders, commisariats, inspectors, storekeepers, and other servants of the king so they would sign the various requisitions attesting to the fact that this amount of stores was duly delivered and paid for at the price specified in advance, when in fact the amount of supplies delivered was usually half of what was ordered. In brief, Cadet's specialty was the falsification of accounts, done with the cooperation of those officials who ordered them—civil and military—and bribed by Cadet by gifts of wine, brandy, or money, or even those pearls of great pleasure, obliging damsels.

The butcher's boy stopped at nothing, and some of his schemes were so odious that most of his accomplices, including Bigot, refused to participate in them. When the British as a "measure of military necessity" began to deport some sixty-five hundred Acadians from their homeland of what is now called Nova Scotia, it was found that many of them were literally starving to death. Hearing of their travail, the compassionate Cadet sent them not wholesome food, but moldy and unsalable salt cod that would probably hasten—rather than prevent—their demise. All this rotten fish was unknowingly paid for at sky-high prices by the king.

Cadet also falsely informed the intendant that the *habitants* were hoarding their grain, and obtained from him an order requiring them to sell the food at a ridiculously low price on pain of having it seized. Thus nearly all of it fell into Cadet's hands, but he did not sell it immediately, waiting until the threat of a famine sent its price rocketing skyward—whereupon he sold it partly to the king and partly to its first owners. Another of his unconscionable "deals" was to sell provisions to the king that were sent to outlying forts, and then falsely reported as having been consumed, whereupon he did send them to their proper destinations, for which he charged the king a second time. Small wonder that an observor of the times could write, "This is the land of abuses, ignorance, prejudice and all that is monstrous in government. Peculation, monopoly and plunder have become a bottomless abyss."

Command of a fort offered so many opportunities of making money, according to Sieur Louis-Antoine de Bougainville, that the mere prospect of a three-year tour was enough for a young officer to marry upon. Such appointments were within the gift of the governor, who was accused of sharing the profits—probably with good cause. Military contractors had swindles of their own, among them contracts for the transportation of military stores issued by a local commandant or the governor. They contained an order requiring the *habitants* to serve him as boatmen, teamsters, or porters, under the promise of a year's exemption as soldiers. This saved the contractor his most costly item of expense, thus increasing his profits in proportion.

Gifts to the Indians to keep them friendly or to send them on the warpath were other outstanding expenses for the crown. The number of recipients was multiplied many times, the surplus being bartered for more valuable furs bringing much higher profits. At one of the posts Colonel Marin and Rigaud, the governor's brother, made a quick profit of 312,000 francs with such tactics. Again shocked, the honorable Bougainville asked: "Why is it that of all which the king sends to the Indians two-thirds are stolen, and the rest sold to them instead of being given?"

Knavery and corruption ran through the life of New France like the warp and woof of the threads in woven cloth, with the exception that French troops of the line were not included in the general contagion of corruption afflicting militia and colony regulars—that is, Canadian-born—as well as the civil service. Most conspicuous among these dishonest soldiers was Major Pean—Le Petit Pean, or Little Pean, as he was called—more celebrated for feats of the boudoir than those of the battlefield. His young wife—Mademoiselle Desmeloizes, Canadian like himself—was famed through the colony for her beauty, vivacity, and wit, qualities that immediately attracted the repulsive Bigot. When Madame Pean accepted him as her lover, the fortune of her husband was made. Major Pean had no real talent as a swindler and was therefore doubly surprised when the attendant loaned him enough money to buy a large quantity of grain; "doubly" surprised because the money came from the Royal Treasury, and the price of the grain was raised beyond the dreams of avarice by his dear friend his wife's lover. On this transaction Major Pean made 50,000 crowns, and within a few more years his personal wealth was estimated at 2 million to 4 million francs.

Madame Pean became a power in Canada, dispenser of favors and offices, usually fed her by her lover and used to extend their dual reign in Canada, the one King of Affluence, the other Queen of Influence. Soon those who coveted the king's gold joined the train of the Queen of Influence, while those who sought merely pleasure and prestige knelt at the throne of the King of Affluence.

What is really amazing about this pack of golden jackals is their resilience and versatility, and—best of all—the incredible thickness of their skin. Thus Pean, jilted by his wife, made profitable love to the wife of his partner M. Penisseault. Though the lowborn daughter of a Montréal tradesman, Madame Penisseault had the calm and benevolent air of a countess, presiding with great dignity and grace in her dining room surrounded by the clerks of Cadet and the lower rank of clerical officials. The chevalier de Levis—among the finest officers in the king's army—was completely captivated by the charms of Madame Penisseault and was seen frequently at her table, although his friends considered that his attendance there was below his station.

As Bigot had succeeded Pean in the charms of Mademoiselle Desmeloizes, and Pean succeeded Penisseault in the favors of Madame Penisseault, the chevalier de Levis succeeded Pean—making certain that when he returned to France there would be no more successions, for he took Madame Penisseault with him.

There may not have been enough paper in all of Canada or Versailles to contain the roll call of those engaged in knavery, peculation, corruption, and unblushing robbery in the colony of New France, or of ink to inscribe them; or to do the same for all the letters of rebuke and reproach, or those threatening arrest and trial or recall, sent across the Atlantic Ocean by Colonial Minister Berryer. Among names of lesser consequence in this carousel of jackals, hyenas, and crocodiles was Varin, commissary of marine, an accomplice of Bigot, and his deputy in Montréal. He was a Frenchman of low birth, short in stature, sharp-witted, conceited, arrogant, capricious, bullheaded, and dissolute. Useless and worthless as he was, he still found a place among the governor's chosen, although in his tireless intriguing to supplant Bigot in the intendancy, he did display a certain unfamiliarity with reality that was not at all surprising in a person of so many small parts. Scenting a visit from the sheriff, he decided to turn informer, but in betraying all his confederates in embezzlement he mistakenly included himself. Among those he delivered to judgment were Deschenaux, son of a Québec shoemaker, and copyist in the office of the intendant; Martel, king's storekeeper in Montréal; the hunchback Maurin, not to be confused with the soldier Marin; and Corpron, an oily clerk dismissed by his employers several times for dishonesty, a skill much prized by M. Cadet, who enlisted him in his service, where he grew rich.

Strangely enough, the name of Marquis Pierre François Rigaud de Vaudreuil, governor of New France, was seldom if ever delated to Versailles as being among the confederates who were steadily and even openly depleting the royal treasury of La Belle France.

When a flow of irate letters of accusation and denunciation from the colonial minister began arriving at Château St. Louis atop the Rock of Québec, Vaudreuil—who was certainly among the peculators—did not carry out his instructions to rebuke the intendant for his "mal-administration," a new euphemism for robbery, but instead became his ardent advocate and defender. He wrote:

"I cannot conceal from you, Monseigneur, how deeply M. Bigot feels the suspicions expressed in your letter to him. He does not deserve them, I am sure. He is full of zeal for the service of the king; but as he is rich, or passes as such, and as he has merit, the ill-disposed are jealous, and insinuate that he has prospered at the expense of His Majesty. I am certain that it is not true, and that nobody is a better citizen than he, or has the king's interest more at heart."

And then Vaudreuil actually requested a patent of nobility for Joseph Cadet: the butcher's boy and King of the Golden Jackals!

In 1758, when Pean went to France, Vaudreuil wrote to the minister: "I have great confidence in him. He knows the colony and its needs. You can trust all he says. He will explain everything in the best manner. I shall be extremely sensible to any kindness you may show him, and hope that when you know him you will like him as much as I do."

In desperation François Bigot was now like a spider trapped in his own web. The corruption that he and Cadet once controlled together had grown like a genie and was now uncontrollable. Again and again Bigot's confederates had dragged him into ventures that seemed to become riskier and more reckless day by day. He did not dare to refuse them in their incessant demands: his connivance and his signature. He wrote to the minister asking leave to retire from office on the plea of ill health, hoping that his successor would be held accountable for the disaster that was now stalking him. But there was no reply.

Little Pean had already withdrawn, sailing back to France with all his plunder, buying land to build a palatial house where he would be safe. But would he? Would any of them? Like a shipwrecked sailor clinging to a spar, Bigot thought that perhaps he, too, would be safe, because of his wartime service to the king. By his administrative skills he might be: his energy, his executive power, his resourcefulness. But he wasn't. He knew that by the tone of the letters arriving from Minister Berryer, full of frightening menace and rebuke. In the last one, he wrote:

"The ship *Britannia*, laden with goods such as are wanted in the colony, was captured by a privateer from St. Malo, and brought into Québec. You sold the whole cargo for 800,000 francs. The purchasers made a profit of 2 million. You bought back a part for the king at 1 million, or 200,000 more than the price for which you sold the whole.

With conduct like this it is no wonder that the expenses of the colony become insupportable. The amount of your drafts on the treasury is frightful. The fortunes of your subordinates throw suspicion on your administration."

In another letter, the same day, the irate minister wrote:

"How could it happen that the smallpox among the Indians cost the king a million francs? What does this expense mean? Who is answerable for it? Is it the officers who command the posts, or is it the storekeepers? You give me no particulars. What has become of the immense quantity of provisions sent to Canada last year? I am forced to conclude that the king's stores are set down as consumed from the moment they arrive, and then sold to His Majesty at exorbitant prices. Thus, the king buys stores in France, and buys them again in Canada. I no longer wonder at the immense fortunes made in the colony."

Some months later—almost sputtering with indignation—the minister wrote again: "I write, *monsieur*, to answer your last two letters, in which you tell me that instead of 16 millions, your drafts on the treasury of 1758 will reach 24 millions, and that this year they will rise from 31 to 33 millions. It seems, then, that there are no bounds to the expenses of Canada. They double almost every year, while you seem to give yourself no concern except to get them paid. Do you suppose that I can advise the king to approve such an administration? Or do you think that you can take the immense sum of 33 millions out of the royal treasury by merely assuring me that you have signed drafts for it? This, too, for expenses incurred irregularly, often needlessly, always wastefully; which make the fortune of everybody who has the least hand in them, and about which you know so little that after reporting them at 16 millions, you find two months after that they will reach 24.

"You are accused of having given the furnishing of provisions to one man, who, under the name of commissary-general, has set what prices he pleased; of buying for the king at second or third hand what you might have got from the producer at half the price; of having in this and other ways made the fortunes of persons connected with you; and of living in splendor in the midst of a public misery, which all the letters from the colony agree in ascribing to bad administration, and in charging M. de Vaudreuil with weakness in preventing."

It is doubtful that the Minister—M. Berryer—unearthed all this incredible record of theft and embezzlement, robbery and graft by his own independent action, but rather that General Montcalm had come to Canada to take charge of the military, which Vaudreuil had almost entirely neglected, and that Montcalm had been writing in cipher for months to his friend Marechal de Belleisle, the minister of war, detailing the contagion of corruption that would soon destroy the colony. Then came these sadly tragic and prophetic sentences:

"It seems as if they were all hastening to make their fortunes before the loss of the colony; which many of them perhaps desire as a veil to their conduct. I have often spoken of these expenditures to M. de Vaudreuil and M. Bigot; and each throws the blame on the other."

Before the general wrote those fateful words, the colonial minister had already written to Vaudreuil and Bigot ordering them to do nothing important without first consulting General Montcalm, "not only in matters of war, but in all matters of administration touching the defense and preservation of the colony."

Next, an investigator knowledgeable in the ways of dishonest public officials was sent to Canada from Bordeaux to conduct an inquiry, and after six months of patient inquisition discovered the existence of four separate combinations for successful plundering of the Royal Treasury. With this Bigot realized that even now his usefulness as a wartime administrator was at an end. The investigator—one Querdisien-Tremais—demanded that the intendant name his confederates. He did not hurry to obey, although he did make a great scene of breaking with Commissary-General Cadet and forcing him to disgorge a paltry 2 million francs of stolen money, after which he and his accomplices became so frightened that they coughed up almost 7 million francs more.

This was done with a great show of sacrifice, repentance, and remorse among them all, as if 9 million francs in penance was anything more than a mere bagatelle. They knew well that the Fool-Killer with his bloody and undiscriminating long scythe was on his way.

CHAPTER 29

Québec I: Before the Battle

"VELL, DEN," the old king said with a growl, "iff Volfe is matt, den I hope he pites some udders of my chenerals."

The duke of Newcastle was surprised and shaken. Nominal head of the British government, though actually only the pussycat partner of the leonine Pitt, the duke had expected that George II would accept his judgment that the young soldier whom Pitt had rashly promoted to major general at age thirty-two was not only inferior to many other officers in years and experience but was also slightly demented.

In fairness to Newcastle, it should be made clear that James Wolfe did not in the slightest resemble the "normal" British officers of the late eighteenth century. Because memories of Cromwell's Roundheads—those pious murderers and hymn-singing regicides—had not entirely faded in the minds of the resurgent British aristocracy, one of the first orders of business was to renew the strength of the armed forces as the guardian of their old way of life—not to say dominance—that the Lord High Protector had come so close to exterminating.

Because of this the exclusive forms of family wealth and influence in British political life took on even more rigid forms in the reborn armed forces. All the higher commands and appointments went either by purchase or recommendation to members of the royal family or the aristocracy, while officers of demonstrated leadership and bravery remained captains and lieutenants during their entire career in the military.

One of these was James Wolfe.

Indeed, Wolfe's origins were neither low nor middling nor high, but rather sketchy and almost obscure, with one foot in Ireland and the other in York. It was James's father, Edward Wolfe, who had caused the family tree to rise above the level plain of nonentity, drawing upon the warrior traditions of two bellicose races. Edward must have been a most unusual man, having enlisted as a private in the Marines, rising rapidly under the duke of Marlborough to the rank of lieutenant, and thence to a lieutenant colonelcy. Following the Peace of Utrecht in 1714, Lieutenant Colonel Wolfe retired, marrying and settling in Kent, where his oldest son—James—was born on January 2, 1727.

James Wolfe considered no career other than the profession of arms. One of the happiest moments of his life was the outbreak of the War of the Austrian Succession in 1740, which he actually hoped would not end before he became eligible to follow in the footsteps of his dashing father. He was then thirteen and a half, just barely eligible for the dubious delights of battle; and his father had heard again the call to arms, becoming a colonel of one of the eight new regiments of Marines that were raised. Colonel Wolfe had hoped to take young James along with him as a cadet when he sailed in July 1740 as adjutant general of a force of ten thousand men bound for the disastrous siege of Cartagena in the Caribbean. James was overjoyed at the prospect of accompanying his father, but he fell seriously ill aboard a troopship at Portsmouth and had to be put ashore.

He recovered, and in the following year he was commissioned a second lieutenant in his father's regiment, but there is no record of active service, which was indeed fortunate, for he was to suffer horribly from seasickness, which, as a Marine aboard the dreadful troopships of the British Navy of those days, was like unto a sentence of living-death.

Before the force embarked for France, it was reviewed by King George II and his two sons—the prince of Wales and the duke of Cumberland—all three of them repulsive with their gargoylelike puffy features and their short, plump bodies, so typical of the German sovereigns and princes from Hanover who ruled the Celtic races of Britain and thus could never be mistaken as fearful conquerors; and yet the slender, boyish ensign who stood before his regiment proudly clutching its colors was, despite his own unwarlike face and features, indeed every inch a soldier. He was gangling, narrow-shouldered, and wide-hipped, and his slanting forehead and receding chin seemed to form a perfect obtuse angle with his sharply pointed nose. But his firm mouth and intelligent, belligerent, dark blue eyes—along with his flaming mop of brilliant red hair and his clear, pale skin—were the marks indeed of the Minstrel Boys going to the wars with "their fathers' swords girded on and their wild harps slung behind them."

Young Wolfe was exalted, almost forgetting his dread of an English Channel crossing that could erupt in a wild, rough sea, and eventually thankful that it was calm and brief: a short and peaceful thirty knots.

Though but a fifteen-year-old ensign, he was proud to be marching with the British Army to fight the French at Dettingen on the Main River and to know that for the last time a British sovereign would command in the field. True enough, roly-poly little George II, dull, miserly, and avaricious though he might be, was nevertheless brave and belligerent.

On the march across Flanders, Wolfe wrote to his mother of his joy on approaching the battlefield, even though his legs were sore and his knees aching—cursing himself bitterly that he was only a lowly infantry officer and not one of those gorgeous Marine commanders from Valhalla he had yearned to be. Nearing the enemy, he wrote: "We are now near forty miles from Frankfurt, which we marched in two days and two nights with about nine or ten hours' halt. The men were almost starved . . . [neither] they nor the officers had little more than bread and water to live on." But instead of complaining of his hardships, he reports with great pride: "I am now doing and have done ever since we encamped the duty of an adjutant." Already his abilities had been noticed and rewarded by Colonel Duroure.

Wolfe had not very much to write home about at Dettingen, for it had hardly been more than a confused brawl—and for a time it appeared that the counterattacking French would cut the British off from their base. But one of the enemy's wings was so badly mismanaged that Duroure's regiment in the center of the British line—by reason of its steady and controlled fire—was able to retrieve the situation. James Wolfe never forgot this bloody, thundering lesson in the necessity of disciplined fire from both muskets and cannon, and thereafter would regard it as the primary purpose of military training.

After the victory at Dettingen he was so exhausted that he had to retire to his tent for a few days, where the regimental surgeon bled him. But he was soon on his feet again, buoyed by his formal appointment as adjutant, and then exhilarated a few days later by his promotion to lieutenant.

James Wolfe had begun his ascent of Mount Olympus.

AT DETTINGEN WOLFE had drunk for the first time the heady waters of a military Pierian spring, and he drank deeply of that magic draught. A year later, at age seventeen, he was promoted to captain. Though his regiment did not fight the French again at Fontenoy, it had relieved a battered one that had, just as he was commissioned a brigade major, and then called home for "the Forty-five," as the Jacobite rising of the Scottish clans under "Bonnie Prince Charlie" was called. There, at the age of eighteen, he was aide-de-camp to the brutal General "Hangman" Hawley at the decisive Battle of Culloden.

Wolfe rather liked Hawley, cruel and merciless as he was to the defeated Highlanders. Like St. Paul, "he was approving everything that was being done against them." There was much of Saul of Tarsus in James Wolfe. He, too, was intense, ugly, and zealous, thirsting to fight for the king, just as Paul hungered to serve the Lord. He was also touched with "divine discontent," exalted in one moment and sunk in despair the next. At first sight some of his comrades undoubtedly must have avoided him as a neurotic caricature of a soldier, picking constantly at his cuffs and buttons with long, tapering fingers. He did not even wear a military wig but allowed his hair to grow lank and long, pinning it together at the back of his head like any jackanapes.

As he had at every battle he had known from Dettingen to Culloden, he earned the respect and affection of two brave young officers of about his own age. The first was Captain Robert Monckton, who had commanded the Acadian operation in 1755 and of whom Wolfe was very fond; the other was a capable young officer named James Murray. Both were blue bloods, though none so purely azure as the fluid that flowed in the veins of the aristocrat George Townshend, whose biting wit and sarcastic artistic skill had made him a merciless critic of young Major Wolfe, though he was but two years his senior in age, and decidedly junior in rank.

George Townshend had also been at Dettingen, acting as an honorary aide-de-camp to Lord Dunmore, who commanded one of the British divisions in the second line. Such honors were taken as a matter of course to this scion of one of Britain's oldest and most influential families. Unlike the vicarage and rented house in which James Wolfe had first seen the light of day, Townshend's home was the family seat at Raynham Hall, an Inigo Jones masterpiece in pink brick built on land they had owned since the twelfth century, and which during the course of half a millennium they had assiduously stocked with one of the finest art collections in the land.

Townshend's uncles were the powerful financier Henry Pelham, first lord of the Treasury, and the duke of Newcastle, secretary of state and master politician who had introduced his glory-seeking nephew to Lord Dunmore with this glowing recommendation: "He has an inclination to the army and intends to serve as a volunteer this campaign in our army in Germany. The favor I have to beg is that Your Lordship would take him particularly under your protection and that he may have the honor and advantage of your advice and direction. I am sensible of the service it must be to a young man of quality who may be desirous of coming into the army to be assisted and favored with Your Lordship's countenance."

Townshend's most famous and powerful relative was his grandfather Charles Townshend, Viscount Raynham, known to the British press as "the Champagne Charlie of British politics" for his fondness for a glass of bubbly. In the American colonies he was also infamous as the author of those oppressive "Townshend Acts" imposing taxes on imports from Britain such as glass, tea, and certain painters' materials, by which he might have earned—but never prized—the sobriquet of "Father of the United States," for his exactions drove the colonists into such a towering rage that they shook off all allegiance to the Crown. His asinine remark that he "understood" the Americans put him in the same class with the pig who taught Sunday school.

Fortunately for James Wolfe, he saw very little of this unblushing plant of the aristocratic hothouse variety, for he would have been close to apoplexy had he been introduced to such a precious "young man of quality" as a comrade-in-arms. Very quickly, Townshend left the Twentieth Foot Soldiers to join the duke of Cumberland's personal staff—an appointment in modern America similar to becoming an aide-de-camp to the chairman of the Joint Chiefs of Staff. But he did reach Flanders for the British Army's last campaign of the war—not, of course, as close to the enemy as James Wolfe had been. At the Battle of Laufeldt, with the British cut in two, Wolfe, though wounded, conducted a desperate rear guard action that enabled the ruptured parts to reunite. For this he received the formal gratitude of the commander in chief, though not, as he had hoped, another promotion.

George Townshend, meanwhile, had been sent home as the bearer of Cumberland's triumphant battle dispatches; and when he landed, he learned that in his absence he had been elected a member of Parliament for Norfolk.

Inevitably and eventually, Townshend found himself lampooned by the waspish Horace Walpole, who described him as "a very particular young man, who, with much oddness, some humor, no knowledge, great fickleness, greater want of judgment and with still more disposition to ridicule, had once or twice promised to make a good speaker." Townshend's wit got him into bad odor with the duke of Cumberland, and the king's son, as commander in chief of the British Army, was not amused by his description of the House of Hanover as a home for murderers (King George I himself), adulterous wives, sauerbraten mitt sauerkraut, and kaduffelglaze. So George Townshend found himself a civilian again, although he was back in uniform when the flames of the Seven Years' War finally engulfed almost all of Europe.

As it did, Townshend learned to his amazement that the despicable Lieutenant Colonel James Wolfe—that lanky hank of a red-haired Irish hostler—had made deliberately sensational attacks on the military establishment, especially on the noble and gracious duke of Cumberland, in order to advance himself above his betters. Well, Townshend thought indignantly, once he was back with his old regiment he would show this neurotic upstart his proper place.

AS HAD BECOME customary, James Wolfe's proper place was at the cannon's mouth, and this time he had been sent there by none other than William Pitt. Lord Chatham—as Pitt was now known—had seen what he thought was another opportunity to chastise his mortal enemy France. With most of the French Army engaged by Frederick the Great in Central Europe, Pitt decided to strike the enemy's weakened rear with an amphibious invasion of the French Atlantic port of Rochefort. Ten thousand troops and six months of supplies aboard a fleet of troop transports and supply ships protected by sixteen ships of the line of battle—as battleships were then called—were concentrated in southern British ports, preparing to set sail in early September of 1757. Pitt also saw this operation as a heaven-sent opportunity to break the backs of the military traditionalists who still chose their senior officers from the ranks of the wealthy or wellborn. So he personally chose as quartermaster-general and fourth in command for the entire expedition the likeliest of all the rising young commanders, James Wolfe—still a lieutenant colonel.

Dropping anchor off Rochefort, the commanding general, Wolfe's sponsor and friend Sir John Mordaunt, called a council of war. He had been an excellent commander in his time but was now a fussy, nervous, and irritable old man. Matching him in his two subordinates was the Honorable Edward Cornwallis, still a lieutenant colonel and only recently the governor of Acadia's silent mists and empty forests, who preferred to address the difficulties rather than the opportunities of the operations, plus an ancient soldier named Conway, who had never believed in the invasion chiefly because he did not understand its purpose.

Bobbing at anchor off the French coasts, this indomitable trio conferred in endless councils without coming to any decision other than the quality of the port served at Sir John's table. Wolfe, who was always present at these exercises in inanition, at last goaded by his

Celtic impatience, called for a rowboat and had himself rowed along the shore, chancing upon a thinly held sandy spit of an island just big enough to accommodate a landing force and seize command of the harbor fortifications. To his delight—and to the confusion of Sir John and his solemn conferees—Captain Richard "Black Dick" Howe, brother of the slain Lord George Augustus Howe, took his warship *Magnanime* right up to the covering French forts to unleash a cannonade lasting thirty-five minutes and bringing the Bourbon lilies tumbling down the flagstaff.

Inspired by this action of a future fleet admiral—whose younger brother would be one of Wolfe's finest officers at Québec—Sir John's commanders boated their troops at midnight on September 28 and sent them plunging through the surf toward the silent forts and the lightly defended little island. But there was a steep sea rising, and after being buffeted about by the swells for three hours, the commanders of the assault decided that the wild state of the rising sea might cut off their retreat, and they canceled the entire operation.

Wolfe was infuriated, almost sputtering upon his return to base in Britain, where he reported: "We have no officers from the commander in chief down . . . and the navy is not much better. . . . If they would even blunder on and fight a little, making some amends to the public by their courage for want of skill, for this excessive degree of caution or whatever name it deserves leaves exceeding bad impressions among the troops, who to do them justice upon this occasion showed all the signs of spirit and good will." Confiding to a friend, he was even blunter and more specific: "There never were people collected together so unfit for the business they were sent upon—dilatory, ignorant, irresolute and some grains of a very unmanly quality and very unsoldierly and unsailorlike."

Wolfe's outburst produced a general outcry in Britain, still brooding angrily after a long season of defeat and retreat. A public inquiry was ordered, and Wolfe was summoned to testify. His testimony clearly indicated that if his superior officers had adopted his plans, success would have been inevitable. His ready replies and depth of knowledge of war, battle, and military affairs attracted widespread attention. No severe rebukes or violent punishments were placed upon the three commanders, but in an effort to reprimand lower officers who had shown initiative, Lieutenant Colonel James Wolfe was promoted above almost all his contemporaries to the rank of full colonel.

THE TREATY OF Aix-la-Chapelle ended the War of the Austrian Succession in 1748 with France slightly weakened and Austria strengthened, and most of the British Army returned to home base, chiefly to put down the Scots rebellion in the Highlands. Wolfe proved himself a merciless enemy once again, describing in a letter to his father how he pursued the famous rebel Evan McPherson: "I tried to take hold of that famous renegade with a very small detachment. I gave the sergeant orders—in case he should succeed and was attacked by the clan with a view to rescuing their chief—to kill him instantly, which I concluded would draw on the destruction of the detachment, and furnish me with sufficient pretext (without waiting for any further instructions) to march into their country, *où j'aurais fait main basse sans miséricorde.*"

Wolfe did not succeed, perhaps because the damp climate—especially in 1749, when the weather was unseasonably cold and wet—brought on a succession of nasty colds and conferred on him the bad health that was to torment his short life. He also despised the work of "military occupation"—more like the "pacification" of the erstwhile enemy—and as a brigade major despaired of any further promotion, for five dreary, weary years shuttling back and forth among Perth, Banff, Inverness, and Fort William to make his regular reports to absent blue-blooded colonels who came north once a year to review their regiments. During this nadir of his fortunes he complained bitterly of his commanding officer, Lord Bury, who "professes fairness and means nothing." Wolfe, ever conscious of how his low birth was a barrier to his promotion—his personal finances had never exceeded £50—whereas unspeakable blue bloods such as Townshend practically waltzed up the ladder of command, was immensely surprised and delighted in 1752 when Bury, realizing that Wolfe's thorough training of his regiment had given His Lordship great credit, at last relented and gave his young surrogate five glorious months' leave in Paris! Moreover, he gave Wolfe a letter of introduction to his father, who saw to it that his shy but voluble guest saw for the first time the great world of the City of Lights. He took lessons to improve his French, rode at the Academy (he was a superb horseman), fenced, danced, attended the opera, and accompanied the British ambassador to the Trianon, where he was introduced to La Pompadour at her toilette. Charmed, Wolfe wrote: "We found her curling her hair. She is extremely handsome and by her conversation with the ambassadors and others that were present, I judge she must have a great deal of wit and understanding."

At last recognition had come to the "ill-born Irish hostler," and he now knew in his heart that—under the patronage of his powerful mentor Lord Chatham—he would soon take another giant step up the heady heights of Mount Olympus.

PITT WAS NOT so much exasperated by the failure of his opportunity to punish the French at Rochefort as he was secretly pleased to chasten the smug self-satisfaction of the lords of the military establishment. In an attempt to end the long-smoldering hostility between the officers and men of the regular army and those of the colonists despised as "general buckskins," Pitt rescinded the rule subordinating senior provincial officers to regular captains. But he did not seek a dangerous harmony between colonial "milishy" and enlisted regulars, for he knew that part-time soldiers with families and occupations could never equal the discipline of seasoned troops trained to advance against enemy fire. Regulars in the colonies closest to Canada would be raised to twenty thousand.

With characteristic energy and enthusiasm, Pitt the opportunist saw the Rochefort debacle as a warning to let Europe alone for a space and resume his focus on North America. At once he began to plan a four-fold operation against the French in Canada. At the turn of the new year of 1758 he recalled the discredited earl of Loudon from North America and replaced him with the inept and bungling James Abercromby, an unfortunate judgment Pitt would never have made had he known that both the colonials and regulars in the New World mocked the new commander as "Mrs. Nanny Crombie."

Under the new fourfold plan Abercromby, accompanied by Lord Howe—from whom Pitt expected great changes for the better—was to attack up Lake Champlain, Brigadier Forbes was to lead British regulars against Fort Duquesne, Bradford with his boatmen and colonials and a few regulars were to raid the French on Lake Ontario, and the decisive blow would be struck in conjunction with the navy up the St. Lawrence against Québec. This last included the earlier reduction of the great fortress of Louisbourg on Cape Breton Island. For this operation the wise and clever Lord Chatham called on no officers higher than army colonel or naval captain, for he still distrusted the great cabal of generals and admirals so pleased with themselves when all about them British ships were being sunk and sailors drowning, while forts fell and those who held them died and bled.

As his senior brigadier the Great Commoner named James Wolfe, who would be second in command to Major General Jeffrey Amherst.

CHAPTER 30

Québec II: The Battle and Betrayal

UPON HIS RETURN to Britain James Wolfe learned to his great joy that William Pitt had chosen him to lead the great amphibious force in its operation to seize Québec—the capital of New France—and therefore all of Canada. Almost at once he approached Field Marshal Lord Ligonier, the British commander in chief. With his customary bluntness— not to say offensive behavior—he informed His Lordship that he wished to appoint his own trio of brigadiers, but Ligonier demurred, having already planned to pay off a few obligations. Unable to understand why he should refuse to honor a traditional privilege, Wolfe replied that unless he had "the assistance of such officers as I should name, His Lordship would do me a great kindness to appoint some other person to the chief direction."

It is not known just how the British war chief received this polite ultimatum, but it is also possible that he suspected that if this brash young major general were to be rebuked, he would probably not hesitate to inform Lord Chatham that the commander in chief was interfering in Pitt's grand plan for evicting the French from North America. So he compromised, allowing Wolfe to pick two of the three brigadiers who would accompany him; and of course Wolfe immediately selected his boon companions of many battlefields: Robert Monckton and James Murray. Field Marshal Lord Ligonier's choice was none other than George Townshend, Wolfe's self-appointed hair shirt.

Wolfe might have objected strenuously if both Monckton and Murray had not informed him that though Townshend's service in the army had indeed been of short duration, he had established a solid reputation for coolness under fire. One remarkable demonstration of this pomaded blue blood's career had occurred at Laufeldt. As he was watching an enemy attack, an exploding shell tore off the head of a German officer standing next to him. "I never knew before," Townshend murmured, cleansing his chest of splattered blood and gore, "that Scheiger had so many brains." That was enough for Wolfe, not so much to embrace his inveterate detractor but at least to accept him, intimating that if his dearest friends would prevail upon this supercilious aristocrat to curb his acid wit and refrain from drawing those savagely funny caricatures that had lost him friends and led him to the field of honor, he would graciously welcome him aboard.

IN FEBRUARY 1759, as Major General Wolfe prepared to sail to Halifax to take command of the Québec operation, he dined one night with William Pitt and his brother-in-law Lord Temple. Toward the end of the meal Wolfe suddenly jumped erect, drew his sword, and rapped on the table for attention. He then began striding around the room, flourishing his sword while boasting of his military prowess and threatening his enemy with destruction, after which he turned and walked from the room without a word.

"Good God!" Pitt exclaimed. "That I should have entrusted the fate of the country and of the administration to such hands!"

The Great Commoner might have felt better for his country had he known that his guest, a teetotaler, had been drinking a little wine.

ADMIRAL CHARLES SAUNDERS commanded the fleet that was to transport Wolfe's army to Québec. In all, he was to have some 170 sail manned by some 18,000 seamen. Part of his force, under Rear Admiral Philip Durell, had been sent ahead to blockade the St. Lawrence so that the French could not reinforce Québec.

But Admiral Durell did not enter the river, choosing to stay clear of its treacherous ice, and the French did get men and supplies into the fortress city on the cliff. With them was Sieur de Bougainville, whom Montcalm had sent to Paris. Bougainville stepped onto the strand of the Lower Town bearing a copy of an intercepted letter from General Jeffrey Amherst.

It revealed the British plan.

MONTCALM CHANGED his plans the moment he read the letter.

He had been prepared to resist Amherst at both Lake Champlain and Fort Niagara. Now, he saw, the major thrust was directed against Québec, the chief operation in another three-pronged campaign with which Pitt intended to complete the destruction of the French in America during the year 1759.

Amherst was to take Ticonderoga and move on Montréal by way of Lake Champlain, General Prideaux was to reduce Fort Niagara on

Lake Ontario and open the way to Lake Erie and the West, and Wolfe was to crack the hard nut at Québec. Now Montcalm remained in the capital.

First, under Vaudreuil's orders, all French ships were sent upriver to be out of harm's way, and to release about a thousand sailors for duty in Québec. Vaudreuil, and Montcalm as well, were confident that Québec guns could prevent the British from getting above the city to cut the supply line westward to Montréal. Confident also that the fortress on the cliff was impregnable, Vaudreuil entrusted its defense to the chevalier de Ramesay with about two thousand men, and allowed Montcalm to move the main body east along the St. Lawrence.

Montcalm built a line about seven miles long. His left rested on the gorge and falls of the Montmorency and his right on the St. Charles. The mouth of the St. Charles was guarded by a boom of logs chained together and two sunken ships mounting cannon. A mile up the St. Charles was a bridge of boats that linked Montcalm's right with Québec. In the center of this bristling line of men and redoubts was the little town of Beauport, and there Montcalm made his headquarters.

Thus Québec's only weak point, its landward flank on the left, had been protected against encirclement. The city with its 106 guns was inaccessible from its sheer front and from its impassable heights on its right. Even if the British landed on the unoccupied south bank of the St. Lawrence, they could not possibly force the stream.

All that Montcalm needed to do was to hold his position until October, when the advent of the harsh Canadian winter would force the British to retire. He had fourteen thousand men, besides his Indians, and Amherst's letter indicated that Wolfe would have only twelve thousand.

WOLFE HAD ARRIVED in Halifax pale and green at the gills from a stormy and sickening voyage. He had found that half of the force of fourteen thousand men there were sick with the measles, and also that Durell had allowed the French to warn and reinforce Québec. A week later, his fury gave way to grief. A letter from his mother arrived informing him that his father had died.

Wolfe at once put on the sleeve of his red coat the black armband of mourning he was to wear constantly and that was to become as familiar to his men as the little ornamental cane he wore slung at his hip like a toy sword.

Going from Halifax to Louisbourg, Wolfe realized that he would have only eighty-five hundred men, of whom many would be those Americans whom he called "the dirtiest, most contemptible, cowardly dogs that you can conceive." He accepted them, nevertheless, and divided his army into three brigades under Murray, Monckton, and Townshend.

On June 5, a foggy, windless day, the British ships began working slowly and with flapping sails out of the harbor at Louisbourg.

THE BRITISH FLEET was sailing up the St. Lawrence flying the French flag. Canadians to the fleet's right about fifty miles below Québec cheered and hugged themselves for joy. Relief had arrived, and their country was saved. Jubilant river pilots quickly launched their canoes and put out to the ships. They clambered aboard, but instead of a smile and the promise of a fee, they met a pistol and a pledge of sudden death if they did not work the vessels through the treacherous Traverse ahead.

A black-robed priest hurried down to the riverbank to watch their progress through a telescope. After enough pilots had been seized, the golden bourbon lilies came fluttering down the mast and the red Cross of St. George was unfurled. The astonished Canadians groaned in despair. They filled the air with curses and lamentations, and it is said that the priest was so overcome with revulsion that he dropped dead.

Aboard *Neptune*, the flagship of Admiral Charles Saunders, General James Wolfe smiled thinly to see how easily the ruse had succeeded. General Wolfe had shared Admiral Saunders' fears for the fleet. Neither officer could forget the disaster of a half century ago, when a similar expedition against Québec under the inept Admiral Hovenden Walker met storm and shipwreck on the St. Lawrence. This time there could be no mistake. William Pitt, the virtual prime minister of Britain, had told redheaded James Wolfe plainly that the conquest of the American continent—exclusive of Mexico—depended upon the capture of Québec. This time the citadel of New France must fall, and that was why Wolfe and Saunders had decided to lure Canadian pilots aboard by flying the enemy flag. Now, the great concourse of about 150 ships manned by eighteen thousand seamen and carrying eighty-five hundred soldiers was entering the treacherous Traverse. Now James Wolfe peered ahead anxiously, while the transport *Goodwill* poked cautiously into the narrow passage. Aboard her an enraged Canadian pilot refused to work her through, and vowed that Canada would be the graveyard of the British Army and the walls of Québec would be decorated with British scalps. Captain Killick, the ancient master of *Goodwill*, angrily pushed the Canadian aside and strode forward to guide the ship through himself. Watching him, the pilot shouted that the ship would be wrecked because no French ship had ever attempted to pass through the Traverse without a pilot.

"Ay, ay, my dear," old Killick shouted back, fiercely shaking his speaking trumpet, "but, damn me, I'll convince you that a Britisher shall go where a Frenchman dare not show his nose."

Behind *Goodwill*, the captain of the *Richmond* was alarmed to learn that *Goodwill* had no pilot.

"Who's your master?" he yelled, and Killick replied, "It's old Killick! And that's enough."

Leaning over the bow, the old man chatted gaily with the sailors in the sounding boats, giving his orders easily while pointing out the different shades of blue and gray indicating the depth of the water, warning of submerged ridges marked by telltale ripples or the sudden disturbance of smoothly flowing waters. Occasionally the men in the sounding boats would shout a warning. "Ay, ay, me dears," old Killick would purr, having seen the danger beforehand. "Ay, ay, chalk it down."

Eventually *Goodwill* emerged from the zigzag Traverse into open water. Killick put down his trumpet and handed the ship over to his mate. "Well, damn me," Killick snorted, "damn me if there are not a thousand places in the Thames more hazardous than this. I am ashamed that a Britisher should make such a rout about it."

Gradually all the following transports were safely through. The fleet was moving now through the North Channel. To the left lay the lower tip of the island of Orléans, an island about twenty miles long and five miles wide in the center of the broad St. Lawrence. Off the island's upper tip was the basin of Québec, and four miles across the water was the city itself.

Here, on the twenty-sixth of June, the fleet anchored. That night, forty American rangers under Lieutenant Meech landed on the island of Orléans and drove off a party of armed inhabitants. In the morning, Wolfe's army began coming ashore to build a base camp. A few days later, General Wolfe went forward to a high point on the island's tip to examine his objective, and it was then that he saw the true magnitude of the mission on which Pitt had sent him.

High, high above him, beautiful and white in the sunlight, was the city. He could see the stone houses, the churches, the palaces, the convents, the hospitals, the forest of spires and steeples and crosses glinting beneath the white flag whipping in the breeze. Everywhere he saw thick, square walls and gun batteries, even along the strand of the Lower Town, straggling out of sight to his left beyond Cape Diamond. To his right as he swung his glass slowly like a swiveling gun, Wolfe perceived the entrenchments of Montcalm He saw the sealed mouth of the St. Charles and the thundering falls of the Montmorency guarding the French left flank. He saw the little town of Beauport and the mud flats before it beneath the grape and muskets of Montcalm's redoubts. From left to right he saw steep brown cliffs scarred with the raw red earth of fresh entrenchments, the stone houses with windows reduced to firing slits by piles of logs, and behind them the tops of the wigwams and the white tents of the regulars. If Wolfe could have seen beyond Cape Diamond to his left, he would have been appalled by natural obstacles more formidable than Montcalm's fortifications. Here for seven or eight miles west to Cape Rouge rose steep after inaccessible steep, ranges of cliffs atop which a few men might hold off an army, all ending at another river and waterfall like the Montmorency.

James Wolfe held his telescope delicately. A soldier near him noticed the marks of scurvy on the backs of his long, thin hands. No one spoke except his engineer. Wolfe listened mutely, silencing him with a gesture and gazing eagerly at what appeared a likely landing place or a flaw in his enemy's line; but then, shaking his head petulantly, he moved on. At last he snapped his telescope shut and strode back to camp.

Wolfe had seen that the plan devised in Louisbourg would not work. He could not land upriver or between the St. Charles and the Montmorency, as the colonists under Sir William Phips had attempted without success six decades ago. In fact, there did not seem to be any place to land. As he was to notify William Pitt, he had gazed upon "the strongest country in the world."

That night a black thunderstorm drenched his troops. After it had passed, sentries on Orléans Point thought that they heard movement on the river. They saw flashes of light and the glow of torches and heard the sound of excited voices—and then the world exploded.

Sheets of fire shot up from the river, roar after roar shook the camp, while the air was filled with flying pieces of burning wood and whizzing bits of metal. The sentries turned and ran. As they did, the flames and the roar pursued them like dragons from hell, belching out columns of suffocating smoke and drenching the air with the sulfurous reek of their breath.

The French had launched their fire ships downriver against the British fleet anchored off the island. Flames ran up masts and sails like fiery snakes, and then vessels soaked in pitch and tar and stuffed with bombs, grenades, old iron, fireworks, rusty cannon swivels, and muskets loaded to the muzzle burst apart like floating volcanoes. The river hissed and roared like a stricken beast, while the night was slashed and crisscrossed with cascades of fire and showers of flying sparks. In that unnatural glare, an excited French soldiery crowded in front of their white tents at Beauport could glance across the glittering river to the beaches where lines of red-coated British were drawn up to repel possible attack.

But the French sailors had applied their torches too soon. Before the fire ships could drift down on the British vessels and ignite them, British sailors had jumped into their boats, rowed bravely within range of the blazing hulks, secured them with grappling irons, and towed them ashore, where they were allowed to burn themselves out.

"Damn me, Jack," one of the sailors called out joyfully, "did ye ever take hell in tow before?"

The fire-ship fizzle was no joy to the marquis de Vaudreuil, watching glumly from the steeple of the little church at Beauport. Against the experienced advice of Montcalm, he had spent 2 million francs on this military bauble, and had hoped, with characteristic naïveté, that it would drive off the British with one stroke. Vaudreuil was also furious with his sailors for firing the ships and jumping clear so soon, although he was later shaken to hear that one captain and seven men, bravely waiting until they had neared the British fleet, were trapped and burned alive.

Vaudreuil returned to Québec, whence, a few days later, he was to look with dismay into the mouth of British cannons.

ACROSS THE SOUTH CHANNEL from the island of Orléans was a tip of land called Point Levi. Between this point and Québec the St. Lawrence narrows to a width of less than a mile.

On the afternoon of June 29 a party of rangers and light infantrymen from Monckton's brigade scaled the point's unguarded cliffs and advanced inland. Monckton followed with the rest of his brigade. Next day the British drove off a force of 650 Canadians and 350 Indians and armed settlers. The French countered on the following day by sending a floating battery to lob shells onto the clifftop occupied by the British. Out in the open, the redcoats began to take casualties. A French warship added to their travail until the British frigate *Trent* sailed upstream with blazing guns and drove off their afflictors.

On rocky soil already reddened with British blood, the soldiers worked desperately to get underground. Now and then, Indians came screeching out of the woods to kill a straggler and take his scalp. Eventually the heights opposite Québec were fortified. And the French made no move to recover them.

Vaudreuil believed a captured British soldier's story that the move at Point Levi was a feint before the major blow fell on Montcalm's line. Montcalm also believed this, until he realized his danger. He wrote to Vaudreuil requesting an attack on the British position before it was too late. Vaudreuil ignored him, and when an assault was finally formed, it was by the Canadian militia, which the Canadian-born Vaudreuil had always favored over the regulars from France. They were repulsed.

Soon the British would have cannon mounted on Point Levi, but even before that happened, the impatient Wolfe had decided to attack Montcalm.

DURING THE DAYLIGHT of July 9 several British frigates and a bomb ketch bombarded the French left flank at the Montmorency. That night Townshend's and Murray's brigades were embarked and set ashore on the east bank of that river. It was an operation carried out against nothing more fearful than the sniping of a few Canadian sharpshooters.

The French were not going to contest possession of ground east of their secure left flank. If Wolfe hoped to cross the Montmorency he would have to move three miles upstream through Indian-infested woods to a ford that was always guarded by a thousand Canadians backed by a line of fortified stone houses linked together by trenches. Wolfe, of course, was attempting to lure Montcalm into decisive battle. Wolfe was confident that Admiral Saunders' fleet could quickly concentrate his separated army at any critical point before a decisive blow could be struck, either against Monckton at Point Levi, the lightly guarded camp at the island of Orléans, or himself on the Montmorency. The chevalier de Levis did not agree. He asked Montcalm to let him cross the river and defeat Wolfe before the rest of his army could come to his rescue. Montcalm refused. He did not fear Wolfe's army as much as the one General Amherst was leading against Ticonderoga. If Amherst could come up Lake Champlain he might capture Montréal and threaten Montcalm's rear. Montcalm was delighted to have two-thirds of Wolfe's army bogged down among the mosquitoes and skulking Indians of the woods across the river.

"While they are there they cannot do much harm," he said. "So let them amuse themselves."

ON THE NIGHT of July 12 a rocket exploded above the river between Québec and Point Levi, and Monckton's cannon roared into life.

Both the first and the second salvos fell into the river, and cries of derision rose from the French. But the British gunners eventually found the range. Shells began bursting among the wharves and streets of the Lower Town, and some even shook the walls of the Upper Town itself. Soon the French batteries were belching back. A furious artillery duel raged throughout the night, and it would continue to roar intermittently for the next two months.

On the night of July 15 a British shell set fire to a building in the Upper Town. High winds carried the fire to the cathedral, which burned to the ground within an hour. A week later another fierce fire all but demolished the Lower Town. Soon the Lower Town was a shambles and the crowded streets of the Upper Town were not safe for passage. One by one, sometimes in family groups, the residents of the crumbling city began to flee to the sanctuary of the countryside.

Meanwhile, the siege continued. Wolfe's batteries on the Montmorency made life unpleasant for the troops on Montcalm's left flank, and Montcalm's sharpshooters cut down the rashly curious British who visited the gorge of the river to marvel at its cataract. Both sides languished in an alternating ordeal of heat and rain, both sides skirmished, and both sides took scalps. The American rangers and soon the British regulars became as proficient in this grisly art as the opposing Indians and *coureurs de bois* until Wolfe had to issue an order prohibiting "the inhuman practice of scalping, except when the enemy are Indians or Canadians dressed like Indians."

Flags of truce passed frequently between both camps. "You will demolish the town," a French emissary told Wolfe, "but you will never get inside of it," and Wolfe replied, "I will have Québec if I stay here till the end of November."

Impatient and impulsive redhead that he was, he could not wait until the end of July.

WOLFE'S BRIGADIERS HAD repeatedly advised him to try forcing the northern shore above Québec, but the general had just as frequently declined; and on July 23 he proposed to storm the very heart of the enemy line.

In front of the gorge of the Montmorency there was a ford during the hours of low tide. Townshend was to cross here with two thousand men. Meanwhile, another two thousand would be embarked upriver and brought downstream opposite Beauport, to make a feint there. Wolfe's true object was the camp of Levis on the Montmorency.

In midmorning of July 31, the sixty-four-gun frigate *Centurion* sailed downriver and anchored off Levis's camp, while a pair of fourteen-gun catamarans worked in close to the shore. It was now high tide, and the river flowed full against the sandy beach beneath the cliffs. *Centurion* and her tiny twins opened up, battering the French redoubts on the beaches. From Wolfe's camp east of the Montmorency and Monckton's batteries to the west at Point Levi came an artillery crossfire aimed at the clifftops. For two hours the thunder of the cannonade continued, and the basin of Québec echoed and reechoed once more to the thump of discharging guns and the crash of exploding shells. Yet Levis, with about eleven thousand men carefully concentrated underground, was barely scratched, demonstrating the imperishable truth that when artillery fires at positions built to deflect it, its bark is worse than its bite.

Montcalm, however, was momentarily perplexed by the boated British force rowing back and forth opposite Beauport. But as the promenade became prolonged, he became convinced that the assault would come against Levis, and he rode down to the Montmorency through ranks of cheering, white-coated men crying, "*Vive notre général!*"

In the afternoon the tide turned to the ebb. Gradually the dark sledge of the mud flats became visible. Wolfe, standing in an open boat, cane in hand, flushed with the exultation of battle, gave the order to attack.

Townshend began crossing the ford, and the first wave of grenadiers and Royal Americans rowed cheering for the mud flats.

But the boats were swept downstream, and many of them were stranded on mud ridges. The French on the heights poured a plunging fire into them. Wolfe in his boat shouted orders to delay the assault. The tide was not low enough. The French fire continued. Three times splinters struck Wolfe, and his little cane was knocked from his grasp by a round shot. At length he ordered the first wave in again. The boats beached on that broad expanse of mud. Shouting and challenging each other, the grenadiers and Royal Americans floundered forward in wild disorder. The French in the redoubt on the sand fled at their approach. The British seized the redoubt, but then the French on the heights delivered a withering fire among the redcoats milling about below.

To the rear, all was confusion. Monckton's men were ashore, and Townshend's troops were already over the ford. Boats were piling up, and no one seemed to know what to do. At that moment, without orders from Wolfe or even from their own officers, the grenadiers took the battle into their own hands.

They went storming up the heights to get at their tormentors above them. Thick, scattered raindrops had begun to fall, and the heat was oppressive as the British swarmed up the slopes. French fire scourged them. Their breath came faster. Sweat poured from their flesh and stained their uniforms, and the ground beneath their boots became a slippery morass. Straining for handholds, using their muskets as crutches, rolling downhill to be stopped by a bush or a fallen comrade, they continued their ascent into the very throats of the twinkling, flashing muskets of the French. And then the skies darkened, the clouds opened up, and a torrent of rain fell on all that wild scene.

It squelched the battle. Wolfe sounded the retreat, and as the last of the living grenadiers and Americans came sliding downhill again, while the entire assault force withdrew in good order to their boats, the rain stopped and the Indians on the heights drew their scalping knives and came clambering down among the fallen.

WOLFE HAD LOST 443 men killed and wounded without harming a single Frenchman in an aborted battle that should never have begun. His plan of attack upon the heart of a fixed position was not only scatterbrained in its conception but also blundering in nearly every detail of execution, down to the boating of troops at flood tide in the morning for an assault to be launched at dusk and on the ebb. By the defeat of the Montmorency, Wolfe lost the respect of almost all his staff officers, including the heretofore intensely loyal Monckton.

Townshend was particularly savage in his criticism, and even Murray, an impatient man himself, regarded the entire affair as stupid and foolhardy. Admiral Saunders was also alienated after Wolfe sent him a copy of the draft of his ambiguous dispatch to Pitt. Saunders accused Wolfe of giving the navy an unfair share of the blame, and Wolfe meekly promised to remove the objectionable parts of the letter. Meanwhile, Wolfe, his health failing every day, vented his rage upon other victims. First, the grenadiers were excoriated in a scathing general order, and next the Canadians on the south banks of the St. Lawrence were informed that because of "the most unchristian barbarities against his troops on all occasions he could no longer refrain from chastising them as they deserved."

East and west, parties were sent forth to scourge the Canadian *canaille.* One of these, under Captain Alexander Ferguson, went to the village of St. Joachim. Robineau de Portneuf, the *curé* there, invited Ferguson and his officers to dinner, but Ferguson declined. The next day, he attacked the priest's house. After Portneuf surrendered, Ferguson had his eighty parishioners shot down in cold blood while the priest was slashed to the ground, scalped, his skull beaten into the earth, and his church and parish burned.

Night after night the residents of Québec could see the glow of burning villages. Montcalm also watched this savaging of his countrymen, but with no intention of ending it. He would not be drawn into open battle under any circumstances, and thus the tormented Canadians were caught between two fires. Whereas Wolfe was wasting the countryside in an effort to starve Québec and force the militia to desert to defend their homes, Montcalm kept the militia in check by threatening to turn his Indians loose on their families.

Even the armed British soldiery lived in daily dread of Montcalm's savages, especially after a private of the Forty-seventh Regiment returned from captivity in an Indian village to tell a horrible story. He had escaped the night before he was to provide the village with a festive meal. For three days before that, the villagers, women and children as well as men, had amused themselves by sticking splinters of wood under his fingernails and into his penis, exploding little charges of powder packed into cuts in his flesh made with a tomahawk, and smashing his toes to a pulp with small stone hammers. Little girls had torn the hair from his chest, and little boys had poked sticks and thorns up his nose. Such details, inevitably exaggerated in the retelling, had the fortunate effect of so terrifying the British that there were fewer and fewer sentries surprised at their post or stragglers relieved of their scalps. In fact, the British had grown so adept at bush warfare that the Indians began to complain of redcoats who no longer stood still to be shot at.

Meanwhile, Québec was collapsing under the hammer of Monckton's artillery. Fires in the Lower Town were a daily occurrence, and in the Upper Town 167 houses were destroyed in a single dreadful night. On August 10 a shell crashing into a cellar set a vat of brandy afire and burned down many buildings, including the beautiful Notre Dame des Victoires. Most of the city fronting on the river was in ruins.

Worse, rations in the town and for the army encamped beside it were growing short. Vaudreuil's assurance that the British could not get upriver had been shattered by the audacity of the British fleet. Beginning on July 18 and with every fair wind thereafter, British ships had run the gantlet of Québec's guns until a sizable flotilla had been assembled upstream under Vice Admiral Charles Holmes. Thus, supply ships coming downriver from Montréal were frequently intercepted by Holmes's ships; while a shortage of pack animals made supply by land along the river's northern shore very difficult.

The ships, however, worried Montcalm most. Wolfe was now able to make thrusts against the northern shore to the west of Québec. To oppose him, Montcalm sent Bougainville above the city with fifteen hundred men. He was to guard about fifteen to twenty miles of clifftop against the British. He did, twice driving Murray off with losses. A third time, Murray landed at Deschambault and burned a building and all the spare baggage of the regular officers. For once, Montcalm was alarmed; but then, his good humor returned. He had received news indicating that General Amherst could not possibly come to Wolfe's assistance that year.

Amherst had occupied Ticonderoga and then Crown Point after the French had blown up the one and abandoned the other. Then General Prideaux had carried out the assault on Fort Niagara. Although Prideaux was killed, the French fort had been surrendered to Sir William Johnson. Thus, with his countrymen driven from Lake Champlain and Lake Erie, it appeared to Montcalm that his right or western flank at Montréal was in extreme danger. Amherst particularly might ascend Champlain to fall on Montréal. To halt him, Montcalm had ordered Bourlamaque to organize the troops from Ticonderoga and Crown Point in defense of Isle-aux-Nois in the middle of the Richelieu River, and had sent Levis from Québec to Montréal with fifteen hundred men.

Now, however, the August skies seemed bright for France. Amherst had dawdled at Crown Point and could not possibly assault Isle-aux-Nois before winter. Some two thousand militiamen could be released to help in the harvest.

"Two months more," Montcalm said of the British, "and they will be gone."

TOWARD THE END of August it appeared that Montcalm was right. Wolfe's army was melting away. He had lost more than 850 men killed and wounded since June, and disease and desertions were daily reducing his strength. Worse, the general himself was gripped by an indecision nearly as destructive to discipline as his own feuding with his brigadiers.

Since the Montmorency repulse Wolfe rarely spoke to Murray and showed an open dislike to Townshend. Townshend, of course, was as much to blame for this as Wolfe. The brigadier could not contain his sarcastic wit nor suppress his habit of seeing the ridiculous in everything. Once, at mess, his officers asked him to entertain them by drawing his famous caricatures. He obliged. Each new one was more uproarious than the last. Then Townshend drew his masterpiece. It was a caricature of Wolfe fortifying a brothel. Every officer who saw it collapsed with laughter, but then Wolfe saw it. His pale face blanched. He crumpled the paper and put it in his pocket. "If we live," he said, his dark blue eyes fixing Townshend, "this shall be enquired into."

Such were the relations among the commanders of the British Army, and then, on August 20, Wolfe fell deathly ill of a fever. He lay in an upper room of a French farmhouse on the Montmorency, his thin body racked and his white face haggard with pain. On the twenty-fifth he began to recover, and on the twenty-ninth he sent his three brigadiers a message:

"That the public service may not suffer by the general's indisposition, he begs the brigadiers will meet and consult together for the public utility and advantage, and consider of the best method to attack the enemy."

Monckton, Murray, and Townshend conferred. They advised Wolfe, as they had often done before, to seize a position on the north shore between Québec and Montréal. Thus he would force upon Montcalm the choice of fighting or starving. Wolfe agreed. He not only embraced this heretofore unacceptable proposal eagerly, he went even further. He would capture the inaccessible heights of the Plains of Abraham, under the very nose of Québec. Montcalm, cut in two, would *have* to come out to fight.

Wolfe did not immediately disclose the details of his plan to his brigadiers. He would divulge it only at their insistence and at the eleventh hour. Nor will history ever know how he came to adopt it, after having previously rejected all counsel to force the stream above Québec.

It has been said that Wolfe was on the edge of despair. He had told his intimates that he would not go back defeated "to be exposed to the censure and reproach of an ignorant population." The very news that he could expect no help from Amherst might have strengthened him in that resolution, so often born of desperation. Wolfe was that sort of soldier: audacious in adversity, delighted to look into the face of calamity and spit in its eye, genuinely determined to triumph or to die trying.

It has also been said that Wolfe was still anxious to make one more attempt on the city before the advent of winter forced the fleet to depart. On September 10 Admiral Saunders assembled his officers and informed them that he thought the time had come to leave. Saunders had about thirteen thousand men under his command. With their ships they represented about a quarter of the strength of the British Navy. He could not risk being frozen into the St. Lawrence. Moreover, the soft, thin floes of ice were already beginning to form in the Gulf of St. Lawrence. All of Saunders's officers agreed, including Holmes; but Wolfe, upon being advised of this decision, rushed to Saunders's flagship and told him of his plan. He advised the admiral that he was going to send 150 picked men up a secret path to the Plains of Abraham. If they could overpower the light guard posted there, then his main body would follow. But if they could not, then Wolfe would agree to return to Britain with Saunders.

Wolfe is said to have seen the outlines of a secret path while studying the heights west of Québec. Examining a little cove called the Anse du Foulon, he is said to have spotted outlines of a path winding up the side of the supposedly inaccessible cliff. Then, observing that there were only a few tents pitched on the clifftop, he is supposed to have concluded that the guard there was light.

Thus the generally accepted explanation of why Wolfe changed his mind about the northern shore and came to choose the Anse du Foulon. But because it assumes too much while accepting the implausible fable of Wolfe suddenly seeing the path "through a glass darkly," and because Wolfe did deliberately destroy the September entries in his diary, it is not too much to posit another explanation.

And that is treachery.

HISTORY SHOWS THAT the key to the postern has as often taken a fixed position as surprise, starvation, bombardment, or direct assault. Although it can never be stated with certainty that Québec had been betrayed to Wolfe, it can at least be suggested that the city could have been. Montcalm himself gave the reason why. He had long ago secretly written to Paris reporting the swindles of the scoundrels Bigot and Cadet, as well as of Vaudreuil's apparent disinclination to restrain them, and Montcalm had said: "Everybody appears to be in a hurry to make his fortune before the colony is lost; which event many perhaps desire as an impenetrable veil over their conduct."

Obviously, with Canada destroyed and records ruined, neither Bigot nor Cadet nor their accomplices could be brought to book—which fact was to be demonstrated at their subsequent trial. *Did* Bigot or someone else, in fact, inform Wolfe of the Anse du Foulon? No one knows. Or *was* Wolfe informed by a French prisoner or deserter? Again, no one knows.

But it is known that Vaudreuil, who was constantly accompanied and advised by Bigot, did countermand an order of Montcalm's and left the Plains of Abraham themselves unguarded. The crack Guienne Regiment under a capable colonel was moved from the plains back to the line of the St. Charles. Moreover, the guard of a hundred men whom Montcalm had placed at the top of the Anse du Foulon was fatally crippled.

It had been commanded by Captain St. Martin, a regular officer handpicked for the duty by Montcalm. With whom did Vaudreuil replace St. Martin in an eleventh-hour change of command?

Vergor.

Duchambon de Vergor, the false chevalier of Beausejour, the craven commander who was court-martialed, though acquitted, for cowardice; and the crony whom Bigot had blandly advised to "clip and cut and rob the king."

Whereas St. Martin had refused to allow the Canadians in his command to go home to help in the harvest, Vergor granted leave to forty men on the condition that they also put in a few hours of work on Vergor's farm. Thus the vital guard was already crippled.

Finally, the clifftops between the Anse du Foulon and Cape Rouge were not even well patrolled on the night of Wolfe's attack. On that night the patrol commander, Captain de Remigny, lost his three horses. One was stolen and two were lamed.

Thus the events suggesting treachery, and although they are far from being conclusive evidence, they cannot be summarily rejected in the interest of preserving that romantic figure of Wolfe on a riverbank suddenly espying the chink in Montcalm's armor. Montcalm himself knew of the path, and he had said to Vaudreuil: "I swear to you that a hundred men posted there would stop their whole army." He was right, but there were not a hundred men and they were under Vergor, and the Guienne Regiment, which was to come to their assistance, had been sent away.

Whether Wolfe knew of this naturally belongs to the limbo of unanswerable questions. What does belong to his lasting glory, however, is the masterly preparation he made for his attack.

First he began the difficult withdrawal from the Montmorency. As he disengaged, Montcalm sent a strong force to fall on his rear. Monckton saw this movement from Point Levi and quickly embarked two battalions to make a feint at Beauport, and Montcalm withdrew.

Next Wolfe made a feint at Cape Rouge held by Bougainville, and during the next few days he drove Bougainville and his men into weary distraction by having the ships of Holmes's flotilla drift upriver with the flood tide and drift downriver on the ebb, forcing the French to march and countermarch to remain abreast of the British fleet. To delude Montcalm into believing that the movement above the town was a diversion for another attack against his fortifications east of Québec, he asked Admiral Saunders to deploy his main fleet in a demonstration off Beauport. Finally, two deserters supposedly told Wolfe that Bougainville was sending a convoy of provisions down to Montcalm on the ebb tide on the night of September 12. Wolfe immediately saw the possibility of sending his own boats down ahead of the convoy so as to deceive the French sentinels, and he gave that order. Wolfe could not know that Bougainville had postponed the provision convoy, but neither did Bougainville inform the sentries below that the familiar store ships were not coming.

On the night of September 12 all was in readiness. The stars were visible, but there was no moon as perhaps forty-eight hundred British began drifting upriver. Bougainville, wearied by the promenade of the past few days, was confident that they would only drift downriver again. In fact, the *sieur* was going to spend the night farther west, at Jacques-Cartier. The desirable and accommodating Madame de Vienne, wife of one of Bigot's subordinates, was at Jacques-Cartier. Below Québec, Saunders was lowering boats filled with sailors and Marines, his guns were thundering, and the marquis de Montcalm was massing troops at the wrong point, ten miles below the Anse du Foulon.

At two o'clock on the morning of September 15, 1759, the tide turned to the ebb. A lantern, its light shrouded from the northern shore, was hoisted to the main topgallant masthead of the *Sutherland*. It was the signal to cast off, and the boats of the British began slipping silently downstream.

General James Wolfe stood mutely in one of the foremost boats. Suddenly the general began to speak in a low voice. He was reciting Gray's "Elegy in a Country Churchyard," which he had only just memorized. His aides listened quietly. Wolfe finished and said softly: "Gentlemen, I would rather have written those lines than take Québec." An embarrassed silence followed. No one believed him. Wolfe said no more. Perhaps he was reflecting on the prophetic line:

"The paths of glory lead but to the grave."

UNCHALLENGED AND ignored, the boats had been gliding downstream for two full hours. Now the tide was bearing the lead craft with

Wolfe's spearhead—twenty-four volunteers who were to surprise Vergor—toward the towering shore. Suddenly there was a shout.

"Qui vive?" (Who goes there?)

No one spoke, and then Simon Fraser, a young Highland officer who spoke French, shouted back:

"France! Et vive le roi!"

"À quel régiment?" the sentry persisted.

"De la reine," Fraser shot back, aware that part of this unit was with Bougainville.

The sentry was satisfied and the boats drifted on, one of the men giggling aloud in relief. Again the challenge. A sentry had come scrambling down the cliff face to stand at the water's edge and demand the password. Again a French-speaking Highlander, Captain Donald MacDonald, gave the answer.

"Provision boats!" he hissed, deliberately disguising his accent with a hoarse whisper. "Don't make such a bloody noise! The *maudit* [damn] British will hear!"

The sentry waved them on. The British could see the gray of his cuff against the black of the cliff behind him.

On the boats drifted, and now the current was running strong and they had rounded the headland of the Anse du Foulon. The sailors broke out their oars and rowed desperately against the tide. But the spearhead boats were swept too far downstream. Undaunted, MacDonald, Fraser, and their men leaped out. MacDonald and Captain William Delaune led the party softly up the cliff face. The figure of a sentry materialized out of the gloom above them. He shouted down at them. Still hissing his hoarse whisper, MacDonald told him that he had come to relieve the post.

"I'll take care to give a good account of the *maudit* British if they land!"

On the shore of the cove below, General James Wolfe and two aides crouched helplessly in the dark—their ears straining for the sound of firing. It came, and Wolfe despaired.

Above, the sentry had hesitated for too long. There were twenty-four shadowy figures around him before he could reply, and then the British charged with blazing muskets. Captain Vergor came dashing out of his tent barefooted and nightshirted. He fired two pistols wildly into the air before he turned and sprinted for Québec at the head of his departing troops. A musket shot pierced his heel and he fell, screaming.

It was then that Wolfe's despondency changed to a fierce, wild joy, for he had heard the huzzahs of his triumphant volunteers. Quickly he gave the order for the second wave to land. In came the boats, and soon the cliff face was crawling with British soldiers. Among them was James Wolfe. Diseased, weakened by bloodletting, never strong, he was climbing on his magnificent will alone; and as he got to the top the empty boats of the first wave were returning to the packed transports for the rest of his troops.

Now the guns at Point Levi and the island of Orléans had joined those of Saunders firing on Beauport. Soon Beauport's batteries were thundering back, followed by those at Québec and at Samos, to the west of the Anse du Foulon. Wolfe immediately sent Colonel William Howe's light infantry against that battery menacing his rear, and the British silenced it.

By dawn, the last of Wolfe's sweating soldiers had struggled up to the undefended Plains of Abraham. Some forty-eight hundred soldiers began to form and to march into a north–south line parallel to and about three-quarters of a mile distant from the western walls of Québec.

That was how the marquis de Montcalm saw them as he rode up in a drizzling rain.

MONTCALM HAD BEEN completely deceived by Saunders' feint. Nevertheless, he rode over to Québec that morning with Chevalier Johnstone, a Scots Jacobite who had been given a commission in the French Army. En route, a messenger informed Montcalm of the British landing. Montcalm set his horse on the path to Vaudreuil's house. From there he could see clearly to those plains that had once been owned by a French pilot named Abraham Martin. He could see the thin red lines of British soldiers stretching from the St. Foye Road on their left—and his right—to the cliffs of the St. Lawrence. Faintly, skirling on the wind, came the wail of the Highlanders' pipes. The enemy array stood motionless, as though awaiting inspection, their regimental colors drooping in the gentle rain.

"This is serious," Montcalm said gravely, and ordered Johnstone to ask Governor Ramesay of Québec for the garrison's twenty-five field pieces. Johnstone clattered off, and Vaudreuil came out of his house. Shaken, he spoke a few words to Montcalm and went back inside. Montcalm rode off to find his command disorganized by a welter of orders and counterorders given in an atmosphere of distrust and dislike. Ramesay would surrender only three of the twenty-five cannons and Vaudreuil had refused to allow the Beauport troops to move up to Québec.

Eventually Montcalm conferred with his officers. Should he attack now, or wait until Bougainville could move on the British rear? If the French waited another hour or possibly two for Bougainville, the British could improve their position. If he attacked now, he would have to do it without Bougainville and the troops withheld by Vaudreuil, but he might also strike the British before they could dig in. His officers, afraid that Vaudreuil might appear at any moment to issue additional hamstringing orders, were for immediate attack.

Montcalm agreed. He sent his troops out to the Plains of Abraham.

Out they marched to the last battle of New France. All that was French, all that Samuel de Champlain had planted 250 years before on the cliff above the river, was to be defended here this day. Golden lily and gilded cross, dream of an empire stretching to the Rockies, fervor and faith and feudalism, all that had nourished or corrupted the martial and colorful little colony along the great river was at stake on the plains beyond. Through the narrow streets they thronged, white-coated regulars in black hats and gaiters and glittering bayonets, troops of Canadians and bands of Indians in scalp locks and war paint; out of the palace gate they poured, the battalions of Old France and the irregulars of the New, the victors of Fort Necessity, the Monongahela, Oswego, Ticonderoga, Fort William Henry, and the Montmorency tramping to the tap of the drum and the call of the bugle for the last time in the long war for a continent.

With them rode their general. He had never seemed more noble to his officers and men. The Canadians might have been more careful, they might have let New France live yet a little longer—but he gave no murmur of complaint. Mounted on a dark bay horse, he was a splendid figure in his green-and-gold uniform, the Cross of St. Louis gleaming above his cuirass. "Are you tired, my soldiers?" he cried. "Are you ready, my children?" They answered him with shouts and as he swung his sword to encourage them, the cuffs of his wide sleeves fell back to reveal the white linen of his wristbands.

In splendid composure, the British watched the French arrive. Since dawn, when the high ground less than a mile away had become suddenly thronged with the white coats of the tardily arriving Guienne, the redcoats had been raked by Canadian and Indian sharpshooters. After Ramesay's three cannon had begun to punish them, Wolfe had ordered them to lie in the grass.

James Wolfe had put on a new uniform: scarlet coat over impeccable white breeches, silk-edged tricorne on his head. He walked gaily among his reclining men, making certain that they had loaded their muskets with an extra ball for the first volley, pausing to chat with his officers. Wolfe ignored the enemy sharpshooters and exploding shells. A captain near him fell, shot in the lung. Wolfe knelt and gently took the man's head in his arms. He thanked him for his services and told him he would be promoted when he was well again, immediately sending off an aide to Monckton to make sure that his promise was carried out should he be killed that day.

The desired battle had arrived, and James Wolfe was exalted. All his black moods and indecision had vanished clean away. His step was light, his voice was steady, and his pale face shone with confidence. Although he did outnumber Montcalm forty-eight hundred to four thousand, it was the quality rather than the number of his troops that gave the British general his assurance. He had trained them personally, and he had taught them to stand in awesome silence until their enemy was close enough to be broken by a single volley.

Toward ten o'clock the French began coming down the hill, regulars in the center, regulars and Canadians to the right and the left, respectively, and Wolfe ordered his men to arise and form ranks. On came the French, shouting loudly, firing the moment they came within range, two columns inclining toward the British left, one to the right.

The British stood still.

Gradually the French lines became disordered by Canadians throwing themselves prone to reload, but they still came on, crying out and pouring musket fire into the silent British.

"Fire!"

A single volley as loud as a cannon shot struck the French not forty yards away. Again a volley, and then a clattering roll of muskets, and then, in the lifting smoke, the British saw the field before them littered with crumpled white coats, and the French, massed in fright, turning to flee.

"Charge!"

The British cheer and the fierce, wild yell of the Highlanders rose into the air, and the pursuit was begun. Redcoats with outthrust bayonets bounded after the fleeing enemy. Highlanders in kilts swinging five-foot broadswords overhead leaped forward to decapitate terrified fugitives with a single stroke and to take a terrible revenge for the insult dealt the tartans at Fort Duquesne.

James Wolfe led the charge. He had already taken a ball in the wrist and had wrapped a handkerchief around it. Now, leading the Louisbourg grenadiers, he was wounded again. He pressed on, but a third shot pierced his breast. He sank to the ground. He was carried to the rear. He was asked if he wanted a surgeon.

"There's no need," he said, gasping. "It's all over with me."

He began to lose consciousness, until one of the sorrowing men around him shouted: "They run! See how they run!"

"Who run?" Wolfe cried, rousing himself.

"The enemy, sir. Egad, they give way everywhere!"

"Go one of you to Colonel Burton," Wolfe said with a gasp, "and tell him to march Webb's regiment down to Charles River, to cut off their retreat from the bridge." Turning on his side, he murmured, "Now, God be praised, I will die in peace!" and he perished a few moments later.

The marquis de Montcalm was also stricken. His horse had been borne toward the town by the tide of fleeing French, and as he neared the walls a shot passed through his body. He slumped but kept his seat, rather than let his soldiers see him fall. Two regulars bore him up on either side. He entered the city streaming blood in full view of two horrified women.

"*O mon Dieu! O mon Dieu!*" one of them shrieked. "The marquis is dead."

"It is nothing, it is nothing," Montcalm replied. "Don't be troubled for me, my good friends."

But that night he was dying. His surgeon had told him that his wound was mortal. "I am glad of it," he said, and asked how much longer he had to live. "Twelve hours, more or less," was the reply. "So much the better," Montcalm murmured. "I am happy that I shall not live to see the surrender of Québec." He died peacefully at four o'clock the next morning, having received the last sacraments of his faith.

Wolfe had fallen knowing that he had won an important skirmish, Montcalm aware that his army was routed and demoralized; but neither knew that all was won and all was lost.

Another year was to pass before the seal was to be placed on the Battle of the Plains of Abraham as the crowning victory in the 150-year war for a continent. Only a few hours after Wolfe's triumph, Bougainville appeared in the west with about two thousand men and was repulsed by Townshend. That night, Vaudreuil panicked. The cowardly governor and archtraitor who had deliberately sabotaged most of Montcalm's wise provisions to defend the Canadian capital—for certainly James Wolfe had already shown that he was a brave but too often an impetuous commander, with little claim to military genius—now abandoned Québec, fleeing to Montréal in the van of a terrified and demoralized army that had hastily quit the Beaufort line to head for Montréal, leaving tents and cannon behind.

Although the infuriated Levis rallied these remnants and prepared to march against the British, the town was surrendered before he could arrive. The British Army, now under Murray, passed a terrible winter in Québec; and in the spring Levis appeared outside its walls with a superior force. Murray rashly left the city to attack him, was driven back after losing a third of his army, and Québec was now besieged by the French.

By then, however, a sea battle perhaps more important than the land war in Canada had been fought between the British and the French. Admiral Sir Edward Hawke met Admiral Conflans at Quiberon Bay, decisively defeating him to break the back of French naval power and to win control of the Atlantic for Britain. Thus it was a British and not a French fleet that sailed up the St. Lawrence on May 16, 1760. Murray was relieved, and Levis was forced to withdraw to Montréal. There, Amherst, now in command in America, applied the final blows.

Murray advanced up the St. Lawrence, Haviland ascended Lake Champlain, and Amherst descended the St. Lawrence from Lake Ontario. Trapped east, south, and west, Levis was force to capitulate.

Canada had been conquered, and the French and Indian War was over. A few years later the Peace of Paris ended the Seven Years' War in Europe. France ceded her colony on the St. Lawrence to Britain, retaining in America only that vast though vaguely defined region called Louisiana. France had emerged from the conflict a wreck: only five towns in India remained to her, her navy was gone, and her finances were in the ruin that was to produce the French Revolution. Britain and Prussia were all-powerful: the one to rule the waves, the other to rack Europe.

Britain had beaten France and had won an empire. And yet she was already in danger of losing the fairest jewel in that imperial crown. As Count Vergennes had warned:

"Delivered from a neighbor they have always feared, your other colonies will soon discover that they stand no longer in need of your protection. You will call on them to contribute toward supporting the burden which they have helped to bring on you, they will answer you by shaking off all dependence."

This they would do indeed.

CHAPTER 31

Retribution

IN DECEMBER OF 1761 the golden jackals, wolves, and hyenas who had done more than the troops of James Wolfe to destroy New France were taken from the Bastille—into which they had been thrown upon their arrival in France, enchained—and brought under guard to their trial at the Chatelet in Paris.

All the principal thieves were there, gilded members of the Bigot-Cadet combination, including Vaudreuil: little Pean whose great estate in France had not given him the protection he had envisioned, Varin, Breard, Le Mercier, Penisseault, Maurin, and Corpron.

At first Cadet the butcher's boy had the gall to plead innocent, until, seeing the mass of evidence against him, he changed his mind and made a full confession, in hopes of clemency. Bigot also denied all the charges against him, until the prosecutor silenced his pleas one by one with the very papers that bore his signature. With the cowardly groveling of trapped criminals everywhere, they defended themselves by blaming each other. Vaudreuil and Bigot—the highest officials of the king—exchanged charges, joining all the others in denouncing Cadet. Bigot was ordered exiled from France for life, all his property was confiscated, and he was ordered to pay a fine of 1.5 million francs by way of restitution, a mere pittance compared to the many millions he had stolen and probably squirreled away somewhere.

Cadet was banished from Paris for nine years and compelled to cough up 6 million francs, which he probably was able to do with ease. All the others convicted were fined sums varying from a low of 30,000 francs to a high of 800,000, and were ordered to remain in the Bastille until the money was paid. Of a total of twenty-one persons brought to trial, ten were convicted, six were acquitted, three were admonished, and two were dismissed as innocent for want of evidence. Thirty-four failed to appear—or to be apprehended, of whom seven were sentenced in default, and judgment reserved on the others.

And what of Vaudreuil?

What of Pierre François Rigaud, marquis de Vaudreuil, what of this cowardly swine, this vulture and viper, Vaudreuil the Vain and Vicious and Vile?

He was acquitted.

It was in keeping that he should be, for this false servant of the libertine King Louis XV of France had undone every wise military precaution of Louis Joseph, marquis de Montcalm-Gozen, St. Veran, which would have saved for this gilded king of the boudoir his great colony of Canada, no fewer than four million square miles of mostly virgin territory, full of mountains packed with minerals—many still unknown and most unexploited—forests, lakes, and waterways, all lost because of the self-love of Vaudreuil, this vainest of human trifles, vainer even than Lucifer, and eager to deliver all this to the enemy if it would embarrass the truly great marquis de Montcalm.

Though unfaithful to his trust, Vaudreuil was constant in the service of La Pompadour, who hated Canada with a passion, who decided to write finis to the steady flow of bad news from across the Atlantic when she sent a hundred thousand French soldiers to the rescue of her confidante and fellow feminist, Queen Maria Theresa of Austria, to defend that tiny kingdom against the blows of Frederick the Great of Prussia, while grudgingly dispatching a mere twelve hundred—and those the dregs of the armed forces—to that vast uncharted and unexploited half continent of New France across the sea.

Thus in sorrow and in shame was concluded nearly two centuries of noble effort to civilize the savages and tame the wilds of this ferocious wilderness; and so also was dishonored the French crown and cross—the oldest civility in Europe—when this seemingly imperishable cavalcade of saint and soldier, martyr and monarch, peasant and prince came to its ignominious end atop the great rock of Québec.

Selected Bibliography

Abercrombie, Thomas J. *The St. Lawrence River and the Sea. National Geographic,* October 1994.

Alberts, Robert C. *The Most Extraordinary Adventures of Major Robert Stobo.* Boston: Houghton Mifflin, 1965.

Ashley, Maurice. *Great Britain to 1688.* Ann Arbor: University of Michigan Press, 1961.

Axtell, James. *The Invasion Within: The Contest of Cultures in North America.* New York: Oxford University Press, 1985.

Beeching, Jack. *The Galleys at Lepanto.* New York: Scribner's, 1982.

Belloc, Hilaire. *Characters of the Reformation.* New York: Sheed & Ward, 1937.

———. *James II.* London: Faber & Gwyer, 1928.

———. *Monarchy: A Study of Louis XIV.* London: Cassell, 1938.

Billias, George Athan. *George Washington's Opponents.* New York: William Morrow, 1969.

Boorstin, Daniel. *The Discoverers.* New York: Random House, 1983.

Brebner, J. Bartlet. *Canada.* Ann Arbor: University of Michigan Press, 1970.

Browning, Reed. *The War of the Austrian Succession.* New York: St. Martin's Press, 1993.

Churchill, Winston S. *Marlborough: His Life and Times.* New York: Charles Scribner's Sons, 1938.

Connell, Brian. *The Plains of Abraham.* London: Hodder & Stoughton, 1959.

———. *The Savage Years.* New York, 1961.

Davies, Bladwen. *Québec: Portrait of a Province.* New York: Greenberg, 1951.

Dupuy, R. Ernest and Trevor N. *Encyclopedia of Military History from 3500 B.C. to Present.* New York: Harper & Row, 1970.

———. *Military Heritage of America.* New York: McGraw-Hill, 1956.

Eckert, Allan W. *Wilderness Empire.* Boston: Little, Brown, 1969.

Flexner, James Thomas. *Mohawk Baronet.* Syracuse, N.Y.: Syracuse University Press, 1989.

———. *Washington.* Boston: Little, Brown, 1969.

Freeman, Douglas Southall. *George Washington.* New York: Charles Scribner's Sons, 1948. Although greatly inflated, Freeman's seven-volume biography remains the definitive work on Washington. Vols. I and II relate to the colonial wars.

Fuller, Major General J. F. C. *Military History of the Western World.* Vol. I, New York: Funk & Wagnalls, 1954.

Gilbert, Martin. *Churchill: A Life.* New York: Henry Holt, 1991.

Guerard, Albert. *France.* Ann Arbor: University of Michigan Press, 1959.

Hamilton, Edward P. *The French and Indian Wars: The Story of Battles and Forts in the Wilderness.* Garden City, N.Y.: Doubleday, 1962.

Hibbert, Christopher. *Wolfe at Québec.* New York: World, 1959.

Irving, Washington. *George Washington.* New York: Da Capo, 1994.

Jones, Archer. *The Art of War in the Western World.* Urbana: University of Illinois Press, 1987.

Josephy, Alvin. *Five Hundred Nations.* New York: Alfred A. Knopf, 1994.

Kraus, Michael. *The United States to 1865.* Ann Arbor: University of Michigan Press, 1969.

Leach, Douglas Edward. *Arms for Empire: A Military History of the British Colonies in North America, 1607–1763.* New York: Macmillan, 1972.

Leckie, Robert. *George Washington's War.* New York: HarperCollins, 1992.

———. *The Wars of America, Revised and Updated.* New York: Harper-Collins, 1968, 1981, 1992.

Montross, Lynn. *War Through the Ages, 490 B.C. to Present.* New York: Harper & Brothers, 1944, 1946, 1960.

Morison, Samuel Eliot. *Admiral of the Ocean Sea: The Story of Christopher Columbus.* New York: Oxford University Press, 1942.

———. *Oxford History of the American People.* New York: Oxford University Press, 1965.

———. *The Parkman Reader.* Boston: Little, Brown, 1955.

Murray, Jane. *The Kings and Queens of Britain.* New York: Charles Scribner's Sons, 1974.

Notestein, Wallace. *The British People on the Eve of Colonization.* New York: Harper & Brothers, 1954.

Oakley, Amy, *Québec.* New York: Appleton-Century-Crofts, 1947.

Parkman, Francis. *France and England in North America.* Boston: Little, Brown, 10 vols., 1887–1888; 2 vols., 1892. Of the 12 vols. cited here, those dealing directly with the colonial wars are *The Pioneers of New France in the New World,* 1894 and *Count Frontenac and New France Under Louis XIV,* 1896. *A Half Century of Conflict,* 2 vols., 1892. *Montcalm and Wolfe,* 2 vols., 1919. *The Conspiracy of Pontiac,* 2 vols., 1894.

———. *The Jesuits in North America.* 1894.

———. *LaSalle and the Discovery of the Great West,* 1894.

Rutledge, Joseph Lister. *Century of Conflict.* Garden City, N.Y.: Doubleday, 1956.

Smellie, K. B. *Great Britain Since 1688.* Ann Arbor: University of Michigan Press, 1960.

Stacey, C. P. *Québec, 1759: The Siege and the Battle.* Toronto: St. Martin's Press, 1959.

Steele, Ian K. *Betrayals: Fort William Henry and the "Massacre."* New York: Oxford University Press, 1990.

Syme, Ronald, *Frontenac of New France*. New York: William Morrow, 1969.

Tebbel, John, and Jennison, Keith. *The American Indian Wars*. New York: Bonanza, 1960.

Thomson, George Malcolm. *The First Churchill*. New York: William Morrow, 1980.

Vagts, Alfred. *A History of Militarism*. New York: Meridian, 1959.

Van Der Zee, Henri and Barbara. *William and Mary*. New York: Alfred A. Knopf, 1975.

Washburn, Wilcombe E. *The Indian in America*. New York: Harper & Row, 1975.

Wolf, John B. *Louis XIV*. New York: Norton, 1968.

Index

Abenakis, 102, 191–92, 199, 203
as French allies, 197–98, 215, 230,
231–32, 289
Abercromby, James, 300, 308, 309,
310–11, 341
Acadia (later Nova Scotia), 46,
68–69, 76, 204, 206–7, 232–33,
235
British assaults on, 237–38, 279
cession to Britain, 243, 247–48
deportation of Acadians, 287–88,
292, 326
See also Port Royal
Ahatsistari, Eustache, 146
Aix-la-Chapelle, Treaty of (1748),
254, 270, 297, 339
Albany, 99, 128, 153, 158, 179,
180–86, 189–90, 203, 236
Albany congress (1754), 273–74, 290
Alderman (Indian defector), 108
Alexander (Wamsutta Indian), 104–5
Alexander VI, pope, 4
Alexander VII, pope, 84
Alfonso XIII, king of Spain, 219
Algonquins, 95, 99, 100, 157, 159
French alliances, 45–46, 68–71,
191
Allegheny River, 274, 275, 281, 286,
312, 313
American Civil War, 54, 208
American Revolution, 159, 295, 311,
317–18
Amherst, Jeffrey, 306–9, 341, 344,
345, 350, 355, 356
Anglicanism, 91, 92, 95, 96, 141,
142, 227, 265, 303
Annapolis Harbor, 47
Annapolis Royal. *See* Port Royal

Anne, queen of Great Britain, 141,
219, 220, 221–28, 230, 235
Anne of Austria, 79–84, 156, 235
Anse du Foulon, 358, 359, 360
Antillia (legendary island), 16
army, 54–57
American historical training in-
adequacy, 213–14
British system, 333, 340, 341
colonial, 58–61
European tactics, 280
Prussian discipline, 245
arquebus, 69, 72, 99
artillery, 52, 55–57, 138–39
Augusta of Saxe Gotha, 257
Augustine, St., 4
Austria, 238, 243, 246, 297, 301–2,
339, 368
Avaugour, Dubois, 169
Awashonks (sachem), 107
Azores, 12, 16, 23, 27
Aztecs, 34

Bahamas, 29
Ball, Joseph, 268
Barlow, Captain, 38
Basques, 66–67, 68
Bastiani, Abbé, 245
Bayezid, prince of Turkey, 35
Bay of Fundy, 11, 47, 50
bayonet, 53, 55, 280
Beaujeu, Daniel, 281, 282, 284, 286
Beauport, 211–12, 213, 345, 348, 349,
352, 358, 359, 361
Belleisle, Marechal, 331
Bernaldez, Andres, 12
Bernard, John, 233
Berryer, Colonial Minister, 328–30

373